W9-CER-245

SELECTED PHOTOGRAPHS BY WALKER EVANS

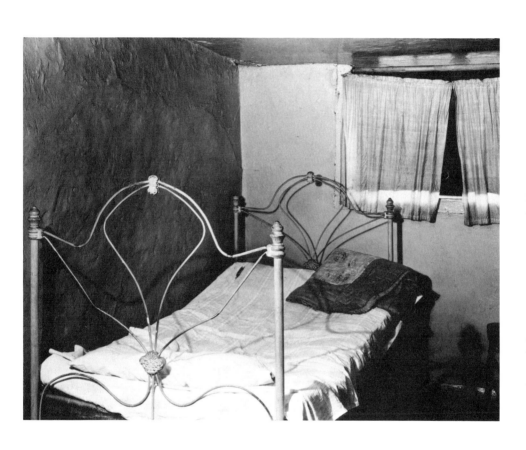

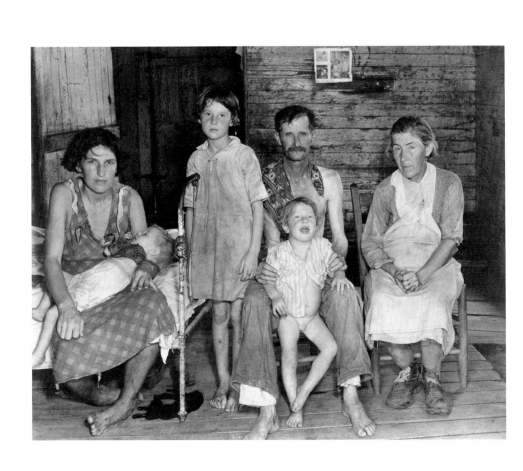

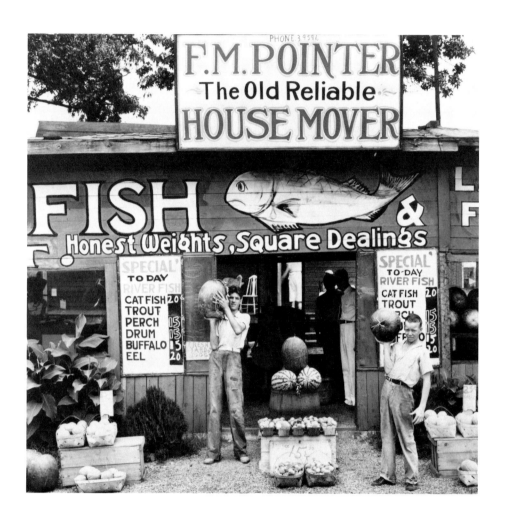

Walker Evans

Belinda Rathbone

Walker Evans

A Biography

HOUGHTON MIFFLIN COMPANY

Boston · New York 1995

Copyright © 1995 by Belinda Rathbone

For information about permission to reproduce selections from
this book, write to Permissions, Houghton Mifflin Company,
215 Park Avenue South, New York, New York 10003.

Library of Congress Cataloging-in-Publication Data
Rathbone, Belinda.
Walker Evans : a biography / Belinda Rathbone
        p.   cm.
ISBN 0-395-59072-8 (alk. paper)
1. Evans, Walker, 1903–1975. 2. Photographers — United
States — Biography.   I. Evans, Walker, 1903–1975.
II. Title.
TR140.E92R38   1995
770´.92 — dc20   95-3711 CIP
[B]

Printed in the United States of America

MP 10 9 8 7 6 5 4 3 2 1

Book design by Robert Overholtzer

The author is grateful for permission to quote from the
following works: Writings by James Agee, used by permission
of the James Agee Trust. Excerpts from *The Bridge,* by Hart
Crane, used by permission of the Hart Crane Estate.
Writings by Walker Evans, used by permission of the Walker
Evans Archive, The Metropolitan Museum of Art. Writings
by Edward Weston, copyright © 1981, Center for Creative
Photography, Arizona Board of Regents. Used by permission.

To my father

Contents

ILLUSTRATIONS ix

PREFACE xiii

1 A MIDWESTERN CHILDHOOD 1

2 PARIS AND NEW YORK 23

3 EXPOSURE 53

4 SOUTH 86

5 THREE FAMILIES 118

6 AMERICAN PHOTOGRAPHS 139

7 LOVE BEFORE BREAKFAST 167

8 FORTUNE 197

9 BEFORE THEY DISAPPEAR 226

10 MESSAGE FROM THE INTERIOR 251

11 A PENITENT SPY 280

NOTES 311

BIBLIOGRAPHY 336

INDEX 341

Illustrations

SELECTED PHOTOGRAPHS BY WALKER EVANS

The Brooklyn Bridge, c. 1929. *J. Paul Getty Museum, Malibu, California. Copyright © Walker Evans Archive, Metropolitan Museum of Art.*

Manhattan (U.S. Rubber), c. 1928. *National Gallery of Canada, Ottawa. Copyright © Walker Evans Archive, Metropolitan Museum of Art.*

Torn movie poster, 1930. *Museum of Modern Art, New York; purchase. Copyright © Walker Evans Archive, Metropolitan Museum of Art.*

Muriel Draper's dining room, c. 1930. *Copyright © Walker Evans Archive, Metropolitan Museum of Art.*

Hudson Street boarding house, New York (detail), c. 1930. *J. Paul Getty Museum, Malibu, California. Copyright © Walker Evans Archive, Metropolitan Museum of Art.*

Ben and Judith Shahn, c. 1933. *Courtesy of Judith Shahn.*

Main Street, Saratoga Springs, New York, 1931. *Museum of Modern Art, New York; anonymous fund. Copyright © Walker Evans Archive, Metropolitan Museum of Art.*

Citizen in downtown Havana, 1933. *J. Paul Getty Museum, Malibu, California. Copyright © Walker Evans Archive, Metropolitan Museum of Art.*

The Breakfast Room at Belle Grove Plantation, Louisiana, 1935. *Museum of Modern Art, New York; anonymous fund. Copyright © Walker Evans Archive, Metropolitan Museum of Art.*

Penny picture display, Savannah, Georgia, 1936. *Museum of Modern Art, New York; gift of Willard Van Dyke.*

A graveyard and steel mill in Bethlehem, Pennsylvania, November 1935. *Museum of Modern Art, New York; gift of the Farm Security Administration.*

Country church near Beaufort, South Carolina, 1935. *National Gallery of Canada, Ottawa.*

Houses and billboards in Atlanta, 1936. *Museum of Modern Art, New York; purchase.*

Sharecropper's family [the Burroughses], Hale County, Alabama, 1936. *J. Paul Getty Museum, Malibu, California.*

Hale County, Alabama [washroom in the dog run of Floyd Burroughs' home], 1936. *Museum of Modern Art, New York; Stephen R. Currier Memorial Fund.*

Fireplace and objects, Floyd Burroughs' bedroom, Hale County, Alabama, 1936.

Alabama cotton tenant farmer's wife [Allie Mae Burroughs], summer 1936. *Museum of Modern Art, New York; the Ben Schultz Memorial Collection; gift of the photographer.*

Sharecropper's family [the Fieldses], summer 1936. *Museum of Modern Art, New York; gift of the Farm Security Administration.*

Roadside stand near Birmingham, 1935. *Museum of Modern Art, New York; purchase.*

Subway portrait, 1938–1941. *Museum of Modern Art, New York; purchase. Copyright © Walker Evans Archive, Metropolitan Museum of Art.*

Corner of State and Randolph Streets, Chicago, 1946. *National Gallery of Canada, Ottawa. Copyright © Walker Evans Archive, Metropolitan Museum of Art.*

Eliza Mabry, c. 1952. *J. Paul Getty Museum, Malibu, California. Copyright © Walker Evans Archive, Metropolitan Museum of Art.*

Robert and Mary Frank, n.d., *Museum of Modern Art, New York; gift of Mr. and Mrs. Richard Benson. Copyright © Walker Evans Archive, Metropolitan Museum of Art.*

Guthrie, Kentucky, New Year's Day, 1970. *Museum of Modern Art, New York; purchase. Copyright © Walker Evans Archive, Metropolitan Museum of Art.*

FOLLOWING PAGE 170

(all photographs by Walker Evans in this section are copyright © Walker Evans Archive, Metropolitan Museum of Art)

Walker Evans Jr., c. 1900. *Courtesy of Charles Lindley.*

Jessie Crane Evans in her wedding dress, 1900. *Courtesy of Charles Lindley.*

Walker Evans, Walker Evans Jr., and Walker Evans III, c. 1907. *Courtesy of Talbot Brewer Jr.*

Walker Evans III. *Courtesy of Charles Lindley.*

The Evans house in Kenilworth. *Photograph by the author.*

Walker Evans III, yearbook picture, Phillips Academy, Andover, 1922. *Courtesy of Talbot Brewer Jr.*

Walker Evans at work, Darien, Connecticut, summer 1929, by Paul Grotz. *Courtesy of Dorothy Grotz.*

Hart Crane, by Walker Evans. *Hart Crane papers, Rare Book and Manuscript Library, Columbia University.*

Walker Evans, 1929–1930, by Paul Grotz. *Courtesy of Dorothy Grotz.*

Paul Grotz, 1929–1930, by Walker Evans. *Courtesy of Clark Worswick.*

Lincoln Kirstein, n.d., by George Platt Lynes. *Museum of Modern Art, New York; gift of Russell Lynes.*

Ben, Judith, and Tillie Shahn, 23 Bethune Street, New York, c. 1931, by Walker Evans. *Museum of Modern Art, New York; gift of the photographer.*

Jane Smith Ninas, Belle Grove, Louisiana, 1935, by Walker Evans. *Courtesy of Clark Worswick.*

James Agee, Old Field Point, summer 1937, by Walker Evans. *Fogg Art Museum, Harvard University Art Museums; National Endowment for the Arts grant.*

James Agee and Mia Fritsch, 1942, by Helen Levitt. *Courtesy of the Laurence Miller Gallery, New York.*

Walker Evans, c. 1940, by Helen Levitt. *Courtesy of the Laurence Miller Gallery, New York.*

Herbert Solow and John McDonald, Croton-on-Hudson, by Walker Evans. *Courtesy of Clark Worswick.*

John Jessup and Wilder Hobson, by Walker Evans. *Courtesy of Clark Worswick.*

Jane's barn with porch addition, Old Lyme, Connecticut, 1940s, by Walker Evans. *Courtesy of Clark Worswick.*

Isabelle Boeschenstein Evans, 1961, by Walker Evans. *Courtesy of Clark Worswick.*

Walker Evans, 1971, by Arnold Crane. *Museum of Modern Art, New York; purchase.*

Walker Evans at work, Hale County, Alabama, October 1973, by William Christenberry. *Courtesy of William Christenberry.*

Walker Evans at his last lecture, Harvard University, April 8, 1975, by Edward Forman. *Courtesy of the Harvard Crimson.*

Preface

I met Walker Evans twice in the early 1970s. The first time was at the opening of his touring retrospective exhibition at the Boston Museum of Fine Arts, of which my father was then director. At the time, I was an aspiring photographer and Evans was already a kind of god to me. His photographs had an indefinable ring of authenticity; to my eye, they seemed to be the essence of the medium. The man himself became all the more compelling when I learned to my surprise that his background was not unlike my own — that he had been born in St. Louis, as had I, and had attended eastern prep schools. His attitude toward his formal education I also found sympathetic: he loved books and literature at the expense of his other studies, such as Latin and mathematics; he had been a bored, disaffected student and had dropped out of college after one year. He believed that the best photographers, like himself, worked from the heart and were self-taught. I was sure that we had much in common.

"I come from St. Louis too" was perhaps my first conversational effort when we met. He explained that he didn't really know the place, that he had left when he was five years old. "So did I!" I hastily (and truthfully) rejoined. I remember that when he asked me which of his photographs I liked especially, I chose without hesitation the wrong one — "Graveyard, Bethlehem, Pa.," one that many others might have singled out, but not the artist. I could tell he was disappointed. Nevertheless, he gave me a copy of his exhibition catalogue and inscribed it "To Belinda, with admiration and with affection."

It must have been several weeks later that he requested my presence at dinner in New Haven, where he was then a professor of photography at Yale. His host, John Atchley, was a graduate student in the photography program, and Walker knew that he and his wife, Nan, were friends of mine. I took along a small black folder of my photographs, which Walker expressed an interest in seeing. He flattered me by asking for a print of one of them — a picture of a doghouse, taken straight on and close up, with a ragged piece of burlap hanging from the door. Not my best, I thought, but with Walker's stamp of approval, I could see that it was perhaps the most direct and unaffected of the lot.

Before leaving, Walker invited me to come to his house in Old Lyme the next day. I was relieved to know I hadn't seen the last of him. His house, I thought, had great style. Against clean white walls there were delicate antique chairs living compatibly with big battered outdoor advertising signs, an unexpectedly elegant mix of old velvet and rusty tin. In its own way, it was impeccable. Through the door to another room — his workroom — I could see that he had also reserved a place for his chaos. There was much to take in. But it wasn't long before Walker whisked me off in his Chevrolet hatchback for a drive, I don't remember where to, with the tape deck running a classical opera at full blast, the dashboard a mess of crumbs and papers. The man is slightly mad, I thought to myself, and I felt the mildest flash of terror.

These personal impressions were always somewhere present over the years as I continued to admire Evans' photographs and to contemplate the depth of their appeal. My interest was constantly refreshed. There seemed to be no aging of the photographs or tiring of the personality who made them. Yet as I closely followed the exhibitions, monographs, and critical writing on Evans over the years, it seemed to me that the gaps in our understanding of the man and his work only grew wider. While other famous photographers of his generation — Ansel Adams, Margaret Bourke-White, Man Ray — wrote of their rise to success in their memoirs, reminiscing about the great times they had lived through, the great people they had known, the great things they had done, Evans maintained his lofty reserve. Rather than attempting to explain how he became the artist he was, he preferred to leave the question open to speculation. "Almost all good artists are being worked through with forces they aren't quite aware of," he said, apparently content in his own case to leave those forces a mystery. Although he foresaw that a biography would be written, he was not especially interested in taking his biographer by the hand.

In the years after his death, while the art market and the academic study of photography expanded many times over, Evans became more and more mythical, inaccessible, and monetarily undervalued. Young scholars picked over shreds of information and inspected brief periods of his career under the microscope. But the resistance of his personality led many to make unsatisfactory conclusions, most notably to attribute too much of his achievement to the influence of powerful (and more available) friends. Evans' frequent assertion that his photography was a compulsive act of passion has been lost in the effort to define its place in history. It was time for a full-scale biography, to see the whole man in relation to the shape of his life, the balance of his friendships, his manner of working, the objects he admired and collected, his haunts and homes — in short, the full range of his associations. By the time I felt ready to tackle the project myself, five years ago, the road was still open; no one had taken it.

This is the first biography of Walker Evans. Like all biographies, it is the product of its special timing. When I embarked on the project, Evans' estate was still unsettled. His negatives, papers, and collections remained in the hands of his executor, John Hill, who provided a few documents to scholars and saw to it that some previously unknown photographs and documents were published in monographs: *First and Last, Walker Evans at Work, Walker Evans: Havana,* and, most recently, *Walker Evans: The Hungry Eye.* Otherwise, the evidence of Evans' life and work was scattered far and wide among museum collections, manuscript libraries, and in the homes and memories of his surviving friends. The situation discouraged several would-be biographers over the years.

My research during the past five years has led me to interview more than a hundred people who knew Evans, ranging from those who knew him intimately, including his two former wives, to those who knew him less well, such as prep school classmates, social acquaintances, colleagues at *Fortune* magazine and Yale, students, assistants, and fellow photographers. In searching out Evans' friends and associates, I have traveled from Taos, New Mexico, to Wiltshire, England. I have studied many collections of his photographs, large and small, public and private, including those of the Library of Congress, the Museum of Modern Art, and the J. Paul Getty Museum, and Clark Worswick, whose private collection includes more than 1,500 photographs. I have searched employment records and city directories for concrete information as to Evans' movements and whereabouts, university collections and various archives for the authentic biographical detail. Before the end of this century, a center for the study of Walker Evans will be organized at the Metropolitan Museum of Art, which recently acquired the estate. This will make the work of future biographers and historians more efficient. But by that time, the life of Walker Evans will be more remote, even to those few people who may still live to talk about it.

I am grateful to the many friends and colleagues of Evans' who granted me interviews, shared documents, and in many cases led me to others who did the same. Some of them, I regret to say, have not lived to see this book published. My thanks are due to Berenice Abbott, Walter Allner, Penny Andrews, Courtlandt and Trini Barnes, Daniel Bell, Varujan Boghosian, Talbot Brewer Jr., Dudley Britton, Charlee Mae Brodsky, Paul Brooks, Slater Brown, Harry Callahan, Dale Callaway, Sam Carini, Bobbi Carrey, William Christenberry, Eleanor Clark, Adele Clement, Susanna Coggeshall, Rosalind Constable, Mildred Constantine, Sage Fuller Cowles, Arnold Crane, Theodore Crane, Jack Delano, Ben deLoache, William DeLuze, Jim Dow, Paul Draper, Andy Dupee, Alvin Eisenman, Barbara and Jason Epstein, Louis Faurer, Miles Forst, Mary Frank, Anne Fuller, Blair Fuller, Emmet Gowin, Paul and Dorothy Grotz, Richard Harrison, Jack Heliker, John Hill, Archie Hobson, Eliza Hobson, Verna Hobson, Walter Hopps, Virginia Hubbard, Lindley Hubbell, Lawrence Israel, Seville Johnston, Joel Katz,

Leslie Katz and Jane Mayall, Alfred Kazin, Barbara Kerr, Mary Knollenberg, Hilton Kramer, Emily Kronenberger, Katherine Kuh, Michael Lesy, Helen Levitt, Charles Lindley, Leo Lionni, Valerie Lloyd, Pare Lorenz, Caroline Blackwood Lowell, Harry Lunn, Russell Lynes, Eliza Mabry, Ben Maddow, Grace Mayer, John McDonald, Walter McQuade, Joel Meyerowitz, Dorothy Miller, Agnes Mongen, Alice Morris, Robert Moskowitz, Carl Mydans, Beaumont Newhall, Elodie Osborn, Eliza Parkinson, Vita Petersen, David Plowden, Davis Pratt, Chris and Esther Pullman, Alston Purvis, Joseph Verner Reed Jr., Nicholas Reed, Permelia Reed, George Rinhart, Marie-Antoinette Robert, Elizabeth Sekear Rothschild, Jane Schoelkopf, Leo Seltzer, Bernarda Shahn, Judith Shahn, Sam and Elizabeth Shaw, Aaron Siskind, Saul Steinberg, Caroline Steiner, James and Tania Stern, Tom Strong, David Swan, David Sylvester, John Szarkowski, Jerry Thompson, Alan Trachtenberg, Diana Trilling, Wally Tworkov, Billie Voorhees, Jack Watson, Tod Webb, Hazel Hawthorne Werner, Lily West, William Hollingsworth Whyte, John Wilmerding, Nancy Tate Wood, Olivia Agee Wood, Mathew Wysocki, Ruth Forbes Young. Most of all, I wish to thank Evans' two former wives, Jane Sargeant and Isabelle Storey, both of whom were forthcoming, patient, and unendingly generous with their time. Their depiction of the man they married was as thoughtful, candid, and fairminded as a biographer could hope for. Without their help, this book would have taken a very different and shallower form.

My special thanks are also due to the three beneficiaries of Evans' estate, Virginia Hubbard, Charles Lindley, and Eliza Mabry, for their support of this project and their permission to publish quotations and photographs. I am grateful to both John Hill and Christina Del Valle at the Metropolitan Museum of Art for seeing my requests through to completion. I also wish to thank the curators, archivists, and librarians who assisted my research in the following collections: the American Institute of Arts and Letters; the Archives of American Art; the Beinecke Rare Book and Manuscript Library, Yale University; the Columbia University Special Collections Library; the National Gallery of Canada; the Mugar Memorial Library, Boston University; the United States Office of Personnel Management; and the archives of Foote, Cone, and Belding. In particular I wish to thank Thomas Tanselle of the John Simon Guggenheim Foundation; Susan Kismaric and Rona Roob of the Museum of Modern Art; Weston Naef and Judith Keller of the J. Paul Getty Museum; David Travis of the Art Institute of Chicago; Greg Bradsher of the National Archives; Alice Hudson, Mildred Wright, and Robert Sink of the New York Public Library; Deborah Wythe of the Brooklyn Museum; David Stirk of the Tamamint Library, New York University; Cynthia Farar of the Harry Ransom Humanities Research Center, University of Texas at Austin; Gail Gilbert of the Margaret M. Bridwell Art Library, University of Louisville; Diane Kaplan of the Yale University Library; John Lawrence of the Historic New Orleans Collection; Rodney Dennis of the Houghton Library, Harvard University; Don Skemer of the Princeton University Libraries; Elaine Felsher of Time Inc.; Amy Cohen-Rose of the Houghton Mifflin Company Library; Patty Stratos, clerk, East Lyme Town Hall; Marilyn Loomis of the Loomis Chaffee School; Meredith Price of Phillips Academy, Andover; Betty Miller of the Mercersburg Academy Archives; and Lynne Fonteneau of the Williams College Archives.

My study of Evans was enhanced by a generous exchange of documents, information, and opinion with fellow scholars, of Evans and others. I wish to thank Beverly Brannan, Scott Donaldson, Maria Morris Hambourg, David Herwaldt, Judith Keller, Douglas Nickel, Jeff Rosenheim, William Stott, David Travis, Robert Ware, Susan Millar Williams, and Clark Worswick. Two treasured colleagues I wish to thank in particular are Eugenia Parry Janis and Ben Lifson, with whom conversations about Evans and photography were always stimulating, challenging, and most of all a great pleasure. Both of them also generously gave their time to reading large portions of my manuscript at different stages of its development. Their criticism and encouragement constantly spurred me on to better thinking and better writing.

A project of this kind is almost impossible to manage without an editor, and I have felt fortunate to have worked throughout this one with Janet Silver, whose expert editing has kept this book on track and whose gentle but constant demands on my writing have made it all the richer. Her assistant, Wendy Holt, has also contributed greatly to the process, and Liz Duvall gave the manuscript a thorough and final editorial review. I am also grateful to my agent, Elise Goodman, for her support and encouragement throughout the undertaking.

The geographical scope of my research outside New York City would not have been possible without the help and hospitality of many friends who took part in the adventure of my work with unstinting enthusiasm and generosity. I wish to thank Bob and Anne Bowie, Christian Brechneff and Tim Lovejoy, Hilary Brest, Anne and Puck Douglas, Eliza and Andrew Hamilton, Christopher and Jamie Hewat, Eugenia Janis, Marion Janis, Ben Lifson, Elise Lufkin, Victoria Munroe and Eric Saltzman, Joe and Jennifer Pulitzer, Peter and Alanna Rathbone, Louise and Caleb Scott, Katya Slive, Martha Love Symington, and Marty and Kim Townsend. My parents' support was constant in every way, and their personal insight into the times I was studying was invaluable. I owe special thanks to my husband, John Ouchterlony — research assistant, proofreader, brainstormer — most of all for his hospitality to Walker Evans, who has always been a part of our life together.

Walker Evans

1 *A Midwestern Childhood*

"PRIVILEGE," said Walker Evans late in his life, addressing a group of well-heeled college students, "is an immoral and unjust thing to have. But if you've got it, you didn't choose to get it and you might as well use it." Looking at the venerable old photographer, his audience might have guessed that he spoke from experience. This small, dapper man in gentlemanly tweeds, gazing down his long nose over a pair of round glasses, appeared to be a living contradiction of the photographs of junkyards, billboards, gas stations, and the main streets of small towns for which he was famous. His encounter with poor southern tenant farmers during the Depression had taught him that privilege was immoral and unjust, but the belief that "if you've got it, you might as well use it" was his escape to the higher ground of aesthetic and intellectual contemplation. He believed that artists like himself made up their own class and were due their own set of privileges. His demeanor, both superior and comfortably informal, and his cultured accent, punctuated here and there by a mumble or stutter, suggested to many that he was an aristocrat, though perhaps not a born one. "He liked to imply that he was very well bred," explained a close friend. "I think he was rather a self-made well-bred man."

Beginning early in his career, Evans' courtly manner and appearance made the point that he was neither poor by birth nor political by nature, and that his photographs, though they often laid bare the reality of poverty and decline, were not driven by social protest. He acted on instinct rather than theory. His depiction of the commonplace and the rejected was a matter of personal taste rather than an effort to change the world. That his work would ultimately come to embody "the moral and aesthetic texture of the Depression era" was to him the unexpected flowering of a purely intuitive act. "This attraction of mine to the camera and its graphic product," he reflected in later life, "was a blind but passionate response to something I could not really analyze or describe. I knew I had to do it."

Born on November 2, 1903, in St. Louis, Missouri, Evans always claimed that his birthdate was November 3. Whether this was his parents' idea or his own, the number three matched the year as well as the Roman numeral III at the end of his name. According to family legend, Walker's great-grandfather, Augustus Heaslip Evans, had had a close friend whose surname was Walker. The two men made a pact to name their first sons after each other; thus one would be Evans Walker, the other Walker Evans.

Little is known of this brief lineage, the last member of which made the name Walker Evans synonymous with the photography of the American scene. All three generations were born in Missouri, their ancestors having been part of the westward migration of tradesmen and merchants in the nineteenth century. Augustus Heaslip Evans came from Woodstock, Virginia; his wife, Mary Anne Lawrence, came from Thetford, Vermont. With a career in clerking, cashiering, and bookkeeping, his son Walker Evans supported his Kentucky-born wife, Emanda Brooks, his daughter, Mabel, and his son, Walker Junior, in Mexico, Missouri. At the time of Walker Junior's marriage to Jessie Crane in 1900, Walker Senior was a secretary at the Mound City Paint and Color Company in St. Louis, where he had begun work as a cashier in 1887.

By comparison to the Evanses, the bride's family was well placed and well-to-do. In 1900, Jessie's father, Charles S. Crane, was the general passenger agent for the Wabash Railroad, a position that rendered him worthy of inclusion in the annual portrait album *Notable St. Louisans*. His origins were more obscure. He was born in Tecumseh, Michigan, in 1847, one of six children of Salmon Crane, a builder, and Harriet Thorp. At the age of sixteen, Charles began his railroad career as a car checker in Toledo, the headquarters of the Toledo, Wabash, and Western Railway, as the Wabash was then called. Within four years he had risen to the position of general ticket agent. By the time he was promoted to assistant general passenger agent in 1879, he was married to Jessie Beach of Northfield, Massachusetts, and the father of a two-year-old girl, also named Jessie. That year the family moved to the new Wabash headquarters in St. Louis, where at the turn of the century more railroad lines converged than anywhere else in America.

Walker Evans Jr. must have seemed a suitable groom to his prospective parents-in-law. At twenty-four, he had successfully embarked on a career in advertising. A photographic portrait of Evans at the time of his marriage shows a handsome man fashionably dressed in a high-collared shirt, with a four-in-hand tucked into a well-cut double-breasted waistcoat. His posture easy and self-assured, his gaze direct, he is clearly a young man on the move.

Even though Evans lacked a college education, he showed a native talent for writing, which he put to work in his advertising career. He was also known to be good with his hands and interested in building. He had once dreamed of becoming a professional architect, but his family had not been able to afford to give him the expensive education it required. To compensate, he took up carpentry as a hobby, for which he had been well prepared at the Manual Training School in St. Louis. For the previous two years he had been employed as a junior advertising agent in the passenger department of the Wabash Railroad, where he worked directly under his future father-in-law. Known to friends and family as Buck, he had pleasant manners and showed every intention of working hard and promoting himself, just as Crane had done, and of living up to the youthful expectations of Crane's first-born child and only daughter.

Anticipating the important occasion of his daughter's wedding, Crane had recently moved his family from their residence of seven years on Washington Boulevard to the more fashionable, recently developed Westminster Place. The Cranes' new home was only a short walk from the opulent gates of Westmoreland Place and Portland

Place, where the elite of St. Louis society lived in houses as big as public libraries. On a smaller scale, Westminster boasted a comparably eclectic panorama of architectural styles — neo-Romanesque, Italian Renaissance, and Colonial Georgian. The Crane residence, at number 4384, was a sturdy three-story brick and wood Greek Revival house with its share of dormers, fanlights, and bays and a large second-story balcony from which the bride might toss her bouquet.

The house was also within easy walking distance of the Second Presbyterian Church, where about six hundred guests — "representatives of the fashionable set of St. Louis" — gathered to witness the evening marriage ceremony in mid-January. The *St. Louis Post-Dispatch* had predicted that the Evans-Crane wedding would be one of the prettiest of the season. Flowers, music, dress, and protocol conformed to the prevailing taste and manners of St. Louis society. An organ concert of Wagnerian themes set the correct mood for the bridal march. Following her fourteen attendants, Jessie Crane, whom the *Post-Dispatch* described as "an exceedingly pretty girl with large, violet eyes," emerged on the arm of her father in a three-tiered dress of lace, chiffon, and satin, dragging a long court train. To the tune of "The Evening Star," bride and groom solemnized their marriage. Less than an hour later, the promising young couple were receiving congratulations in the bow window of the empire drawing room at Westminster Place, under a festoon of smilax and pink carnations.

Shortly after the match was sealed, the Cranes moved from Westminster Place to the slightly less fashionable McPherson Avenue, as if to say that their showpiece had served its purpose. During the next four years, both the Cranes and the newlyweds transplanted themselves as often as once a year, and Evans' advertising jobs changed with comparable frequency. The young couple were living with Jessie's parents in a two-story frame house on Cates Avenue when their first child, Jane Beach Evans, was born in February 1902. Not quite two years later, Jessie gave birth to their second child at home at 4468 McPherson Avenue. They named the boy Walker Evans III.

Six months before Walker Evans III was born, President Theodore Roosevelt arrived in St. Louis to dedicate the buildings of the Louisiana Purchase Exposition. In April 1904 the fair opened to the public. Like a scene of ancient Rome before the fall, the "Ivory City" was an extravaganza. Visitors could stroll down the "Ten-Million-Dollar Pike," past cycloramas of the Galveston Flood, the Battle of Gettysburg, the Tyrolean Alps, the Wild Animal Show, and the Creation of the Earth, at ten to fifty cents a thrill, or travel by electric streetcar to the promenade of white exhibition palaces — Forestry, Agriculture, Mines and Metallurgy, Electricity, Education, each elaborately and variously capped with steeples, towers, domes, obelisks, arches, and globes. "A phantasm," Henry Adams called it, especially by night, when the Ivory City was "exquisitely lighted by thousands on thousands of electric candles, soft, rich, shadowy, palpable in their sensuous depths." At the same time, Adams scorned the sheer extravagance of the fair, and the way "a third-rate town of half-a-million people without history, education, unity, or art, and with little capital . . . threw away thirty or forty million dollars on a pageant as ephemeral as a stage flat."

With this labyrinth of temporary plasterwork, St. Louis sought to disprove that its status as a major economic crossroads was gently falling. Business was gravitating to centers north and west of the Mississippi, and Chicago was winning the battle for midwestern supremacy. In St. Louis the roads needed paving, sewer systems needed upgrading, and the smoke from the Illinois soft coal burning in every home and factory cast the city under a constant pall. But "Meet Me in St. Louis, Louis" was the song of the season, fairgoers poured into the city from every direction, and for the brief period of this great festivity, St. Louisans could afford to believe that the lights were not shining "anywhere but there."

Walker Evans Jr. was by this time vice president of H. E. Leson and Company, an advertising firm for which he had served as a junior secretary three years earlier. In those early days of advertising, the job consisted of selling magazine and newspaper space to businesses; the advertisements themselves did little more than name the product and tell the reader where to purchase it and at what price. As a man near the top of the agency, Evans probably did his share of traveling by train, stopping in dusty midwestern farm towns to chat with tradesmen pushing everything from tricycles to toilet seats.

Evans must have proved himself an able salesman, for in 1905 he left

H. E. Leson to become a local representative for Lord and Thomas, a Chicago company, at that time one of the largest advertising agencies in America. Lord and Thomas already represented Anheuser-Busch in St. Louis, with a campaign so successful that it ultimately helped to put 150 smaller breweries out of business. With the St. Louis Fair, Lord and Thomas was positioned to take advantage of the new businesses the city would attract, and young advertising men like Walker Evans Jr. were needed on the spot. Although this assignment lasted only a few months, it led to Evans' full employment as a copywriter for Lord and Thomas three years later. In 1908, when his son was nearly five years old, Evans moved his family from St. Louis to Chicago.

When Evans joined Lord and Thomas, twenty-eight-year-old Albert Lasker was the director and owned the company jointly with the aging Mr. Lord. Although the firm had been successful under the steady direction of its two Yankee founders, it was Lasker who turned it into one of the three largest in America, and at the time of Evans' appointment, there was no job as a full-time copywriter to be had anywhere else. To join Lasker's exclusive staff of nine or ten promising young men was to graduate to the top of the profession in a single move.

Lasker was among the first men in advertising who systematically attempted to decipher and make use of mass psychology. He perceived the potential of salesmanship in print and was a pioneer of the "reason why" approach to copywriting. He had a special knack for creating for his product a scientific-sounding argument, however fanciful, that would capture the faith of the typical American consumer. Lasker was able to convert an overproduction of oranges in California into orange juice, a novelty at the time, while promoting the health benefits of vitamin C. Sales of Palmolive soap soared into the millions when his campaign suggested that the ingredients — the oils of palms and olives — were those used by Cleopatra. For the Van Camp company in Indianapolis, Lasker gave canned pork and beans the stamp of reliability by promising that the food was "uniform right through the can." And he turned the disturbingly inauthentic taste of Van Camp's canned milk product into an asset by claiming, "If it has not the almond flavor, it is not the genuine!" An illustrated ad for this product showed a cow made entirely of tin cans, underscored by the slogan "You can have a cow right in your kitchen."

In 1908, the year that Evans was hired for Lasker's staff, Lord and Thomas got the Quaker Oats account, and Lasker put Evans in charge of the Aunt Jemima pancake flour campaign. This assignment made an indelible impression on his son, who was later to cringe with embarrassment at the thought of it. Under a picture of a plump and smiling mammy in a kerchief was the reassuring cry, "I'se in town, honey!"

At the end of the day, Walker Evans Jr. commuted home by train from downtown Chicago to the North Shore suburb of Kenilworth. The smallest village in America in 1896, Kenilworth had been incorporated only twelve years before the Evanses moved there from St. Louis. The town was the idea of a well-to-do Chicago businessman named Joseph Sears, who had dreamed of creating a suburban American village on the model of Kenilworth in Warwickshire, England. To reinforce its British associations, the founding residents named all the streets after places or characters in Sir Walter Scott's *Kenilworth* and other historical novels; thus Essex Road, Devonshire Lane, Tudor Place, Exmoor, Warwick, and — after Scott's own Victorian residence — Abbotsford. Along the straight and spacious avenues they planted sugar maples, catalpas, ginkgoes, and copper beeches. Under a gathering arch of American elms, Kenilworth Avenue led from the railroad station half a mile to the bathing beach on the shore of Lake Michigan — the unobstructed view of fathers coming home to the suburbs.

In Sears' Anglophilic village there were two churches, the Episcopal church and the Protestant Union church, "dedicated to the worship of God over and above all minor differences of opinion." Minor doctrinal differences may have been tolerated in Kenilworth, but more was not. The town bylaws stated unequivocally, "Sales to Caucasians only." Residents could participate in a ladies' social club, the Kenilworth Neighbors' Association, card parties, and dances for all ages. There was a public school, a nine-hole golf course by the shore, and a boathouse on the sandy beach. For the socially ambitious young Evanses, admission to Kenilworth was as good as membership in an exclusive country club. This was not just a village; at the turn of the century, Kenilworth was "the Tuxedo of suburbs."

At the far end of the well-tended front lawns along Kenilworth Avenue loomed Italian villas, Georgian mansions, and French chateaus. The Evanses' house, which stood at the corner of Richmond and Woodstock avenues and had just been completed when the family moved into it, was modest compared to many of those around it; it was a standard midwestern bungalow, shingle upstairs and stucco below.

In the days of Walker's childhood, nothing but a field stood between his house and the railroad tracks. A few brief essays he later wrote show the great impact the railroad had on his imagination. "He who travels by rail over the lesser lines of the U.S.A. clangs and shunts straight into his own childhood," he wrote in middle age. From the dining room window, he could watch his father board the train every morning and disembark every afternoon onto the platform of Kenilworth's rusticated Romanesque railroad station. Since the train from Chicago passed through every hour, Walker's day was measured by its mournful whistle and pounding arrival, "and the ting ting ting . . . of the warning bell — that heart-rending tinny decrescendo which is an early lesson in the relativity of the senses." On summer days Walker would play with his best friend, Jimmy, on the hot tracks; their favorite game was to leave a penny on the rails for the next train to flatten into a pure copper round. They also had plenty of opportunity to memorize freight car insignia, "like old ditties beating in the back of our heads. We once knew them all by heart," Walker recalled. "They were with us like the weather, like the backs of books we collected, and like the streets we walked in."

For the children of Kenilworth, summer was formless and without end. Day after day they could idle about on the beach or around the boathouse or retreat into the shade of the willows. They could trail after their parents across the golf course, retrieving balls and caddying clubs, occasionally getting their chance at a swing. There were blackberries to pick in the south woods, hickory nuts and hazelnuts all around the village. They could follow the iceman down the road when he came over from nearby Winnetka or go fetch the mail at the village store by the station.

Everyone knew everyone within the boundaries of Kenilworth's one square mile, and almost all doors were open to children. Walker had especially fond memories of Fanny Phelps, a young married woman with no children of her own, who was the first person to instill in him the joy of reading. In her large house on Leicester Road overlooking the golf course, she gathered children after school and read aloud to them. Though he had long since forgotten which books they read, Walker remembered in middle age how this wonderful woman had made them come alive, and how, through her, the world of literature had opened up to him effortlessly.

At home there were the standard books of the day, beginning with nursery rhymes, then classics by Charles Dickens, Sir Walter Scott, Robert Louis Stevenson, and Ernest Thompson Seton, and on to the popular serials, the Rover Boys and the Motor Boys. But Walker's parents did not read books with the warmth and intelligence of Mrs. Phelps. They were talented in other ways. His father, the frustrated architect, built an elaborate dollhouse. His mother played the piano by ear and liked to attend the opera. Their taste was conservative; their motives, especially his mother's, were social. Jessie Evans was more interested in making her way into suburban Chicago society than anything else. In spite of the family's average income and rather small house, she employed two servants, a girl to cook and clean and a black manservant, whom they referred to as the butler. Jessie was able to keep up the appearance of comfort and prosperity, but she could not hide her feelings that she deserved more than she had and that her upbringing had led her to expect better. Although her husband did his best to meet her high expectations, she was coquettish, pouty, and extravagant. While conveying to her children a sense of privilege and entitlement, she undercut that sense by suggesting that they were partly to blame for her trials.

A few surviving photographs of Walker as a child show his striking resemblance to his mother, from the downward slant of his hazel eyes to the impish curl of his pert little mouth. Walker confessed to his first wife that as a child he was in love with his mother but that she was perpetually out of reach. He cried out for her embrace and was repeatedly spurned with the impatient rebuff, "Oh, dry up!" One evening when she was dressed up for the opera and lit a cigarette, he felt the first stirrings of sexual arousal.

Walker's sheltered life in Kenilworth came to an abrupt end in the fall of 1914, when his family moved to Toledo, Ohio. The decision to move was swift and unexpected. Less than a year earlier his father had bought the house they had leased for five years at 430 Woodstock Avenue. Thus settled, he had also become involved in community debates and petitions having to do with the quality of life in Kenilworth. In June 1913 he was one of a committee of ten neighbors who protested the lengthening of Richmond Avenue. In hopes of saving the untended field in which his son loved to play, Evans suggested that the road be moved to the other side of the tracks. These were hardly the thoughts and actions of a man who expected to leave town in just over a year.

But an opportunity came up in Toledo that Evans couldn't afford to turn down, one that would soon make him a specialist in one of the fastest-growing American industries: the automobile. In 1914, Toledo was enjoying a boom year, with a good share of the automobile business to its credit, led by Willys-Overland; advertising followed quickly behind. Evans' first job was on the Willys-Overland account at an agency called C. H. Fuller. The family settled into Chesebrough Dwellings, a new housing development. Two years later they moved to 637 Winthrop Street and Evans left C. H. Fuller for Martin V. Kelly, where he was remembered for creating the slogan for Fisk tires, "Time to Re-Tire."

As his father moved up in his career, Walker, at the brink of puberty, was abruptly wrenched from idyllic Kenilworth, from the lake and the golf course, the train tracks and the open field, from his best friend, Jimmy, and from reading with Fanny Phelps. Toledo was a big industrial city. It was racially mixed; for the first time Walker was exposed to people unlike himself — Poles, Italians, blacks, Jews — and learned that their circumstances differed as well. He had never seen the slums of Chicago; his occasional trips into the city had consisted of visits to the natural history museum or Marshall Field's department store. And even though he had attended a public school, the little wooden three-room schoolhouse in Kenilworth, filled with the well-mannered children of the well-to-do, was like *Babes in Toyland,* he later reflected, compared with the big public school he entered in Toledo.

In summer Jessie and her children would escape the heat and crowds of Toledo to relax at resort hotels. Walker later reminisced about the summer hotels of his youth, remembering their "atmosphere of flannels and flirtations, of ice-water pitchers and corn-fed gaiety, and the gazebo that was off limits to the unchaperoned after dark." When he was about fifteen years old, they went to the Bedford Springs Hotel in Pennsylvania, famous for its medicinal springs, mountain views, and vast acreage of unspoiled forest. Within the safety of the hotel grounds and surrounding countryside, Walker was free to take off on his own, to stroll along the causeway idly searching for the source of the legendary springs. He was also able — in his fertile imagination, if not in fact — to dodge the proprietary gaze of his mother and lose his virginity with a chambermaid.

At about this time his father began a love affair with their next-door neighbor on Winthrop Street, Louise Hower, who was the wife of Henry Hower, a Willys-Overland executive, and the mother of two young boys. Evans was attracted to her good looks and intelligence; compared to Jessie, she was independent, authoritative, well read in politics and world affairs, and supremely capable of running her household as well. Yet it was clear that she was unhappily married, and Evans could not help wanting to alleviate her pain. If he was not solely responsible for her divorce, he gave her more reason to see it through. When she divorced Henry in 1918, Evans left his family and moved in with her and her sons. This odd arrangement was never discussed openly at home. Walker lived under the shadow of his estranged parents' silent hostilities, wondering why his father would want to desert them and whether he really had.

Walker turned inward. He wrote in a diary "confessions and descriptions of things I didn't want anyone to see." He also acquired a Brownie camera and took pictures of the neighborhood, like a detective in search of clues. He taught himself the rudiments of photographic printing and developed his pictures in the bathroom. At school he was starved for lessons in more visual subjects than the requisite Latin and arithmetic. He became interested in geography and mapmaking to the point of obsession; when instructed to draw one map, Walker would draw twenty, and he covered the wall of his bedroom with maps. In other subjects his powers of concentration flagged and his schoolwork suffered. Except in English, he earned barely passing grades. Latin, which he had just begun to study, was especially hard. He became moody and lethargic and could not be persuaded to make a greater effort.

All of the Evanses were due for a radical change of scene. In January 1919, it was decided that Jessie and Jane should move to New York City, where Jane would enroll at Finch, a private day school for girls, and that Walker should be sent to an eastern boarding school. At the suggestion of their Toledo neighbor Edward Cady, Jessie applied for Walker's admission to the Loomis Institute, in Windsor, Connecticut — a new school, reasonably priced, reasonably good, where Cady's son had gone. The application stated candidly that Walker's schoolwork was very poor; he was, as it explained, "bright but inattentive."

At that time, an inattentive student who wished to board had a better chance at getting into Loomis than into many more established schools. In the fall of 1919, when Walker was admitted, Loomis was only ten years old. Its classes were small, each consisting of fewer than twenty boys, the majority of whom were day students from nearby Hartford. In his first year, Walker was scheduled to repeat his sophomore year of high school. When asked to indicate on his application which college he was preparing for, Walker, undaunted by his poor grades, decided that he would aim for Yale.

The Loomis campus was built on a farm and included a few acres of farmland by the Connecticut River. Students were offered courses in agriculture and farm management as well as in the sciences and humanities. Each year on a fine October day they left their desks to harvest the corn, an activity the headmaster, a man named Batchelder, believed would build character in the city boys who predominated at Loomis. "Mr. B." was the quintessential boys' school headmaster, as one of Walker's classmates recalled: he was firm but kindly, he expected his students to take a healthy interest in sports as well as in their studies, and he was apt to remind them, whenever the opportunity arose, that he was himself a Harvard man.

Walker took an immediate dislike to Mr. B. and to the school in general. Having weathered the big-city high school in Toledo, he found his Loomis classmates from sheltered backgrounds like "a bunch of babies" and the Christian-gentleman ethic the school aspired to teach them as hypocritical as his parents' failing marriage. He felt closed in, bored, and rebellious. His alienation can be readily detected in the Loomis yearbook photograph of the sophomore class. Seated in the front row, he is the only boy in his class who does not have his ankles crossed or heels together. His hands fall limply between knickered legs (his classmates are all in trousers), his hair is parted in the middle and slicked down with ointment (in the style of his father's), his lumpily tailored, hunched shoulders are tucked behind those of his nearest classmates, and he peers at the photographer with menacing eyes and the trace of a smirk.

Dudley Britton, of the Loomis class of '22, remembered Walker as something of a slob, a loner, and not at all a typical prep school boy — in fact, "rather a strange fellow." Britton recalled that as a student, Walker "got by" but tended to get into trouble for sneaking into the village, smoking cigarettes, or hoarding pornographic magazines under his bed. Whatever his misdemeanors, those that were discovered by the Loomis faculty were not grave enough to call for serious punishment, but Walker clearly had a bad attitude.

After earning lackluster grades, including an F in Latin, in his first year, Walker spent part of the summer of 1920 living with a Latin tutor and taking his meals with the farm superintendent. At the beginning of the fall term, Headmaster Batchelder felt that his efforts to improve his academic performance were an encouraging sign. But the year got off to an unfortunate start. The classmate with whom Walker had hoped to share a room failed to return to Loomis, leaving him unexpectedly bereft of his best friend. At the end of the term he failed Latin again, after all of his hard work over the summer. His disappointment fed his increasingly negative attitude toward the school and his classmates.

It could not have helped matters that his parents' separation was now firmly established; his father had moved to Cleveland with Louise Hower, her two boys, and, for the sake of appearances, her parents. So that he could finance trips to New York to see his family, Evans was holding a job in the Cleveland office of a New York–based advertising agency called the Blackman Company. However much or little Batchelder knew of the Evanses' family troubles, he noticed that Walker's mind had begun to work in circles. The boy's depression was so great that it began to affect him physically. It was, Walker was to realize only much later, a kind of nervous breakdown, a crisis of faith that would have sent parents and faculty in a later decade in search of psychiatric help. But none was recommended.

In November, Batchelder sent Walker home to New York, where his mother and sister now lived at 112 East 74th Street. His father, who was visiting at the time, agreed that Walker was "out of adjustment to such a degree" that it was necessary to explore alternatives to Loomis. The impression among some of Walker's classmates was that he had been expelled. More precisely, it had been suggested that he should make a change. He left Loomis with the headmaster's "cordial consent," as did a few other troublemakers — a group of three or four boys who, like Walker, had become, as Batchelder phrased it, "a decided detriment to the school."

Batchelder did his best to find Walker an alternative. In a letter to the Reverend Mr. Mulford of the Ridgefield School, in Ridgefield, Connecticut, he patiently explained that Walker was "in no sense bad or dull" but "somewhat subject to moods, and . . . likely to become more depressed than circumstances warrant." He also suggested that although Walker had been heading for the academic department at Yale, he had better shift his sights to Sheffield Scientific School or some smaller college. He hoped that Ridgefield might have room for Walker as early as the forthcoming January. Apparently it didn't.

Thrown back into the lap of his fractured family, Walker enrolled for the remainder of the fall term in a New York City public high school. If he was unhappy there, it was nonetheless preferable to staying at home with his lonely mother and older sister, to whom he had never been especially close. Now just seventeen, he awakened to the discomfort of losing step with his prep school contemporaries.

In December he took it upon himself to write to the headmaster of Mercersburg Academy, in Mercersburg, Pennsylvania, requesting a catalogue and an application. Mercersburg was a large school, whose aim was to reach the "typical American boy" and give him every opportunity to develop his powers. The faculty promised "by warm personal interest to convince boys that we desire to help them."

Suitably impressed with the catalogue, or perhaps aware that his choices were narrowing, Walker decided to make every effort to get into Mercersburg directly after Christmas. "I am *very anxious* to come," he wrote to the headmaster, Mr. Irvine. "I feel very strongly that Mercersburg is the place for me." In a tone of humility and fresh resolve, he pleaded his case. He admitted to doing poorly at Loomis and realized that the fault was his own. "I am now just seventeen and am anxious to get a fresh start before it is too late." He expected now, he said, "to use former mistakes to advantage."

Recommendations were hurriedly solicited from friends in Toledo. Edward Cady posited that Walker was a boy "of good habits and character" and added, even less accurately, that "his home influences have always been very good." Harvey Robison, a real estate broker, assured the admissions board that Walker was "certainly bright enough if he applies himself." And from Loomis, Mr. Batchelder delivered a lengthy and considered account of his former student. He admitted that Walker Evans "gives the impression of being rather sour and fault-finding, and of being rather sophisticated and supercilious. We talked with him repeatedly about this, and his father talked with him as well. I think he made some efforts to correct the appearance which he always claimed was not an expression of his real attitude, and there were times when we were distinctly encouraged." But Batchelder was cautious not to promise that he was anything more than an average student at best: "I think his ability for abstract intellectual work is limited, but no more than that of many boys who have done accept-ably . . . I am sorry not to be more specific, but I certainly cannot recommend the boy with any heartiness, while at the same time I feel that he has a good deal of good in him, and that thrown in the right environment, with a new attitude, he may come out well."

On January 8, 1921, Walker entered the third form at Mercers-burg Academy, and he proved within the next few months that Mr.

Batchelder's hopes were well placed. His Latin score rose to 78; English, always his best subject, was 83. With a B average, he tasted the small triumphs of good scholarship. But he was not sure he was in the right school. In popular boys' books of the period such as *Stover at Yale,* Walker had read about Phillips Academy in Andover, Massachusetts, which at the time had perhaps the highest number of Yale-bound graduates in the country. During the summer of 1921 he applied for a transfer to Andover for his senior year.

He spent the summer in uncertainty. While Mercersburg politely asked whether or not he was planning to return, Andover, privy to his poor record at Loomis, wanted to know more about his bearing and attitude and whether his weaknesses were now viewed as "merely temporal or permanent." In late July, a letter from Mr. Irvine, an Andover graduate himself, persuaded the school to admit Walker for his senior year.

Walker entered Andover in the fall of 1921, at the start of what became known among loyal alumni as "the Golden Twenties." The school was then under the headmastership of Albert Stearns, who made a point of reminding his students of their great privilege in having a superior education. Academically, Andover was tougher than the Ivy League colleges most of the students went on to, but its regimen encouraged a high degree of self-discipline. To Walker's liking, his new faculty had the sense to leave the boys alone. A large library encouraged reading beyond the required textbooks, and Walker was able to spend hours in the stacks by himself. Although the school encouraged team sports, he was relieved to discover that participation was not required; as long as a boy could shinny up to the top of the flagpole, he was qualified to graduate. Even Latin was probably a less painful subject under the tutelage of the charming Charles Henry Forbes. Virgil's *Aenead* was on the program for every Andover senior; Forbes taught it not only as verse but as a guide to Augustan Rome. He loved puns and mimicry and never tired of inventing new and amusing ways of teaching dactylic hexameter. As one student remembered, Forbes' "manner in the classroom was that of a gentleman entertaining us at home."

For the first time since leaving home, Walker was happy. He made a good impression on his classmates, in spite of the fact that he was not an athlete or an exceptional scholar, and he liked Andover, even though he felt poorer than most of his peers and more provincial than those who had grown up in Boston or New York and could boast fathers and grandfathers among the proud alumni. But in the troubling interim between Loomis and Andover, Walker had made himself over. He had become fastidious about his style and appearance. At least to classmates like Jack Watson, who knew him casually, Walker seemed to be "a nice fellow who dressed well and behaved himself." Indeed, he was voted one of the vainest boys in the senior class poll.

Walker was also pegged, along with his friend Joseph Verner Reed, as being among the most eccentric in the class of 1922. His addiction to tea in his later years might easily date back to afternoons spent in the dorm room of his worldly friend Reed, who was known for the habit of drinking tea. Reed, whose father was an oil tycoon, was exceedingly rich, even in comparison with his well-to-do classmates. He carried the majority of the "vanity" vote and was also voted best dressed, perhaps partly for being the only senior in possession of his own full-length raccoon coat.

That Walker was noticed at all as an entering student in a class of 150 boys suggests that his character and demeanor were striking. There was something seductive about him, but it was hard for his classmates to identify exactly what it was. With his slight figure and natty dress, his small, effeminate mouth, his long, impertinent nose, and eyes that slanted downward like those of a faithful, melancholy dog, he embodied intriguing contradictions. "E is for Evans, they call him a snake, and his innocent stare is only a fake," the seniors wrote for the class alphabet, with the weight of presentiment.

Snake here carried a double meaning, being the nickname of the secret society Walker joined at Andover, otherwise known as Phi Lambda Sigma. Unique among prep schools and eventually banned for being undemocratic, Andover's secret societies were the students' nearly private domain. For its lucky members, Phi Lambda Sigma was an oasis from the rigors of academic life, a sanctuary from their roommates' Victrolas, and the only place they were allowed to go after the Saturday night movie and stay as late as ten P.M. The height of club members' privileges was the freedom to partake of soda pop, ice cream, and even cigarettes. These benefits seemed worth the humiliation of hazing, which was the lot of every willing candidate for membership; the ritual included obedience to the command to "take the position" — bums up with hands around ankles — for a good swat with the adjustment rod from the nearest Morris chair.

Walker also joined the choir and the glee club. Every morning at 7:45, after breakfast in the Beanery, he took his stand in the chapel's front choir stall, where he had an unobstructed view of hawk-eyed Headmaster Stearns, who delivered the news of the world with an emphatically Republican slant and then kneeled, shut his eyes tightly, and prayed for the forgiveness of his boys' sins.

The Andover Glee Club was very popular in the 1920s, even among those who were not particularly musical, mainly because it meant giving concerts at the nearby girls' schools, followed by dancing. Contact with girls was otherwise a rare event in the life of an Andover boy. Although Abbott Academy, Bradford Hall, and Rogers' Hall were just a stone's throw away, the amount of preliminary paperwork involved in a brief chaperoned visit — letters from parents and faculty on both sides — was discouraging to all but the most determined young lovers. To make matters worse, Stearns banned all dances at Andover for two years during Walker's time, so alarmed was he at the style of postwar dancing. Thus, casual meetings with girls were a privilege open only to those willing to sing for them, and Walker Evans was among them.

In his last and happiest year of school, Walker remained an unexceptional student. He had a C average in English, French, and history, barely passed mathematics, and failed Latin once again. It is therefore not surprising that he was not on the final list for Yale with Joe Reed and about seventy other boys from the class of 1922, although his yearbook entry states that he expected to be. Owing to an administrative mix-up, he arrived in New Haven in the fall of 1922 fully expecting to enroll, only to be told by the dean that his scores hadn't added up and he had not been admitted.

On the spot, without having his parents available to discuss it,

Walker switched his sights to Williams College, in Williamstown, Massachusetts, drove up there, and, as he described the casual way it was done in those days, "just walked in." A small college, Williams was only a slight change from the large prep school he had just left. Situated in the Berkshire hills, the college retained a strong sense of community, being at a safe distance from cultural and social distractions. With a student body not much larger than Andover's, it had just as many rules of conduct, mainly having to do with enforcing respect for upperclassmen and keeping a low profile in town. College loyalty was foremost in the shaping of a Williams man, and to help engender an interest in becoming one, upperclassmen concocted little rules for entering freshmen, who were forbidden to wear the school color (purple) and to sit in the front row of Jesup Hall or on certain outdoor benches, and who always had to yield to upperclassmen on the street or when entering buildings.

To reinforce in the freshmen the idea that they were starting at the bottom again, the sophomore class stormed them within a few days of their arrival, a traditional event that was usually ended just short of serious injuries by the carefully scheduled arrival on the scene of juniors and seniors. Kidnappings were also popular. Most of all, the Williams man was measured by his abilities on the playing field, and those who weren't varsity material were expected to be enthusiastic spectators and join the ranks of the raccoon-coated loyalists on the bleachers. Whether or not a student played ball, he had to submit to the Physical Trials every October — the broad jump, the fence vault, the baseball throw, and the quarter-mile run. Walker was among the large percentage of his class who failed this test completely.

If Walker had formed any romantic attachments by the time he entered college, he was far from prepared to commit to them. Certainly his parents' example would have given him pause; his sister's was no more inspiring. In the middle of his freshman year, Jane married Talbot Magruder Brewer, a Williams man himself, class of 1916. Brewer had served overseas in the First World War as a lieutenant in the 306th Machine Gun Battalion. He now had a job as a personnel manager on Wall Street, but he would not always have to work for a living; his grandfather had founded Metropolitan Gas, the forerunner of Con Edison, and the family was well off. As Walker perceived it, the marriage was arranged by his mother, who was anxious for Jane, who had graduated from the Finch School, to be married and secure. In Talbot Brewer she saw a considerate and hardworking fellow who might provide the kind of stability, financial and otherwise, the whole family needed. Her hopes, as it turned out, were well placed in the young lieutenant.

Unlike her mother's, Jane's January wedding was a modest affair. Finances, not to mention gaiety, were strained by the fact that the bride's father, who traveled in from Cleveland, was supporting two families. Adding a somber note to the event, the Evans family was in an official state of mourning for Charles Crane, who had died in Pasadena just a few days before the wedding. Thus the darkly dressed Evanses and their Brewer in-laws were the only witnesses to the ceremony, which took place at the groom's parents' townhouse, at 313 West 91st Street, while outside an army of plows scraped seven and a half inches of wet snow off the pavement.

As far as Walker could see, the American dream of a happy family life, one of the targets at which his father had learned to aim his subliminal advertising persuasions, was neither pure nor true. In his attempt to remain loyal to two lives, his father was presenting false fronts to everyone. He felt too much guilt to divorce the helpless Jessie but not enough courage to marry the capable Louise.

In a voracious program of reading having almost nothing to do with his freshman English course, Walker was beginning to learn that he was not alone in his doubts. It was during his freshman year at Williams that he became what he later described as "a pathological bibliophile." He skipped classes to spend time in the library alone or to pursue through a network of like-minded classmates the latest issues of the new literary journals, including Margaret Anderson's *Little Review*, Scofield Thayer's *The Dial,* and T. S. Eliot's *Criterion.* To Walker's generation of college students, it was a novel idea that art or literature might have anything to do with real life. They "were taught to regard culture as a veneer, a badge of class distinction — as something assumed like an Oxford accent or a suit of English clothes," as one contemporary explained. This was a condition held

over from the era of Victorian prosperity, the vestiges of which came
to an abrupt end following the First World War. The poets and writers
emerging at the time expressed their ironic detachment from a society
based on material greed, a corrupt church, and the false security of
negotiated world peace. Instead they explored the meaning of the
ordinary and the depths of the human psyche.

Evans was reading books now considered classics of the twentieth
century almost as they rolled off the presses. "Just look who was
publishing then!" he later exclaimed. "That's who I was reading . . .
You can be sure that Williams didn't teach you those. You had to go
and get them. We did." T. S. Eliot was becoming recognized as a poet
of revolutionary dimensions; "The Love Song of J. Alfred Prufrock"
was a cry of rage against the petty bourgeoisie. Virginia Woolf was
upsetting the literary canons in England with her stream-of-con-
sciousness method in *Jacob's Room.* Perhaps the most talked-about
book of the time was James Joyce's epic *Ulysses,* which described
twenty-four unexceptional hours in the life of an unexceptional man.
Joyce's detachment from and lack of moral stance toward his hero's
drinking, politics, and sexual desire, and his candid descriptions of
normal bodily functions, shocked his Anglo-American readers and
led to the book's being banned as obscene in the United States and
Britain. Meanwhile, the work of D. H. Lawrence was shocking for the
opposite reason; his vivid descriptions of sexual passion in books like
Women in Love were thought to be dangerous. Walker's French instructor, perceiving an eager and open mind, gave him Lawrence to
read on the sly.

For Evans, the work of modern writers was a passport out of his
family's world; it liberated him from his past. Through the books of
the literary avant-garde he acquired the critical distance he needed
to see that the social façades of his childhood might be false, his
father's profession manipulative, if not mendacious, his mother's ambitions naive, and her dependence on her scattered family pathetic.
As for his own future, in the rapture of his burgeoning passion for
literature, he could picture himself only as a writer.

This dreamy vision of the future had little to do with his course
of study at Williams, at which he did poorly. His English and French

classes rarely sparked his interest, and he flunked Latin twice during his first year. If he returned as a sophomore, he would have to repeat that tormenting subject. With Latin a recurring and insurmountable hurdle ahead of him, for all he knew, he might never graduate. Leaving Williams for the summer vacation in June 1923, Walker decided that in his own mind he had graduated from college and would never return.

2 *Paris and New York*

IN LATER YEARS, Walker Evans explained that he left Williams after his freshman year in order to continue his education in Paris. If this was indeed his clear intention, it was frustrated for three long years. Apparently his father was not immediately willing to support the plan, nor could he afford to carry it out on his own. Instead he pursued an ambition of almost equal intensity but closer to home — to get into the stacks of the New York Public Library. As he later recalled, he simply went to the head librarian and told him that he was longing to work there, that he was even willing to work without pay. As it turned out, as a page in the stacks he would earn the respectable wage of $75 a month. On March 1, 1924, Evans reported to work at the main reference library, at Fifth Avenue and 42nd Street. Two weeks later he was transferred to the Map Room, a subdivision of the Department of American History. He was out of the stacks, but he had seen them, and given his teenage passion for mapmaking, the move was not altogether disappointing.

In Room 312, where Evans went to work, the shelves were stuffed with maps and atlases, and the long viewing tables were often filled to capacity with visitors. Much of his job was routine — helping an agent from a telephone company who was laying plans for new lines, a U.S. Air Mail Service agent searching out possible landing strips, and, almost daily, real estate men who were studying the detailed maps of New York City for information on the location of sewer systems and electricity lines. Occasionally an artist, writer, or historian appeared, in search of authentic detail, geographical grounding, or insight into the past. Within the four high walls of Room 312, studded with fading leather and gold leaf, there was a mix of fantasy and hard practical fact that appealed to the visual as well as the literary mind. For a self-proclaimed pathological bibliophile with a fondness for geography, there was the pleasure of handling the lavish old volumes of such treasures as the *Blaeus Atlas*. At the very least, even on a bad day, it was an escape from home.

In the spring of 1925, Evans was joined in the Map Room by Lindley Hubbell, a young poet three years his senior. Evans and Hubbell both believed that they had better things to do — namely, writing — and when they became friendly they alternated day and evening shifts to make that possible. Hubbell was preparing his first book of poems for the Yale University Press. Evans was struggling with short stories. Hubbell was sympathetic to Evans' literary efforts, and they talked of his plans to join the steady stream of American writers moving to Paris. If he could be supported for one year abroad, he promised his father, he would take care of himself from then on. As for an American college education, he had lost interest in having one.

Evans quit his job in the Map Room in the fall of 1925. At about the same time, his sister, Jane, and her husband moved to a small farm on Somerstown Road in Ossining, New York, forty miles north of the city, up the Hudson River. With Jane now beyond easy visiting distance for her mother, it must have been obvious to the whole family that Jessie Evans might make dangerous emotional demands on her only son. Walker's father finally agreed to finance his trip to Paris. He was to enroll at the Collège de France in a course for foreign students, "La Civilisation Française," and audit classes at the Sorbonne. His main objective, he said, was to study the French language and its great literature. With the promise of $15 a week from his father, he set sail for Cherbourg at noon on April 6, 1926, aboard the RMS *Orduna*, probably in third class. Among his belongings he packed his brand-new six-dollar vest-pocket camera, a compact black box with a lens that unfolded on an extendable bellows, the most popular amateur camera of the period.

Like many young writers from America, Evans imagined that by immersing himself in the rich artistic atmosphere of Paris, he would break free of the old-fashioned conventions and personal inhibitions that reined him in. The palpable sensuality of the city might awaken him to feelings he had never known before. He would live for the moment, let experience take him where it would. "Paris was a great machine for stimulating the nerves and sharpening the senses," the writer Malcolm Cowley remembered. "Paintings and music, street noises, shops, flower markets, modes, fabrics, poems, ideas, everything seemed to lead toward a half-sensual, half-intellectual swoon."

Evans had been raised to think of artists as forbidden fruit and the life they led abroad as charged and erotic, and he was longing to get a taste of it. Maybe he would fall in love; surely he was more likely to find opportunities for casual sex than he would find at home. Compared to New York in the 1920s, Europe offered a liberal atmosphere in which to lose his sexual inhibitions, indulge his fantasies, and test the strength of the moral code he was raised with. He was off to a place where extramarital affairs like his father's were not only tolerated, they were taken for granted.

Most of all, his year in Paris would give him a fresh perspective on his own country, a tradition as old as Thomas Jefferson's *Notes on the State of Virginia* and as new as Gertrude Stein's *The Making of Americans*. In the 1920s, the French were also enjoying their share of American popular culture. Evans traveled to Paris in the wake of Josephine Baker's pink flamingo feather dance and Charlie Chaplin's *The Gold Rush*. He also followed a growing number of American poets, writers, artists, and composers who had more or less transplanted themselves in Paris. Ernest Hemingway, Ezra Pound, Virgil Thomson, T. S. Eliot, and Dorothy Parker were all in Paris in the spring of 1926. On April 20, they signed the leather-bound guest book at Shakespeare and Company, where their fellow American, Sylvia Beach, was hosting a memorial exhibition of Walt Whitman artifacts.

Evans most likely made Shakespeare and Company, a bookshop and lending library, one of his first objectives upon arriving in Paris

on April 17, for Sylvia Beach was already well known to him by reputation. Her shop had been a haven for English-speaking expatriates
in Paris since it opened, in 1919. Three years later the determined
young woman had secured her place in modern literary history by
publishing Joyce's *Ulysses*. With the aid of subscribers she had solicited from the growing ranks of Joyce's avid readers, she had done
what no one else dared to do, simply by taking the book to the printer,
with every word just as he wrote it. In 1922 *Ulysses* came out in an
edition of one thousand copies. The book, according to the critic
Cyril Connolly, "lay stacked like dynamite in a revolutionary cellar."
The American journalist Janet Flanner told how "it burst over us like
an explosion in print whose words and phrases fell upon us like a
gift of tongues, like a less than holy Pentecostal experience."

Though *Ulysses* was banned in the United States, Evans was well
acquainted with it, for the book as it had appeared in a series of
installments had passed from hand to hand among curious young
readers and writers; its very title was a code word for literary freedom.
The fact that Bloom, its central character, was an advertising man, a
family man, and an adulterer — an ordinary man with a repressed
desire to break free from his conventional middle-class life and the
demands of his marriage — would surely have made him a compelling figure to Evans, whose image of his own father as a social coward
entangled in the conventions of his profession and upbringing loomed
large. Joyce seemed to know Bloom's every heartbeat. And he described his daily movements with ice-cold impartiality, in a language
unintelligible to all but the initiated. To Evans, Joyce was so powerful,
he seemed not of this world. That they now breathed the air of the
same city was nothing short of miraculous.

Evans soon became a regular visitor to Shakespeare and Company.
On fine days, an open shelf of new books was set just outside the
window, where it was presided over by a black cat named Lucky.
Inside, the shop was comfortably and modestly decorated in a style
that both charmed the French and reminded Americans of home.
There were black-and-white Serbian rugs on the floor and antique
chairs from the flea market. Standing amid her densely packed shelves
was Sylvia Beach herself, a sharp-eyed, broad-shouldered young woman
habitually clad in a velvet smoking jacket, with a cigarette dangling

between two fingers. Evans discovered that she was easy to talk to, especially if the visitor proved himself well read. "She sensed that I knew my Joyce," he recalled.

At the time of Evans' stay in Paris, Joyce was in the habit of appearing at Shakespeare and Company at least once a day. From across the cluttered room Evans could have studied his slight, slumping figure — wearing a dark blue suit, with a black felt hat cocked on his head, a black patch over his right eye, and dirty white tennis shoes — perusing the shelves or checking the latest accounts of *Ulysses* with Beach. But most often, as soon as Evans saw him entering the shop, he slipped away.

One day Beach offered to introduce Evans to Joyce; in terror, he declined. He might have known by then how freely Beach extended her introductions, and how inevitably awkward their outcome was. Almost every young writer who expressed an interest in Joyce was invited to shake hands with Shakespeare and Company's main exhibit and to test his or her talents at making him speak. Dwight Macdonald, a writer and recent Yale graduate, found the invitation irresistible but the test impossible. "Yes," "No," "Who?" and "Mmmmmmm" were all he could elicit from the genius in one desperate hour. "It was like trying to open a safe," Macdonald later said, "without the combination."

Though Evans never did shake Joyce's hand, he repeatedly spoke of this nonevent in later years, perhaps because it was the only time during his year abroad that he came within range of the literati he had spent so long preparing himself to meet. Having arrived at the center of modern culture, he found himself wide-eyed, tongue-tied, and lonely. For some the 1920s may have been the city's golden age, but "not for me," he later admitted. Bohemian Paris was in itself an establishment, and he was just a student, "a nobody." Even if he was well informed and could recognize André Gide in his broad-rimmed Stetson, having an apéritif at the Café des Deux Magots, or knew which regulars at the Café Sélect were the models for the main characters of Hemingway's *The Sun Also Rises,* just published that year and the talk of literary Paris, he was too shy and too proud to push himself on people who had no reason to care who he was.

As it happened, several of his future friends and acquaintances

were in Paris that year, though they didn't meet at the time. Among
them was Berenice Abbott, a young American photographer from
Springfield, Ohio, who, along with her former teacher Man Ray, was
the official portraitist for what was known as "the Crowd." Her work
and Man Ray's monopolized the walls of Shakespeare and Company,
and her portrait of Joyce, which she made in 1926, might have been
among the latest additions around the hearth during Evans' year in
Paris. Harry and Caresse Crosby, whom Evans was later to meet in
New York, were also in Paris at the time. Wealthy Bostonians, the
Crosbys had recently started the Black Sun Press with the intention
of publishing their favorite young poets (as well as Harry's own
poems) in tastefully designed, bound, and boxed limited editions, a
pleasure to the hand as well as to the eye. Their home, at 19 rue de
Lille, was the casual meeting place of well-known poets, models for
the couturier Patou, bookies and whores, artists, photographers, and
miscellaneous young Americans. But Evans was not among them. Nor
was he aware that a recent Harvard graduate named Thomas Dabny
Mabry, eventually to become an intimate friend, was roaming the
same halls and dozing in the same lecture rooms of the Sorbonne.

Evans would have to return to New York to meet his fellow expatriates. For the time being, he had to be content with the friendship of the other foreign students staying at Madame Thuilier's pension at 5 rue de la Santé, where he was obliged to speak French. He
got himself a few jobs translating, and he struggled with his writing.
But he was humbled by his own high standards, and Paris only made
them higher.

The level of candor and self-revelation then required of young
writers of fiction came no more easily to Evans in Paris than it had
in New York. The deceptions and secrecies of his family life made
him more inclined to be a spy than a confessor. To Evans, the very
act of seeing belonged to the fascinating realm of the forbidden. But
in Paris he encountered a respect for the visual arts unknown in
America, and a corresponding tolerance for staring that he had never
imagined possible. "Stare," he advised his admirers years later. "It is
the only way to educate your eye, and more. Stare, pry, listen, eaves-
drop. Die knowing something. You are not here long." In the early
1960s, he recalled the pastime he had perfected in Paris:

I remember my first experience as a café sitter in Europe. *There* is staring that startles the American. I tried to analyze it and came out with the realization that the European is *really* interested in just ordinary people and makes a study of man with his eyes in public. What a pleasure and an art it is to study back, and a relief to me as a young more or less educated American, with still echoing in the mind his mother's "Don't stare!" . . . But I stare and stare at people, shamelessly. I got my license at the Deux Magots, . . . where one escaped one's mother in several other senses, all good, too.

Hoping not to be taken for an American, Evans worked on his French accent and idiom. He studied the way the Frenchmen dressed, the inflections of their movements and speech, their manner of sitting, standing, smoking a cigarette, drinking an apéritif. Believing himself well disguised as a native, he could sit with an air of confidence at the Deux Magots, order a lemonade, and spend the better part of a warm afternoon. He discovered the pleasure of sitting still, not knowing what or who would next come into view, while the wicker chairs around him were rearranged to accommodate an impromptu party, a lovers' meeting, or a solo reader and the waiters in their starched white aprons hurriedly circulated among them. When fall came and the days became shorter and cooler, the terrace was heated with coal fires in braziers, and the party went on.

In the absence of a social life, Evans had plenty of time to read. His companions were the classics of Baudelaire and Flaubert, whose modernism and melancholy made them relevant to the postwar ethos. "Who could be more wonderful masters?" he later asked, though at the time he had no idea how essential and far-reaching their observations would be in training his eye.

From Baudelaire he learned that his museum was the street. He learned to see, as Baudelaire taught him, that the age he lived in had "a deportment, a glance, a smile of its own." He learned how to study the difference between the native and the foreigner, the shopkeeper and the concierge, the nouveau riche and old money, observing how each individual's idea of beauty, in Baudelaire's words, "imprints itself on his whole attire, crumples or stiffens his dress, rounds off or squares his gesture, and in the long run even ends by subtly penetrating the very features of his face." Beauty, Evans was learning, was not an absolute. It was "of a relative, circumstantial element, which will be either severally or all at once, the age, its fashions, its morals, its emotions."

Flaubert was also deeply attentive to the material expression of society. In *Madame Bovary* he described in painstaking detail the modes of dress, the arrangement of interiors, the order of provincial towns, and the ubiquitous signs of commerce on the industrial landscape of mid-nineteenth-century France. He described the chemist's house in Yonville as "plastered from top to bottom with advertisements — in running hand, copperplate, or block capitals for Vichy, Seltzer, and Barèges waters, blood purifiers, Raspail's medicine, Arabian rachout, Darcet's pastilles, Regnault's ointment, bandages, fomentations, medicinal chocolate, and whatnot." In order to expose the bourgeois society that he knew intimately and despised, Flaubert noted its visual evidence with a strict dedication to realism. He was determined to avoid the cliché, the overstatement, or the personal feeling that might contaminate the clarity of his writing and its underlying morality.

Flaubert achieved an impartial style in *Madame Bovary*, but the book resonated in personal ways for Evans. The description of advertisements exposed his father's profession as a long line of noisy competitors with souls as flat as billboards. And in Flaubert's brutal depictions of the heroine's sentimental taste — "She loved the sea only for its storms, green foliage only when it was scattered amid ruins" — Evans would have recognized the weaknesses of his own mother, whose taste for schmaltzy operas was like Emma Bovary's appetite for cheap novels, with their images of "damsels in distress swooning in lonely lodges . . . horses ridden to death on every page, gloomy forests, troubles of the heart, vows, sobs, tears, kisses, rowing boats in the moonlight, nightingales in the grove, gentlemen brave as lions and gentle as lambs."

For the first time, Evans was able to see his family at a critical distance and to know that he could survive without them, however lonely he might be. But this new and precarious sense of independence was challenged before the year was out. Casting restlessly between her estranged husband and her married daughter, Jessie Evans could no longer bear to have her son so far away. She may also have had her own fantasies about life in Paris, where she had never been. Whatever her inspiration, her arrival in Paris was a shock to her son, and her insistence on staying in the very same house, however briefly, must have made it worse. But Evans at last felt prepared to confront her. At the peak of his impatience, he sat his mother down on a park bench and told her, as if she were a naughty dog, to go home.

In the spring of 1927, after his mother was gone, Evans traveled to the South of France. After a week in Juan-les-Pins, he took a midnight boat from Villefranche to Genoa, and he spent most of April traveling through Italy in what the surviving snapshots suggest was a party of three. One picture shows a swarthy young man with mustache and beret, a slightly plump young woman with a fashionable bob, and the slender, bow-tied Evans standing together and beaming, with their arms across one another's shoulders. In another, the young woman is seated on a stone wall while the two young men lounge on the grass below her. Evans holds a chianti bottle at his hip and wears a triumphant smirk on his face, while his foot straddles his friend's leg in a gesture of brotherly abandon.

Evans used his camera to record the sights as well as his friends. Often vertical in format, the photographs are at first glance typical amateur travel snapshots — casual, nondescript, disappointing. But on closer view they reveal a more than ordinary consciousness of the camera's graphic possibilities and an aversion to the obvious land-marks as subjects. Instead, Evans seems to have been on someone's trail, taking pictures from behind a shrub or through the decorative stonework of an old building. In Juan-les-Pins he photographed his own shadow on the wall, frontally and in profile — the fuzzy gray silhouette of a tentative young spy.

In spite of an array of disappointments, Evans' creative ambitions were intact, even stronger, by the time he returned to New York in May 1927, after one year abroad. Fulfilling his promise to his father, he set out to make his own living. One evening not long after his re-turn, he wandered into a bookstore on 57th Street "and sort of asked for a job and got it," as he later told the story. The woman who ran the shop, he soon discovered, didn't know much about the business. He took charge of its French department, ordering books from France ("I had made my connections") and taking some pride in arranging window displays of the recent arrivals.

Among Evans' customers in the fall of 1927 was a serious young social worker named Dorothy Rogers who was intent on reading Proust in French. "He was a little gentleman," Rogers remembered, but she sensed that beneath his cocky wit and fastidious dress, he was lost. She gave him her phone number, and Evans once or twice accepted her invitation to dinner at the apartment she shared with college friends. On one occasion he invited her along to help him endure lunch with his mother in Ossining. "I was clean, I knew how to use a knife and fork," said Rogers. "Everybody took me home in those days." As she recalled, Evans appeared dressed like a schoolboy, in white knickerbockers and golf socks, and promised that his mother would give them strawberries and cream.

At the time Evans was living alone in an apartment in the west twenties, in the district known as Chelsea, but it was not long before he moved to Brooklyn Heights, where stately brownstones stood directly across the East River from downtown Manhattan and low rents had lately attracted the young and unattached. At the far end an avenue named Columbia Heights, where it abruptly slopes down to the river, he took two rooms in a small clapboard townhouse. From his window he had an unobstructed view of the Brooklyn Bridge, with its cathedral-like pylons, rising above riverside warehouses and billboards.

Because he worked the evening shift at the bookshop, Evans was free during the day to explore the city. His many hours in the Map Room had made him intimate with New York's geography, but it was only after his year abroad that he understood how to explore the city, to see its rising skyline, its rigid contours, and its hurried pace with the eyes of a stranger. He felt a growing obsession with seeing it all, and the little black instrument — the camera — lured him onward.

In the late 1920s, the center of culture was perceptibly shifting from Paris to New York. Those who had been to Europe and come back infused the city with their newly acquired sophistication and regard for art as a vital component in their lives. They were also better prepared than those who stayed at home to perceive the unique qualities of American culture — what the critic Van Wyck Brooks had in 1918 despairingly prescribed for American artists and writers: the search for "a usable past." But their numbers were still few, and it was not hard for them to recognize one another. In certain neighborhoods, such as Greenwich Village and Brooklyn Heights, and among poor students and artists, New York was like a small town, where people struck up conversations and made friends in bookstores, libraries, coffeeshops, and on the street. Evans began to lead the kind of life he had expected to lead in Paris, casually meeting fellow readers, Francophiles, and transient Europeans. In the two and a half years following his return from Paris, between 1927 and 1930, he met many of the people who in different ways helped to encourage his growing interest in photography.

For the most part, his new friends were not photographers themselves but artists, architects, and writers. In about 1928 Evans met a German artist named Hanns Skolle. With his huge dark eyes, shock of dark hair, and narrow jaw, Skolle had the look of a mad romantic. Charming and rootless, he was by nature a nomad. As a painter he subscribed to the machine-age aesthetic of the *neue Sachlichkeit,* or the "New Objectivity," one of a variety of abstract movements embraced by the Bauhaus, the famous German school of architecture and design which flourished in the 1920s. The sharp angles of the new buildings in New York City and the onslaught of signs in the streets and subways provided fresh visual material for Skolle's experiments in scale and geometry. As a follower of this school of thought, Skolle respected photography as an instrument of objective seeing, and he encouraged Evans to take it seriously.

At about the same time Evans met Paul Grotz, a gentle, handsome German with dazzling blue eyes and a hesitant grasp of the English language. He also shared Evans' interest in photography. Grotz was originally from Stuttgart and had studied modern architecture and landscape design in Munich. Hoping to expand his professional experience, he was looking for a temporary job with an architectural firm in New York.

Grotz had brought with him from Germany the latest camera, a

Leica. This instrument, coveted by serious young photographers, had been introduced in 1925 and was still relatively rare in the United States. Lightweight and pocket-size, it was designed for inexpensive 35mm film. With one loading, the camera held enough film for thirty-six pictures, enough for a day's outing. Perhaps most important, its fast lens enabled photographers to make brief exposures in an extraordinary range of available light.

Grotz was frankly awestruck by the skyscrapers then under construction in New York: the Chrysler, the New York Central, the Daily News. The work in progress interested him even more than the finished buildings. Although Evans was terrified of heights, on more than one occasion he and Grotz managed to persuade the construction workers to allow them onto the scaffolding with cameras, and they climbed the outdoor stairways to the highest possible point. While Grotz admired the steel beams of the rising Chrysler Building, Evans took pictures looking straight down, testing his courage against the irresistible tug of the vertiginous view.

For Grotz and Evans, taking pictures was a way to tour the city — downtown, Brooklyn, and Coney Island — and the camera helped to sharpen their visual acuity. Under the then powerful influence of European modernism, they practiced the bird's-eye view and the worm's-eye view, which distorted depth and form, and they learned to see shadows as elements in the composition that could flatten the foreground and background into a single plane. "We just had fun," Grotz said of his tours with Evans. But for his American friend, he felt, there was more at stake. Evans, he recalled, "was full of ideas."

Evans' early photographs show his awareness of current fashions in European photography, but he was also following more personal instincts, which had a lot to do with his experience as a café sitter in Paris. As he explored the city with his camera, he tried to capture a spectrum of society with its guard down. Surreptitiously, he photographed gangling schoolgirls in sunbonnets, workmen in overalls eating their lunch on the sidewalk, frowning women shoppers clutching their handbags or adjusting their coifs, a Communist with his shirtsleeves rolled, raising his fist in angry protest — any subject that he felt had the potential to reveal candid human emotion. At Coney

Island he photographed the electric-light hearts and fans of Luna Park, the fake Florentine towers, the fun-seekers enwebbed in the Ferris wheel's wires, and the mass of overheated humanity on the beach.

Like Baudelaire's quintessential painter of modern life, Constantin Guys, Evans was after "a sketch of manners," executed, as Baudelaire recommended, with "an aristocratic reserve." Nothing could have been more suitable to the quick sketch Evans was interested in making, nor to the reserved distance he wished to keep from his subjects, than Paul Grotz's miniature Leica. The camera was his notebook. Photography was becoming a substitute for writing.

Among his acquaintances in Brooklyn Heights was a young doctor named Iago Galdston who was also an amateur photographer. One day Galdston accompanied Evans on a photographic excursion around Brooklyn and was impressed with the sureness of his eye, the way he might single out an iron gate because of a certain slant of light across it, a street drain for its pattern of deep holes, or the shape of a construction crane, black against a white building. "Both of us looked, but he saw the better," Galdston recalled. But when it came to technique, Galdston considered himself better informed. "Evans, at that time, knew practically nothing about the physics of light," he said. "He did not understand what the f stop and focal length meant, or why the lesser apertures gave greater depth of focus, etc. This I humbly expounded to him."

Though he owned and studied the standard technical manuals, Evans was impatient with learning the mathematical aspect of his medium, which did not come to him any more naturally than his Latin studies at Loomis had. Furthermore, no example had prepared him to take himself seriously as a professional photographer. Neither his conservative middle-class upbringing nor his literary aspirations could show him the way. He pursued his new artistic passion "somewhat guiltily," he later admitted. "Photography had about it a ludicrous, almost comic side . . . A 'photographer' was a figure held in great disdain." At the same time, this aura of unrespectability around photography attracted Evans to the medium. "My poor father, for example . . . decided that all I wanted to do was to be naughty and get hold of girls through photography, that kind of thing. He had no idea I was serious about it. And respectable, educated people didn't. That was a world you wouldn't go into. Of course, that made it more interesting for me, the fact that it was perverse."

Others who were practicing photography in a serious way did not necessarily agree. At the time, art photographers generally followed two aesthetic lines of theory and practice, each with its own high standards. The style known as pictorialism, which emerged and flourished at the turn of the century in both Europe and America, sought to legitimize photography by imitating current trends in academic painting. Instead of taking advantage of the camera's ability to capture everyday life, the pictorialists, in an effort to bring photography under their complete artistic control, created their own world before it, posing nudes or figures dressed in flowing classical robes in gardens or woods or sunny interiors. They used soft-focus lenses and manipulated their negatives to achieve the look of a painterly surface. On city streets and country lanes, they sought the effects of smoke, rain, or fog to soften the edges of real life.

This style still prevailed in America in the early 1920s, but in Europe artists were coming to terms with the senseless carnage of the Great War in new ways. At the Bauhaus, students of architecture and design were interested in photography less as an art than as a brave new visual language uniquely capable of dissecting the modern world. Theoretically, to artists such as Laszlo Moholy-Nagy, Lux Feininger, Alexander Rodchendko, and El Lissitzky, photography was the opposite of self-expression; it was an exercise in objectivity and the manipulation of light. Subject matter was supposed to be irrelevant. Everything within their frame of reference, from the Eiffel Tower to a hen's egg, was reduced to formal experiment. While the pictorialists preferred to use the view camera, a cumbersome instrument requiring dark cloth and tripod, the modernists favored the hand-held 35mm camera, which encouraged them to view the world from new points of view, including upside down and sideways. Eager for the medium to take them by surprise, the modernists also studied microscopic and aerial photography and experimented with techniques inherent to photographic chemistry, such as solarization, a tone reversal caused by exposing the print to light in the middle of processing, and photograms, made by placing objects on photographically sensitized paper under the enlarger.

By the late 1920s, such experiments had spread into commercial application on both sides of the Atlantic and had become stale. "Modernistic photography is easily recognized by its subject matter," wrote M. F. Agha, art director of Condé Nast: "Eggs (any style). Twenty shoes, standing in a row. A skyscraper, taken from a modernistic angle. Ten tea cups standing in a row. A factory chimney seen through the ironwork of a railroad bridge (modernistic angle). The eye of a fly enlarged 2000 times. The eye of an elephant (same size). The interior of a watch. Three different heads of one lady superimposed. The interior of a garbage can. More eggs . . ."

At the same time, the values prescribed by the pictorialists and taken over by local camera clubs across the country — "restful" compositions, "atmospheric" light effects, and "pleasant" subject matter — had become predictable to the point of banality. Even the most inventive photographers of this style, such as Gertrude Kasebier, Clarence White, and Alvin Langdon Coburn, lacked relevance to the embattled postwar era. These two opposing camps — modernism and pictorialism — were beginning to have much in common. Both stressed composition over content or meaning. Both were bankrupt of ideas.

Alfred Stieglitz, who had begun his career as a leader of the New York camera clubs, was still the reigning mentor of art photography in America. Charismatic and combative, Stieglitz had placed himself at the center of aesthetic debates on photography and loudly campaigned for its legitimacy as an art form. As early as 1907 he had grown tired of these issues and begun to promote instead the art of the European avant-garde. At his gallery at 291 Fifth Avenue, he introduced to the American public the work of Rodin, Picasso, and Braque. By the late 1920s he was devoting himself almost exclusively to the work of his small stable of contemporary American painters, including that of his wife, Georgia O'Keeffe, who had captured the imagination of the New York art world with her giant and suggestive flower paintings.

In his own photography, Stieglitz synthesized a spiritual modern-

ism based on the ideas of the artist Wassily Kandinsky and the philosopher Henri Bergson, and he concluded that photography was
nothing less than an affirmation of life and of the self. Few photographers, in his mind, lived up to this lofty standard. The young Paul
Strand was the only one whose work he followed with intense interest
and from whom he thought he still might have something to learn.
In his photographs of New York, Strand had proven himself capable
of integrating the lessons of modern painting with the unique possibilities of the camera. Technically masterful, he was also a theorist.
Like Stieglitz, Strand was dedicated to photography as a revelatory
art and, in his case, a search for the real America.

Evans was not interested in falling to his knees before the great
Stieglitz in exchange for guidance, even if Stieglitz was the only
known mentor in the field. He was put off by what he took to be
Stieglitz's high-flown "artiness." Stieglitz's recent photographs of clouds,
into which he believed he had projected the very meaning of life,
seemed to Evans phoney, pictures of nothing. But eventually, at the
urging of his Brooklyn neighbor Stefan Hirsch, a painter of the precisionist school, Evans visited Stieglitz's third and last gallery, An
American Place. Armed with a small portfolio of his recent work —
most likely an assortment of street portraits as well as views of skyscrapers from high and low vantage points, all made from negatives
no larger than $2\frac{1}{2}$-by-$4\frac{1}{4}$-inch roll film — and a note from Hirsch
asking Stieglitz to consider it, Evans took the elevator to the seven-
teenth floor of 509 Madison Avenue.

The room was quiet, stark white, and brightly lit; there was an
uncomfortable atmosphere of holiness about it. Stieglitz was not
there. Georgia O'Keeffe, who was minding the desk, explained that he
would be back soon. Meanwhile, perhaps she could have a look at
the young photographer's work. Evans had seen enough of O'Keeffe's
painting to know that he didn't like it. But face to face with O'Keeffe
herself, he was charmed. As she looked with apparent interest at his
presentation, her perceptive eyes and graceful hands attending exclusively to his work, he felt the thrill of her unaffected naturalness and
sensitivity. She commented on the photographs with intelligence and
warmth, and he found himself opening up and talking to her about
what he was trying to do.

When Stieglitz entered half an hour later, the mood abruptly changed. Gruff, gray-haired, and beady-eyed through a pair of round spectacles, he gave Evans' photographs a cursory run-through, uttered not much more than "Very good, go on working," and sent him on his way. Then sixty-four, Stieglitz made photographs only of subjects with which he had a long and thoughtful relationship. He had recently embarked on a series of city views, taken mainly from the rooms he and O'Keeffe shared on a high floor of the Shelton Hotel, whose windows gave onto the rapidly changing skyline of midtown Manhattan. These contemplative and technically flawless photographs were mature and stately compared with Evans' efforts, which probably appeared to Stieglitz as tentative imitations of the European avant-garde or, worse, the technically uneven attempts of a misguided amateur.

From this, his only encounter with Stieglitz, Evans confirmed his opinion of the man as egotistical and cultish. At the same time, he had to admit that Stieglitz's influence on photography was good, not least because Stieglitz presented a powerful figure to rebel against. Most of all, Evans used the older man to define what he himself was not. Yet there remained the question of what he was.

It was perhaps as a result of this unsuccessful interview that Evans went to the New York Public Library and called for the most serious journal of creative photography yet to be published, Stieglitz's *Camera Work*. Through all fifty issues (from 1903 to 1917) of this deluxe art journal, generously illustrated with hand-pulled gravures tipped into the pages, Evans searched for guidance. He sped past the best and the best-known of the photo-secessionists, whose soft-focus images of gentle domestic scenes, impressionistic nature studies, and mythical tableaux vivants left him cold. It was not until he reached the last issue, devoted to the work of Paul Strand, that he slowed his pace. He was arrested by a single photograph of a blind woman, taken on the Lower East Side of New York. One of her eyes was sealed shut, the other open and vacant; a crudely hand-lettered sign bearing the single word *Blind* hung about her neck. "That's the stuff, that's the thing to do," Evans thought to himself, and he left the library charged with fresh inspiration.

Though Evans found almost nothing of interest in the rest of

Strand's work, the image of the blind woman represented a landmark
in the formation of his vision. The picture implied an encroaching
crisis of the American dream of prosperity, but it showed no obvious
emotion. The fact that the photographer had stolen his photograph
was pointedly expressed by the stark sign hanging around the woman's
neck, as if the subject had come with her own caption. Was the portrait cruel or sympathetic? It was the fact that it was neither, that it
appeared not to reveal the photographer's feelings at all, that intrigued Evans.

In the late 1920s Evans could not easily imagine how to turn his calling into a career. For the time being, having quit the bookshop, he
accepted his brother-in-law's offer of an entrée into the lower ranks
of stock brokerage. In 1928, Talbot Brewer was personnel manager
for Henry R. Doherty and Company, on Wall Street. For Evans he
secured an evening job, checking stocks from six to eleven P.M.

Evans' financial outlook was also improved in the fall of 1928 when
Paul Grotz, now working for a landscape architect, moved into his
apartment on Columbia Heights and began sharing the rent. Grotz
went to work by day, Evans by night. As Grotz recalled, Evans liked
to rest while others were working and to work while others were
resting. On Sundays they bought the *New York Times* for the sake of
its supplement of news photographs printed in brown-toned rotogravure, which they devoured with equal enthusiasm. They also engaged in occasional impromptu portrait sessions, assisting each other
in the pursuit of self-revelation or disguise. They beamed a strong
artificial light into the room, adding dramatic shadows to the walls
and deepening the contours of their faces. In tinted glasses, Evans
struck philosophical poses, his long-fingered hands cupping his chin
or playing across his forehead in feigned pensiveness.

That same fall, the young poet Hart Crane moved into a building
across the street and a few doors to the south of Evans' apartment.
Crane hoped that by living close to the waterfront he would find fresh
inspiration for his epic poem *The Bridge,* which he had begun six
years earlier. In Crane's work, the Brooklyn Bridge symbolizes a
mystical journey across the North American continent, beginning at
dawn and returning at midnight. In the course of this journey, the

rush of life in the big city — the office tower, the elevator, the subway, the burlesque — is woven into the legends of American history — Columbus, Cortés, Pocahontas, Rip Van Winkle, and the gold rush — using references to Shakespeare, Marlowe, and the Bible to evoke the connecting layers of the American frontier. With this monumental effort, Crane sought to champion the culture of America's past and to deny the worldly cynicism of T. S. Eliot's *The Waste Land.*

With its more than mile-long walkway arching high over the rumbling eastbound traffic, the Brooklyn Bridge was a regular beat for both Evans and Crane. They had both ventured under the bridge to study its massive structure from below or to watch the steady movement of tugboats and barges. As Evans later told the story, he and Crane first met under the bridge, Evans with his vest-pocket camera and Crane with his notebook. They recognized each other as kindred spirits and fell naturally into conversation.

Crane was fascinated by photography, and with the idea that a machine was capable of revealing unexpected harmonies between inanimate things. He was a great admirer of Stieglitz's work and ideas, but he also appreciated the modest beauty of what Evans was doing with the camera, and he would carry on about it, Evans said, "in his raving way."

As they quickly learned, the two young men had much in common beyond their love of writing and photography. Hart Crane (who was no relation to Evans' mother) had grown up in Warren, Ohio, where his father ran a successful canning business. Later, in Cleveland, Clarence Crane became a candy manufacturer, invented Life Savers, and established the Crane Chocolate Company and several retail stores. As a Cleveland businessman, he was acquainted with Evans' father, who had been in advertising there since 1920. Both men had a deep faith in American capitalism, and both had hoped that their only sons would follow in their tracks to success. But their prescription for life was flawed by at least one common complaint: both were unhappily married and, by the time Walker and Hart met, separated from their wives. The wives too had similar hopes and disappointments. Grace Crane and Jessie Evans had imagined marriage to be a continuous courtship, with material comforts ever multiplying as their husbands marched steadily up the business ladder. Upon finding that her dreams were not coming true, and in the eventual absence of her husband, Grace Crane had pursued her only son like a desperate lover, in much the same way that Jessie Evans had followed Walker to Paris. In the late 1920s, the pressure of their loneliness was still a constant threat to their sons' independence.

That Hart Crane was homosexual was by now well known to most of his friends. He confessed to Evans that he had been seduced as a boy by an older man. In New York he spent his nightlife on the fringes of society; he was as intimate with sailors as he was with poets and artists. A heavy hit of bathtub gin or a quick round at the speakeasy and Crane was on his way from one of his small worlds to the other. The ease with which he moved among various circles of friends, and the complementary talent he showed for keeping them separate, was another quality he shared with Evans. Both had been erratic students, both lacked a college degree (Crane hadn't finished high school), and neither had managed to shake a recurring sense of inferiority. Sometimes they made up for their scholastic failures or artistic uncertainties by blurring the truth about the past or creatively blending fiction and fact. Crane was fond of telling people that his family had founded Hartford, Connecticut; Evans is known to have said that his family came from Boston and that he was descended from the Adamses.

In fact, Crane had already made a name for himself as a very promising young poet. He was not shy about introducing himself to the people in the art and literary world he believed he should know. He was not only well connected, he was four years Evans' senior, and with his wiry gray hair he looked even older. But Evans, in his own way, acted more mature. While Crane sought approval and guidance everywhere, Evans practiced his photography with an air of nonchalance. And while Crane made no effort to hide his drunkenness and sexual escapades, Evans' drinking habits in the days of Prohibition were modest and cautious, and his sexual adventures, if he had any, were a matter he kept to himself. Paul Grotz remembers Evans once showing him into a speakeasy, but he knew next to nothing about his friend's sex life.

For a few weeks in the fall of 1928, Evans and Crane saw a good deal of each other. Crane was a fascinating companion. His talk was a performance, vivid with puns and crazy metaphors, and his laughter could fill a room. He could talk poetry for hours, reciting passages from memory or discussing endlessly how poetry related to the other arts — "how a Bach fugue, a Chinese painting, a Donne sonnet, all irrationally illuminated each other," as one friend recalled, and ultimately, how his words could find their spiritual equivalent in pictures.

Like many of his friends, Crane loved to walk at all hours of the day and night through the ethnic neighborhoods of lower Manhattan, where the streets were busy with vendors and children and where women, bracing their elbows on window ledges, perused the scene. He was a connoisseur of the five-and-ten — of kitchenware, cheap toys, pencil sharpeners, hair curlers, repair kits, shoelaces — and of secondhand shops, where he might purchase the odd Chinese porcelain teacup or chipped plate to decorate his temporary rooms. Evans, who was to become an ardent collector of castoffs, was no doubt inspired early on by his strolls with Crane. They cultivated their eye for cheap wares not only because they could not afford the quality shops of Madison Avenue, but because it offered an opportunity to establish what Crane called an "aristocracy of taste" among the crass and vulgar stuff of industrialized America.

Evans and Crane brought to their observations a keen and ironic eye for the false promises of the advertising man. Both had been raised on them, and Crane had taken several jobs as a copywriter, most recently with the agency Griffin, Johnson, and Mann. As the crude commercial parallel to writing poetry, the experience of writing ad copy was not wasted on him. In "The River," a section of *The Bridge,* he successfully incorporated "the loud-speaker stuff of the day," as he called it, into his introductory passages, borrowing snatches of well-known advertisements of the time. The result is a construction of sight and sound impressions that subjects both senses to an onslaught of pressure to buy, to have, to consume.

> Stick your patent name on a signboard
> brother — all over — going west — young man
> Tintex — Japalac — Certain-teed Overalls ads
> and land sakes! under the new playbill ripped
> in the guaranteed corner — see Bert Williams what?

Minstrels when you steal a chicken just
save me the wing, for if it isn't
Erie it ain't for miles around a
Mazda — and the telegraphic night coming on Thomas

a Ediford — and whistling down the tracks . . .

Evans also had an intuitive grasp of the ad world, a sense of the immediate present, and a talent for puns and double-entendres much like his father's gift for the catchy phrase. But unlike his father, he shared with Crane a sense of the emptiness and pathos that such things so quickly acquire with age. Perhaps it was on one of his walks with Crane that he searched out a rooftop view of the U.S. Rubber Company's giant company sign, revealed close up in broad daylight to be nothing but a piece of scaffolding dotted with light bulbs.

In the fall of 1928, with the help of his brother-in-law, Evans secured Crane a job much like his own at the Doherty company, "sorting securities of cancelled legions ten years back," as Crane described it to his friend Malcolm Cowley, "with Wall Street at 30 per — and chewing gum for lunch." For breakfast, Crane often had no more than a cup of coffee in the automat after a rowdy all-nighter, with no time to change out of the clothes he had worn to work the day before. He quickly became fed up with the job. One morning after roaming the city all night, he marched into the office, headed straight for the window, and, addressing the entire financial district, shouted the name emblazoned on the nearest electric billboard several times at the top of his lungs. Then, with a burst of profanities, he marched out of the office, scattering stocks and bonds, past the astonished clerks and secretaries, never to return.

In his ultimate effort to finish *The Bridge,* Crane decided that a change of scene was all he needed. Soon after the Wall Street incident, he sailed for Europe with $5,000 he had inherited from his grandmother. Before sailing, he gave himself a going-away party in a Second Avenue speakeasy. Evans was there, along with the regular crowd of poets, essayists, and booksellers that Crane gathered around him, including Malcolm Cowley, Solomon Grunberg, E. E. Cummings and his wife, Lorna Dietz, Sam Loveman, Slater Brown, the Gorham Munsons, and the Isidor Schneiders. Crane was in form. He danced with all the ladies and played popular tunes such as "Too Much Mustard" on the piano, as well as (with a whisper to Evans, "I fake it") something that resembled Debussy. The next day he was off to Europe, carrying an unfinished manuscript and a string of addresses.

Having played the responsible role by comparison to Crane, Evans was now left with a gathering sense of frustration, toiling without his friend through the daily doldrums of Wall Street. With Crane's example so vividly before him, he resented the amount of time and energy his mundane job was stealing from his art. The night view from the twentieth floor began to make him dizzy. He asked to be transferred to the vaults. There, feeling increasingly isolated, he fantasized about planting a bomb to obliterate the business machine that might drain him of his talents.

It was probably sometime in the spring of 1929, if not sooner, that Evans quit his job at Doherty. The downward spiral of Wall Street was already gathering speed and may have rendered his position superfluous, but it is unlikely that he could have sustained himself much longer there in any case. For the time being, he was free to pursue his photography. With Paul Grotz, he planned a train journey up the East Coast and into Canada, to look at architecture and take pictures. Dorothy Rogers would have liked to join them; she had admitted defeat in capturing the heart of Evans, "always a very cocky person," but his handsome roommate was more approachable. After helping them pack and still lacking an invitation to go along, she threw a grapefruit out the window at them, and missed.

The trip was restorative for both Evans and Grotz. They practiced their French in Quebec and admired early American architecture throughout New England. When they came through Williamstown, Massachusetts, on their way south, Grotz was enchanted with the unspoiled architectural coherence of the main street. But for Evans, it was still the college town he had only recently escaped from. Well before Grotz had satisfied his visual curiosity, Evans announced that they had already been in Williamstown too long and if they stayed any longer, they were bound to run into someone he owed money to.

With no job and no immediate prospect of getting one, Evans had reason to feel nervous about his debts, even those perhaps long since forgotten. Soon after he quit Wall Street, his father came up with a plan that combined his own latest hobby, horticulture, with Evans' need for a job. He bought a small acreage in Darien, Connecticut, on which he planned to raise a new hybrid gladiola. Though Evans knew little and cared less about horticulture, he and Grotz were happy to use the two-story cottage on the property throughout the summer of 1929, along with Evans' wire-haired mongrel Aspasia, named after the ancient Greek courtesan. His father rarely looked in on the flower enterprise, and there was plenty of time off from gardening for Evans to read, lounge in the sun, and take pictures. With the added mobility of his own Ford, he was able to go where he chose and explore small towns in Connecticut and Westchester County, occasionally stopping for a meal with his sister in Ossining. There was also time to enjoy visits from friends. Dorothy Rogers, who had successfully become attached to Grotz, joined them on weekends.

The gladiola project was abandoned as quickly as it had been taken up, although Walker's father continued to practice his hobby ardently in Cleveland. Paul and Dorothy were married in the fall of 1929, and Walker was alone again in the apartment in Brooklyn Heights. But soon there were new friends with whom he could share photographic equipment, compare notes, and talk ideas.

It took a sophisticated eye to perceive what was brewing in the apparent plainness of Evans' photography. Ralph Steiner, whom Evans met at about that time, was one of the few who did. A small man with a large nose, an acerbic wit, and forthright good humor, Steiner was hard to resist once he had decided to make someone his friend. He had been at work in advertising photography since 1923, having received his formal training at the Clarence White School in New York. The school gave its students a rigorous background in formal design and picture composition while preparing them to make a living in photography.

In the photographs Steiner made during the summer of 1928 and in others made even earlier, he showed the best of his training in both pictorial and modernist methods as well as his eye for particularly American subjects — a Victorian rocker struck by late afternoon

sun on a farmhouse porch; the dusty wheel and fender of a Model
A Ford; a movie poster depicting a scantily clad woman clinging in
terror to a dark-skinned, bare-chested man, beneath which lies a
veritable sea of trash. Steiner's quick wit and eye for typical American
juxtapositions marked him as an individual; his lighthearted play on
the conventions of Victorian gentility amid the industrial scene and
his accomplished but unobtrusive use of the eight-by-ten view camera elicited Evans' unguarded admiration. Steiner was so interested
in Evans' creative potential that two years after they met, he gave
Evans one of these view cameras, together with various lenses, luxuriously encased in their own velvet-lined, fitted trunk.

At about the same time Evans met the portrait photographer
Berenice Abbott, who had recently returned from Paris. Abbott must
have struck him as someone to know. In her determined way, she was
unencumbered by the constraints of conventional femininity. The tall,
freckled, blue-eyed young woman from Ohio had met everyone in
Paris from Joyce to Edna St. Vincent Millay and persuaded many of
them to sit for her. But most important for Evans, she had befriended
the reclusive old photographer Eugène Atget, whose photographs of
Paris at the turn of the century and through the 1920s were as appealing to surrealist poets as they were informative to urban historians. Along with Man Ray and other artists, Abbott had often spent
an evening at Atget's studio at 17 bis, rue Campagne-Première, looking through his many albums of photographs. After his death, in 1927,
she collected the remains of his estate and imported it to New York
with the help of the art dealer Julien Levy.

Atget's photographs made up an exhaustive visual record of Parisian culture. Rising early, Atget photographed Paris before its streets
were disturbed by people. His work is a catalogue of features unique
to the city's old sections (hand-painted shop signs, wrought-iron ban-
isters, door knockers, and courtyards), its *ancien regime* (the formal
parks and gardens, some, like Versailles, well tended, others, like the
Parc de Sceaux, a romantic ruin), and the ephemera of modern times
(shop windows, cafés, street fairs, and carousels). Where others saw
nothing but the commonplace or depressed, Atget found beauty. His
careful and thorough documentation showed his love and respect for

his subjects, and in its very plainness it also left room for the free-wheeling meanderings of the surrealist imagination.

In the late 1920s, Abbott was beginning to make prints from among the thousands of Atget's negatives she had rescued. Evans was among the photographers who had the privilege of seeing the work in her studio on Horatio Street, and he was especially interested in them. The experience was similar to his first encounter with Strand's photograph of the blind woman. There was a shock of recognition. In Atget, it seemed, all of his latent instincts were combined: a straight cataloguing method imbued with an inscrutable melancholy, a long look at neglected objects, and an unerring eye for the signs of popular culture in transition. Atget's methodical, all-embracing approach to his surroundings confirmed and enlarged Evans' sense of photographic subject matter. Whereas modernist photography had shown him how to see form, Atget vastly enriched his sense of content.

Abbott also had much to learn from Atget. Her recent photographs of the older neighborhoods of New York City were inspired by his work. At the time she met Evans, she was learning to use a small view camera, which considerably enhanced her flexibility in making architectural views. Just as Paul Grotz learned from Evans' example, Evans gleaned a few technical refinements from the more experienced Abbott, who was organized and thorough about her work. While she admired Evans' eye, she found his darkroom technique sloppy, his prints improperly fixed and washed, and in general she regretted his cavalier attitude toward what she had come to respect as the rules of the game.

Evans' most lasting friendship of the period began one evening at Dr. Galdston's house on Willow Street in Brooklyn Heights, where he met the young artist Ben Shahn. A stocky Lithuanian-born Jew raised in the rough neighborhoods of New York's Lower East Side, gregarious, passionate, and full of articulate argument, Shahn cut a figure refreshingly alien to Evans' sheltered middle-class background. He had just returned from a year in Paris with his wife, Tillie Goldstein, and their baby girl, Judith. His paintings reflected the influence of Matisse, Dufy, Picasso, and Klee, but he was beginning to feel disinclined toward the art-for-art's-sake mentality of current European art. In

Italy he had fallen in love with early Italian painting, especially the work of Giotto. He longed for a subject as spellbinding and meaningful to his own time as the Crucifixion had been to medieval Italy.

Five years older than Evans, Shahn had greater confidence as an artist, and greater drive. To Evans, he embodied the passion of the struggling artist and the tough confrontational power of images like Strand's blind woman. Evans could also perceive that under Shahn's peasant features lay sensibilities as refined as those of a highly educated aristocrat. At a glance Shahn could distinguish a coat that cost fifty dollars from one that cost only twelve dollars, or between Ukrainian and Estonian lace curtains; he was attentive to posture and the movement of hands as indications of class or character, and he was determined to make these subtleties a part of his art.

Evans' Anglo-Saxon reserve and quiet cynicism were equally attractive to Shahn, who was in flight from the provincialism and domination of his extended family. Both rebels, Evans and Shahn quickly recognized that they might form an alliance of opposites that would enlarge their scope, and before long they were talking about finding a studio together in Manhattan. By nature they shared a sense of mischief, a tendency to thumb their noses at authority and tease the self-satisfied. As artists they sensed their common ground, especially in what they hoped to avoid — self-conscious artiness, the tyranny of modernism as much as the cloying sentimentality favored by their parents. While an earlier generation of artists had wanted to *épater le bourgeois,* Shahn wished to *épater l'avant-garde.*

As Evans and Shahn made plans to leave Brooklyn, Crane returned from Europe, with his poem still unfinished. In Paris he had been adopted by Harry and Caresse Crosby, who were now planning to publish a deluxe limited edition of *The Bridge* as soon as it was completed, "on sheets as large as a piano score, so none of the lines will be broken," Crane wrote excitedly to a friend. In Paris the Crosbys had introduced him to all their artistic friends, fed him on oysters, absinthe, and opium, and set him up in their country estate outside Paris to write in solitude between weekends of wild house parties.

Anticipating the publication of his poem at last, Crane began a search for its perfect visual complement. The year before, his friend

Charmion Von Weigand, a painter, had urged him to look at Joseph Stella's multicolored cubist painting of the Brooklyn Bridge. Crane was instantly enamored. Stella's masterpiece surely belonged with his own mystical synthesis of the same subject. In January 1929 he wrote to Stella from Paris, asking his permission to use his painting of the bridge as a frontispiece to his poem. "It is a remarkable coincidence," he wrote, "that I should, years later, have discovered that another person, by whom I mean you, should have the same sentiments regarding Brooklyn Bridge which inspired the main theme and pattern of my poem."

Stella was pleased to oblige, and when Crane returned to New York, Stella sent him to the Brooklyn Museum, where the painting then hung, to study the logistics of photography. Having looked into the cost of a five-plate color reproduction and found it to be $200, "which would be too steep for any of us," Crane explained to the Crosbys, he began to consider the idea of reproducing the painting in black-and-white. He was even ready to believe that the painting, an extravaganza of color effects, might be improved by the black-and-white reproduction process. At the end of September, he sent "a fine clear photograph" of Stella's painting to Paris.

Meanwhile, he agonized over the completion of *The Bridge*, now in its seventh year. The poem, which he had approached from both ends, refused to meet in the middle. In his dilemma, he drank more heavily than ever. Friends were subjected to increasingly frequent midnight calls for help, nagging confessions, withdrawal symptoms, and violent behavior. Broken chairs, if not bodily harm, were the result of many of Crane's nocturnal visits. In Evans' opinion, his friend had lost his head in Paris, had gone to pieces "à l'americain." Crane would call Evans in the middle of the night after being beaten up by sailors, crying, "Save me!" But Evans was put off by such histrionics and showed him little sympathy. Hoping to shake him off, he changed his telephone to an unlisted number. But the more he rejected the midnight raids, the more vigorously Crane pursued him.

In the fall their friendship cooled, but by December, when the Crosbys arrived in New York to finalize plans for the publication, it had warmed again. For reasons that are now obscure, Evans' photographs were suddenly to take the place of Joseph Stella's painting. (Harry Crosby's recent interest in photography might have been a factor in the decision.) Now, instead of using a single image as a frontispiece, Crane wanted to intersperse three of Evans' photographs of the bridge as separate plates within the text. Perhaps in the end Evans' oblique, stealthy little black-and-white pictures matched Crane's sense of the poem's incompleteness better than Stella's monumental painting. And by approaching the bridge from below, Evans' photographs complemented the poem's soaring upward lift as well as its dark passages.

To celebrate the final plans for *The Bridge* and to make a grand gesture for the Crosbys, who would shortly return to Paris, Crane threw a party on December 7. The E. E. Cummingses, the Malcolm Cowleys, and the Slater Browns were there, along with the principals of the book production and a few sailors nobody but Crane seemed to know, who got drunk on gin. Toasts were raised to Crane, to the Crosbys, and to the Brooklyn Bridge itself. But the gaiety only half concealed a wave of growing tension. Harry Crosby's enduring suicide wish emerged when somebody produced a pack of cards. Asked to choose a card from the pack, Crosby crossed himself, prophesied that he would draw the ace of hearts, and did. It was the signal he had been waiting for. Three days later, he shot himself and the New York socialite Mrs. Albert Bigelow to death in a room of the Hotel des Artistes.

Crosby's suicide, long feared by his wife, did not stop the progress of the Black Sun Press. Caresse immediately took up the reins, and plans for *The Bridge* continued apace. Crane and Evans were equally anxious that the publication be perfect, and they communicated their instructions in no uncertain terms to Caresse. A minimum of fuss — no rules or printing of any kind — should appear on the pages with the images.

Crane's epic poem was finally published in the spring of 1930, and Walker Evans' photographs were published for the first time. The trade edition of the book, published by Liveright, appeared a few weeks later, with one photograph by Evans opposite the title page, and the Black Sun edition did not receive much critical attention. But

the meticulous elegance of that edition set a standard for the reproduction of Evans' work that he would be at pains to achieve from
then on. And that was not all. His collaboration with a poet who was
determined to exercise the connections between words and images
confirmed what he had hardly dared to believe — that his photographs could be the equal companion to poetry.

3 *Exposure*

MONTHS AFTER the stock market crashed in October 1929, many
Americans still believed that the economy would spring back into
shape of its own accord. They did not see, nor did they wish to see,
that the style of living they fondly believed was an American right
was not going to survive as they knew it. The awful truth of the
matter was more easily accepted by those in the bohemian circles of
Walker Evans' generation than among their parents. Since they were
already poor, their material well-being was hardly threatened by the
coming depression. And while the downward-spiraling economy put
a tight squeeze on the job market, for artists, being jobless was one
of the accepted facts of life. The most satisfying point of all to these
young dissidents was that the dreadful turn of events had proved
them right in suspecting that the American business world was not
the most reliable road to financial security, to say nothing of happiness. So great was their sense of dispossession that Evans and his
friends cheered when they heard the latest horror story, of how a
young businessman who had watched his fortune dissolve hurled
himself from the thirtieth floor of his office building in downtown
Manhattan.

Youth itself had previously been a bond, but the depression made
it stronger. When the economy showed no signs of improvement, a

small number of like-minded artists and writers helped to house, feed, or introduce one another to potential clients or impresarios. Evans embarked on the unpromising road to making his living as a photographer. Byard Williams, who had been his roommate at Williams College, bumped into him one day in 1930 and was impressed to learn that he had become a "professional" photographer. After visiting him in the dark little apartment he shared with Hanns Skolle at 92 Fifth Avenue, on the corner of 14th Street, Williams reported in the alumni magazine that Evans was "in fact quite a success, artistically if not monetarily; and as I saw him feeding tea to a lady, I suppose that he is keeping the wolf from the back stairs anyhow."

For Evans, no one could have been a better ally at that moment than the energetic and canny Ben Shahn. Shahn's vitality was an antidote to Evans' frail constitution and spells of doubt and inertia. He was full of talk and ideas about how they would make themselves known and how the art world was going to change. "All he had to do was come into the room," remembered Evans, "and you felt tired." While living at 92 Fifth Avenue, Evans kept a studio in the house where Shahn lived, at 21 Bethune Street in Greenwich Village, two blocks east of the Hudson River. Evans' studio was in the basement, and the Shahns lived on the two floors directly above it. Shahn painted in the living room. Evans was frequently invited upstairs for supper in the kitchen; as Judy Shahn recalled, he was like a member of the family.

Evans was also the Shahns' guest in Truro, on Cape Cod, where the Shahns had recently bought two small farmhouses for the modest sum of $500. They made the one with a better view of the sea into their own summer house and sold the other to their former Brooklyn neighbor, Iago Galdston. Evans spent most of the summer of 1930 in the Shahns' little white clapboard saltbox in the dunes. In return for this hospitality, he provided transportation to and from Cape Cod in his Model T and gave Shahn driving lessons along Truro's relatively safe sandy roads.

With money in short supply for all, meals at the Shahns' were the result of creative scavenging, wit, and personal charm. A dairy farmer up the road gave the Shahns his sour milk; children of eastern Europeans, Tillie and Ben preferred this to the fresh milk they would have had to pay for. The fruit and vegetable trucks on their way through Truro to Wellfleet were another source of free food; Evans and Shahn would trail after them, picking up the overflow as it tumbled onto the road. Occasionally a bag of groceries from a more fortunate friend brought relief. And clams were always plentiful — cherrystones and giant quahogs were free to anyone willing to dig them out of the sand. Clam pies, clam fritters, clam chowder, and steamed clams were the constant fare from Tillie's summer kitchen.

It was during the summer of 1930 that Shahn began to work on a project that would liberate him from his former artistic influences once and for all — a series of watercolor portraits of the characters involved in the Dreyfus affair. The story of the unjustly convicted Jew, a case that divided French society in the 1890s, was the kind of real-life material he was looking for. He had participated in political demonstrations and protests in Paris over the more recent Sacco-Vanzetti scandal, the case of "the good shoemaker and the poor fish-peddler," anarchists who were convicted of murder near Boston on flimsy evidence. The Dreyfus case represented a similar story of modern-day persecution. Using books, old magazines, news articles, and photographs, Shahn studied the villains and heroes of the case. The resulting series of thirteen portraits in gouache, like pages from an old book, each one with a title and a legend, have the lightness and the quick, confident gestures of caricature.

In a similar spirit of satire, Shahn made a watercolor portrait of Evans that summer, slouching gracefully in a battered wicker chair, his shoulders hunched, his hands digging into his pockets, his legs crossed at the knees, and his expression characteristically pensive, vividly suggesting what he himself would have admitted at the time was "a certain malaise." The portrait also suggests his general attitude of aloofness and the difficulty Shahn faced in prodding him into action.

Evans' apparent disengagement was the striking opposite of Shahn's constant talk about forging his art out of real social and political issues. In fact, as Shahn was well aware, Evans was equally intent on using his photography as a weapon and a protest against the rich and the self-satisfied. But while Shahn expressed his political beliefs in his own hand, Evans' approach was more circumspect, and also better suited to his medium; he discovered an unintended political irony in the unwitting hands of others. On Martha's Vineyard, he found an aging campaign poster for President Herbert Hoover, his face frowning with the rugged individualism he continued to promote to the public. But in Evans' photograph, the poster is framed by the evidence of poverty and disenchantment. Between the panes of a weathered window frame, with an old cardboard box and a tired arrangement of fake flowers at his elbow, Hoover appears to be slated for the trash.

The ability to step back and view his culture with reserved judgment, without appearing to comment on it, was a talent that Walker Evans was beginning to recognize as the key to his photographic style. He used it not only to express his feelings about the tainted and false aspects of his society but to celebrate the beauty of the pure and unaffected. An example of the latter was provided by the DeLuzes, a family of black-skinned Cape Verdean Portuguese who lived fifty yards from the Shahns' house, down the hill and over the dunes. Ten or twelve children, ranging in age from infancy to adolescence, all somehow fit into the narrow, shingle-sided saltbox on the other side of a weathered picket fence. And as if her family weren't enough, Mrs. DeLuze always kept a couple of spare rooms for paying guests. "She couldn't say no to anyone," remembered her son Bill. Judy Shahn thought of Mrs. DeLuze as "a kind of saint."

Evans soon became a favorite of the DeLuze children. He took them for rides across the dunes in his Model T and rocked the car back and forth to their screams of pleasure. To him, the whole family possessed a kind of folk authenticity, as did the details of their house, with its kerosene lamps and cold-water plumbing and its lack of decorative pretension. In the DeLuzes' low-ceilinged front parlor he observed how a prickly cactus plant was at home among framed family portraits, a souvenir American flag, and a vase of dried flowers. In the kitchen he admired the water pump attached to the sink, the worn buckets and pans, and the stained flowered wallpaper. And he gained the senior DeLuzes' permission to set up his view camera in a corner of their bedroom to photograph its wrought-iron white bedstead, seersucker bedspread, and old parlor stove.

So welcoming were the DeLuzes that they lent Evans and Shahn their barn for a two-man exhibition. Shahn hung his Dreyfus portraits and Evans his photographs of the DeLuze family. Though the audience for the show consisted primarily of locals, summer visitors, and a few nearby artists (a group that included the painter Edward Hopper), both men were impatient to build their reputations in whatever way seemed possible. "I am going to publish some photographs in order to become known and make someone exhibit me and sell prints and make money," Evans wrote to Hanns Skolle in June.

Evans' photographs in *The Bridge* had been an auspicious beginning. His intention to publish and exhibit his work in artistic circles was further realized in the fall, when the September issue of *The Architectural Record* devoted no less than five pages to his photographs, all architectural studies. With their deep shadows and bold diagonal lines, they made an elegant, if not entirely original, presentation, suggesting Evans' efforts to prove his competence in modernist photography.

He published a slightly less coherent group of four photographs in the December 1930 issue of *Creative Art*. The selection, according to the text, was an attempt to capture "the blended babel of such a modern city's life." It opens with an explosive typographical collage of the words *machine, camera, speed, wonder,* and *$,* no doubt designed by Evans himself. The first of the photographs in the sequence is an image of a giant electric sign spelling the single word DAMAGED being loaded onto the back of a truck. The portfolio then jumps to a multiple exposure of city lights, to the prow of a ship in port, to a busy lunch counter. An anonymous statement offers the reader the vague explanation that Mr. Walker Evans "has been in Europe where he studied modern Continental methods" but that he is "now interested in making 'records.'" While Evans' message was still foundering in the disparity between "modern Continental methods" and "records," he was beginning to shed the self-consciousness and exaggerated angles of his early work and to see his way clear to the most transparent and ephemeral of photographic styles: straight documentation.

Most magazine editors at the time were inclined toward the clean

lines of "modern Continental methods." But there was one who was
more interested in Evans' efforts to make "records," and who furthermore perceived the particular appropriateness of those records to his
own literary journal. Lincoln Kirstein, editor of the quarterly *Hound
and Horn*, selected three photographs by Evans for publication in the
fall of 1930. All three represented Evans' emerging straight style. The
strongest by far is a period piece as well as an intricate and subtle
composition, an informal portrait of a plump black woman cloaked
in an abundant fox collar, standing near the entrance to the Third
Avenue el. Cars rush by on the avenue behind her, and each step to
the elevated advertises Royal Baking, all under a pattern of receding
triangular shadows.

Kirstein had established *Hound and Horn* three years earlier, when
he was an undergraduate at Harvard, with funds from his father. At
first he called it "a Harvard Miscellany," intending its pieces to make
up an ongoing historical survey of the college. The majority of the
contributors were or had been at Harvard; T. S. Eliot and Ezra Pound
gave the magazine a boost by contributing to the first issue. But soon
the journal branched out, borrowing elements from the famous literary magazines of the early years of the century — *Criterion, The Dial,
transition, The Little Review*. In his choice of poetry, fiction, art, and
criticism, Kirstein specifically avoided the political front, and when the
Great Depression hit and the little magazines were all but finished,
Hound and Horn remained an island of epicureanism in a sea of
conflicting political viewpoints.

Evans recalled first meeting Kirstein when he was a customer in
the midtown Manhattan bookshop where Evans worked in 1928. One
evening, arrested by a display of French literature that Evans had
arranged in the window, Kirstein strode in and demanded to know
who was responsible for it. Later, not realizing that they had already
met, Evans sent a few of his photographs to Kirstein, hoping to be
published in *Hound and Horn*. In the fall of 1930, having graduated
from Harvard and moved the offices of his magazine to New York,
Kirstein began to develop a special interest in Evans and his work.
Once he decided someone was worthy of his attention, he was irre-
pressible. His energy for promoting talent was boundless, and his

conviction, as long as it lasted, was total. "He invaded you," said Evans. "You either had to throw him out or listen to him."

Kirstein was a fascinating figure to Evans. A towering six feet three inches (next to Evans' five feet seven inches), he had daringly close cropped hair, full lips, and a more or less permanent frown. Although he was five years younger than Evans, even as a student he seemed to know more, and he was infinitely more confident in his opinions. "This undergraduate was teaching me something about what I was doing in my work," recalled Evans of his friend. "It was immensely helpful and hilariously audacious. Professor Kirstein."

Kirstein, who grew up in Boston, was raised with a vivid sense of history and culture. His father, Jewish by birth but not in practice, had made a fortune as a business partner in Filene's department store and took proper Bostonianism more seriously than the Brahmins themselves did. As president of the Boston Public Library, he had initiated the cleaning of its famous Puvis de Chavannes murals. An amateur historian, he was especially well read in the American Civil War, collected books on the subject, and named his only son Lincoln after its greatest hero. He taught the boy that history was alive; it was not only the story of battles but a matter of daily life and culture, and its evidence was all around in the buildings and museums of Boston. He nurtured Lincoln's creative interests and had the money to support those interests as well. He backed not only *Hound and Horn* but the Harvard Society for Contemporary Art, which Lincoln and two of his friends established on the top floor of Harvard's student emporium, the Coop. How enviable, how as things should be, this seemed to Evans.

Kirstein had tried his hand at writing poetry, harbored dreams of becoming a dancer, and most of all aspired to being a painter. Yet with too many abilities to choose from and — the common plague of Harvard men — too keen an awareness of the greatness of others, his creative efforts lacked a certain potency. He actively sought out people who lived on the fringe, who could connect him to a genuine artistic temperament. He perceived this temperament in Walker Evans — in his natural artistic narcissism, which infused his manner, in his graceful catlike movements, and in his occasional hesitant, spellbinding stutter. Beneath Evans' impassive, almost ghostly façade and apparent lack of initiative there lurked a powerful creative urge, and Kirstein was determined to draw it out.

By 1930, both men were regulars at Muriel Draper's Thursday afternoon teas. Kirstein, who had known Draper since 1928, took Evans to her salon. Muriel was the abandoned wife of Paul Draper, a tenor and a gambler. For most of their married life they had lived abroad, first in Florence and later in London, where Muriel had entertained a literary crowd including Henry James and Oscar Wilde. By the time she returned, penniless, to New York, she was an experienced *saloniste*. With a son almost the same age as Kirstein, she increasingly welcomed young people to her home, delighting in their youthful enthusiasms and budding talents. She wrote on interior decoration, but talk was her medium. She had a talent for monologue, and she was full of opinion and audacious metaphor, which encouraged others to open up and speak their minds. From her gilded throne (salvaged from a theatrical warehouse) in the dining room of her dilapidated townhouse at 312 East 58th Street, she bestowed as much appreciation on the obscure as on the famous. The Armenian philosopher George Gurdjieff was a close friend, and his disciple A. R. Orage had once been a regular visitor. When Evans was visiting, other guests included his fellow photographer Ralph Steiner, the painter Mark Tobey, and the music critic Carl Van Vechten, a champion of jazz and Negro spirituals and a habitué of Harlem nightclubs. In the gathering of earnest and unconventional minds, Draper's tea parties were as invaluable for Evans as they were for Kirstein.

To Evans, Draper herself had an unusual allure. The meandering poetry of her speech was like that of no other woman he knew of his mother's generation. With her strangely sculpted face; her full lips, loudly painted; her nails, bright blue to match her brilliant blue eyes, her figure, clad in loosely flowing garments befitting an aesthete, Evans found her intriguing and even strangely attractive. Once, tipsy on champagne from a wedding party, he made a pass at her, but she pushed him away, tossing her beads over her shoulder, and begged him not to spoil their lovely friendship.

But if Draper fascinated Evans, the reverse was also true. She and Kirstein agreed that Evans had a kind of hypnotic hold over the

Thursday afternoon teas, without appearing to exert a fraction of energy. He sat back and observed, and was occasionally persuaded to express his opinion on the current state of photography. At the time, he was beginning to think that the possibilities of his medium were limitless and that no other photographer, with the exception perhaps of Ralph Steiner, was taking advantage of its most valuable quality: its ability to describe the extraordinary visual reality of their own day. In the street, on the subway, everywhere he looked, there was movement, gesture, irony, emotion. At times he felt himself going almost mad with the possibilities. No one had addressed what seemed to him to be the single most intriguing challenge to the photographer: how to capture the essence of a moment — "swift chance, disarray, wonder," that obscure aspect of a place or a person that would most unexpectedly and vividly recall its moment in history. Surveying the gathering evidence of the Depression and the rank edges of a resistant American culture, he found that he cared less about the present than about discerning what the present would someday look like as the past.

Kirstein, with his passion for history and his drive to bring the past to life, was primed to respond to these ideas and to encourage his passive friend to realize them. It is likely that he pointed Evans in the direction of Mathew Brady's photographs of the Civil War and expounded on their immediacy, the sophistication of their restraint and subtle order, and the palpable detail rendered by Brady's big plate camera. "Contemporary photographers might with profit again look at Brady," wrote Charles Flato for *Hound and Horn*. "They may be refreshed to see the enormous possibilities of simplicity and directness." Kirstein might also have recommended Walt Whitman, if Hart Crane hadn't already, as offering a poetic equivalent to Evans' photography. Whitman's radically plain poetic voice, forged out of the idiom of the folksong and the daily newspaper, proved the expressive potential of the ordinary. As Whitman wrote in his notes to himself, he aimed to achieve "a perfectly transparent plate-glassy style, artless, with no ornaments."

The crystallization of Evans' ambitions for photography coincided fortuitously with the opening of the Museum of Modern Art in New York. By the late 1920s a growing number of Americans were ready to advance their taste beyond impressionist painting to the fanciful palettes and radical compositions of the Fauves and the School of Paris, and to graduate from beaux-arts architecture to the new international style, which was already gaining ground in New York. The museum — virtually the first of its kind anywhere in the world — was the idea of three well-to-do, art-loving women: Mrs. John D. Rockefeller Jr., Miss Lillie P. Bliss, and Mrs. Cornelius J. Sullivan. Gertrude Stein, who said that you can have a museum, and you can have modern art, but you can't have a museum of modern art, was proven wrong. On November 8, 1929, several thousand visitors came to the museum's first day, cramming the elevators to get to the twelfth floor of the Heckscher Building, where the galleries were temporarily housed, to see the exhibition of paintings by Gauguin, Van Gogh, Cézanne, and Seurat.

In search of the museum's first director, the founders had sought the advice of Paul Sachs, who taught what came to be known as "the museum course" to Harvard graduate students. Sachs immediately recommended his former student Alfred Barr, who was then teaching art history at nearby Wellesley College. As a teacher of modern art, Barr was an anomaly. Instead of relying on books and slides and trips to museums, he instructed his students to ride the train from Wellesley to Boston in order to study the stations designed by H. H. Richardson along the way. To train their eye for modern design, he sent them to the local five-and-ten with a dollar each and told them to bring back the best-designed objects in the store. At the college art gallery, he mounted an exhibition of mass-produced posters he had brought back from Europe. The posters had cost him $125; the only other expense for the show was thumbtacks. In considering the program for the new museum, Barr came up with the idea that all of the disciplines of art and design — postimpressionist painting, architecture, mass-produced objects, poster art, photography, and film — should be collected and displayed as equals.

Lincoln Kirstein was well placed to become an important figure in forming the museum's policies and exhibition program. Alfred Barr had been his tutor at Harvard, and Nelson Rockefeller, who was among the first trustees of the museum, had taken note of his enterprises at the Harvard Society for Contemporary Art. In the spring of 1930, Kirstein was invited to serve as a member of the museum's first advisory council, along with a few of his fellow Harvard men, including the audaciously modern young architect Philip Johnson.

In the early days of the museum, exhibitions were conceived, decisions were made, and plans were carried out with amazing speed and spontaneity. The very young staff, which numbered only five when the museum opened in 1929, hired their college classmates and parents' friends. The new museum was also the base for a kind of informal social club. Barr and his wife, Marga, would regularly gather their friends and the staff on Saturday mornings in their apartment at 424 East 52nd Street, and from there set out on a tour of the midtown galleries; the latest works at Julien Levy's, John Becker's, and Weyhe's galleries were of the most intense and regular interest. Back at the Barrs', everyone compared notes over lunch and a drink, seated on the most modern American chairs.

Evans was a member of this elite group, probably as a result of knowing Kirstein and, through him, Alfred Barr. He was also one of the first photographers to be hired by the museum. Early in 1930 he was assigned to photograph some of the sculptures to be included in an upcoming exhibition of the work of Lehmbruck and Maillol, and these were published in one of the first of the museum's handsomely produced catalogues.

Kirstein also suggested that Evans photograph a selection of lesser-known objects in the Metropolitan Museum to form an esoteric guidebook, an idea that may have appealed to Evans but that never got off the ground. More successfully, Kirstein hitched Evans up with the young architect Lyman Paine to make photographs of the Red Cross Building and the New School for Social Research for Paine's article in *Hound and Horn,* "Is Character Necessary?" In exchange for these introductions, Evans gave Kirstein a taste of the low life, taking him to his favorite speakeasies and *bals musettes* and to lunch at cabmen's shelters, and introducing him to the untrained literary talents of one of Hart Crane's sailor friends, in the form of a bundle of dog-eared, typed yellow pages.

In 1931, Kirstein had an ambitious project in the works that had originated with his friend John Brooks Wheelwright, a poet and an architect, and included Evans in its grand plan. As early as mid-February, Kirstein spoke to Evans about the idea: a book on neglected American architecture, particularly the eclectic variety of Victorian house that could be found in almost every town in New England and New York State. With a murmur of interest from Evans, Kirstein immediately wrote to Wheelwright in Boston, informing him that he knew a very good photographer who could go up to Boston whenever they needed him.

Jack Wheelwright came from an old Boston family that could directly trace its ancestry to seventeenth-century Puritans. To Kirstein, the son of a self-made Jewish businessman, he was the exemplary man of breeding — always neatly dressed, shoes polished, hair kempt and combed. He presented an air of calm sophistication, and he also possessed an acute critical mind, particularly about architecture. His father had been a prominent civic architect in Boston, responsible for monuments, bridges, subway stations, and the anthropocentric clubhouse of the Harvard Lampoon. Jack had an eye for public buildings and the wit to call on a range of visual experiences to summarize their effect. The Lincoln Memorial, he said, was badly lit and made Lincoln look like a jack-in-the-box; Pennsylvania Station resembled a Roman bath; the east front of the Boston Public Library was a frontispiece of abstract expression and manipulated scale, and the north front was its parody. In the company of Wheelwright, ten years his senior, Kirstein began to question everything he had learned in the course of what he thought was a reliable education at Harvard.

The book on American architecture was to be previewed in a series of articles in *Hound and Horn*. Wheelwright's plan was encyclopedic. "My first article," he wrote to Kirstein, "will deal with wig-wam hut and shed, temporary ramshackle building, Holmes' Chambered Nautilus, the Americans as speculative nomads. City, country and seashore speculative building, the railroad, the industrial jungle, tourists, bohemians, E. E. Cummings living in a corrugated iron shed. Walt Whitman, Blackstone, Johnny Appleseed, the Lords Brethren and the Lords Bishop, Thoreau, the Simple Life, solitude and society (Emerson), Nature's Picture Gallery, rustication, naturalistic parks." He admitted that this was a good deal of material for one or even two articles, but he insisted that it was essential background for the study of American architecture.

For Kirstein, in contrast, the project was a campaign to save a dying breed of nineteenth-century domestic building, particularly the Victorian style of Abraham Lincoln's era, which had lately been discredited by the post–World War I vogue for undecorated modernism. The project offered Kirstein an opportunity not only to work with both Evans and Wheelwright but also to further his investigation into his own past in Cambridge and Boston — which he had begun in an autobiographical novel, *Flesh Is Heir,* in which he described the heartaches and shocks of boarding school and first jobs, striving to make them into sharp-focus "photographic" episodes, "like postcards, dashed off to be mailed home or to friends."

Early in April 1931, Kirstein and Evans traveled slowly up to New England, stopping in Fall River, Massachusetts, then Naushon Island, the private enclave of the Forbes family of Boston, to see the modern redwood house that Lyman Paine had built for himself and his wife, Ruth Forbes. Henry Russell Hitchcock, the architectural critic, had declared that it was the best new house on the East Coast.

Already Kirstein was beginning to realize that Evans was as resistant to taking direction as most artists, with perhaps a greater than usual wariness of being turned into a hack photographer. At Naushon, he seemed to be more interested in photographing an old fisherman in the harbor than in Paine's masterpiece. Kirstein began to bristle at his arrogance; Evans' bad manners, he decided, were a way of compensating for his small size and lack of physical strength.

In the second week of April they joined Wheelwright in Boston. For five days, in Kirstein's Ford coupe, the three men drove through Boston's neighborhoods — Beacon Hill, the South End, South Boston and East Boston, Charlestown, Dorchester, and Brookline — and on to its suburbs — Salem, Swampscott, Beverly, Revere, Arlington, Medford, Chestnut Hill, Dedham, and Somerville. And of course they thoroughly explored Cambridge. Kirstein and Wheelwright had certain targets in mind, but they left most decisions to the process of exploring, following their well-trained eyes to an unusual roofline or chimneypiece. With Kirstein at the wheel and Wheelwright in the passenger seat, conversation was lively and ongoing, not only about architecture but about poetry, painting, the Russian ballet. Evans was in the rumble seat with view camera and tripod, and the noise of the engine kept him from hearing his companions' stream of conversation, so his thoughts could drift away to the passing scene.

The discussion about what to photograph and why one house and not another was continuous. Wheelwright favored a survey approach toward the entire Victorian period as background to his book; Kirstein thought it urgent to document the oldest and most endangered examples; and Evans followed his own inner romance, which did not adhere to the concerns of either history or conservation. Here the scrolled brackets along the roofline of an Italianate house attracted his eye, there the smooth white pillars of a Greek Revival portico or the slant of clean April sunlight across a clapboard façade or sagging porch. For Evans, signs of disintegration had a poetry, a personal resonance, that directly opposed a preservationist zeal like Kirstein's. While Kirstein entertained visions of happier days, when the houses were bright and new, Evans felt an affection for their present ghostly air of decay.

Given the three men's differing points of view, it was impossible for them to steer a logical course through Greater Boston. Often, once Kirstein and Wheelwright had chosen a building to be photographed, Evans would refuse to perform. Perhaps as much to assert his own artistic will against his Harvard-trained companions as to make a better picture, he would suggest returning at another time of day, and then, having returned, suggest returning again. Hedging his bets against the unknowns of his view-camera technique, he demanded to work in strong sunlight, preferably at midday, which would give a shadow outline to every detail.

At each location Kirstein became the photographer's assistant, carrying the film plates, helping Evans to set up the camera, assessing the view through the lens, and tidying up after the exposure was made. Although he was intermittently irritated with Evans, he felt a certain thrill in catering to his friend's superior air of exactitude; it seemed to honor the architecture as much as Wheelwright's ongoing verbal critique did. The whole process felt to Kirstein like an adventure, even a dangerous one at times, a mission to rescue these buildings as if they were forgotten souls. Sometimes, when the owners peered out of their doors suspiciously, the three men felt like thieves.

Evans and Kirstein took the train back to New York just in time for the opening of Evans' first gallery exhibition, which took place on April 22 at the John Becker Gallery, at 520 Madison Avenue. Becker, who was specializing in modern French art, had been Kirstein's classmate at Harvard, and so had his partner, the strikingly handsome, red-haired Tom Mabry, writer, dancer, and southern gentleman from Clarksville, Tennessee. In addition to Evans' work, the exhibition included photographs by Ralph Steiner and Margaret Bourke-White, a rising star of magazine photography. Evans showed his photographs of big electric signs and a series of pictures from Luna Park and Coney Island. Mehemed Fehmy Agha of Condé Nast, or "Doctor" Agha, as he preferred, contributed a brief essay to the brochure. As if to apologize for the disparity between Evans' uneven technique and the darkroom wizardry of his two coexhibitors, Agha typed Evans as "one of these glorified reporters supremely indifferent to the technical side of their trade."

With the prospect of further work on Kirstein's nineteenth-century houses and other architectural assignments, Evans decided to get a better grip on his view-camera technique. Seeing that he was gaining enthusiasm for the refinements of the eight-by-ten, Ralph Steiner offered some free instruction, which Evans gratefully accepted. "I will let [Steiner] work on me as much as he likes," he told Hanns Skolle, as if this were a privilege for Steiner.

The bulky, old-fashioned view camera is essential equipment to the photography of architecture. Its flexible bellows between lens and plate enables the photographer to correct for the distortion of the vanishing point and to bring everything, near and far, into focus at once. Since the camera is positioned on a tripod, the photographer can make long exposures at minute apertures (as small as f 64), which give extremely fine detail and tonal range to the negative. These advantages are well worth the effort of carting the heavy equipment around, fiddling with a myriad of adjustment knobs ("swings" and

"tilts"), and composing the picture on the ground glass (which reg-
isters upside down and reversed) while hunched under a dark cloth.
Once the exposure is made, there is further room for error in the
darkroom, most crucially in the development of the negative. If the
chemical baths are not well mixed or the temperature is not well
controlled, the print will be less than perfect.

The photographic results of Evans' first tour around Boston were
better than Kirstein had dared hope. Some detail had been lost in the
shadow areas, and it was clear that Evans had not yet mastered the
swings and tilts that corrected perspectival distortion and brought
the entire image into the same plane of focus. But on the whole, the
photographs were sharp and informative. Toward the middle of June,
Kirstein and Evans returned to Boston for a week's work. The plan
was to go back to places in South Boston and the South End which
they had been unable to photograph in April. Wheelwright was to
join them every morning at seven.

Kirstein was increasingly questioning his attraction to his obstinate
photographer friend, but he was determined to see their project published and publicized. Since Wheelwright's book was still not in clear
sight, he began searching for other ways to publish Evans' photographs. The young poet Archibald MacLeish, then a senior editor at
Fortune, seemed genuinely interested and brought the matter up
with his editor-in-chief, Parker Lloyd-Smith, but nothing came of
it. Wasting no time, Kirstein next wrote to Lewis Mumford, taking
the liberty of suggesting that Mumford's forthcoming book *The Brown
Decades* (which Kirstein hadn't yet read) might be enhanced by a
collection of Victorian house photographs, even though the "brown
decades" were the end rather than the middle of the nineteenth
century. Mumford politely declined. (When *The Brown Decades* appeared that fall, Kirstein asked Wheelwright to pan it in *Hound and
Horn,* but not to go on at any length, as the book did not deserve
much attention.)

In spite of these discouragements, the Victorian house project
moved ahead. Later in that summer of 1931 the tireless Kirstein
traveled with Evans to Northhampton and Greenfield, in western
Massachusetts, and over the New York border to Poughkeepsie. There

they found a Gothic Revival gatehouse in excellent condition, which so impressed Evans that he took its picture even though the day was overcast. In the fall they traveled to Saratoga Springs, where the horse-racing season had ended and the great old Victorian hotels on Main Street stood practically empty. They took a room on a high floor of the United States Hotel, with a corner view of the equally imposing Grand Union. The next morning Evans was dismayed to wake up to a rainy day. The sidewalk along Main Street was slick with rain, and the leafless elms receded into the mist. Wet black cars were parked in a solid row diagonally along the curb. It was hardly the view they had come all the way to Saratoga to capture, but there it was. At Kirstein's suggestion, Evans later admitted, he set up his camera in the hotel room, composed his photograph through the window, and squeezed the shutter.

The result was a picture that brought an entirely new element to Evans' photography. Exploring the full power of the view camera's facility for the long vista, the picture shows legible detail as far as the eye can see. But its real subject remains elusive. It is not a photograph of Victorian architecture, nor of a main street, nor of cars, nor of trees. Rather, it expresses the feeling of being there, and the heart of a young man facing the monotonous prospect of a rainy day in a town that isn't home.

"Suddenly," Evans wrote in his review of six photography books for *Hound and Horn* in the fall of 1931, "there is a difference between a quaint evocation of the past and an open window looking straight down a stack of decades." He was attempting to analyze the elusive element of time in photography, which Atget had so mysteriously mastered. "His general note is lyrical understanding of the street," Evans wrote of Atget, "trained observation of it, special feeling for patina, eye for revealing detail, over all of which is thrown a poetry which is not 'the poetry of the street' or 'the poetry of Paris,' but the projection of Atget's person."

In the same review, Evans roundly dismissed the work of the highly successful portrait and fashion photographer Edward Steichen. Making explicit the distinction between what he considered personal and impersonal photography, he declared that Steichen's "general note is money, understanding of advertising values, special feeling for parvenu elegance, slick technique, over all of which is thrown a hardness and superficiality that is the hardness and superficiality of America's latter day." He saved his toughest blow for the end, concluding bluntly that the work "has nothing to do with any person."

This elusive "personal" quality of a photograph, Evans firmly believed, could not be concocted in the commercial studio or, for that matter, have any relation to material profit. The camera was far more likely to yield a work of art in the hands of an amateur than in the hands of a pro. In the book *Photo-Eye*, an anthology of the "new" photography, Franz Roh shared this conviction. The photographs of a trained professional, wrote Roh, "will always appear uninteresting, though he be skilled in technique, while photographs by the other, who considers himself an amateur and whose work is not technically perfect, yet invariably are of forcible effect." Thus Evans would be guided by instinct and intelligence through the narrow straits between the look of an amateur and the force of a master.

In drawing a distinction between the sentimental photography of the preceding generation and the pure documentary style that would soon overtake it, Evans made notable use of the metaphor of an open window and evoked a penetrating vista down through a "stack of decades." The receding vista, common to many of Atget's photographs, was becoming a particular interest of his. In Saratoga, he had composed his pictures not only down the street but along the hallways and porches of the old hotels. In the town of Oak Bluffs, on Martha's Vineyard, he shot a series of neighboring porches straight through from one side, so they seem to unfold like his camera bellows. That his photographs saw through windows and porches and around corners gave them a new dimension and power and even an aura of revelation. They seemed to bring him closer to seeing into the past. In an old house in Copake, New York, he made a picture through one small room into another, which suggested a secret conversation between the dresser, the chair, and the Victorian portrait on the wall.

Like Atget's views of old Paris, Evans' photographs quietly animated the inanimate. Evans was becoming a keen observer of interiors, and in everything he observed lay the possibility of a photograph. In his pictures of rooms he was learning to suggest the personality and even the psychology of the inhabitants, as if the walls could speak. For instance, his photograph of the bedroom of Cary Ross, an eccentric young poet and devoted volunteer at the Museum of Modern Art, hints at a certain madness behind the room's clinical decor. Twin beds with polished steel frames are positioned under two identical prints by Georges Braque; a double gooseneck lamp sits on a bedside table between them. It has been said that Ross, who committed suicide in 1932, was a schizophrenic. Whether or not Evans knew this, his description of Ross' bedroom tells us as much if not more about the man's condition than we might have seen in his boyish, terror-stricken face, which Evans also photographed.

Evans also took pictures of Muriel Draper's dining room in the aftermath of one of her gatherings, aiming the harsh light of a flashbulb on her empty wine bottles, tired flower arrangements, and chipped gilt-edged chairs. The photographs suggest a sadness and poverty beneath Draper's worldly allure, as well as Evans' private opinion that she was "phony to the fingertips."

A boarding-house bedroom on Hudson Street was in stark contrast to Draper's townhouse stagecraft. Beaming a strong artificial light into the cramped room, Evans spared none of its poverty: the sagging bedsprings, the crudely bent iron bedframe, the coarsely plastered walls, and the cheap wrinkled fabric of the window curtain on a string. In itself this mean resting place was emblematic of hard times, but it was given more personal interest by the man who then slept in it, a young writer named John Cheever who had just arrived in New York from Boston.

Like Evans, Cheever was a small, neat man whose middle-class upbringing and prep-school education had not prepared him for the squalor of boarding-house living. But Cheever's father, like Evans', had not been able to dissuade his son from his risky creative ambitions. Evans no doubt sensed a common ground with Cheever, who was almost nine years younger. He also detected his latent homosexuality, a fact that attests to his own homosexual curiosity at the time.

Some of the most aggressively creative men Evans then knew were homosexuals, Crane and Kirstein being prime examples; others, less highly charged, moved around them like satellites. Evans was aware that they were erotically drawn to him but stayed clear of the whirlwind. His sensuality and fascination with the forbidden, his affinity for secretive, backstairs sex, was tempered by his fear of violence and of letting his guard down. Overall, there was his perpetually low fund of physical energy. Though sex was often on his mind, he seemed to get as much pleasure from fantasy as from acting on his desires. He loved to look but not always to touch. Yet with the young Cheever, he felt an irresistible urge to experiment. As Cheever recalled many years later,

> When I was twenty-one Walker Evans invited me to spend the night at his apartment. I said yes. I dropped my clothes (Brooks). He hung his (also Brooks) neatly in a closet. When I asked him how to do it he seemed rather put off. He had an enormous cock that showed only the most fleeting signs of life. I was ravening. I came all over the sheets, the Le Corbusier chair, the Matisse lithograph and hit him under the chin. I gave up at around three, dressed and spent the rest of the night on a park bench near the river.

This halfhearted foray into homoerotic seduction did not, as far as we know, lead to a love affair between Cheever and Evans, although they did remain friends. Evans' friendship with Kirstein also survived some awkward moments. One winter afternoon early in 1931, Evans told Kirstein that the trouble with them was that they were just a couple of lesbians. This cryptic statement was followed by a portrait-making session — Kirstein's idea — in Evans' 14th Street apartment. It began with Evans making convict-style mug shots of Kirstein's head — front, left side and right — and escalated into a kind of mad boxing match between photographer and subject, with Kirstein stripped to the waist. The results of the session, artistic and otherwise, didn't live up to Kirstein's expectations.

Kirstein nonetheless remained devoted to the promotion of Evans' photography. At the time, he was particularly enamored with Evans' photographs of circus posters and movie bills and impressed by his eye for the damaging effects of weather that added a twist of the macabre. The best-known of these photographs is an image of a movie poster depicting a respectable-looking young couple cowering in the face of an unknown danger. Cropped and severed from its context and any clues to its scale, the poster leaves the viewer stranded. Evans slyly implies that the threat is purely superficial. A violent tear through the poster takes a gouge out of the woman's forehead and places a terrible scar down her face, while the man is defaced, less horribly, by the large letters SA, the remains of a Saturday past. Perhaps when Evans made the photograph, Hart Crane's line from *The Bridge* "under the new playbill ripped in the guaranteed corner" was playing in the back of his mind.

Just as Walker Evans' professional career began to blossom, Hart Crane's began to fade. Since the publication of *The Bridge,* Crane had been casting about for new inspiration, agonizing over his limitations as a writer, and drinking heavily. In 1930 he was commissioned by *Fortune* to write an article on the George Washington Bridge, which was then nearing completion. He began the project excitedly and spent a lot of time on the site interviewing engineers and workmen, but somehow the article refused to take shape. Crane complained that he was incapable of conjuring up the words in a style suitable to *Fortune,* and finally, fitfully, gave up.

Evans was aware of Crane's disappointment with the final passages of *The Bridge* and his torture over his lack of new inspiration. He was also alarmed not only by Crane's excessive drinking but by his occasional references to suicide. One late night when Evans and Crane were crossing the Brooklyn Bridge in a taxi, Crane said about his death, "When it comes, it will be with a bang, by God!" as if to deny once and for all the cynicism of T. S. Eliot's famous whimper.

In 1931, having won a Guggenheim fellowship, Crane decided to head for Mexico. The night before his ship sailed, Evans had dinner with him and decided that without his help, Crane might never get off. The next day Evans took it upon himself to see that Crane bought his ticket, got his luggage on board, and secured his cabin.

A few months later Evans himself was on board a ship heading south from New York. Through Crane, he had met the Opferr brothers, Ivan and Emil — Ivan a cartoonist, Emil a poet, both experienced

sailors — and their poet-sailor friends Tommy Thompson and Carl
Carlsen. It was probably through one of these connections that Evans
met Oliver Jennings, who (apparently unaffected by the economic
crisis) had hired a schooner for a four-month cruise to the South
Seas. Like many sophisticated New Yorkers at the time, Jennings and
his party believed that an escape to the islands and an encounter with
primitive culture would be an antidote to their world-weariness.
Jennings invited Evans to go along as the official cruise photographer,
with the hope of having a picture album fully documenting their
adventure. He also wanted Evans to take some 35mm movie film. The
idea of spending the winter in a warm, sunny place would certainly
have appealed to Evans, and the suggestion that he try his hand at
filmmaking no doubt made the offer even more interesting.

The party set sail just before New Year's Day 1932, on the *Cressida*,
a luxurious 170-foot schooner. Ben Shahn, Paul Grotz, and Lincoln
Kirstein saw Evans off on his journey. As a practical joke, Shahn and
Grotz stuffed an extra suitcase with toilet paper and several pounds'
worth of the New York telephone book. Kirstein's farewell present
struck a more studious note: pocket editions of Virgil, Marcus Aure-
lius, and Dante. As it happened, the *Cressida* had a library of its own.
George Moore, Beerbohm, Boswell, Conrad, Lewis Carroll, Schopen-
hauer, Willa Cather, Samuel Butler, Knut Hamsun, and Shakespeare
were all available on board, Evans reported to Hanns Skolle on his
first day out, adding that there were four tiled bathrooms.

Other than these introductory details, little is known about Evans'
voyage to the South Seas. He hardly spoke of it afterward, and the
several reels of film he shot were scarcely viewed by anyone. From
scant evidence, it can be surmised that he had little to do other than
read and gaze at the horizon. Having just become fascinated with
spacial depth, he would have found nothing less appealing to his
visual imagination than a perpetual seascape. Somehow the sky, the
sea, the clouds, were too formless, too out of time. Like a prisoner
studying his captors, Evans slyly made pictures of the sailing party
when they were not looking, and shot a few more pictures up the
mast, which he swore to himself he would dare to climb before the
trip was over.

When the cruise reached Tahiti, Evans found richer subject matter.

With his movie camera, he recorded the harbor scene and native ritual dances. He also made several still portraits with the view camera, bust-length studies of the Tahitian male physiognomy. Escaping his party of rich Americans, he wandered around the island alone and became friendly with a ten-year-old boy and with a native named Metaia, who had starred in F. W. Murnau's film about the South Pacific, *Tabu*. Evans attempted to introduce Metaia into the sailing party, which turned out to be awkward. Mataia was out of step with Western manners. Jennings jeered, which did not improve what Evans later confessed to Kirstein was a strained relationship. Whether or not Jennings was satisfied with the photographer's results, Evans considered the project on the whole a write-off. Except for his portraits of the natives, the photographs had little to do with the kind of photography he was now eager to pursue. "Romantic journalism, the beautiful tropic isles, etc.," he wrote to Hanns Skolle, but "not up to my usual great work," and the film was only "good in spots."

As the *Cressida* neared New York Harbor toward the end of April 1932, Hart Crane was a few days in its wake, on his way home from Mexico on board the *Orizaba*. Around noon on April 27, 275 miles north of Havana, Crane quietly dropped himself overboard. A passenger saw him jump and lifelines were immediately tossed out, but he had already vanished.

By 1933, at the age of twenty-nine, Evans had learned that the creative life was uncertain at best, at worst suicidal. He was also well acquainted by then with the difference between privilege and poverty. In the worst year of the Depression so far, survival was a matter of daily concern. "I am beginning to understand what sort of a period we are living in," he wrote to Skolle in May. His idealistic notion of accepting only those photography assignments that he considered honest and interesting would have to be modified if he was to make enough money to live on. He was ready, he told Skolle, to accept jobs from people "in such bastard trades as advertising and publicity."

But Evans was also on his way to becoming known on the gallery circuit as a promising young artist with a camera. During his absence in the winter of 1932, his photographs were exhibited at the Julien Levy Gallery, along with those of George Platt Lynes. Lynes' studio portraits, which made use of artificial lighting and such otherworldly effects as superimposition, could not have been farther from Evans' plain documentary approach, but both photographers interested Levy as representing opposite but equally vital avenues to surrealism: Lynes was a conjuror of dream imagery, while Evans was in charge of the accidental poetry of real life. Levy was also partly responsible for placing Evans in an international show of photography at the Brooklyn Museum. There Evans' architectural photographs appeared in a mixed display of the latest in advertising, fashion, and portrait photography, including work by Imogen Cunningham, Lee Miller, Paul Outerbridge, and André Kertész. Evans was also included in "Modern Photography," an exhibition at the Albright Gallery in Buffalo, which was more or less borrowed whole from an exhibition Kirstein had organized at the Harvard Society for Contemporary Art in 1930.

In fact, though he might have dreaded it daily, Evans was hardly forced to accept jobs from people in "the bastard trades." He took a few commercial assignments, briefly from the ad agency N. W. Ayer, but increasingly his work came from the cultural sector and from the kinds of people he would call friends. In 1931 he had the good luck to meet Charles Fuller, a young architect. Bright, athletic, and likable, Fuller had been a star student at Groton and Harvard. Adding to his attraction was a visible streak of the naughty boy, the tease. Like Evans, Fuller was driven by a desire to shed "the barnacles of Victorianism" that had hung on through the years of his childhood. His liberation was aided by a family history that included eight generations of artists from Cornish, New Hampshire. By the time Evans met him, Fuller was married to one of the three rich and beautiful White sisters of Bedford, New York, favorites of the social columnists. He was also the father of three small children and the master of a pet monkey. The family lived in Bedford, in a large, comfortable house of classical proportions and decorative details that Fuller himself had designed.

In the 1930s Fuller did not hesitate to use his wife's fortune to employ his less fortunate friends. With Evans he instigated a project to photograph Greek Revival buildings, a style from which much of his own domestic architecture derived, in New York State. He also employed Evans to photograph his architectural projects around Bedford and Long Island. And whether or not he was paid to do so, Evans made portraits of the entire Fuller family.

While Evans was becoming a more experienced photographer of architecture, he was also cultivating opportunities to photograph art. Shahn secured him a job at the Downtown Gallery, where, in addition to showing the work of young artists like Shahn, Edith Halpert was beginning to monopolize the current vogue for American primitive art — whirligigs, weathervanes, shop signs, and the work of itinerant portrait painters. Evans' job was to photograph American folk paintings and objects. He was also assigned to photograph objects of Mayan and Aztec culture for an exhibition at the Museum of Modern Art called "American Sources of Modern Art." While he regarded these assignments as work for cash, he enjoyed his growing familiarity with the objects of old or ancient civilizations. His trip to the South Seas had taken him closer to the source of their inspiration.

In the 1930s, the artists of revolutionary Mexico were models for Americans in search of a form of art that would speak to the masses. In the spring of 1933, Diego Rivera arrived to paint a mural in the spectacular new building complex called Rockefeller Center. Commissioned by young Nelson Rockefeller, Rivera was planning a panoramic exposition of "Man at the Crossroads Looking with Hope and High Vision to the Choosing of a New and Better Future." Ben Shahn, who was eager to learn the technique of fresco painting, volunteered his services to the Mexican master. He was joined by Lou Block, an artist who had recently moved into a studio at 22 Bethune Street. Evans often went uptown to watch Shahn and Block at work and to see the mural take shape. He brought along his eight-by-ten view camera and took pictures of several panels. As the figure of Lenin emerged on the central panel, grasping the hand of a black American on one side and a Russian soldier on the other, people began to talk. Journalists made the image into a minor sensation, and Rockefeller lost his courage. If he couldn't keep the central figures, Rivera insisted, the whole mural would have to be sacrificed, and it was. Evans' photographs were among the small remains of the project.

As Lou Block recalled, "Mural controversy at that time was almost a daily item in the papers." Lincoln Kirstein was also caught up in the crusade, not having forgotten his father's conservation of the Puvis de Chavannes murals in the Boston Public Library. In 1932 he had organized an exhibition called "Murals by American Painters and Photographers" for the Museum of Modern Art, hoping to stimulate interest in further projects. Shahn was included, with his latest attack on social prejudice, a triptych called *The Passion of Sacco and Vanzetti*. Kirstein also included photographic mural designs by Berenice Abbott, among others, which had only recently been made possible with the perfecting of photosensitive paper in large sheets. Kirstein stressed the comparative ease and quickness of producing photo-murals compared with fresco. Alert to any opportunities for Evans, he suggested to the manager of the new Bloomingdale's department store that he install a photo-mural over the first-floor elevator bank, and Evans produced a model for it. But like many of Kirstein's efforts on Evans' behalf, nothing came of the scheme. Furthermore, Kirstein's exhibition at MoMA turned into a fiasco when some of the artists' works — Shahn's triptych in particular — proved to be too politically radical for the museum's trustees.

It was at about this time that Evans and Shahn met Ernestine Evans, a literary agent, freelance editor, and occasional writer whose contacts and connections with writers and artists appeared to be limitless. She counted herself a close friend of Diego Rivera and his wife, the artist Frida Kahlo, and had written an introduction to a book on Rivera's paintings. Like Rivera, Ernestine Evans had a voice as large and intimidating as her figure, and she was never unsure of her opinions, nor of imposing them on others. Walker, who appreciated Ernestine's intelligence from the start (not the least evidence of which included her appreciation of him), was always quick to point out that they were not relatives.

As a member of the international set that congregated in Mexico City in those days, Ernestine also knew Carleton Beals, an American journalist who had been passionately involved in the Mexican Revolution. In 1932 Beals shifted his journalistic concerns from Mexico to Cuba, then suffering an economic depression under the corrupt dictatorship of Gerardo Machado. In the fall of 1932, Beals spent two months in Cuba, scouting behind the scenes of the civil war raging between Machado and his local enemies. *The Crime of Cuba,* as Beals named his resulting full-length book, was intended to implicate American imperialism in Cuba as much as to expose Machado's cruel dictatorship; Beals meant to stress that the American government was also to blame for Cuba's economic disaster.

By March 1933, Beals' publisher, J. B. Lippincott of Philadelphia, was ready to make production plans for the book. When the question of illustrations arose, Ernestine suggested to Lippincott's art director, Walter Goodwin, that Walker Evans be sent to Havana to make photographs. She also arranged for Beals and Evans to meet, though it seems that their interest in each other as collaborators was neither immediate nor strong. Nevertheless, Goodwin liked the idea of a handsomely illustrated book and was ready to argue for it against matters of cost and practicality to J. Jefferson Jones, Lippincott's managing editor.

A less expensive plan for illustrations, suggested by Beals, was to obtain news photographs of street demonstrations and violence in Cuba from the *New York Mirror.* But Goodwin continued to push for Evans' contribution. "I feel perfectly sure," he wrote to Beals, "that Evans has the possibilities for [being] another Margaret Bourke-White" (a comparison that would have curled Evans' toes), and he speculated on how fine it would be to place publicity illustrations in the newspapers' rotogravure sections, "if he did as good a job on Cuba as [Bourke-White] did on Russia." Conveniently for Evans, it seems that Goodwin mistook him for an aspiring magazine journalist. By early May the decision was made. Evans was scheduled to leave for Havana before the end of the month, with strict instructions to keep his expenses to a minimum. "I am sure the boy will do a fine piece of work," Goodwin promised Beals.

Evans later confessed, without remorse, that he never bothered to read the book his photographs were slated for. He insisted before leaving that he should not be expected to make literal illustrations for the text, that he should be left alone. For one thing, Beals' writing style was not to his taste. The book was full of purple prose and overwritten passages such as "Beneath the tropical opulence of Cuba, hidden in the tangled jungle of her present cruel political tyranny, are the fangs of bitter discontent." Evans was equally unmoved by

Beals' political passions. Cuban politics interested him only insofar as it influenced the look and the feel of the contemporary Cuban scene. He went to Cuba in search of its Latin culture, its social ambiance, its visual idiosyncrasies.

Equipped with a collection of addresses and letters of introduction provided by Beals, Evans arrived in Havana at the end of May 1933. He was prepared for warm weather, dressed in a lightweight suit, a straw boater, and a pair of perfectly round dark glasses. Ever alert to sartorial style, he was more than occasionally arrested by his own reflection. But Latin culture had something new to show him. The cobbler, the barber, the candy vendor, were all part of the street life of this exotic town. Women in thin sleeveless dresses cooked in courtyard kitchens. Men dozed on the benches in the plaza. A tall, slender Afro-Cuban in a suit of pure white paused furtively in front of a shoeshine stand. At the harbor, Evans engaged a group of dock-workers in an extensive portrait session. He positioned them individually and as a group face to face with his view camera under the hot sun. They were a crew of ethnically mixed men, young and old, united in the blackness of their sooty faces and the grime of their shirts, under a collection of hats as motley as they were tattered. To Evans, Havana felt "half savage, forgetful and unsafe." It was full of chances for the kind of camera work he was eager to master. In a note to himself he wrote, "I have been drunk on this new city for days."

Thanks to Beals' introductions, Evans did not lack for social life in Havana. He was in touch with American journalists from the *New York Times* and the United Press as well as with a Cuban journalist, Jose Fernandes de Castro. These men entertained him, offered him insiders' knowledge of the city, and pointed the way to subjects that might interest him. It was through one of his journalist friends that, halfway into his stay, Evans met Ernest Hemingway, at the time holed up by himself in a northeast corner room of the Hotel Ambos Mundos.

Evans had stared in awe at Hemingway from across the café tables of Paris in 1926. Now, on closer view, Hemingway was not only approachable but sympathetic, and the two men often got together in the evenings for a drink. Hemingway was lonely and depressed.

His marriage to Pauline Pfeiffer was in trouble, and he was beginning to find distraction from his personal trials in deep-sea fishing every day with his friend Joe Russell.

During Evans' visit, Hemingway was engaged in a fierce exchange of letters with *The New Republic,* where Max Eastman had recently reviewed Hemingway's *Death in the Afternoon,* his book-length account of the meaning and methods of the Spanish bullfight, published the previous September. Eastman criticized the book as having more to do with the author's sexual insecurity than with bullfighting. Archibald MacLeish, in an angry letter to Eastman, defended the book and succeeded in igniting Hemingway's indignation against Eastman. A furious sequence of letters followed, with Hemingway loudly defending himself against the implication that he was a "fairy." There can be little doubt that Evans was privy to the drama, since Hemingway was consumed by it. Perhaps he played the role of Hemingway's sounding board. But he also found that Hemingway was interested in his photography. When the day neared for Evans to sail home, Hemingway persuaded him to cancel his ticket and stay for another week at his expense.

By mid-June, J. Jefferson Jones, of Lippincott, was growing concerned. He had not heard a word from Walker Evans since he had sailed for Cuba nearly a month earlier. From Ernestine Evans he learned that Walker would be leaving Havana on June 17 and arriving early the following week, bearing (Jones hoped) a satisfactory batch of photographs.

Very few of the photographs Evans made for *The Crime of Cuba* could be considered powerful arguments against an oppressive dictator or proof of the island's desperate poverty. Basking in the lazy ambiance of a hot climate, Evans had admired the decorative lettering on the walls, the crude mural paintings, the old-fashioned horses and buggies. "It's a grand place and I'd be sorry not to go there again," he wrote to Beals shortly after his return.

The stimulation of being a stranger on a tropical island and the bonus of spending evenings in the company of Hemingway were at least as fascinating to him as his own photography. "I often felt presumptuous," he wrote to Beals, "having so much to do with another's careful work." But this rather obsequious line was quickly overtaken by his polite demand that his photographs be published in exactly the sequence he designated, clearly separate from Beals' text.

Evans was just as concerned about his idea for a dustjacket design as he was about his photographs. In Havana he had discovered an old muralist, a former sugar-plantation worker, whose paintings of local scenery, including one of a bullfight, covered the walls of many *fondas*. The painting Evans had in mind for the jacket was, he promised, "a real Cuban primitive . . . naive, true, pure, sound, and a work of art as well as a document," qualities that he aspired to and was beginning to meet in his own photography. The mural was a sugar-mill scene, with "the mill, animals, carts, a train, men cutting cane, palms and blue water of a stream running through," and there was plenty of room in the sky for the title. "It could not be more appropriate for your book," Evans stated summarily. He had armed himself with a watercolor copy, made by the artist at his urging.

The Crime of Cuba was published in August 1933, two weeks after Machado fell from power; Fulgencio Batista officially took over the following January. Beals' impassioned exposé suffered a slight mistiming, but his sentiment struck the right chord. The book was well publicized and generally well reviewed, though criticized by some as being carelessly researched and — typical of Beals' writing — burdened with literary effects. On the dustjacket was not the sugar-mill mural but one of Evans' photographs, a scene of an ambling crowd taken from above. Another photograph by Evans, of a straw-hut village on the outskirts of Havana, dominated the cover of the *New York Times Book Review* on Sunday, August 20, under the headline "Cuba, the Crucified Republic."

The critical results of *The Crime of Cuba* were perhaps ultimately more rewarding for Evans than for Beals. Though his photographs were not in the company of the artistic or literary elite with which he was becoming identified, Lippincott was a high-profile publisher that took him beyond his own small circle and established him as an accomplished documentary photographer. Yet to the observant reader, the photo section, "A Portfolio of Photographs by Walker Evans," contained a surprise. Following his instincts, Evans had fished out a few photographs from the local agency in Havana and deftly slotted them in with his own. This he had done partly to supplement the newsworthiness of the photo section — especially the bloodier aspects of the civil unrest, which he had missed, if not consciously avoided — and partly out of his own delight in searching picture files for the anonymous curiosity or obscure masterpiece.

Anonymous art was a rapidly growing passion for Evans. With Ben Shahn, he was becoming a regular visitor to the New York Public Library's picture collection. The collection, conceived and directed by an energetic young woman named Romana Javitz, was made up of throwaways — old books with broken bindings or soiled pages, motion picture stills, greeting cards, postcards, and clippings. Javitz and her team cut up the old books and sorted the plates by subject into big wooden bins, where they were available for browsing and borrowing. To publicize the collection and demonstrate its breadth, Javitz organized exhibitions in the library corridors. "The Romance of Railroading," "Peddlers and Vendors," and "Arrivals and Departures" were some of the free-spirited thematic collages of her mixed treasures.

For the social historian or researcher, the picture collection was invaluable, but Javitz's favorite customers were artists. The solitary sculptor Joseph Cornell was a regular visitor, and Javitz often gave him material for his assemblages and collages. Diego Rivera made use of the collection while preparing his mural for Rockefeller Center. Ben Shahn and Berenice Abbott were regular bin browsers.

For Evans, the library's postcard collection was a profound source of delight as well as information. As a budding connoisseur, he singled out cards produced at about the time of his birth, circa 1900, when postcard publishing was in its heyday and the scene was the predictable main street of a small town, the local church, or the Civil War monument, all tinted in fading pink and blue, the inked message from the sender still clinging to the surface. Evans was becoming, like his friends Hart Crane and Carl Carlsen, a collector of printed ephemera, of "baseball and cigarette cards, old valentines, tobacco boxes, trademarked paperbags, and twine," as Lincoln Kirstein noted. With Judy Shahn and her younger brother, Ezra, Evans could spend hours in the sun under his straw hat sorting out treasures from the beach. For him, things that were cast off, washed up, were there to be rescued by the sensitive eye. They contained clues to the transparent simplicity he was trying to achieve in his photography.

In his dogged pursuit of an anonymous style, Evans was beginning to define his personal aesthetic. His rigorously straight approach reflected the value he placed on revealing the naked truth; his lack of commentary in the face of a disintegrating culture suggested a Baudelairean melancholy, through which he perceived the end of civilization, and the belief that there was nothing to be done about it. His aversion to the new or modern and his particular eye for the telltale signs of cultural apathy were becoming apparent to those who followed his work closely. And they could identify his subject matter, wherever they happened to see it. For Kirstein, the sight of a Salvation Army band, drums only, on a wet December afternoon was "pure Walker Evans." For the wealthy young art collector James Thrall Soby, who briefly employed Evans as his private photography instructor, Evans' attraction to the decrepit, his razor-sharp eye for homemade fenestration, peeling billboards, industrial towns whose day had passed, expressed his "probably incurable sense of noblesse n'oblige pas." To the writer Morris Werner, John Cheever's windowless Ford, its paint and upholstery well tempered by the wind and the rain, was "out of Walker Evans."

As he began to develop his reputation, Evans weighed the relative benefits of exposure. On the one hand, he wished to become known and to make some money. But the benefits of success, he suspected, were gained at the risk of letting go of one's secrets. At the time his ideas were germinating so rapidly that he was not confident that he was in total command of them. Margaret Bourke-White, for example, was the kind of photographer who might steal his ideas and make a lot of money from them, leaving him in obscurity. He confided these terrors to Kirstein, who told him they were exaggerated. Kirstein even wondered if his sudden spells of paranoia were a result of his physical weakness. Perhaps he just wasn't getting enough to eat.

Evans' father lived long enough to know that his son's talents were recognized, at least by a few people well placed in New York's art world. But he died on May 1, 1933, before Evans' first museum exhibition. In November, Lincoln Kirstein finally found a way to show his Victorian house project. Philip Johnson, the adviser on architecture to the Museum of Modern Art, agreed to display thirty-nine of Evans' photographs in the museum's architecture galleries. Opening on November 16, the show fortuitously coincided with a retrospective of the paintings of Edward Hopper, whose views of Victorian houses reinforced the interest of Evans' work. Most of Evans' photographs had been taken two years earlier under Kirstein's guidance.

For Kirstein, who was still holding out for Wheelwright's monumental history of American architecture, the exhibition was primarily an argument for architectural conservation. "These wooden houses disintegrate, almost, between snaps of the lens," he wrote in the museum *Bulletin.* "Many shown in these photographs no longer stand." Evans was as drawn by the houses' decay as Kirstein was intent on reversing it, but his photography, as far as Kirstein was concerned, contained the right moral virtues: "patience, surgical accuracy, and self-effacement." Kirstein concluded his brief essay with a toast to the project's future, in which he still expected Evans to figure: "Detroit, Cleveland, Chicago, St. Louis and Philadelphia," he wrote, "await the tender cruelty of Evans' camera."

4 *South*

DURING THE LAST few months before Franklin Delano Roosevelt took office as president in March 1933, America suffered its sharpest economic decline since the stock market crash in 1929. The Great Depression had taken hold of the economy and showed no signs of releasing its grip. Unemployment increased across the board among skilled as well as unskilled workers, reaching an unprecedented total of 48 million, and no group was exempt from wage reductions. Railroads and the building trades were among the hardest hit in 1933; farm income in the previous two years had declined by more than 40 percent. With his first crucial executive acts, FDR sought to reverse the tide of despair. In Washington the architects of the New Deal literally worked around the clock, brainstorming and plotting how to put their ideas for revitalizing the economy into motion. Still, banks closed, construction projects were canceled, office workers were laid off, and farmers were driven off overused land.

Evans read about the deepening economic crisis and Roosevelt's New Deal strategies with some concern, but he was drawn more to articles about people, such as the dashing Prince Edward of England (whom he had been told he resembled) and an exceptionally fortunate young American girl who had just inherited $53 million. The reform activities in the capital were exciting, he was sure, but despite his own hardship, he confessed that he felt a certain emptiness in the face of the political momentum gathering around him.

By the time his photographs of Victorian houses went on view at the Museum of Modern Art in November, Evans had been hard pressed to find paying jobs for several months. Nor was there any family money to draw on. His father had left him with little inheritance, and from the sale of his grandfather's property in St. Louis he inherited the paltry sum of $6.75. Like many of his friends, he was getting used to skipping meals. He didn't resort to soup kitchens, but at times he was desperate enough to accept a friend's offer to share what everyone knew as "one of those government relief boxes of groceries." Meanwhile, the streets of New York were filling up with subjects for his camera. Paul Strand's blind woman seemed to appear on every other corner.

With plenty of free time on their hands, Evans and Ben Shahn took to strolling around the Lower East Side with cameras, photographing the street life of its overcrowded neighborhoods. Shahn had recently learned the basics of photography from Evans. ("Look, Ben, there's nothing to it," Evans had called to him on his way out the door to catch the boat to Havana. "F 9 on the shady side of the street, f 45 on the sunny side, twentieth of a second, hold your camera steady!") In order to catch their subjects unposed, Shahn and Evans used a periscopic lens on their Leicas (not unlike the one Strand had used on the Lower East Side almost twenty years earlier), so that they appeared to be aiming at each other rather than disturbing the natural flow of events in the street. They imagined themselves to be like Daumier with his sketchbook in the third-class carriage, interested in the coarse social weave of contemporary urban life, and in using their cameras to arrest threads of telling gesture, like "that split second of action in a guy stepping onto a bus, or eating at a lunch counter."

Many of Evans' friends had become Communist sympathizers. Shahn was one, at least in theory, and Jay Leyda, a young filmmaker, was perhaps the most dedicated. But Evans felt in no way compelled to join them. Leyda had urged him, unsuccessfully, to join the Communist-oriented Film and Photo League in New York, which had formed in response to the Depression. The members of the league scorned the commercial movies of Hollywood, aspiring instead to make the kinds of revolutionary films being made in Soviet Russia by Sergei Eisenstein. They believed that if they could match Eisenstein's grasp of powerful narrative and innovative technique, their films would be capable of changing the world. But Evans declined to join them; he did not share their idealism, which he thought was naive. To him, the insularity and dogma of the Communist movement seemed just as oppressive as his father's business world. "The problem became one of staying out of leftist politics and still staying out of the [business] establishment," he reflected much later. Neither one, it seemed to him, would make the world a better place, only a duller one. Their postulations were just an effort to make matters tidier than they actually were.

While he maintained his independence from the Communist party, Evans was nonetheless keenly interested in Leyda's trip to Moscow in the fall of 1933 to study film with Eisenstein. Ever since his first experience with the movie camera in the South Seas, Evans had wanted to make films. He had recently befriended Irving Jacoby, a film producer who had established a small production company with the help of his wife's inheritance. Jacoby was regarded as a lightweight by some of the more politically minded New York filmmakers of his generation, but from Evans' point of view, this could only have meant that he kept a reasonable distance from politics. That autumn, Jacoby thought he might have a job for Evans as the cameraman on a world cruise to make a series of short travel films. Hendrik Willem Van Loon, a Dutch-born writer famous for his best-selling *The Story of Mankind*, was to be the scriptwriter. According to Jacoby, this was a rare chance for Evans to advance his cinematic technique at someone else's expense.

Like many other projects that involved funding in 1933, Jacoby's world cruise fell through. But by February 1934, Jacoby had come up with a modified plan. He had raised enough money, he claimed, for him and Evans to go around the world on a cruise ship and pay for their own equipment. He would be the business mastermind, Evans the photographic director, and Van Loon — though something of "a fathead," in Evans' estimation — would draw the crowds. They would make ten or twelve short travel films in Europe and America, call it *Van Loon's Occident* or some such thing, and, in lieu of a salary, take a percentage of the royalties. Perhaps Leyda could meet them in Europe in the spring, Evans suggested, if he could break free from his film course.

As these plans were taking shape, Evans had plenty of leisure in which to contemplate them, as well as to enjoy the rare comforts of good food and warm weather. His old Andover classmate Joe Reed had recently acquired a resort hotel called the Island Inn in Hobe Sound, Florida. Alert to the ways in which he might employ his less fortunate friends, Reed had invited Evans down to make some publicity photographs. For several weeks that winter, Evans enjoyed the temporary security of hotel living, eating regular meals and drinking iced tea while reading Jules Romains' multivolume *Les Hommes de bonne volonté.* He found the books so absorbing that they were almost a substitute for living, especially where he now sat surrounded by bridge players and golf conversations. "Florida is ghastly," he wrote to Ernestine Evans, "and very pleasant where I am, away from the cheap part . . . This island a millionaire's paradise and I'd like to be a millionaire as you know."

Evans wrote to Leyda about his film prospects, but to Ernestine he composed his thoughts on another possibility. Sometime before he had left for Florida, the two had discussed his ideas for a picture book. Ernestine, in her capacity as literary agent, was aware that the American public was eager for firsthand documentary evidence of the nationwide Depression, which the daily newspapers kept off the front page. People wanted to witness the real lives of their fellow Americans, to know better the common ground not only of their crisis but of their culture. Photography seemed the most natural medium for communicating this message, but it was not at all obvious how to use it, for while the effects of the crisis were felt across the country, they were not so easily seen. The Depression was, in the words of one historian, "an oddly invisible phenomenon." It consisted of things not happening, of a subtle slowing of the pace on the street that was more easily described in words and statistics than in pictures.

Evans envisioned his photographic picture book as a study in con-

trasts. He was interested in capturing not so much a material poverty as a poverty of spirit. He would look for evidence of the slow,
reluctant disintegration of the American business mentality, the nervous middle class side by side with the homeless. The cities of the
Midwest were his most promising targets. Perhaps Ernestine could
persuade some of her influential friends in Washington to fund the
project. "American city is what I'm after," he explained to her.

> So might use several, keeping things typical. The right things can be
> found in Pittsburgh, Toledo, Detroit (a lot in Detroit, I want to get in
> some dirty cracks, Detroit's full of chances). Chicago business stuff,
> probably nothing of New York, but Philadelphia suburbs are smug
> and endless.
>   People, all classes, surrounded by bunches of the new down and out.
>   Automobiles, and the automobile landscape.
>   Architecture, American urban taste, commerce, small scale, large
> scale, the city street atmosphere, the street smell, the hateful stuff,
> women's clubs, fake culture, bad education, religion in decay.
>   The movies.
>   Evidence of what the people of the city read, eat, see for amusement,
> do for relaxation and not get it.
>   Sex.
>   Advertising.
>   A lot else, you see what I mean.

While his mind was mainly on cities, the road trip to Florida had
also opened Evans' eyes to the photographic possibilities of the rural
South. In the roadside stands and simple frame churches of Georgia
and the Carolinas remained the traces of a preindustrial age and the
beauty of things improvised and handmade. On the way home, Evans
decided to linger, and with an introduction to Ernestine's friend the
writer Julia Peterkin, he stopped to spend several days at Lang Syne
Plantation in South Carolina, which was still carrying on much as it
had before the Civil War.

By the time Evans arrived back in New York, his film prospects
with Jacoby had diminished, and nothing could yet be made of his
plans for a book. Fortunately, other jobs were in sight. For the September 1934 issue of *Fortune*, Dwight Macdonald was scheduled to

write a piece on the Communist party in America, and Evans was invited to make the photographs.

Fortune, the first magazine to be devoted to American business, had been founded in 1930 by Henry Luce, the aggressive young publisher of *Time.* With an unprecedented newsstand price of one dollar a copy, *Fortune* was a sumptuous magazine, generously illustrated, printed in sheet-fed gravure, its text set in old-fashioned letterpress type. If the idea for the magazine had occurred to Luce a few months later, when the economic tide had turned, *Fortune* would probably never have appeared. Almost immediately it was caught at the ideological crossroads of the Depression. The editors felt compelled to provide a multifaceted view of the economy, acknowledging the detractors as well as the champions of business. The senior writers were well equipped for this problem; many of them, ironically, were political radicals. As far as Henry Luce was concerned, their political beliefs made no difference, and their knowledge of the business world was immaterial as long as they could write. If they happened to be graduates of Yale, as Luce himself was, so much the better.

Hunting for subject matter on a warm Saturday in July, Evans, Macdonald, and Geoffrey Hellman, a writer for *The New Yorker,* drove up to Beacon, New York, to visit a Communist summer camp. The photographs Evans made "during a prowl through Camp Nitgedaiget (Yiddish for carefree)" of half-naked campers — earnest, sweaty, crowded together and frowning under the hot sun — aptly suggested, Macdonald wrote, "the human side" of the American Communist movement, namely that "Communists made great campers. No one doubts the party's social success." Macdonald's careful wording only thinly disguised his disgust with the whole experience, which he confessed to his future wife, Nancy Rodman, almost "made a fascist" out of him. He was more of a snob — and perhaps an anti-Semite — than he realized, and he discovered during the course of the weekend his "fundamental dislike of living in a herd. The comrades," he told Rodman, "were 99^{44}/$_{100}$% pure Yiddish and they had that peculiar Yiddish love of living in each other's laps that you can observe any day on Coney Island." This kind of group mentality was equally repellent to Evans. Having survived Sunday morning at

Camp Nitgedaiget, Macdonald, Evans, and Hellman escaped for brunch and a Tom Collins at the Westchester Embassy Club and "bathed in the clean capitalist pool."

Before the September issue of *Fortune* went to press, another opportunity for Evans came up in a story more closely matched to his instincts. The article, called "The Great American Roadside," was by a young staff writer named James Agee. Like most *Fortune* articles, it had a clear business slant, being concerned mainly with the emerging business of roadside cabins, soon to be labeled motels. But in his description of the American highway, Agee successfully merged the duties of a magazine journalist with a prose style of sumptuous description:

> How it scraggled and twisted along the coast of Maine, high-crowned and weak-shouldered in honor of long winter. How in Florida the detours are bright with the sealime of rolled shells. How the stiff wide stream of hard unbroken roadstead spends the mileage between Mexicali and Vancouver. How the road degrades into a rigorous lattice of country dirt athwart Kansas through the smell of hot wheat (and this summer a blindness and strangulation of lifted dust). How like a blacksnake in the sun it takes the ridges, the green and dim ravines which are the Cumberlands, and lolls loose into the hot Alabama valleys.

"The American Roadside" was generously illustrated with drawings by John Steuart Curry, a popular genre artist, but perhaps because the article was longer than the editors expected it to be (managing editor Ralph Ingersoll finally cut it short at eight thousand words), a few photographs supplemented its later pages. One of these was a photograph of a solitary roadside cabin with a sign bearing its name — MISS FLORIDA — over the door, by Walker Evans.

No doubt Agee preferred this straightforward little photograph to the paintings that illustrated his article. The camera, he believed, was, "next to unassisted and weaponless consciousness, the central instrument of our time." He also believed that it was very often misused. It was immoral, he thought, to use photography the way most journalists did, as a tool of persuasion. But in the way that Evans used the camera, in an effort to perceive the subject simply and candidly, bathed in "the cruel radiance of what is," Agee found the match to his own efforts as a writer and felt most keenly the inadequacy of mere words.

It was probably at about the time the roadside article was published that Agee and Evans first met; no one remembers exactly how. There were many links between the circles of artists and writers in Greenwich Village, and as Evans later reflected, "People do get drawn together when they're sort of meant to." The two men soon recognized their shared instincts and aesthetic sensibility and their opposing, complementary talents, which would ultimately lead to the most ambitious and self-revealing artistic collaboration either man would ever undertake.

Agee had hitchhiked to New York immediately after graduating from Harvard in 1932 to join the staff of *Fortune*. He had already shown promise as a poet during his student years at Phillips Academy in Exeter, New Hampshire. At Harvard he was a writer and the editor of the literary journal *The Advocate*, for which in 1931 he edited a brilliant parody of *Time* magazine. Dwight Macdonald, who had carried on a correspondence with Agee since his Exeter days, had recommended him to Henry Luce.

Agee was married to Olivia Saunders, known as Via, a spirited redhead and graduate of Bryn Mawr College. Via was the daughter of a chemistry professor at Hamilton College whose passion for music involved his entire family and circle of friends. Agee had spent an idyllic summer with the Saunderses in their large, comfortable house in Clinton, New York, joining in chamber music, games of charades, and lively intellectual conversation. He was in love with the whole family, and married the younger of Saunders' two daughters, six years his senior, as soon as he graduated from Harvard.

As Via recalled, Walker and Jim saw a good deal of each other in the early days of the Agees' marriage, and Walker often went to visit them in their basement apartment on Perry Street in Greenwich Village. On warm nights they would sit outside on the small patio, talking and drinking under the ailanthus trees. Jim, who was known to be extremely quiet in the office during the day, by night became so animated in talk — about art, books, people, music — that it was almost impossible to interrupt him. Whatever the subject, he wanted to become it, to empathize with all his senses, to know how it felt to be that thing, and his whole body was involved in the effort. "He seemed to model, fight, and stroke his phrases as he talked," Walker wrote. "Agee did a great deal of writing in the air. Often you had the impulse to gag him and tie a pen to his hand." Jim also spent many evenings with Walker on Bethune Street. Then Walker might suggest that he walk Jim home while they continued their conversation; the conversation not being finished, Jim would follow Walker back to Bethune Street, and so on, until Walker would finally collapse with mental and physical exhaustion sometime in the early hours of the morning, while Jim carried on, he knew not where, until dawn.

Agee was tall and big-boned, and he walked with a great loping stride. He changed his clothes as infrequently as possible, and Evans observed that "in due time the cloth would mold itself to his frame." His teeth were bad and his dark hair a tangle. His total lack of personal vanity made him a striking contrast to the figure of Evans, whose keen self-awareness exuded an air of indisputable correctness. Both men in their different ways wished simply to fade into the background unnoticed and watch. But they did not go unnoticed. Evans all buttoned up and Agee all undone, Evans with his fine frame and sloping, shady eyes and Agee with his broad shoulders and cocked smile — each in his own way was exceedingly, if not irresistibly, attractive to both men and women, young and old.

Different as they were, Agee and Evans shared a fundamental attitude that sealed their friendship. Both deeply distrusted organized movements of any kind — in art, politics, or both. They suspected anything highly structured or neatly labeled, including the very word *art*. Both had an instinctive love for the aesthetically rejected object. And while others became involved in social protest, their protest was of another kind — an almost complete intolerance of outside authority over their creative work. Agee occasionally fantasized about shooting poker-faced Henry Luce, who had the habit of stopping his writers in the halls with meaningless questions such as "How many blocks are there in Manhattan?" Agee was to become extremely adept at satisfying Luce's obsession with hard facts in many of the articles he wrote for *Fortune,* but this was not his line. His natural impulse was to turn a given subject every which way and inspect it from all sides. With the sharp-eyed and philosophical Via, Agee played "the metaphor game," which consisted of equating an inanimate object with a personality — a secondhand silver flute was Leslie Howard, a Grand Rapids easy chair was Carl Sandburg, and so on. Agee could give soul to a lamppost, and wax about it without end. But as Dwight Macdonald noted of his colleague's work, "The weariest river of Ageean prose winds somewhere safe to sea."

Where Agee rambled, Evans was concise. While Agee's fascination lay in his ability to temporarily embody the person or thing he was talking about, Evans' charm was in his split-second response to the situation at hand, his dry wit and nimble plays on words, as quick and cool as his camera eye. Evans was good at introductions but remained emotionally reserved; Agee appeared awkward and shy but was capable of an almost overwhelming intimacy. Both of them, Evans reflected with pride, were "old Americans," meaning that they each had southern ancestors; Agee's were farming folk in Tennessee, Evans', on his father's side, from Virginia and Kentucky. In a way that was deeply intriguing to them both, the South held not only the mysteries of their past but the key to their own tumultuous, blues-filled era.

In the winter of 1935, Evans had a second opportunity to go south. Charles Fuller had recently traveled to New Orleans and discovered its wealth of Greek Revival buildings, many of which were in dire need of restoration. With a young colleague named Gifford Cochran, who seemed to have plenty of money and not much to do, Fuller developed the idea of producing an illustrated book about the architecture around New Orleans, with the thought of stimulating interest in saving it. In particular, they wanted to document the old plantation homes along the Mississippi River. Having worked with Evans on a similar project in upstate New York, Fuller asked him to make the photographs. Cochran would foot the bill, make suggestions, and go along for the ride.

Fortunately for Evans, Cochran knew how to travel in style. At the end of January 1935, the two of them set off for Louisiana in a chauffeur-driven car. They took at least two weeks to reach New Orleans, stopping on the way in Savannah, where Evans, driven by James the chauffeur, took his camera to explore the Negro quarter, the waterfront, and the open market. In New Orleans, Cochran had arranged for them to live temporarily in the Upper Pontalba Building, one of a pair of large brick apartment buildings that flanked Jackson Square, in the heart of the French Quarter, and to have the daily services of a housekeeper. All was in place for them to explore the town.

The weather was balmy and the pace of life unhurried. The French Quarter, an island of stylish architecture that alternated Ionic columns with lacy ironwork, was the domain of immigrant Italians, barnyard animals, artists, and Negroes as well as some of the more prominent members of New Orleans society. Evans felt its aura of decay and, in its particular Franco-Latin cultural cross, a libertine atmosphere that he found strangely threatening.

Less than a week after they arrived, Cochran abruptly left for New York by train. On his own, Evans sought out the company of Paul Ninas, a local artist whom Fuller had suggested he contact. Ninas was a successful painter of regional scenes, a teacher, and a prominent member of the New Orleans Arts and Crafts Club. When Evans met him for lunch, the tall, angular painter was accompanied by his pretty young wife, Jane Smith, a promising artist herself at twenty-two.

Jane was not a native of New Orleans, but she had family ties in Louisiana: her grandmother's plantation home in Natchitoches had burned to the ground in the Civil War. She had grown up in Fond du Lac, Wisconsin, but she reconnected with her southern heritage by attending Sophie Newcomb College in New Orleans, where she studied painting. Since her marriage to Paul Ninas, she had become something of an art-world insider. Although she was shy, Evans immediately felt comfortable with her; her proper midwestern upbringing put him at ease in the exotic and slightly seedy atmosphere of the French Quarter. There was an inscrutable air of sadness about her, but he quickly learned that he could make her laugh. When she laughed, her blue eyes sparkled and her high round cheeks lifted and he saw that she was beautiful. Over lunch that very day, he invited her to accompany him up the River Road to photograph the old plantations, and with hardly a moment's hesitation she said yes. During the next few weeks, before setting out for each day's work, Evans would ask his housekeeper to pack sandwiches for two. Jane, who was just as interested in the shanties along the river as she was in the mansions, took along her sketchbook.

The appalling state of the southern economy could not have been more poignantly revealed than it was along the River Road. The dramatic fall in the price of sugar in the early 1930s — the same one that hit the Cuban economy — had destroyed whatever vestiges of the aristocracy remained. Here were summed up the tatters of the Gilded Age. A scant few antebellum mansions still stood where less than a century before they had literally crowded the riverbank. Now the poor occupied the desolate sugarcane fields in crude makeshift houses, and a growing population of squatters had begun to invade the old mansions.

Evans did not manage to photograph all of the remaining plantation homes, but he photographed enough to reveal their common architectural elements as well as their need for attention. The possibility of disturbing the inhabitants kept him from getting too close to the buildings, but he also kept his distance for other reasons. By standing back, as he had when photographing with Kirstein around Boston, he was best able to reveal the stateliness of the architecture and the baldness of its demise. His pictures of the Uncle Sam Plantation, Seven Oaks, and Belle Hélène document the prevailing style — classical columns surrounding a square, symmetrical structure, hipped roof, and wraparound second-story veranda. At Uncle Sam, the late afternoon sun cast a shadow of columns on the crumbling façade and the rotting porch, where once the plantation owner might have rocked contentedly at the sight of his richly planted property; now there was nothing but weeds.

A few miles north of Belle Hélène, on the west side of the river, stood Belle Grove, among the grandest plantation houses along the river. From the far end of an untended field, where Evans made a photograph, it stood like a giant solitary tombstone. Its two huge front porticos loomed high above the ground; when Evans moved closer, he could see the pale pink remains of the original exterior paint still in evidence. The house was completely deserted.

With his Leica, Evans made a picture of Jane seated beside one of the massive stone columns on the front portico. Dressed in a fitted jacket, full skirt, and shoes with modestly high heels, she hugged her knees and avoided his direct gaze. With teasing admiration for her neatly folded legs, he also photographed her from below, peering over her knees, and close up from the side he captured her piquant profile and plaited chestnut hair.

They ventured inside. Time and neglect gave intimacy to an interior that had once been ostentatious in the extreme. One room was especially striking in its state of semi-ruin. Perfectly symmetrical and generously fortified by a march of Corinthian pilasters, it led through a pair of columns to a small semicircular room beyond. The hazy Louisiana sunlight filtered gently through the rotting shutters, exposing chipped paint and crumbling plasterwork, and spread its even glow over all. Aiming his lens at the little room beyond where they stood, Evans imagined the mansion's former glory, when each chapter in the day was accented by its own formal setting. He called his picture *The Breakfast Room*.

At Belle Grove, Walker's usual emotional reserve was tempered by a new spirit, a romance with the South's decline inspired by the presence of his thoughtful companion. By the time he made this picture, he was in love with Jane — with her natural modesty, her ready laugh, and her occasional devastating candor. Furthermore, she came from the same midwestern background as he did and like him had childhood memories of Chicago, of eating chicken pie at Marshall Field's and taking the Chicago-Northwestern Railroad home again. Jane was the girl next door. But like Walker, she had fled her stultifying background to become an artist.

The fact that she was married did little to keep Walker from pursuing her. His mild sense of shame was easily overcome by the pleasure of making her smile. Jane also felt little remorse as her feelings for Walker turned amorous. Although she wasn't absolutely sure, she suspected that her husband was having an affair with a young designer named Christine Fairchild. The days of motoring along the river with Walker gave Jane a new sense of freedom and confidence. He had distracted her from her doubts and boosted her sinking morale. His enthusiasm for what he saw was exhilarating to her, his commentary was sophisticated, full of wit and unexpected turns of phrase, and there was irresistible mischief in his dark sidelong glances.

They were not always alone. For several weeks that winter, Walker, Jane, Paul, and Christine made an awkward party of four, dining and drinking together night after night, each one pretending not to notice the subtle signs of betrayal as their excitement rose. They danced to the music of the big bands on the decks of a retired Mississippi paddlewheel steamer and huddled in the smoky corners of the jazz clubs along Decatur Street. By the time Walker left New Orleans on March 23, he was determined to see Jane again.

The photographic results of Evans' trip to New Orleans were mixed. Processing his negatives in the darkroom, he was excited by the success of some of the plantation pictures and shocked by the technical shortcomings of others. In some the sky was streaked because he had overdeveloped the negative; in others the lens shade had created an unexpected dark halo, which he had not accounted for when raising the lens. Furthermore, he felt he had not taken advantage of many opportunities to photograph in the French Quarter, which made him long to return. But within a few weeks Fuller's book project went to pieces over arguments with Cochran, mostly having to do with money.

Just before the project was dropped, Tom Mabry, who had recently been hired as assistant treasurer of the Museum of Modern Art, came up with another big commission for Evans: to photograph the entire contents of the museum's forthcoming African sculpture show. Opening in the spring of 1935, the exhibition was among the first to present African sculptures as works of art rather than anthropological curiosities. Altogether there would be almost five hundred pieces — sculpted masks, weapons, utensils, ornaments, musical instruments, and figures made of wood, ivory, bronze, gold, iron, stone, and terra cotta.

Mabry's intention for the show reached beyond the museum's walls. Two years earlier he had been teaching creative writing to black students at Fisk University in Nashville, at the invitation of James

Weldon Johnson, one of the prime movers in Negro education at the time. Mabry had become keenly aware of the American Negro's lack of a tangible cultural history, and he felt strongly that African sculpture should not be limited to a privileged urban museum audience. Backing this idea, Alfred Barr sought funding from the General Education Board to make a group of photographs of the objects that could be sent to black schools and colleges throughout the South. At the end of the tour, the photographs would be donated or sold at cost to the schools. Altogether the project would require the photographer to make about five hundred exposures and sixteen sets of prints.

For several weeks while "African Negro Sculpture" was on view, Evans arrived at the museum every evening at closing time with his eight-by-ten view camera and two assistants, one to prepare each piece for the exposure, the other — Dorothy Miller, of the museum's curatorial staff — to help with camera and lighting. The objects were of widely varying sizes. Evans fussed over their exact placement in front of his camera, and over the position of the lights; many of the pieces had to be photographed from three points of view, and some then had to be photographed all over again. Scheduled to photograph six objects each evening, the three workers rarely got through all six before quitting, exhausted, at midnight.

As painstaking as it was, the task did not seem like drudgery to Miller. Evans, she quickly learned, was captivated by the sculptures and expressed unabashed wonder and curiosity at each piece. To do each one justice with the camera, he studied it carefully, determined what the most original quality of its surface or form was, and devised a way to bring it fully to life. Not wishing the source of the artificial spotlight to show, he asked Miller to move the light in a circular motion for the duration of each lengthy exposure.

Engrossed as he was in his work, Walker's thoughts often turned to Jane Ninas. Hoping to tempt her northward, he had written to say that he had been given the run of a small townhouse for the summer, located, appropriately enough, on Jane Street in Greenwich Village. He knew that it was Paul Ninas' habit to spend two months of every summer teaching in west Texas while Jane visited her parents in

Wisconsin. Would it not be just as easy to travel first to New York, Walker ventured, and pick up a ride west from there? Perhaps anticipating objections from Ninas, he included Christine Fairchild in his invitation to blur his intentions. Less than two weeks after he returned to New York, he received a letter from Jane with the news that she was thinking of coming.

At the same time, aware of the dangers of getting more deeply involved with a married woman, Walker was cultivating some romantic interests closer at hand. While he was in the South that winter he kept in touch by postcard with Irving Jacoby's sister Beatrice. By the spring he was enjoying her exclusive company almost once a week. They took evening walks in the park, went to the movies, held hands in the front seat of his car, and went dancing in Harlem. When Jane's letter arrived, Walker was also in the midst of a brief love affair with Jim Agee's sister, Emma. An aspiring poet, Emma had followed her older brother from Knoxville to New York, where Jim had helped her get a clerical job at *Time*. Like Jim, she was fond of staying up late, talking, drinking, and listening to jazz. The affair, which lacked passion on Walker's part, made him feel embarrassed and guilty; he vigorously scribbled over all of the entries in his diary about Emma coming to spend the night with him.

Jane was, in Walker's mind, his "best girl," even though she was another man's wife, and he was full of excitement over seeing her again when she arrived with Christine on June 7. Paul Grotz, who had not seen Walker since his trip south, remembered the day when he came to call with two young women, one on each arm. "They looked like twins," he recalled. Later, Walker took him aside and jokingly boasted that he could not decide which one to marry. But he was not to have a woman on each arm for long. Within a few days Christine had disappeared with a German, Freedie Von Helms, leaving Jane and Walker to their privacy on Jane Street, where, with the easy passage between neighboring bedrooms, they had already become lovers.

Evans still shared space on Bethune Street with Ben Shahn, but they had moved their studios into a larger building at numbers 20 and 22, on the other side of the street, where the artist Lou Block was also working. Encouraged by Evans' example, Shahn and Block had both become avid photographers and in the summer of 1935 were using the camera to make studies for a mural they had been jointly commissioned to do for the prison at Riker's Island. In order to accommodate their extra photographic activity that summer, including Evans' African sculpture project, the three men organized a new darkroom. Having moved his family to West 11th Street, Shahn also used 22 Bethune Street to carry on his love affair with a spry young artist and journalist named Bernarda Bryson, who had originally come to New York from Ohio to write about the Diego Rivera mural in the making. One of Bryson's first impressions of Evans was the sight of his photographs floating around in a bathtub and hanging up to dry on a string like the day's laundry.

To fill the huge order for the Museum of Modern Art, Evans hired extra help in the darkroom. Through Shahn, he found Peter Sekear, a young Dutch artist who was making a living as a commercial sign painter. Sekear also had some experience as a museum photographer, and Evans made him second in command. John Cheever, who was beginning to publish his brilliantly sad short stories in *The New Yorker* and other magazines, was desperate for money and was also willing to be trained as Evans' darkroom assistant.

While Walker was occupied with African sculpture, Ernestine Evans was busy prodding her contacts in Washington, D.C., to get work for him and Shahn in one of Roosevelt's new work-relief programs, possibly through the Works Progress Administration (WPA). Under the directorship of Harry Hopkins, who was a close friend of Walker's sister and brother-in-law, the WPA combined the need for civic improvements throughout the country with the even greater need to get the unemployed back to work. During the 1930s it built interstate highway systems, dams, bridges, boardwalks, schools, and playgrounds. But just as bridge builders needed jobs building bridges, artists needed jobs making art. Through Hopkins' enlightened management, actors, musicians, writers, and artists were also invited to apply their talents to the works. Music and theater were effectively spread beyond the big eastern cities to small towns, writers were assigned to develop a series of guidebooks covering every state in the union, and artists painted easel paintings or murals for public buildings, earning as much as $100 a week.

The WPA made official what the artists already knew — that culture did not belong exclusively to Europe. The idea that art was as useful to society as any other profession was revolutionary. And it was not long before many artists employed by the WPA took government sponsorship for granted. If they had once believed that the world owed them a living, now they were sure of it. For the first time, a community of artists from all over the country gathered in Washington. Bernarda Bryson remembered how cheerful everyone seemed to be in the capital during the Depression. To many young people, the city felt like a big college campus. Everyone was in shirtsleeves and knew everyone else. Artists, bureaucrats, and politicians waved to one another on the Mall. "We were full of hope," remembered Peter Sekear's wife, Elizabeth. "We were going to reform the whole world."

The WPA had the highest profile as an agency that included artists in its programs, but others quickly followed its example. One of these was the Resettlement Administration (RA), a division of the Department of Agriculture. Hoping to revitalize a number of existing farm relief and housing programs, Roosevelt corralled them into one ambitious new organization. On April 30, 1935, under a hastily passed emergency relief act, he established the Resettlement Administration and appointed Rexford Tugwell, then undersecretary of agriculture and a member of Roosevelt's original three-man economic team, known as the Brains Trust, as its chief administrator.

Tugwell was not the kind of person one would expect to see on a farm. He was urbane, well-spoken, and handsome, and he liked to dress in a white suit. He was also better known for his theories than for his practical experience. One of his first ideas for the RA came in response to the dust storms in the Midwest and the resulting devastation to the nation's most valuable farmland. He conceived of a grand plan by which the government would reorganize land and farm families to their mutual benefit, leaving fallow land to rest and recover from overproduction and offering farmers interest-free loans to stake out a new living on better soil, often on cooperative homesteads. His plan was based on the problems of small and tenant farmers, who he believed were at the center of the crisis.

Grace Falke, Tugwell's wife-to-be, was the driving force behind the Resettlement Administration's involvement with the arts. She originated a program called Special Skills, to encourage the inclusion of American folk arts and crafts as an integral part of cooperative homesteading. As much as Americans needed to brighten their economic outlook, Falke believed, their communities would benefit from a better knowledge of their common cultural past. Special Skills sent artists, artisans, and musicians to instruct newly settled families in basket weaving, quilting, furniture making, and folk music. The program struck a chord with the eastern intelligentsia and quickly became a favorite of Eleanor Roosevelt's.

One of many agencies absorbed by the Resettlement Administration was Subsistence Housing, created by Eleanor Roosevelt in 1933 for the Department of the Interior. Ernestine Evans was working for Subsistence Housing in 1935. At the same time she was badgering Adrian Dornbush, head of the fine arts section of Special Skills, to hire Ben Shahn. She also had access to John Franklin Carter, director of the RA's Division of Information, and with her forceful recommendation, Carter was eventually persuaded to give Evans a trial run as a photographer for the agency.

Jane was still in New York when Walker received the good news. On June 15, 1935, the Resettlement Administration notified him that he had been appointed to the position of assistant specialist in information, at a very respectable salary of $7.22 per day. His appointment was for an initial period of three months, effective June 24. He was to report to Washington immediately to sign the oath of office. Unwilling to cut his visit with Jane short, he begged her to go along for the ride. She told her husband she was on her way to Wisconsin by car and left with Walker for Washington.

Tugwell had inherited a number of unfinished projects when he pulled together his collection of farming and housing agencies, including those of Subsistence Housing. The agency's particular area of concern was the coal-mining district of West Virginia and southwestern Pennsylvania, where mines had been closing for lack of business, leaving a growing number of families on government relief. Mrs. Roosevelt's idea was to build a homesteading community in the mining district as a model of Yankee self-sufficiency. She would put the miners back to work building their own homes and supply each family with its own dairy cow and vegetable garden. She would attract new businesses to the area to help the economy grow again. She chose Arthurdale, near Morgantown, West Virginia, for a model community, upon which several others in the vicinity were to be based.

But from the beginning the project was poorly organized. The prefabricated houses taken into Arthurdale didn't fit the foundations already in place, and the cost of the buildings was underestimated; it was not easy to get industries to move in, and just as difficult to nudge the homesteaders into a cooperative spirit. Before long, Arthurdale was overrun with government employees trying to make the idea work. The embarrassments of Mrs. Roosevelt's homesteading project rippled throughout Washington, and the conservative press made a feast of them. When Tugwell took on Subsistence Housing, the controversy had not subsided. From the point of view of public relations for his new Resettlement Administration, Arthurdale was a high priority.

Walker Evans' first assignment therefore was to document the progress of the homesteads and industries in West Virginia and, by way of contrast, the poverty that the new communities were supposed to alleviate. Evans ordered the best equipment available, a Deardorff eight-by-ten view camera, a tripod, and plate holders, all together weighing about fifty pounds. He also asked for a Leica, and he packed his own detachable right-angle viewfinder. Days passed in Washington while he waited for the delivery of his equipment, stalled in a bureaucratic mixup. Finally, late in the afternoon of June 26, he and Jane started out from Washington. They stopped for the night in Leesburg, Virginia, then went on across the mountains to Aurora and Reedsville, West Virginia.

The challenge most perfectly suited to Evans' talents was never more clearly before him than it was now in the hills and valleys of the West Virginia coal country. In the mining towns, deserted and depressed, the monotonous rows of frame houses marching up and down the hills, workers' strikes brewing, Evans immediately saw a rich landscape for his photography. In the small company towns sprawling over the landscape, once thriving, now bankrupt, he saw through the American dream of an egalitarian society to its core of melancholy. In Morgantown he photographed the housing along the train tracks and over the hills, as evenly spaced and rhythmically dull as railroad ties, with a sense of stillness that seemed to anticipate a massive change.

Known as the photographer sent from Washington, he struck up conversations with the locals to learn more about his subject and how to get closer to it. A politician, a schoolteacher, or a man without a job might take him to the housing project or tell of an imminent miners' strike. With the help of one new acquaintance or another, he won his way into some of the miners' homes, as Eleanor Roosevelt had done before him. There he not only fulfilled his duty to describe the material poverty of the region, he made art out of its lowly interiors, made order out of the unrelated stuff of people's lives. In one photograph he took inside a miner's house in Scott's Run, a pale, sad-eyed little boy slouches barefoot on a hard chair while a collage of advertisements and life-size figures of the American mother and Santa Claus pop up from the table, beaming, and sidle out from behind the cupboard. Looking at this drab little room through the ground glass of his big camera, Evans found it full of life and interest, and a perfect opportunity to weave together the strongest elements of his photography — straight portraiture, an intimate interior, and the ironic presence of advertising, which insinuates its way into the bleakest corners of American life.

The boy from Scott's Run elicited a sympathetic portrait from Evans, but he took a more jaded approach to the crowd at a Fourth of July picnic in Terra Alta. Using his periscopic camera and pretending to photograph Jane, who smiled obligingly, Evans made pictures of fat, vacant-eyed young women and toothless old men. In his diary he noted the degeneracy of rural poverty and the hideous evidence of inbreeding. Needing an injection of comic relief, he and Jane spent the evening at a W. C. Fields movie.

If the people Evans was instructed to visit were difficult to look at, they were also great savage material for his photography. The more he photographed them in their plight, the greater was his own sense of well-being. He found beauty in the monotony of the old company houses across the narrow valleys, the railroad tracks and power lines, the gas stations placarded with advertisements. Moving north into Pennsylvania, he photographed the little streets of Mount Pleasant in the brightness of a summer afternoon, making pictures of such clarity and depth that the viewer could almost be persuaded to walk into them. Under the high July sun, he used his view camera to its fullest capacity for detail and resolution, looking for opportunities to make the most of foreground and background elements. Positioning his camera right behind a war memorial in Mount Pleasant, he aimed the lens straight down the main street in front of it, following the lines of the electric trolley as far as the eye could see, with every detail, near and far, in sharp focus. It was hot work. Whenever he saw a river, he would immediately strip and jump in, and he would come out brimming with renewed affection for Jane, for everyone.

By early July their time was up. Walker was scheduled to return to New York to process his photographs. Jane's parents were waiting. The lovers spent their last few nights together at the Mayfair Hotel in Pittsburgh. On the last day they went to the Carnegie Institute, where they looked at cast replicas of Greek architectural elements and what Walker thought were some very bad paintings, and both he and Jane developed headaches. After obtaining a cheap excursion ticket through Chicago for Jane, they sat and cried in the hot dirty station until it was time for her to depart. As the train pulled out of the station, she was afraid to look back, reminding Walker of the way he himself sometimes feigned indifference when his passion was at its peak. Days later he was still plagued by the memory of her profile in the window, and he confessed to his diary that he felt slightly lost and ashamed.

On his way back to Washington, he continued to work and to meet people. In Mount Pleasant he stayed in a company boarding house and the next day was invited into a mine, which he found cold and frightening. Evans' travels into the heart of coal country prompted him to peer into his own sheltered past, a reminder of which was right on his route. As he neared Bedford Springs, Pennsylvania, before the end of the week, he couldn't resist stopping for the night at the old summer hotel where he and his parents and sister had stayed before his parents separated. Driving up to the door, he recognized the classic front portico, but he had forgotten the gingerbread wings. He pictured himself as a fourteen-year-old in white flannel pants, strolling along the causeway by himself, surrounded by mountains, and thought about how space seems to shrink as one grows older. Nearing Baltimore the next day, he passed through the campus of Mercersburg Academy, deserted in midsummer, and felt a mild rush of memories not entirely unpleasant.

John Franklin Carter was impressed with the results of Evans' trip. On August 1 he wrote to say that the photographs were indeed of value to the Division of Information and that Evans' temporary assignment might be extended. On August 17 Evans cordially wrote back, thanking Carter for the opportunity to work on such an assignment, "which seems to me to have enormous possibilities of precisely the sort that interest me." He also felt confident enough of Carter's sympathies to insist on maintaining control over his negatives, even if it meant spending more time on them than the government might think necessary. "You will appreciate a certain craftsman's concern on my part," he suggested. Whatever future employment there might be for him with the RA, he promised to allow ample time for his darkroom work.

During the summer, Tugwell had introduced a new member into the staff of the RA: Roy Emerson Stryker, one of Tugwell's economics students at Columbia University and for the past ten years his teaching assistant. With Stryker's help, Tugwell had produced the first photographically illustrated textbook, *American Economic Life*, in 1933. Tugwell had his economic theories, but Stryker could think only in terms of real experience. Jowly, gray-haired, and thickly spectacled, he had grown up on a ranch in Colorado, had punched cattle and worked in the gold mines. His interest in economics had been motivated by what he had witnessed, not by what he had read, and he took this attitude into the classroom. "I wanted the kids to see things for themselves," he said later, "and that's where the use of pictures really began. I got impatient because the bright boys at Columbia had never seen a rag doll, a corn tester, or an old dasher churn. I dug up pictures to show city boys things that every farm boy knows about."

Searching out the visual material for a course in urban economics, Stryker became very interested in photography, particularly the work of the turn-of-the-century photographers Jacob Riis and Lewis Hine, whose images of city slums and child laborers had directly influenced changes in housing and labor laws, respectively. Stryker believed the time had come for photography to be a tool of economic and social change again. The only way to make the public understand the agricultural crisis was to take them there with pictures. Advances in phototechnology made this opportune. The small camera eased the photographer's movement, and flashbulbs synchronized with the camera's shutter greatly enhanced his or her flexibility and speed.

As chief of the historical section of the RA, Stryker was expected "to direct the activities of investigators, photographers, economists, sociologists and statisticians engaged in the accumulation and compilation of reports, statistics, photographic material, vital statistics, agricultural surveys, maps and sketches necessary to make accurate descriptions of the various phases of the Resettlement Administration." Given this jumble of commands, he continued to ask Tugwell to define precisely the purpose of his job for many years to come.

At the start of his tenure, Stryker had to look no further for guidance than the first photographs to be made on assignment for the RA. Just as Evans' photographs of West Virginia arrived freshly printed from New York, Stryker began to articulate the scope of the agency's picture collection. He was immediately impressed by the rich factual detail of Evans' photographs. They exuded an austere faith in pure record; at the same time they possessed a warmth, and an almost haunting sense of familiarity. They helped Stryker to imagine how the nationwide economic depression might be described in pictures. The RA collection might distinguish itself by avoiding the sensationalism and packaging of the latest newspaper headlines, offering instead a broader statement about the contemporary American scene; it would be full of telling sociological detail. It would serve as a visualization of the facts and statistics of middle-class American life, the kind of background that Robert and Helen Lynd had provided in *Middletown* in 1929. Its mission would be not necessarily to reform, but to reflect in the ordinary detail of American life the state of the nation's mind.

In the freewheeling atmosphere of New Deal Washington, Ernestine and Walker swiftly corralled Ben Shahn into the Information Division. Shahn, who had been designing posters for the Special Skills Division, was also looking for a sponsored trip to the South to collect material for his various new mural projects. In no time, he and Evans were telling their new boss how to run his program. Shahn had Stryker "at his knee," Evans recalled, "saying 'What shall we do next, Mr. Shahn?'" as Shahn explained pictorial methods of political persuasion, where to look for subject matter, and how to organize a filing system. When the photographer Russell Lee joined the Information Division that fall, he thought (until someone corrected him) that Ben Shahn was in charge of it.

On September 16, 1935, Evans was notified that he had been appointed to the permanent position of assistant specialist in information. He was not completely satisfied with his promotion. Now certain that he was in demand, he requested a better title — senior information specialist — and an annual salary of $3,000. To earn his new title, he was required to furnish professional recommendations. Charles Fuller stated unequivocally, "Mr. Walker Evans' photographic work is of the highest order," and Wilfred S. Lewis, secretary of the New York City Housing Authority, agreed that "he showed the greatest talent as a photographer," adding, not irrelevantly, that he was "a cultured gentleman." Despite a sudden cut in Stryker's photographic budget in October, the division granted Evans his request, with a plea that he keep his expenses to a minimum.

Evans' request not only reflected his material need; he knew the raise and the title would help to distinguish him from the growing ranks of RA photographers, none of whom shared his art-world connections or the high standard he had set for himself and his medium. Stryker had just recruited Arthur Rothstein, a chemistry student from Columbia University who had done picture research for

him and Tugwell on their textbook. Dependable and organized, Rothstein was immediately placed in charge of setting up a darkroom for
the Resettlement Administration. Carl Mydans, another early information specialist, was a journalist and amateur photographer from
Boston. In the fall of 1935 Stryker also brought in Dorothea Lange, a
successful portrait photographer from San Francisco. Lange had recently turned her attention from formal portraiture to the real-life
drama of workers' strikes and had proven herself even more capable
of photographing people in the field than in the studio. Her enno-
bling photographs of migrant workers in California came to be considered exemplary of the RA photographic team's mission.

With differing temperaments but equally strong visions, Evans,
Shahn, and Lange exerted the greatest influence on Stryker's staff of
photographers. All fostered a straight documentary approach and a
disdain for obvious propaganda. "*No politics* whatever," Evans had
vowed before accepting the job in the spring of 1935. His conviction
about this was more absolute than his companions'. While Lange's
and Shahn's photographs of migrant laborers and displaced farmers
openly declared their humanistic concerns, Evans retained an emotional distance from his subject matter. Guided by his aesthetic sense
in the face of all possible distractions, his photographs had a rigor, a
beauty, and a certain edge that made them stand apart. "A bitter
edge," Lange called it. "I liked that bitter edge."

At the time, Evans was passionately interested in the graphic possibilities of his medium. For his return trip to Pennsylvania he
ordered a Zeiss "triple convertible" lens to fit his Deardorff, with three
different focal lengths, normal, long, and longer. The longer the focal
length, the farther he could see down the road or across the river and
the more he could condense a complex scene into a sturdy graphic
structure.

In early November, armed with his new lens, he headed for the
steep banks of the Delaware River. Choosing a strategic position from
which he could condense a long view, he made a photograph that
looks right into the back yards of Phillipsburg, New Jersey, and at the
same time offers a clear vista across the river to the houses and
factories of Easton, Pennsylvania. On the other side of the river, he

photographed from Easton to Phillipsburg, integrating the eclectic architectural geometry on the far bank with the structure of the bridge between the towns. On the outskirts of Easton, Evans came upon an automobile dump. Junked cars were ubiquitous in those days, but this was a treasure trove, right beside the railroad tracks, with a blank field sloping upward just behind. Magnifying the effect of so many cars with their identical profiles, Evans telescoped the dump into a coherent mass, the hill beyond a blank canvas.

The hilly terrain of Bethlehem, Pennsylvania, was abundant with opportunities for telescopic photography as well. Peaked windows and towers broke up the monotony of the town's middle-class housing. Standing on a hill, Evans took aim down a cascade of matching rooftops, punctuated at the end by a church tower. And he could not resist the obvious irony of an arrangement that showed a hilltop graveyard in the foreground with a clear view of the faceless Bethlehem steel mills in the distance. Deliberately choosing the most ordinary of views, he was achieving pictures of heroic proportions — a perfection in his careful positioning of the camera and attention to light, born of an effort so understated as to be nearly invisible. He was mastering the view camera and using it in the grand manner of Mathew Brady, encompassing the scope of near and far, structuring his pictures with as much expanse and depth as could be found in Old Master paintings.

From Bethlehem, Evans drove south through western Pennsylvania, Ohio, and Kentucky. He sent no evidence of his photographic work back to Washington and not a word of his whereabouts until mid-December, when, from somewhere in Tennessee, he wired Stryker for money. On December 10, Stryker sent a gently reproachful letter to Nashville, where Evans awaited his reply. "We were quite concerned about you," Stryker wrote, "thinking that perhaps you had been waylaid and were sleeping in a ditch somewhere in the South." He enclosed a check and suggested that the RA might expect something in return for it. But already it was clear to Stryker that he could never be sure of his footing with Evans. He urged him to get as much done "in as short a time as is commensurate with good work," but he tried to cushion his demand in affectionate teasing: "How your artistic soul must like to hear me ranting on about quantity production!"

Indeed, Stryker's requests for subject matter specific to the Resettlement Administration's interests seemed relatively trivial, if not incomprehensible, to Evans. What mattered now was that he had suddenly hit his artistic stride. Furthermore, at least one untold purpose of his travel southward was to reach Jane in New Orleans in time for Christmas. Since July they had carried on a correspondence. Through the late summer and into the fall he had sent her books (including *Look Homeward, Angel*), drawing pads, and some silver buttons he had found in a junkshop on the Lower East Side.

Soon after Walker arrived in New Orleans, on December 20, the odd foursome of Walker, Jane, Paul, and Christine was back in position, but now the sexual intrigue reached a higher pitch. Christine, who was narrowing her sights on Paul, had possibly hinted that Jane had been unfaithful to him in New York. As if to force a confrontation, a few days after Christmas, she invited them all to stay at her family's vacation house in Waveland, Mississippi. In that once grand but now decrepit Victorian "cottage," the two couples carried on a painful charade, each married person too guilty to accuse the other of infidelity. On January 12, Walker took the Pullman train from Gulfport, Mississippi, straight to Washington, but he left his car in New Orleans, as if to promise his return.

For his next photographic field trip, to begin in February, he asked for $600 to cover daily expenses and travel for two months. His request was only partly filled. He was told to return by the end of February and promised only $300. He informed Stryker that he planned to start out from New Orleans (where his photographs of African sculpture were on view at Dillard University), retrieve his car, and travel through Louisiana, Mississippi, Alabama, Georgia, South Carolina, North Carolina, Virginia, West Virginia, Kentucky, and Tennessee.

He might have also told Stryker that he would be traveling with Peter Sekear, who had already joined him on one of his brief trips to Pennsylvania. As an associate of Evans', Sekear was hoping to be hired onto the photographic team of the Resettlement Administration. For his part, Evans enjoyed Sekear's admiration, even though it usually came by way of a barbed comment. Sekear was tough, unrefined, and waggish, and he was fascinated by the way the stylish Evans "kept his white gloves on" as he aimed his camera into the slums of Atlanta and Birmingham. But the two men shared certain enthusiasms, in particular for the art of sign painting. Both photographed hand-painted signs they admired, and Sekear occasionally went as far as to steal one from the site. His wife remembered him bringing home from a southern rooming house one that said, in crude hand-painted letters, KNOCK ON PIPE FOR GIRLS. But as he struggled to master a documentary style, he was frustrated to find that anything he felt the urge to photograph, Evans had reached first. Not only that, Evans was constantly hogging the better point of view for himself. When he photographed, he seemed to draw an invisible line around himself and his camera, and his companions learned never to cross it.

Arriving once again in New Orleans, Walker was eager to see Jane. By this time they were tempted to run away together. Over drinks one afternoon with Jane and Peter Sekear, Walker asked Peter, "Do you think Jane's coat is warm enough for a New York winter?" Meanwhile, Paul Ninas had decided that it was time to put his rival to the test. One evening when Walker was visiting them in their new apartment on the top floor of the Lower Pontalba Building, Paul pulled out a gun and started waving it in the air. If Walker was man enough to take his wife away from him, he could go ahead; if not, his time was up, and he could leave them alone. Terrified and unprepared for this dramatic threat, Walker slunk away.

For his next encounter with Jane, Walker decided he needed a disguise. From a garage mechanic in the French Quarter he borrowed a boiler suit and a visored cap with the inscription "New Orleans Auto Supply Co." across its front; then he drove the mechanic's truck to the Ninas' apartment where he waited at the wheel for Jane to come out. By evening she still had not appeared. With gathering paranoia, Walker began to wonder if Paul had killed her in a fit of jealous rage.

Later he learned that she was only sick in bed. But Walker was by now alert to his own real fears. The love affair had become too serious. The charade was over. There were real consequences to his actions that he was not prepared to take on. Before long, to Jane's great disappointment, he admitted defeat and slipped out of town.

Two weeks later, in Vicksburg, Mississippi, he wrote Jane a long, apologetic letter, attempting to explain how it had all become too serious and too upsetting and that it was more than he could face.

By the second half of February it was clear to Roy Stryker that Evans would not be returning to Washington by the end of the month, as he had been instructed to do. To justify Evans' employment to an increasingly challenging Congress, Stryker made a more concerted effort to direct his errant employee. A two-page letter full of specific orders regarding subject matter and location reached Evans at the Carroll Hotel in Vicksburg in early March. Ernestine Evans, in her role as roving adviser and researcher for the Resettlement Administration, was to meet Walker in Birmingham, Alabama. Stryker instructed him to head for Birmingham by way of Tupelo, Mississippi, and to photograph the eroded farmland and the poor state of Negro housing. He also asked him "to show deterioration of some of the fine old mansions of the South" and to track the progress of several RA housing improvement projects. Throughout his travels, Evans was supposed to keep in touch with Stryker by night letter and develop his negatives on the road, sending them to Washington as soon as he possibly could. "I realize this is a nice big order," Stryker concluded, "but remember you've got to deliver or else I'm going to catch the devil."

But Evans would not be rushed. He and Sekear, who shared his view that Stryker was just "a big Boy Scout," were taking their time in Vicksburg. The longer he could stay in one place, Evans felt, the better his photographs would be. If he saw potential in the subject but was discouraged by the quality of light, he would go back on another day. While other photographers on the RA team used portable press cameras, Evans had to spend time setting up his view camera, and once it was arranged to his satisfaction, he never failed to make more than one exposure. (Sometimes he did this to expose the negative with more than one setting of the lens, but very often he did it to supply himself with an extra set of negatives.)

Evans and Sekear spent almost three weeks in Vicksburg, where Evans found a wealth of subject matter. With Sekear trailing behind him, he photographed shopfronts in the Negro quarter, rivermen in rowboats and an old paddlewheel ferry on the Mississippi, and the Civil War battlefield — none of which filled any part of Stryker's request. But on his travels northeast from Vicksburg, he made a conscious effort to meet Stryker's demands. In Tupelo, he documented soil erosion on farmland. In Birmingham, while he waited for Ernestine Evans to arrive, he made several photographs of the steel mills, the company houses, and the miners' shacks on the outskirts of town. After he and Ernestine were finally united, following a series of missed connections and frantic telegrams from Stryker, they went with the architect Tom Hibbon to visit two RA projects in the Birmingham vicinity. In Putnam County, Georgia, Evans made several rather ordinary pictures of another RA housing project under construction, swearing that this would be the last time he would waste his talents on his duties to the government.

Along the way through Mississippi and Alabama, Evans grasped a wealth of opportunities to follow his instincts, to reveal the unexpected beauty of the ordinary. He could not have explained what drew him so surely to set up his camera where he did. It was not so much a conscious choice as an irresistible tug from inside, "like magic," he said. "It's as though there's a wonderful secret in a certain place and I can capture it. Only I, at this moment, can capture it, and only this moment and only me." Where others saw degradation, he saw perfection so brilliant that he sometimes lost control of his technique in his hurry to capture it. Certain kinds of subject matter he by now knew were his quarry — rows of matching houses marching to infinity; wooden country churches, their steeples the only element to distinguish them as a place of worship, not of work; storefronts crowded with wares and tin signs. Everywhere he hunted billboards — for the circus, the minstrel show, the movies — often faded and torn, blending seamlessly with the billboard they had superseded beneath. In Atlanta, below a pair of matching wooden houses with identical oval-framed upstairs porches, Evans immortalized a movie poster advertising *Love Before Breakfast.* Carole Lombard, gazing seductively over her shoulder with a prominent black eye, suggested a condition of love he now understood better than before.

During that winter, Evans was working in such a frenzy of excitement and producing so many fine pictures that he could not find time to develop his film at the rate Stryker had asked him to. But by the end of March, Stryker was at the end of his tether. Discovering that Evans was in the coastal town of St. Marys, Georgia, he wrote in more threatening tones: "Your monthly expenditures look pretty large and unless I can lay down lots of pictures with your name on them each month, I am afraid I am going to be in for some difficulty." And as though Evans had not understood that he was actually on assignment, Stryker condescendingly reminded him, "After all, the Resettlement Administration is putting out to you each month a pretty nice sum of money and they have a right to request certain returns." Nevertheless, Evans apparently continued to have his way, asking for additional expense money and staying out in the field long after he was due back in Washington.

His last request was to stop at Julia Peterkin's plantation on his way home, which he did one afternoon in early April. Then he traveled steadily north through the Carolinas and Virginia toward Washington, reviewing the countryside that had set his mind at work on vast photographic projects two winters before. "Carolina and Georgia, a revelation," he had written to Ernestine Evans. "Have to do something about that too."

5 *Three Families*

WHILE EVANS WAS in the South during the winter of 1936, James Agee was taking a six-month leave from *Fortune* in Florida and seriously contemplating quitting his job as soon as he returned to New York. He had been with the magazine for four years and was growing bored with his assignments on such lifeless topics as glass, jewelry, and Colonial Williamsburg. His most recent assignment, a story on the orchid industry, had left him feeling especially cynical and weary. If these were the kinds of subjects *Fortune* deemed worthy of his devoted attention, it was time to quit.

Agee was understandably sympathetic to Evans' complaints about the demands of his boss in Washington. "Very sorry you have been having so bad a time," he wrote to Evans in March. "Govmt is certainly showing its ass off the higher it puts it in the air isnt it. Needs wiping, kicking, clotting, and elimination." He urged Evans to extend his road trip, to join him and Via in Florida, and to "bring Jane," whom he had met only briefly in New York. Alternatively, he hoped that Evans could join them somewhere on the drive north in late spring; he and Via were going to New Orleans and along the Mississippi River to his home state of Tennessee. After that he fully expected to be spending the summer in New York, "and very much hope you'll be," he added.

Evans was no doubt tempted by Agee's invitation, but by the time he reached the Florida border in late March, he had already stretched Roy Stryker's patience to its limit. As soon as he arrived back in New York in April, Stryker began making plans for his next field trip, to West Virginia. Evans wanted to take some time getting there, touring and making pictures through Pennsylvania, New Jersey, and Maryland. On June 19 he proposed to extend his travels north to New York State and throughout New England. But these plans came to an abrupt halt when Agee, having just returned to New York, called on Evans for an assignment of even greater interest.

In response to the deepening Depression, *Fortune* had been running a series of human-interest articles on the ways in which the blighted economy was affecting individuals in the working class, a series the editors dubbed "Life and Circumstances." Over the past several months, in terms they thought palatable to their generally conservative readership, *Fortune* had recounted the hard-luck stories of various blue-collar workers — an employee of the New York Telephone Company, a paint sprayman in the Plymouth Motor Plant in Detroit, hard-working family men who deserved their share of the company pie and hadn't been getting it. For the next story in the series, the managing editor, Eric Hodgins, wanted to find a typical white tenant farmer and his family somewhere in the South. The perfect writer for this assignment was Jim Agee. As the boy from Knoxville, Agee understood the mentality of southern country folk better than most of his colleagues. Furthermore, Hodgins figured, he was the least likely of any *Fortune* writer to balk at the idea of spending two of the hottest weeks of the year in the heart of cotton country.

When Agee heard about the assignment, he decided to postpone his resignation. Here was just the kind of story he had been wanting to write, a story about people, not commerce, not merchandise. He was familiar with the agricultural issues involved, having written two well-received articles on the Tennessee Valley Authority and another on the drought of 1934. Those assignments had been too large in scope, though, for him to get as close as he wanted to the people affected. He had already given a good deal of thought to the subject of tenant farmers, an exceptionally damaged group of people hidden from society, and had even considered pursuing it on his own. But traveling "in disguise" as a journalist would give him the excuse he needed to probe into the lives of people wary of intruders. His ambition was to make the people he wrote about not just real, but "full of vitality and the ardor of their own truth." He would treat them with a respect and dignity never before known to journalism, forcing his readers to face them as equals and thereby exposing the superficiality and condescension of so much Depression reportage. He would reveal the injustices of society, not necessarily those bound to his own time and country but those with a universal aspect.

Agee's one request was for Walker Evans to be sent with him to make the photographs. No other photographer, he believed, would be as sensitive to the delicacy of his new assignment. He wanted to move gently, almost invisibly, into the culture of southern poverty, to take away the clearest and truest possible reflection of the reality before him. He was well aware of how easily such an assignment might slip into exploitation and invention, political bias and calculation, and how the photographs, like those Bourke-White had made for his story on the drought, might come out as hackneyed Depression propaganda, all windblown fields and starving livestock and concerned looking farm folk. Evans was the only photographer he knew who understood that the camera could lie just as easily as it could reveal the truth.

While Evans' qualifications were obvious to Agee, he was not so confident of his employers' ability to recognize what to him was crucial to the undertaking. Then "one day," his friend and *Fortune* colleague Robert Fitzgerald recalled, "Jim appeared in my office unusually tall and quiet and swallowing with excitement." It appeared likely that his wish had been granted. "He was stunned, exalted, scared clean through, and felt like impregnating every woman on the fifty-second floor."

If the project did not inspire the same delirium of excitement in Evans that it did in his friend, it was certainly intriguing. Not since his trip to Cuba had he produced a documentary photo-essay, an in-depth description of a place and people. The prospect of traveling with Agee, one of the few people, he believed, who understood the real value of his photography, made it especially attractive. He could trust Agee not to skim lightly over the subject; he would be encouraged to take his time making the photographs. Furthermore, Evans no doubt suspected that with Agee he was likely to get closer to the lives of the people than he would have either the energy or the daring to do alone. The only snag was how to hold on to his job with the Resettlement Administration while taking on a job for a commercial magazine.

Fortunately, the subject of this assignment proved to be of even greater interest to the RA than it was to *Fortune*. Nothing was more pertinent to the improvement plans of the Department of Agriculture than the problems of cotton farmers in the South. One of the priorities of the Resettlement Administration was to rescue destitute tenant farmers from exploitative landowners and overworked soil. Lately, critics had complained that the RA was spending too much time on soil erosion and not enough on the human factor. The photographs that were bound to result from this expedition would be ideal publicity material and invaluable stock for the RA files.

At the end of June, Roy Stryker and Eleanor Traecey, *Fortune's* art director, struck a deal. Evans would take a leave without pay from the RA and be on loan to *Fortune*. The magazine would pay his fees and have first rights to publish his "sharecropper" photographs, but the publishing rights and the photographs, like all of the work Evans had done for the RA, would ultimately belong to the government. The two agreed that Evans should return, just as Agee was expected to do, by July 15.

By the time Stryker wrote his letter to Traecey, Evans and Agee were already on the road.

Midsummer was the ideal time to witness a cotton tenant family at work. By July the cotton plant has split open its multichambered pod and is ready for the picker to reach into its tough, prickly interior and pull out the fluffy white fiber. In the 1930s, cotton was still sown and harvested entirely by hand. No machine had yet been developed to take the place of the men, women, and children who made their meager living in the backbreaking business of cotton farming.

Part of what interested Agee in the tenant system was the way that it persisted while fostering such primitive conditions. Its issues were not bound to those of FDR's New Deal; little had changed since the 1860s. After the Civil War, plantation owners had replaced slave labor with tenancy, an alternative that served them almost as well. In return for the use of the landowner's fields, the tenant farmer owed the landowner one quarter to one half of his cotton crop. It was nearly impossible for him to make a profit from the remaining share, or to save enough money to buy his own land. By the time he saw any income, he already owed money to the landlord, at a high interest rate, for rations and supplies purchased over the year. Often the tenant farmer was not even allowed to use a portion of his small acreage to grow his own food.

The people of the region Agee and Evans now headed toward, known as southern Appalachia, including parts of Florida, South Carolina, Georgia, and Alabama, were predominantly of Scotch-Irish ancestry. The original economy of the region was based on subsistence homesteading, small independent farms buttressed by a wealth of forests. Now the timber was heavily cut, the soil was overworked, and many of the farmers were at the mercy of large landowners. The Depression only intensified the difficulty of these conditions. In 1936 the Resettlement Administration estimated that in no other region in the United States were more people economically "stranded" than in southern Appalachia.

Agee already knew that his interest in the subject was too great to be contained in the limits of a magazine article. His idea was to research his story in three sections, using three families, perhaps in different parts of the South. While he harbored doubts about his ability to do the subject justice by his own high standards, he was even less confident of *Fortune*'s ability to publish his work as he saw fit. As he wrote to his old schoolteacher Father James Flye, just before departing from New York, "Feel terrific personal responsibility toward story; considerable doubts of my ability to bring it off; considerable more of *Fortune*'s ultimate willingness to use it."

To Evans and Agee, notably warier of their calling than most journalists, it was not immediately obvious how they were to find a "typical" or "average" tenant family, especially since they intended to show that what the magazine thought was average was in fact as extraordinary as any family could be. In conversations with locals along the road, Agee got a feeling for the region and the character of its inhabitants, the local dialect, and the special problems of farmers, hoping that one of these conversations might lead him to the kind of family he and Evans were looking for. But the rural southerners they met regarded the two journalists from New York with suspicion. Approaching the outskirts of towns along their route, Agee began to dread "the pressure upon us, the following, the swerving, of the slow blue dangerous and secret small-town eyes." His hope that they would move invisibly into the culture of southern poverty was gradually dissolving. After more than three weeks on the road, with their allotted time nearly up, they were still traveling in search of their story.

By the middle of July, Evans and Agee had narrowed their search to south-central Alabama, a large part of which was known as the Black Belt for its exceptionally dark, rich soil. This was the heart of cotton country; it was also the region where white tenant farmers were to be found in the greatest numbers. On roads more often dirt than asphalt, Agee and Evans traveled over gently rolling hills, past fields of cotton and corn and grazing cattle, occasionally spotting a rambling derelict antebellum mansion.

Along the roads of Alabama, Evans often wanted to stop to photograph a building that caught his eye — a roadside store, a filling station, a one-room schoolhouse. One day, when they came upon a roadside church, wrote Agee, "the light so held it that it shocked us with its goodness straight through the body, so that at the same instant we said *Jesus*." They stopped the car, and after a few minutes of meditating on its stark, classical, handmade simplicity, Agee helped Evans set up his camera to make a picture. Having the highest respect for his friend's creative instincts, Agee indulged him and assisted him in arranging his heavy equipment just so. At the same time he began to despair of ever finding the lifeblood of his story. It was "hotter than hell," he wrote home to Via, "drought; not showers enough to wet a shirt through." In his frustration, he decided it was Evans' fault they weren't getting anywhere, and he began to doubt the wisdom of their decision to travel as a team. Even though he felt "all kinds of pleasure seeing Walker and traveling around with him," as he wrote to Via in early July, their progress, it seemed to him, was alarmingly slow. "I should . . . have had the sense and foresight to go alone," he confessed.

In Alabama, they sought the direction of a New Deal executive and landowner by the name of Harmon, who introduced them to several other landowners, but his efforts yielded no suitable candidates for their piece. Agee recalled one of Harmon's introductions with acute embarrassment. They had traveled a few miles "up a loose wide clay road to the northwest of town in the high glittering dusty sunday late morning heat of sunlight" to a stranger's plantation. Past the cotton fields, Harmon directed them to a group of shacks and prodded them forward into one, where a family gathering was in progress. The family and their friends were black, some of them, Agee wrote, "of that sootiest black which no light can make shine," and they were all dressed in their Sunday best. Harmon had apparently not realized that Agee and Evans were looking for a *white* tenant family. And though it seemed to Agee that their presence there was a terrible intrusion, the people stood before them "as if they had been under some sort of magnetic obligation to approach just this closely and to show themselves." Three men sang; at the close of their songs, Agee, struggling to relieve himself of his awkwardness and guilt, gave the leader fifty cents, "trying at the same time, through my eyes, to communicate much more," and left with Evans, feeling more than ever the impossibility of their mission.

A few days later Agee's editor contacted Harmon, inquiring anxiously after Agee's whereabouts, but Harmon had no answer. Toward the middle of July, Roy Stryker received a request from Evans for an extension of his leave from the RA. On July 15, the day he was due back in Washington, he was notified that he had been granted a furlough without pay for two months, until September 16. Agee was granted a similar reprieve from *Fortune*.

Now in Hale County, Alabama, a particularly poor and desolate part of the state, the travelers stopped to revise their plans in the county seat, Greensboro. In front of the courthouse, Evans struck up a conversation with a farmer who was there seeking government relief. Agee discovered them sitting together at the base of a Civil War monument outside the courthouse, the farmer talking and nervously laughing, explaining how he and his fellows from up near Moundville couldn't make a living off the soil because it was so overused it was infertile, but they were not eligible for government relief since technically they were employed tenant farmers. As Agee joined the conversation, Evans made some photographs with his angle-finder.

The man Evans had struck up a conversation with was Frank Tingle. He was accompanied by Bud Fields, his brother-in-law, and Floyd Burroughs, who was married to Fields' daughter. Seizing on the idea that these two northerners were government men and might be able to help, Tingle invited them back to meet his family. From the front seat of their car he directed them along the highway seventeen miles from Greensboro to where the road changed to dirt and finally onto a branch road marked by two posts, which led up a steep incline, past Tingle's blighted cornfield, onto a small plateau called Mill's Hill.

Tingle's house was a dilapidated single-story frame construction that had once belonged to a small farmer, since bought out by a larger one. A barn stood in the background, and in the distance Agee and Evans could see the crude pineboard shack where the Fields family lived. Tingle invited the two journalists to sit on the wide front porch, which was caving in here and there under the pressure of a rocking chair, and offered them, as Agee vividly remembered that day, a glass of water from the cistern and "small sweet peaches that had been heating on a piece of tin in the sun." Children emerged from behind bushes and "hid behind one another and flirted at us." Tingle called out to them and to his wife to say they had visitors, and asked them to fetch their neighbors, the Fieldses from next door and the Burroughses from over the hill, "children sent skinning barefooted and slaver-mouthed down the road and the path to corral the others."

Evans brought out his eight-by-ten view camera, and the Tingle family prepared itself for a group portrait. Frank laughed about how his face would break the camera while his wife combed her hair and nervously smoothed her sackcloth dress, full of holes and stains. With mounting excitement, Agee observed the family and "Walker setting up the terrible structure of the tripod crested by the black square heavy head, dangerous as that of a hunchback, of the camera; stooping beneath cloak and cloud of wicked cloth, and twisting buttons; a witchcraft preparing, colder than keenest ice, and incalculably cruel."

Believing that the photographer was testing his equipment and setting up his shot, the rest of the Tingle family — seven children with matching Anglo-Saxon features, ranging in age from four to twenty — groomed themselves in front of him. Catching them unaware, Evans made his first photographs with his small Leica. The older Tingle girls, barefoot and dressed in tattered and filthy cotton, combed and combed their hair, while little William Fields screamed with excitement and clutched his handmade doll. Agee tried to ease the tension of the moment and reassure them all with his smile and his quiet casual talk as he searched their faces for signs of trust.

Mrs. Tingle then posed for her portrait, embarrassed before the big camera, "in a one-piece dress made of sheeting, that spread straight from the hole where the head stood through to the knee without belting." Before Evans made his picture of Frank Tingle, he waited for his subject's nervous smile to wear off, to be overtaken by a questioning frown, his deeply lined face illuminated by the late afternoon sun. Mrs. Tingle then posed with her seven children, "as before a firing squad," remembered Agee, "the children standing like columns of an exquisite temple."

Meanwhile Floyd Burroughs had assembled his family. His house was out of sight, even more remote and primitive than the other two, down a rutted lane that was often impassable by car or truck. But Burroughs' wife, who did not appear, had washed and dressed the children in clean clothes for the occasion, and Burroughs was looking for a good place to have their picture made, as far as possible, Agee and Evans noticed, from the mess and depravity of the Tingles' front porch. The family organized itself in front of a tall bush, where Evans photographed them in the anonymous style "of family snapshots made on summer sunday afternoons thirty to forty years ago, when the simple eyes of family-amateurs still echoed the daguerreotype studios."

When they finally left, Agee noted with chagrin that he and Evans had kept the families an hour late from their supper.

Agee and Evans were not sure whether this was the first or the last of their visits to Mill's Hill. But of one thing they were certain: having spent the afternoon there, they were closer to capturing their subject than they had ever been. And having already intruded on the families' privacy, they felt drawn back, as much by guilt over their intrusiveness and a wish to make up for it as by the desire to see and know more. After a few days in the Greensboro area, they found it impossible to pass the branch road to Mill's Hill without turning onto it and driving up to that particularly secluded community of houses. And with each successive visit they felt more welcome. Agee talked, mostly to Bud Fields, who at fifty-nine was the oldest of the three farmers, while Evans took photographs around the Tingles' house and barns and eventually felt comfortable enough to enter the house to photograph its stark interior.

Although it was Evans who had made the initial contact with the Burroughses, the Tingles, and the Fieldses, in later years he insisted that Agee deserved all the credit for winning their hearts. Agee treated them with the utmost cordiality and took a sincere interest in the daily problems of their lives. He spoke to the children as if their thoughts and feelings mattered to him. They quickly realized that they didn't "have to act any different from what it comes natural to act," Mary Fields told Agee, whose accent, Evans noticed, had begun to veer toward country southern.

After several days of returning to the hill, observing, talking, making pictures, and taking notes, Agee and Evans retreated to Birmingham for a break, checking into the Hotel Tutwiler, the best in town. Their job was way overdue: "According to our employers' standards of speed," Agee wrote, "I should have been back at my typewriter and Walker at his tanks." But their work had just begun, and Evans was anxious to see how well his pictures were turning out before he went any further. The interiors of the farmers' houses were dark; he was not sure if he could get the detail he wanted using only available light, but he was just as concerned that using artificial light would give a harsh effect. During their break in Birmingham, he hoped to make one of the hotel bathrooms dark enough to develop some test negatives.

Agee and Evans, still open to finding new leads on their story, also planned to look up the architect Tom Hibbon, with whom Evans had traveled that winter, and "some Communists" Agee had met nearby.

Overall they looked forward to talking with people more like themselves and to relishing briefly the taste of city life and the "provincial
slickness" of hotel living after weeks in the hot and desolate countryside. But after one night at the hotel, feeling a great need to reflect
on his experience at Mill's Hill alone, Agee took off in the car by himself, leaving Evans ("almost equally glad on his account") alone with
his darkroom work.

Evans might have thought a few more day visits to Mill's Hill would
be enough to gather the material they needed, but Agee would not
be satisfied until he had actually moved in with the families, to become one of them as much as possible, in order to experience their
lives with greater immediacy. He had discussed the possibility with
Bud Fields, who was the oldest and, Agee thought, the wisest of the
three farmers, politely inquiring if he and Evans might pay one of
the families for their room and board. Fields suggested that they stay
with the Burroughses, where there was more room, and not with him,
partly, as he explained with a glint in his eye, out of his sense of
propriety for his much younger wife. "You understand, taint I don't
trust yuns, but I know, young feller git too nigh a womurn, may not
know hisself what he's lible to do next."

Agee had not yet seen the Burroughses' house, but he had found
that Floyd was especially helpful in talking about farming and local
issues. The Burroughses were half-croppers, which meant that they
gave half their crop to the landowner, and they were even poorer than
the Tingles and the Fieldses, who gave only one third. Their cabin
was typical of sharecropper dwellings, a split rectangular design made
of the cheapest unfinished lumber, with an open breezeway, or "dog
run," through its center. Only one window had a glass pane, and one
other had a screen. Otherwise the house provided no better shelter
from the wind, heat, insects, and rain than an old crate.

Gathering his resolve against guilt and shyness as he drove away
from Birmingham after that first night, Agee approached the Burroughs house for the first time. Floyd Burroughs welcomed him in
and invited him to spend the night. Agee's first instinct was to flee,
and he drove away in the darkness, but a violent thunderstorm
reversed his course. With his car mired in mud at least half a mile
from a decent road, he had to return to the Burroughses' for help.

Accepting their offer of a supper of burned eggs and a flea-ridden bed, Agee began his brief but extraordinary episode as a member of the Burroughs family, and it was not long before he persuaded Evans to join him there.

In Moundville, the nearest town, people began to talk. The Civil War was still vivid enough in the minds of the people of Hale County for them to wonder what a pair of Yankee journalists were doing snooping into the lives of the common folk. Landowners and police watched for clues that they were actually labor organizers in disguise. Agee dreaded walking down the main streets of Hale County's small towns, where "all the narrow, mean white faces . . . turned slowly after me watching me and wishing to God I would do something that would give them the excuse." Yet he would have been the first to agree that he and Evans were up to no good. "It seems to me curious, not to say obscene and thoroughly terrifying," he was later to write, ". . . to pry intimately into the lives of an undefended and appallingly damaged group of human beings . . . for the purpose of parading the nakedness, disadvantage and humiliation of these lives before another group of human beings, in the name of science, of 'honest journalism.'" But however terrifying it might have been, prying is exactly what they did.

On weekdays, the Burroughses would leave for the fields by the crack of dawn, when the temperature would already be climbing into the upper nineties, to spend the day gathering cotton, their backs bent, their sacks dragging along behind them. Back at the house, Agee explored bureau drawers, storage trunks, kitchen cupboards, and closets, making a thorough inventory of their contents. Meanwhile Evans analyzed and composed his surroundings through the ground glass of his view camera. They worked in silence, out of a faith in each other and a respect for the privacy of their separate creations. They resisted the idea that one medium might serve to illustrate the other, or that either might dominate. What would result, they were sure, would be morally and aesthetically equal and compatible, reflecting their shared belief that what lay before them was not a sociological set of statistics but the bare bones of a great work of art.

What is striking in Evans' photographs of the farmers' dwellings is not the poverty but the purity of these homes. In the images' unsparing realism and devotion to detail, they suggest that everything in the Burroughs house was sacred. Under the impartial gaze of the camera, the house, furnished with the bare necessities, is revealed to be beautiful, suggesting not so much that poverty should be abolished as that its victims should be respected exactly for what they were — old pioneer stock, whose connection to their ancestors was so undisturbed by modern times that they still spoke a kind of Elizabethan English — and that the culture of their backwoods existence — no waste, no disguise, not a trace of pretension — should be preserved.

The unconscious beauty Evans perceived in the Burroughs house was no doubt intensified by the presence of his impassioned friend, but he was better prepared to deal with it. Evans moved about the place decisively, setting up his camera with a total confidence in the unwitting perfection of what stood before him. Agee, meanwhile, was trying to deal with the enormity of the experience, to become a part of it while remaining outside of it, determined "to see or to convey even some single thing as nearly as possible as that thing is." As a writer, he would also have the advantage of later reflection. Evans' photographs would carry away the clear picture of that moment in time, but Agee would be working on his prose long after Evans had developed and printed his negatives, and he would rely on the pictures to renew his inspiration and assist his memory in his exhaustive verbal cataloguing of the house's every object and its arrangement.

In the dog run, Evans composed a view of the washstand: a wooden shelf with a bucket, a dipper, a basin, a bar of soap, and, hanging from a nail above, a towel made of an old flour sack. The photograph shows distinctly, as Agee would later write, that the basin is graniteware, that the bucket is dented, that the soap is a cheap white gelatinous face soap. Through his fine lens Evans could make the wooden siding of the house almost tangible; the texture was so intensified by the camera that it carried Agee's imagination into "wild fugues and floods of grain, which are of the free perfect innocence of nature, are sawn and stripped across into rigid ribbons and by rigid lines and boundaries, in the captive perfect innocence of science." The vortex of Evans' photograph is a rectangular vanity mirror, grimy and barely large enough for a face to study itself, hanging above the washstand. With punctilious accuracy, Agee noted that it was more often to be found on the Burroughses' bedroom mantel.

Evans' photographs of the bedrooms are equally detailed. On the surface of a double bed is what Agee described as "a thin constellation of perhaps a dozen black flies"; the ironwork is "dark and smooth and the pattern is plain"; above the bed, "suspended on two forked sticks nailed to the wall, is a light-gauged shotgun." On a mantel above a fireplace, Evans exposed the objects as Mrs. Burroughs had arranged them in what she told Agee was "her last effort to make this house pretty"; the photograph shows the arrangement to be not pretty but beautiful, in a way that Mrs. Burroughs would never see. Agee called this the altar, as if it contained all the symbols of the Burroughses' humanity, and he described it in unmitigated detail: "two small twin vases, very simply blown, of pebble-grained iridescent glass," and between them, "a fluted saucer, with a coarse lace edge, of pressed milky glass," and a fringe of white tissue paper across the mantel, which Mrs. Burroughs "folded many times on itself and scissored into pierced geometrics of lace." Above the mantel hung a calendar "depicting a pretty brunette with ornate red lips, in a wide-brimmed red hat, cuddling red flowers"; and to the right of the mantel, ten-year-old Lucille Burroughs, her hand covered in paint one day, had added her own decorative whimsy: "in whitewash, all its whorlings sharp, the print of a child's hand."

In Evans' eyes, the Burroughs children seemed as content as any children who are sure of their parents' love, and certainly more so than he was at their age. To watch the two-year-old Squeakie Burroughs by his mother's side, heading for the farm buildings to feed the chickens in the late afternoon, was to know that no amount of privilege could make up for the little boy's confidence in his place in his mother's world.

At night, after the family went to bed, while the crickets sang and in the distance foxes warbled, Evans and Agee talked, sharing their thoughts and their responses to what they had witnessed during the day. To sleep, they alternated with each other every night between the rear seat of a Chevrolet sedan and a thin piece of cotton quilting on the wooden floor of the dog run.

Evans survived this arrangement as long as he felt able, perhaps as much out of a sense of loyalty to Agee as out of a belief that living among the sharecroppers would improve his ability to describe them with his camera. After a few days, having done his best to feign tolerance of conditions that he could hardly bear to witness, much less live under, he moved into a room in a nearby hotel, where he could sleep through the night free of bugs and lice and where the food would not bring him to the brink of gagging with every bite. Meanwhile, Agee, whose intense desire to empathize with lives outside his own outweighed the physical revulsion that he too felt toward his surroundings, stayed on, writing late into the night by the light of an oil lamp, covering page upon page with his tiny, illegible script.

The three families on Mill's Hill, related by blood and by marriage, differed in many ways, and the observant northerners found the very concept of "average" in this context absurd. Agee and Evans devoted more of their attention to the Burroughses than to the other two families, partly because they lived with them, but also because they were closer to them in age; Floyd was thirty-four, and Allie Mae was twenty-seven. But perhaps most important, the Burroughses, as Agee observed, had an "earnest wish that everything shall be as pleasant and proper to live with as possible," while their relations, the Fieldses and the Tingles, were "disheveled and wearied out of any such hope or care." To the writer and photographer, the Burroughses had the greatest dignity, and thus the greatest potential for dignified portrayal.

Early on in their stay with the Burroughses, Floyd asked Evans to take a picture of his family in their Sunday best. Evans was glad to oblige, since it helped to win the family's favor and get them accustomed to facing the camera. In his portrait, he evoked the style of family photographs that Agee referred to when he spoke of "family snapshots made on summer sunday afternoons thirty or forty years ago." Since it was Floyd's picture, he let Floyd direct it, telling each member of his family where to sit or stand, crowding them neatly together as if to make sure they would all fit into Evans' view. In fact, Evans left a generous margin of wooden clapboard behind them, emphasizing their solidarity and innocence before the camera. The children are arranged in the foreground, standing or sitting on a bench, while Floyd, "master of the brood," dominates the rear, one arm over Allie Mae's shoulder, the other over her sister Mary's.

Agee perceived that Floyd Burroughs was attracted to Mary and admitted that he, too, was drawn to her. Mary was eighteen, a big girl whose build was "rather that of a young queen of a child's magic story" and whose eyes and demeanor were "resolute, bewildered, and sad." Mary, whom he called Emma in his text, after his own sister, was married to an older man up in the northern part of the state, and everyone dreaded the day when he would come back to fetch her. Agee fantasized a more pleasurable alternative for her, and for himself: "If only Emma could spend her last few days alive having a gigantic good time in bed, with George [Floyd], a kind of man she is best used to, and with Walker and with me, whom she is curious about and attracted to." At the same time, he suspected that should this orgy occur, the "inferior parts of each of our beings would rush in, and take revenge."

Evans would later cringe with embarrassment at Agee's words and at the idea, which had never, he insisted, crossed his mind. Though the Burroughs Sunday portrait might be seen to reveal the sexual tension between Floyd and his sister-in-law, it more obviously shows the Burroughses' extreme propriety, their God-fearing purity and righteousness. The children, neatly buttoned and combed, are doing their best to sit or stand still. Mary, with a modest frill across the bodice of her dress, swerves slightly outward at the hip away from Floyd. Allie Mae stands straight and tall in pure sunlight ("the long vertical of a Chartres statue"), in black buttoned shoes and with her hair combed and pulled severely back from her face.

Though Evans was shy about making people pose for their portraits and aware of how easily the process could slip into manipulation, in Alabama he was ready to forgo his doubts. With his view camera he made individual portraits of Bud Fields, Floyd, Allie Mae, and their daughter Lucille, and once he was absorbed in the process, his excitement rose and his shyness disappeared. The portraits show them to be people of character and distinction, whose "life and circumstances" seem irrelevant in relation to their presence as individuals. Their faces show not despair but expectation, not inbreeding but pure breeding. The photographs are in the same plain style as his portraits of friends, and as intimate as any he would ever make. As his subjects sat or stood before his camera, he waited for them to return his penetrating gaze — searching, intelligent, complex, a revelation of selfhood usually limited to the photography of loved ones, and even then achieved rarely.

The Burroughses wished to be photographed outdoors, away from the inescapable poverty of their home, but the Fieldses did not mind posing amid the filth and shabbiness of their wooden shack. In his portrait of that family in the parents' bedroom, Evans encouraged his subjects to arrange themselves until they felt comfortable. Mrs. Fields sits on the bed, cradling the sleeping Lilian between her spread knees, her bare ankles crossed and bent under the bed, her gaze without a trace of reserve ("[her] eyes go to bed with every man she sees," said Agee). Next to her stands her eight-year-old daughter by a former marriage, dazed, knock-kneed, one arm draped over the iron bedstead. Bud Fields holds the center of the picture, his lean body seated on a chair as steady as a tripod, his chest bare except for a kerchief draped around his neck to hide his skin cancer, while three-year-old William, naked except for a ragged shirt fastened by a single button, restlessly hangs from his knees. Mrs. Fields' mother sits beside them, fists clenched together, one eyebrow raised questioningly. She is the only one in shoes, though they are worn beyond repair. Finally, under the bed is a cat so thin that it looks like a splatter of black ink on the floor.

In the Fieldses' portraits, neither the photographer nor his subjects tried to conceal from the camera what they knew to be the signs of terrible human degradation — tattered and filthy clothing, tangled hair, soiled bedclothes, sore feet. The Fieldses looked frankly upon the man under the dark cloth, without shame or suspicion. By endowing the occasion with formality and allowing them to strike their own pose, Evans conveyed a stately proportion and pride of family worthy of the Old Masters of royal portrait painting.

The kind of respect Evans showed his tenant farmer subjects was not only unusual for a photographer of his generation, it was beyond the imagination of any other. At the time, to dramatize the conditions of the poor was the only conceivable approach to powerful (not to mention responsible) photojournalism. The difference between Evans and his contemporaries becomes clear when his work is compared to that of Margaret Bourke-White, whose tenant farmer pictures proved to be, in commercial terms, far more successful than Evans'.

Less than a month before Evans and Agee started out, Bourke-White and the writer Erskine Caldwell had headed south to take pictures and prepare the text for a book on rural poverty during the Depression. Caldwell, a southerner himself, had made southern poverty the subject of many of his recent articles in the *New York Post* as well as in his popular novels *Tobacco Road* and *God's Little Acre.* He was interested in collaborating with a photographer who could prove that what he described was not exaggerated, who could bring people face to face with the shocking reality of the poverty he had witnessed. For this, Margaret Bourke-White was his perfect match, even though, with the exception of her 1931 book, *Eye on Russia,* most of her work to that point had been advertising photography. As she once said about photographing soup, "It must out-soup any you ever dreamed of, with fragrant fumes rising straight from the film gelatin." For her, the goal was the same with sharecroppers. She was after the most extreme signs of poverty and degradation she could find.

Through Arkansas, Tennessee, Mississippi, Alabama, Georgia, and South Carolina, Bourke-White and Caldwell traveled in search of their subject. Like Evans and Agee, they were regarded with suspicion by the people they met. But Caldwell's southern accent and knowledge of the territory helped, and they made up stories about periodicals or agencies they were working for, on whatever assignment they thought would make them appear most trustworthy. Bourke-White relied on Caldwell to guide her to the people she wanted to photograph, but once there she went to work "like a motion picture director," remembered Caldwell, telling people where to sit, where to stand, and waiting for a look of worry or despair to cross their faces. Under her direction, passive, weatherbeaten, and cross-eyed sharecroppers were turned into characters in a play, playing themselves. With a battery of flash equipment attached to her $3\frac{1}{4}$-by-$4\frac{1}{4}$ Linhof camera, she achieved the eye-popping sculptural effect of stage lighting.

The more the subject appeared to be off-limits, the more Bourke-

White hungered for it. She and Caldwell had no trouble getting into a Negro church. "Visitors were always welcome," she recounted later, "even a visitor who came loaded with cameras." The rural churches of the white folk were not so welcoming, but this was hardly a deterrent. In South Carolina, "we made our great find on a Sunday morning," Bourke-White wrote in her memoirs. "Everyone was already in church. I tucked a small camera into my jacket, and Erskine filled his pockets with flashbulbs. Finding the church door locked from the inside, we leaped through the open window and started taking pictures at once, Erskine changing flashbulbs as though he had been assisting a photographer all his life." Reflecting on her experience of "that bleak and splintery church on its plot of stony ground," she concluded, "It is obvious this shoddy little ceremonial, re-enacted each week in the name of religion, was the very antithesis of religion . . . It illuminates the spiritual poverty of people who have no other emotional release."

Where Bourke-White barged in, Evans hung back. The religious fervor of Southern Baptist or Methodist services was of no interest to him as subject matter for his camera, and not only because the emotional heat of an excited crowd had always frightened him. He knew how easily the scene could be misinterpreted or reduced to a primitive curiosity that amused the northerner. Nothing could be a clearer statement of his wish to keep his distance than the many photographs he made of the undecorated exteriors of rural southern churches, their sacred rites protected from nosy intruders behind firmly shut doors. His attitude toward manipulating the scene for the sake of his photograph was the same. Bourke-White recalled rearranging the little handmade things she found on a woman's makeshift dressing table and later being scolded by Caldwell for doing so. Evans' strict policy was "I never touch a thing!"

Bourke-White was not the only photographer who developed directorial techniques to dramatize the Depression. Arthur Rothstein manipulated his subjects to achieve desired facial expressions. For example, he photographed a ragged, pregnant sharecropper talking with a neighbor, but by leaving the neighbor out of the picture, he implied that her worried frown was the result of private thoughts about her terrible circumstances.

While Evans disdained this kind of photojournalism, he was perfectly able to respond to the requirements of a magazine story, and in the case of the tenant farmers, much more so than his companion. Going about his work with self-directed practicality, he made a sequence of pictures, following the process of cotton farming from the gathering in the field to the loading of the mule wagon, then riding into town with Frank Tingle to the local cotton gin. On other days he branched out and took the car to Greensboro or Sprott or Moundville or wandered along the country roads to photograph subjects less intimate and less demanding than the three families. He photographed roadside stores, filling stations, and restaurants decorated with signs for Coca-Cola and Camel cigarettes. He was arrested by ragged posters for minstrel shows and Barnum and Bailey's circus, and by the light on the silvery surface of a corrugated tin façade of a contractor's shop.

As far as Evans was concerned, he and Agee could have returned to New York sooner than they did. The sharecropper story was a great story, but it wasn't his story, and he did not feel the compulsion to live it that Agee did. He might even have wondered sometimes if Agee wasn't getting too absorbed in the families' lives, if he wasn't too eager to shed his sophistication and become, like them, a primitive. For their part, the Burroughses had come not only to accept but to enjoy and even depend on the journalists' presence. When it was time for Mary to leave her sister to go north with her husband in mid-August, she shyly approached Agee, who was sitting on the porch, to say, "I want you and Mr. Walker to know how much we all like you, because you make us feel easy with you; we don't have to act any different from what it comes natural to act, and we don't have to worry what you're thinking about us, it's just like you was our own people and had always lived here."

When they finally made their departure at the end of August, Agee and Evans felt as much guilt as they had setting out. But now their guilt was real rather than simply anticipated. They knew that what they had done would not really change the families' lives for the better, and they knew that the families were under the innocent impression that it would. They promised to send money, clothes, toys for the children, and they promised that they would return. What they carried away was much more than the material for a magazine article, and the love they had invested and the love they had inspired was too great to dispense with in a timely piece of journalism. A few months later, back in New York in midwinter, Walker received a letter from Flora Bee Tingle, who wrote, "I Sure was heart broken to see you leaving down hear i was all ready heart broken but you Broken My Heart worser."

6 *American Photographs*

BY THE FALL OF 1936, the Resettlement Administration had the largest staff of any government agency in Washington, in offices spread out among twenty-seven different buildings. But this was not necessarily a sign of its success. "Tugwell Has Staff of 12,089 to Create 5,012 Relief Jobs," read an ironic headline in the *New York Times* in November. The liberal press complained that in his grand plan to make better economic use of the land, Tugwell had lost sight of "the human element." The conservative press, in that election year, made Rexford Tugwell "Roosevelt's clay pigeon," the target of what it called New Deal overspending. Everything about Tugwell seemed to point to his extravagant tendencies. Ernestine Evans made no secret of the fact that one day she had happened to peer into his closet and discovered a small army of brand-new shoes.

As Roy Stryker's staff grew in number and his photographic material multiplied, Congress increasingly pressured him to prove the worth of the historical section. Skeptics about the Resettlement Administration questioned the value of a rapidly growing photographic archive, from which only a handful of photographs had ever been used, the same ones over and over. The photographers themselves were discouraged by this trend. Dorothea Lange disparagingly labeled those often-used photographs "cookie-cutters." Her famous portrait of a pensive migrant mother framed by her three huddling children was a perpetual favorite of the press, while others just as good were never printed. At the same time, there were significant gaps in the material, especially in the area of farming. Unfortunately for Stryker, Carl Mydans, who had been the most dedicated photographer of agricultural subjects on the RA team, left in the summer of 1936 to join the staff of *Life* magazine, which was to publish its first issue in November of that year.

The reputation of the historical section had not been improved by a recent incident involving a photograph by Arthur Rothstein. Overtly symbolic of the terrible condition of midwestern farmland, the photograph depicted a cow skull on a dry alkali flat somewhere near Fargo, North Dakota. It appeared just in time for Tugwell's public relations tour of the Midwest. But when the press discovered that Rothstein had moved the skull from the grassy hillock where he found it to the parched flat, the image immediately lost its validity. Furthermore, observant viewers noticed that the skull was well bleached by the sun and had obviously been around for years. This was hardly the documentary approach to photography that the Resettlement Administration had declared was its mission. While conservative congressmen and the press used the incident to poke fun at Stryker's "historical" collection, Rothstein, still hoarding the skull in the trunk of his car, explained that he had only been testing exposures and had not expected the picture to be used. It was too late; the photograph had taken on a life of its own. It had evolved from positive propaganda to political cartoon, symbolizing everything that was not right about the RA. In Erie, Pennsylvania, the *Dispatch Herald* put it bluntly: "The revelation that Dr. Rexford Tugwell's 'Resettlement Administration' . . . has been guilty of flagrantly faked 'drought' pictures . . . is a highly instructive, but not especially surprising development. The whole resettlement program is a ghastly fake, based on fake ideas." By the time Walker Evans arrived back in Washington, Stryker was exceedingly eager to see the photographs he had made in Alabama. There was nothing Stryker needed more than fresh, untampered material on a vital New Deal topic.

But Evans was even more reluctant to cast his photographs into the indiscriminate files of Stryker's picture collection than he had been before he left. He was shocked to hear about the Rothstein episode. He also noticed that the historical section's staff was growing, as was Stryker's ambition to photograph virtually all of America. New members of the RA staff such as Edwin Locke, John Vachon, Theodore Jung, and Russell Lee were quickly learning how to photograph the kind of American scene that Stryker was looking for. Stryker gave his less willful photographers as much direction as they could take, including what he called "shooting scripts," guiding them to make the most of the ordinary. "Bill posters; sign painters — crowd watching a window sign being painted, . . . parade watching, ticker tape; roller skating; spooners — neckers; mowing the front lawn" went a typical Stryker script, "the kinds of things that a scholar a hundred years from now is going to wonder about." His notions about what was key to the period had been guided by Evans' photography, but Evans had no interest in joining the informal discussions about them in the office. He liked John Vachon, who had been a graduate student in Elizabethan poetry when he joined the RA staff as a messenger, but on the whole he remained aloof. In fact, he was hardly ever there.

Fortunately for Evans, his Alabama photographs were on reserve for *Fortune* and had to be kept apart until they had been used as commissioned. Thus he was temporarily excused from any responsibilities other than lavishing attention on the printing and arrangement of his newest work, most of which he did back in New York on Bethune Street.

In two looseleaf albums, Evans arranged his Alabama photographs in four chapters, one for each of the three tenant families and an appendix of photographs of the surrounding towns and countryside. It was not the first time that he had arranged his work in sequence, but the Alabama albums show his growing sense of photography's potential for narrative, not unlike a film. Evans' interest in the problems of cinematic structure was no doubt enhanced during his many hours in the company of Agee, an avid film enthusiast, and by his own conviction that no single photograph should be pushed into performing as the exemplary image, as some hackneyed Depression icon. The Rothstein incident was a perfect example of how wrong such an idea could go. The Alabama albums Evans was now laying out would make it clear that each picture was but a part of the whole, and that in their cumulative effect the viewer would come closest to feeling the reality of the subjects' circumstances.

In his first section, on the Burroughses, Evans approached his subject from a distance, as if slowly tracking in with a movie camera, beginning with the buildings — the tool shed, the chicken house, and the main house from the rear. Moving in slowly, the photographs reveal figures on the porch. Then the details — the washstand, the view through the porch door into the kitchen, the bed, the fireplace. Finally Evans introduced his characters, one by one: Floyd with a quizzical frown, Allie Mae gazing squarely into the camera, Lucille in a straw hat, Floyd Jr., Charles, and Squeakie, the baby, napping under an empty flour sack. The chapter ends with a still life of Floyd's field-weary shoes.

Evans gave similar treatment to the Fieldses and the Tingles. In the final chapter he presented a number of photographs of rural towns in southern Appalachia, the outer limits of the families' provincial world. Throughout the albums he interspersed two kinds of photographic prints, using a semigloss paper for his eight-by-ten negatives, so as not to diffuse the hard-won detail of his larger scenes and formal portraits, and a softer-grade, matte-finish paper for his 35mm negatives, mostly of the children. Showing an unmistakably cinematic sense of narrative, Evans' "sharecropper albums," as they came to be known around the RA office, were to be seen but not used.

Tugwell was not immune to the concept of film as a powerful arm of public relations. Earlier that year he had commissioned a documentary film on the Dust Bowl. The film critic Pare Lorenz, who had brought the idea to Tugwell, was hired as director, and he drew around him a solid team. As cameramen he brought in Leo Hurwitz, Ralph Steiner, and Paul Strand (Steiner and Strand had become as practiced at filmmaking as they were at still photography), and he commissioned the celebrated young composer Virgil Thomson to write the musical score. Taking its title from a Sioux Indian saying, *The Plow That Broke the Plains* tells the story of the deterioration of the Great Plains. Moving from images of virgin grassland to hasty homesteaders and their farm machinery to dusty, sun-baked desert, the filmmakers reenacted the decline of the land to the mournful strains of Thomson's music. The twenty-five-minute film won widespread critical approval as an epic documentary. It was certainly as staged and manipulated as Rothstein's skull photo, but the elegance of the camerawork and the powerful narrative theme apparently overwhelmed any problems the audience had with its authenticity.

Given the success of *The Plow*, Tugwell felt that more films would help to spread the message of his good works and intentions. That fall he commissioned a film on a suburban housing project the RA was in the process of building in Berwyn Heights, Maryland, a few miles outside Washington. Ben Shahn and Walker Evans offered to make the film together, as long as they were able to maintain complete control over its direction. For Evans it was an opportunity to continue his work in film, even if the subject matter was of little interest to him. "It's not perfect, of course, and won't be, even with all our dreams inviolate," Evans wrote to Jay Leyda, now back from Russia with a job as a curator in the Museum of Modern Art's film department and camping at 22 Bethune Street.

By the fall of 1936, Ben Shahn had left his wife, Tillie, and their two children, Judy and Ezra, to live with Bernarda Bryson. Both Shahn and Bryson were on the payroll of Special Skills, Bryson as a graphic artist, Shahn as a printmaker, photographer, and now filmmaker. Bryson remembered that Shahn and Evans were excited about making their film at first, rising early to shoot the site in the misty hours of the morning. But the two artists differed on certain ideas, now forgotten, as early on as the opening scene, and they quarreled. With the film still fragmentary, they screened it for Tugwell, who gave them "a properly negative response," Evans reported to Leyda. Having already concluded that Tugwell knew nothing about art, Evans managed to press him into a radical revision of the script, "leaving out all that crap about Washington," he told Leyda, "and that special precious little housing project out in Maryland. So we have quietly gotten together a sort of prospectus . . . of a film about *people*, people and unemployment, people and slums, using an employment office interviewer and questionnaire blank as a device to jump off into various backgrounds, into unemployment, housing, child labor, farm tenant problems, any damn social situation you want."

As Evans struggled with his film project in Washington, Agee confronted a major upheaval on the staff of *Fortune*. Dwight Macdonald had quit the magazine over a series of articles he had written on the United States Steel Corporation. Having spent the winter before on a leave of absence reading Trotsky and Marx, Macdonald was more than usually primed to detect and broadcast capitalist greed. As his U.S. Steel series evolved with greater daring, Henry Luce became increasingly nervous, and he eventually called on Ralph Ingersoll to step in and write the steel chairman's profile and "substitute for my sparkling gem," Macdonald reflected later, "a leaden, ill-written, and nervously adulatory portrait." Macdonald resigned after that final insult to his efforts. At the same time, his roommate from Yale, Wilder Hobson, a *Fortune* writer better known for playing the slide trombone, left the magazine in the midst of a serious case of writer's block. Meanwhile, Luce had replaced managing editor Hodgins with Russell Davenport, who discontinued the series "Life and Circumstances." Thus abandoned by the editor who had assigned him to the sharecropper piece, and by two treasured colleagues, Agee had even greater reason to doubt, as he had from the start, *Fortune*'s willingness to publish the article he wanted to write. He felt stultified, and wrote to Father Flye that he was sure the article was "impossible in any form and length *Fortune* can use." To Evans he wrote, "This little number, now typed up, runs to a few over eighty pages. So now I tunnel beneath the cellar with dynamite. God damn."

Dwight Macdonald recognized trouble signs when he first read the article. It was neither conservative nor liberal enough for *Fortune;* it had no clear political point of view. It was, in Macdonald's opinion, "pessimistic, unconstructive, impractical, indignant, lyrical, and always personal." Robert Fitzgerald also saw that it was too long, too personal, and too violent. But Evans perceived a motive behind Agee's presentation: he knew that his incorrigibly self-destructive friend "half consciously made the article so it would not be acceptable." As predicted, Russell Davenport, the new managing editor, rejected Agee's first draft.

As Agee toiled over subsequent drafts in December, he conceived of greater plans for his subject. The material, he believed, ultimately deserved book-length treatment. He and Evans might have to return to Alabama to delve more deeply into their subject. They also might want to make a film. With the encouragement of Jay Leyda, he wrote to Evans in Washington, "J. Leyda has seen or written you of possibility of short you and I might make for Nykino (what a name). I keep thinking a swell 20 minutes could be done out of tenant families, detail and country in the dead of winter." He also wondered if Evans would like to join him and Via in sending Christmas presents to the Burroughses, Fieldses, and Tingles. "I will in any case be shopping Woolworth's today."

Agee was not the only one toying with the idea of making a tenant farmer film. Not long after expressing interest in making a film with Evans, he met the German film director Fritz Lang and wrote to Evans that Lang wanted to make "a tenant movie (or more likely a tenant background for Silvia Sidney)." He also reported that Lang was "extremely wowed" by Evans' photographs. In Agee's opinion, Lang was "a smart guy and a likeable one" and had "about 4 times as good an eye for 'american' stuff as most of the indigenes give any sign of." Meanwhile, Evans had managed to interest Tugwell enough to agree to discuss the prospect of another film for the RA.

By January, it had occurred to Roy Stryker that not since the previous spring had Evans contributed anything usable to the historical collection. The sharecropper photographs remained on reserve in their two albums, and his film efforts had amounted to nothing more than rough footage and unworkable ideas. There had been quite enough dallying in Washington, as far as Stryker was concerned. It was time to send Evans on the road again, this time on a specific assignment. Just to make sure he did not stray from his duties, Stryker sent Edwin Locke, who had already played the answer man in the Rothstein fiasco, as his travel companion. Their assignment was to go to Arkansas and Tennessee and cover the disaster areas affected by the great floods of the Mississippi that winter.

Evans and Locke left Washington in Locke's car on January 30, 1937; by February 2 they had reached Memphis, not far from where hundreds of flood refugees were camped in Forrest City, Arkansas. The roads were impassable between Memphis and Forrest City, but they could approach the area by train. Like a tightrope, the tracks bore the photographers through a surreal landscape of flooded farms, houses, and cars. In the camps of Forrest City, the refugees were mostly tenant farmers, the majority black. Locke described to Stryker how he and Evans made pictures in a Negro shelter in an old cotton warehouse, where the victims lay dazed or ill with pneumonia and influenza, hopelessly attempting to guard their privacy. Outside the shelter Evans and Locke photographed the food lines — men, women, and children in ragged winter coats pressed together, clutching their tin plates and buckets. On February 4 Locke reported to Stryker from the "Locke-Evans HDQS.," in the Hotel Chisca in Memphis. "So far all goes well," he said. "I had a job annoying Walker out of his lassitude, but," he added reassuringly, "today in Forrest City, Arkansas, he worked as I am sure he never has before."

To Evans the flood "was damned interesting, highwater refugees and all that," but the lines of destitute figures waiting for plates of soup were less compelling to him than the three families in Alabama, and passing through on a quick assignment didn't compare with the feeling of standing alone and staring for as long as he wished at the interior of a tenant farmer's cabin. And without Agee there to remind him of how delicate the assignment was, and how worthy of his undivided attention, it seemed less so. With Locke he made two visits to Forrest City and did another shoot farther along, in Marianna, Arkansas. All day they toured the camps in Marianna with cameras and flashbulbs. The work was exhausting; lighting conditions inside the shelters were difficult. By the time they returned to flooded Memphis, Evans had become ill. "I am in a hell of a dilemma," Locke wrote to Stryker from their hotel. "Walker is down with the flu and has a good dose of it." Locke was eager to get on with his work, but Evans could not stand to be left alone in his sickbed. Locke suggested to Stryker that he and Evans might split up as soon as Evans' health improved, "me to go to Reedsville and Tygart Valley and Evans to continue here." Locke admitted, though, "He probably won't like that."

For ten days Evans and Locke were holed up in the hotel, Evans unwilling to move and Locke unable to leave him. Their boredom was briefly alleviated by the arrival of Pare Lorenz and Willard Van Dyke, at work on *The River*, a documentary film about the flood. On February 17 Evans wrote to Leyda that he and Locke would be starting back slowly toward Washington, "working along the flooded river towns, taking about ten days." He was not sure what awaited him in Washington, but he suspected there was trouble in the air. "Affairs very dubious in Washington, I don't know what I'll be doing in March," he confessed, reiterating his keen interest in making a film with Leyda and Agee.

Evans was right in sensing trouble in Washington. Tugwell had resigned. Dorothea Lange, one of Stryker's more independent employees, had been moved to a freelance position. Stryker's budget had been cut again, and money-minded bureaucrats such as Max Wasserman, director of finance, wanted to know exactly which employees really earned their pay. For photographers, this meant only one thing — they would be judged on the quantity rather than the quality of their production. Evans was the only photographer on the staff using a view camera, which limited him to considerably fewer pictures per day than the other staff photographers, with their Leicas and press cameras. But Wasserman was not likely to understand this subtlety.

Sensing Evans' precarious position, Locke left the attribution of his negatives of the flood ambiguous, in case Evans needed to boost his numbers. But it was too late. Faced with the question of which photographer on his team he could best live without, Stryker had one and only one choice: Walker Evans. Soon after arriving back from Memphis, Evans was invited in for what Stryker would have called "one of his little talks." On March 23, he was given official notice that his appointment with the Resettlement Administration had been terminated. "Reasons for action: Services no longer needed."

Evans could hardly have been surprised. He had knowingly tormented the hardworking Stryker for almost two years with his moody independence and his blatant disregard for the schedules, budget, and specific needs of the RA. He had decided quite consciously that his creative freedom was worth the risk of negligence. But there was no doubt that working for the RA was the best job he'd ever had, and it was a shock to learn that he no longer had it.

One issue was still unsettled between Stryker and Evans — the sharecropper albums. With the interests of the historical section in mind, as well as perhaps a personal sense of remorse, Stryker now joined in the effort to see that the photographs were properly published.

The bulk of Evans' photographic output now resided with the United States government. This unfortunate arrangement may have prompted Evans to attend to the organization of his own archive, which, thanks to his foresight, did include many near-duplicate negatives he had made on assignment for the RA and squirreled away for himself. His efforts to take stock of his work also coincided with his move in April 1937 from 22 Bethune Street to a new apartment at 441 East 92nd Street. Jay Leyda had reserved apartments for both of them on the second floor of this four-story building. Leyda took the front apartment with his new wife, Si-Lan Chen, the daughter of the Taiwanese ambassador to Moscow. Evans took the flat in the rear, which included a small rooftop accessible through the back window. There he could enjoy the kind of view he liked best, over the backs of houses and laundry lines and, to the right, the East River.

The calm and order Evans maintained in his bachelor apartment made a striking contrast to Jim and Via Agee's domestic chaos in Greenwich Village. To Via the contrast epitomized the difference between the two men and underlined Jim's need for Walker's control and discretion. As Jim's bond to Walker grew stronger, his closeness to Via was coming undone. Having sworn undying devotion to her only four years earlier, he was growing restless and dissatisfied with his marriage and had fallen in love that spring with a violinist, Alma Mailman. They had met before; like Jim, Alma was one of the talented young people gathered by the Saunders family in Clinton, New York. Alma, who was from a middle-class Jewish family in Utica, had always felt the Saunderses' a mild social condescension toward her, but the fact that she was musical made up for her provincial manners and slightly garish way of dressing. By the time she and Jim met again in New York City, Jim found her to be not only "exceedingly pretty" but also refreshingly innocent compared with the older, more widely read, more conventional Via. Now, as he attempted to abandon his intellectual trappings and plunge into the depths of the primitive, Alma seemed closer to the source of his creative self.

In the midst of their disintegrating marriage, Jim invited Via to accompany him on his next assignment for *Fortune,* one that was sure
to underline the pitfalls of their feigned happiness. The assignment
was a typical *Fortune* filler — a travel piece on a cruise to Havana,
to add an entertaining note to a special issue on U.S. shipping. The
cruise was aboard the turboelectric liner *Oriente,* of the New York
and Cuba Mail Steamship Company, carrying freight, mail, and 132
passengers, most of whom were on a pleasure trip. Agee, who used
the assignment as an opportunity for his most acerbic prose, persuaded the editors to send Evans along as photographer.

Reflecting on their role as journalists, Agee had begun to think of
himself and Evans as a pair of spies. Their experience in Alabama
had made them feel most acutely the subversive nature of their craft;
from now on they would operate as undercover agents in the field of
journalism. In May 1938 Agee articulated this notion in the form of
a poem. In the draft he sent to Evans, he suggested that he and Evans
were the metaphoric "younger sons" of the world. Like Edgar in *King
Lear,* they were "spies, moving delicately among the enemy," with a
special ability to outwit the strength of their elders with a blend of
craft, magic, and art. In various forms of disguise, they would signal
to each other across the enemy landscape, baffling "the eluded sentinel."

The idea of the spy helped to make the Havana cruise more bear-
able. On board the *Oriente,* in a mood of playful but pointed irony,
Jim, Walker, and Via agreed to conceal their personal relationships
to one another from the other passengers. By posing as strangers
rather than as the friends, partners, and allies that they were, they
hoped to convey an air of critical indifference. As an ultimate act of
disguise, Via removed her wedding ring.

By day they dispersed themselves among their fellow passengers,
most of them "representatives of the lower to middle brackets of the
American urban middle class," Jim and Via taking notes, Walker
taking pictures. Capturing the passengers mid-stride at shuffleboard
or beaming in party hats, Walker made photographs that betray the
awkwardness and discomfort of their effort to enjoy themselves. He
observed the predominant group of passengers on board, the low-
salaried office girls reclining in deck chairs and looking for romance,
if not lifelong partnerships. His photographs revealed their frank dis-

appointment; Jim's prose left them thoroughly exposed, "skull-eyed in goggles; their cruel vermillion nails caught at the sunlight." The blond and well-built young men they lay in wait for, appearing in "naughty trunks" and furiously engaged in a game of deck tennis, reminded Jim of Airedales. Spinsters and retired married couples made up a smaller segment of the passenger list, and finally there were a number of Cubans, on board for the simple purpose of getting home. At dinnertime the three spies convened in the dining room and felt the quizzical gaze of the others upon them as they dined on "turgid, summer-hotel type food" and anticipated an evening of bad entertainment.

In Havana, Evans had less than twenty-four hours to renew his acquaintance with his old haunts and share them with the Agees. Bound to their assignment, they toured the city with the ship's passengers "in a noisy flotilla of open cars," racing from site to site too hurriedly to taste the variety and ambiance of that exotic place. As passengers off the *Oriente,* they felt like embarrassed intruders.

As the ship departed and Havana shrank from view, Agee observed how the passengers seemed to sink slowly into a depression, aware that their vacation was half over. But, he wrote, despite their lack of inner resources and dependence on the program of fun and games, they seemed to be sure that they were having as good a time as the brochure had promised them they would. He heaped his cynical wit upon his unknowing victims, identifying their strongest common trait as "their talent for self-deceit," but he might meanwhile have pondered his own ability to live a lie in his relationship with his wife. Meanwhile, Walker and Via had begun to form their own private alliance. As the three travelers approached New York after six long days at sea, they all faced an ambiguous future.

Walker, Jim, and Via had other outlets during the summer of 1937 through which they could try to channel their uncertainties. Wilder Hobson and his wife, Peggy, had rented a large house on the beach at Old Field Point, on the north shore of Long Island. Wilder's father had died suddenly that spring, and his marriage was on shaky ground. He desired nothing more than the distraction of friends. Walker and the Agees were among the Hobsons' regular guests, joining in the highly unprogrammed fun of nude bathing, beachcombing, and all-night talking and drinking, with Wilder's mournful trombone improvisations underscoring their formless days and nights. Walker took photographs of Jim on the beach. In one, Jim has a towel draped around his bare shoulders, his chin needs a shave, and he looks at the camera with sleepless, trusting eyes, like a subdued prizefighter before his trainer.

From the Hobsons', Walker and Via took off for day trips to explore the small towns of Long Island. Via was heartbroken over her decaying marriage, but she also felt herself dangerously close to falling in love with Walker as their friendship turned into an affair. She found him an unusually attractive man, but she cautioned herself against getting too deeply involved. For Walker, the affair was not threatening. Knowing that Jim was in love with another woman, he felt absolved of guilt. And being quite sure that Via was still in love with Jim, he felt little threat to his independence. "With Walker you knew you were never the only one," Via later recalled. "He was discreet about it, but I knew there were others."

By the time Via and Walker began their affair, Walker was also involved with Frances Strunsky Collins, a striking brunette with a Roman nose and eyes like daggers; her admirers said that she resembled Queen Nefertiti. Married to Pete Collins, an obscure novelist, Frances was the head of publications at the Museum of Modern Art and a great friend from Vassar days of Marga Barr's and Dorothy Miller's. It was Miller's impression that Frances and Walker were very much in love. But while Walker was fostering his various affairs in New York, he was thinking about Jane in New Orleans. They hadn't corresponded since the day he left New Orleans in January 1936, but in the midst of his current romantic involvements, he continued to allude to his "best girl," who was nowhere in sight.

A year had passed since Agee and Evans had returned from Alabama. *Fortune* had rejected three drafts of Agee's article and finally given him permission to do what he wished with it. He now began work on a full-length book, still determined to combine Evans' photographs with his writing. Hoping for unconditional support for their

creative efforts, Agee and Evans both applied for Guggenheim fellowships in the fall of 1937. In his application, Evans stated that he wished
to continue his work on the tenant farmers, which meant returning
to Alabama to make more pictures. He expected to make a photo-
essay of between one hundred and two hundred images, which might
take the form of a narrative sequence, describing a day in the life of
one family. As written in his application, his intention was to "present
the most exhaustive possible visual catalog of the facts of this life."
The photographs would ultimately be published in book form with
Agee's text, not as literal illustrations but as a visual analogue.

Evans also stated his plans for a second project, to which he would
apply not only the vision and technique of the photographer but the
position of "the anthropologist, the sociologist, and the historian."
This was to be a photographic catalogue of contemporary American
society. Although he confessed that the outcome of his study was
somewhat unpredictable, he would be concentrating on the city —
faces, buildings, interiors, shopfronts. Like the Alabama project, it
would be an exhaustive visual document of the contemporary everyday.

To what extent Agee would be involved with the second part of
Evans' Guggenheim proposal was not made clear, but it is likely that
he was very much a part of its genesis. His own proposal to the
Guggenheim was an interminable ramble of half-formed ideas, including an analysis of faces and news pictures, experiments in caption
writing and recorded fragments of overheard conversations, "notes
for color photography," "conjectures on how to get 'art' back on a
plane of organic human necessity, parallel to religious art or the art
of primitive hunters," and a new kind of sex book — "as complete
as possible a record and analysis . . . from early childhood on." As
far as Agee was concerned, Evans was an essential partner in almost
everything he would now undertake, and vice versa. Together they
were a font of ideas, certain that between them they had what it
would take to inject quality and intelligence into the documentary
literature of the day. Both were loath to be pinned down as to exactly
what indescribable magic they possessed, as if limiting it to bald
statement might make it disappear.

Life magazine, then exactly one year old, appeared to be the perfect target for their creative takeover. In the fall of 1937, Archibald MacLeish encouraged Agee to propose himself as an editorial adviser to the magazine. Agee wrote to MacLeish that he was interested in the prospect but only if he could work in partnership with Walker Evans, on the theory that "two men strike many ideas out of each other which one alone would miss and which three or more would make chaos of." And in case *Life* should suggest another partner, Agee offered a daunting recommendation of Evans, who "has the best eye I know, and the force and ramifications of brain in and behind the eye that would inevitably go with it . . . the cleanest and strictest theory, meaning knowledge, of what the eye and a camera . . . can and can not do. Which means among other things: a great freezing and cleansing of all 'art' and 'dramatic' photography and of the plethoric and flabby ends of Leica photography." In conclusion, Agee said that Evans understood the power of the photograph as "historian, arrestor of matter and of meaning and as social- and psychoanalyst." As partners and editors, Agee suggested, they would produce a special category of piece, immune to and exempt from the usual pressures of a weekly newsmagazine. They might also engage the talents of other photographers. Agee had heard that Henri Cartier-Bresson had been talking to *Life* editor Ralph Delahaye Paine. Perhaps the three of them could collaborate on an occasional project. Without wishing to limit his concept with irksome details about what these articles would concern or how often they might appear, Agee explained simply that he and his partner would be in charge of every detail "from the ground up." All they needed was an office to share and $100 a week each.

Back in Washington, meanwhile, Roy Stryker was concerned that the sharecropper photographs, which had been dropped by *Fortune,* had now fallen into a murky bureaucratic muddle of rights and ownership. To make matters even more complicated, the Resettlement Administration had been renamed the Farm Security Administration (FSA) as part of the effort to wipe the slate clean after the resignation of Rexford Tugwell. At a loss for a clear mandate, Stryker developed a proprietary attitude toward the photographs.

As various publishers came through the offices of the Resettlement

Administration expressing interest in the pictures, Stryker joined the effort to see them published in the careful arrangement Evans had made of them. In November he wrote to Evans that a Miss Kitty Wickes from Scribner's had been in. "She happened to see the share-cropper books, and pleaded for one or two pictures, but I was adamant — no one is going to get them unless he is prepared to take them in their entirety, or at least to make a very definite offer, publishing them in a worthwhile way." Stryker then suggested that Evans might approach Scribner's to publish his and Agee's book.

Agee had meanwhile been in touch with C. A. Pierce, an editor at Harcourt, Brace and Company. But on the first of December he received the discouraging reply that competition for the book was too stiff: their nemesis, Margaret Bourke-White, and her collaborator, Erskine Caldwell, had beaten Evans and Agee to the finish with their documentary book on the South, *You Have Seen Their Faces.* "Viking have made such a handsome job of the Bourke-White and Caldwell opus that competition would be ruinous," Pierce wrote to Agee. He expressed his sympathies and his recognition that the bad timing had been the fault of *Fortune*'s editors, not of the authors, adding encouraging words of praise for both of them. "I have rarely seen such a fine bunch of pictures . . . And then your own job of reporting is one of the most concise, informative, and human of documents."

Stryker followed with the suggestion of another interested publisher, the University of North Carolina Press. By that time, Via Agee had introduced the idea to Edward Aswell, who had just married her college roommate and had recently been hired as an editor at Harper & Brothers. Aswell was not only impressed with the work; he was willing to act on it. In January 1938, the beginnings of a contract began to take form.

Negotiations with Harpers staggered along over several weeks that winter. Agee insisted that Evans be given equal status as coauthor and receive the same advance and royalties as himself. Evans argued that he did not deserve more than one quarter, although he had begun to fret that he had no money to do any further work on the photographs. He told Roy Stryker that he and Agee would try to get as much money as possible out of "those eighteenth-century gents" at

Harpers, and he wondered if he would be obligated to share it with the government.

At the end of February, Agee and Evans signed with Harpers for a book tentatively titled *Three Tenant Families*. They were disappointed with the small advance, Evans wrote to Stryker, but they had won most of their editorial points. Evans' photographs were to constitute a separate but equal portfolio to the text, he was to have complete control over the layout and sequence of the pictures, and he would even be allowed to oversee the engraving and reproduction in the printer's shop. "Extra work, but worth the trouble," he wrote, pleading with Stryker not to let the government bureaucracy make a mess of their plans.

To devote himself full-time to perfecting his book, Agee had recently moved out of New York to Frenchtown, New Jersey, a small town near the banks of the Delaware River, where Evans had found him a house to rent. After months of vacillation, with floods of desire for his new lover alternating with pangs of guilt, he had gathered his courage to leave Via once and for all. The dark-eyed Alma was to be his part-time companion in Frenchtown. She would listen attentively to passages from his writing, stimulate his sensuality, entertain his wildest instincts, and play the child to his older man.

Like Agee, Evans was attracted to younger women, whose admiration helped to fortify his ego. At about the same time that Agee retreated with Alma to Frenchtown, Evans welcomed a new female disciple into his life. Helen Levitt had grown up in a middle-class Jewish neighborhood in Brooklyn and as a teenager had developed an interest in photography. Her subject was the street, especially in poorer neighborhoods, where she could capture children playing freely among parked cars and fire hydrants. Levitt was in search of that rare breed of photographer who worked in her vein, whose method was documentary but whose concerns had more to do with art than reportage. She noticed that photographers who worked in the documentary manner were rarely taken seriously enough to be exhibited or published as artists. Henri Cartier-Bresson, whose work she had seen at the Julien Levy Gallery, was for some time her only true role model. Searching for other sources of inspiration, she came upon *The Crime of Cuba* and discovered that Walker Evans might be another. She looked him up in the phone book, and without hesitating, he invited her over.

Agee dropped in on Evans the day Levitt went to show him her portfolio, late in 1937 or early in 1938. Looking quickly over her photographs, Evans commented on a few and showed a special interest in her pictures of graffiti and public signs. Agee looked slowly, carefully; the photographs seemed to give him ideas. For Levitt, the visit was encouraging beyond all expectation. By her own account, she was just a kid from Brooklyn, and these two immensely attractive, sophisticated older men had taken her seriously as an artist.

Levitt met Evans when he was thirty-four years old, and for the first time he was reviewing his photographic work in its entirety. He had been photographing for ten years, and though he had achieved some respectable critical attention, he was not well known. Nothing had come of his proposal to *Life*. In March both he and Agee were turned down by the Guggenheim Foundation; Agee's proposal of no fewer than forty-seven possible projects could not have helped the judges to focus on the Alabama project. Outside his circle of friends and acquaintances, Evans believed, his work was undervalued, misunderstood, and in grave danger of being indiscriminately classified with the growing mass of American documentary photography. Having set the example for Stryker's team, he was pained to see the FSA continuing on without him, applying a broad interpretation of the aesthetic he had formulated. The recent publication of a volume called *Land of the Free* further dampened his spirits. The book was a portfolio of photographs culled from the FSA files, with a poem by Archibald MacLeish running through like a soundtrack on every other page. The documentary-style Depression book was already becoming a genre of the period, and Evans had not yet made his decisive contribution to it.

Fortunately for Evans, enough of his friends were well placed to rescue him from his mounting fears and disappointments. Tom Mabry demonstrated his loyalty once again in the spring of 1938 by arranging for the Museum of Modern Art to buy a group of Evans' photographs for its permanent collection. The museum was still lacking a department of photography, but Beaumont Newhall, who joined the staff in 1935 as the librarian, had organized an enormous history-of-photography exhibition the year before. This landmark exhibition, called simply "Photography: 1839–1937," filled the entire gallery space of the museum, and on the strength of it Newhall was soon charged with establishing a photography department. He was already acquainted with Evans through lunches at the Barrs', and on more than one occasion they had photographed around town together. But although Newhall was genial and studious, Evans subtly resisted his friendship, perhaps because although Newhall admired his photography, he didn't seem fully to appreciate its superior intellectual edge.

For some time the idea of an exhibition of Evans' photographs had circulated in the museum, with Kirstein as its strongest advocate. In 1938 MoMA was in the process of constructing a modern building on the site of the museum's second location, 11 West 53rd Street. During construction, the museum held its exhibitions in temporary galleries in the underground concourse of Rockefeller Center. Taking advantage of a gap in the exhibition program, Mabry hastily scheduled a Walker Evans retrospective as one of the opening events of the 1938 fall season.

As soon as the exhibition was on the schedule, Mabry began to organize publicity to establish Evans as the leading American photographer of his time. In a conversation with the critic Gilbert Seldes, he mapped out an aggressive publicity strategy, beginning with a discreet "whispering campaign," to carry the news of the museum's first one-man photography show by word of mouth. Then on to the literary journals, the Sunday papers (offering one exclusive photograph to the rotogravure sections of the *New York Times* and the *Herald-Tribune*), and the picture magazines, such as *Harper's Bazaar, Popular Photography,* and *Life* ("work for at least three pages," Mabry noted in his memorandum). But publicity in itself was not enough. It was essential that Mabry instruct the critics in the subtle difference between Evans' work and that of the growing numbers of documentarians and "candid" cameramen. He made it clear that the exhibition was equal in importance to all other artists' retrospectives the museum had undertaken, and the first to honor a photographer.

While Evans longed for the critical recognition Mabry was pressing for, he wanted to be sure that it was directed toward the photographs themselves and not toward himself or his career, providing fodder for a photo-world success story. He refused to pose for a publicity photograph, and he offered the barest autobiographical outline. Mabry felt compelled to explain to the press that it was Evans' "retiring temperament" that kept him from pursuing a more commercial line of photography and becoming, until now, better known. Furthermore, he said, "It is because his work is untouched by any personal ambition that it ranks among the first of our time."

With Evans' friend Frances Strunsky Collins in charge of museum publications, plans for a book accompanying the exhibition quickly fell into place. Collins and Mabry wanted Evans' book to reach the widest possible audience, and they aimed to give it a prominence equal to the exhibition itself. The book would be bound in plain black Bible cloth, printed in an edition of five thousand, and distributed to bookstores across the country. The photographs were to be reproduced in halftone engraving; Evans specified that they be printed one to a page, with a blank page opposite each, and undisturbed by captions, which would be listed at the end of each of the two sections of the book. Finally, here was a chance for Evans to realize an ambition he had been mulling over for years: a sequence of photographs that would, in its entirety, compose a critical portrait of America's historical present, at once resolutely unspectacular and shockingly real.

The responsibility for selecting the photographs would not be his alone. Lincoln Kirstein was to become his closest collaborator in the realization of his exhibition and book. Although Kirstein was by then devoting most of his promotional talents to bringing the Russian ballet to New York and creating an American ballet of comparable stature, he remained loyal to his convictions about the special value of Evans' photography. And in spite of other pressing projects, he took on the task of writing the book's critical essay. On April 29 Mabry wrote an urgent letter to Kirstein, who was on the road with the Russian choreographer George Balanchine and his troupe, the Ballet Caravan: "Don't forget that you said you would write an article on Walker Evans' photographs," an essay of anywhere from three thousand to eight thousand words, due at the end of May.

Kirstein began his essay by addressing the question likely to be the exhibition's biggest critical stumbling block: whether photography could really be an art. He was not impressed with most of what had been widely taken for "photographic art" in recent years. "The inventors of the process," he wrote, "were less pretentious for it than their modern heirs." He criticized the turn-of-the-century, soft-focus salon photography all too recently out of fashion, as well as the newer craze for the "candid camera," which was, in his opinion, "the greatest liar in the photographic family." Setting the stage for the singular achievement of Walker Evans, he then stated that "the real photographer's services are social, the facts of our homes and times, shown surgically, without the intrusion of the poet's or the painter's comment." In his measured opinion, not since Mathew Brady's photographic chronicle of the Civil War or Atget's Paris of the Belle Époch had there been photography of the distinction and importance of Evans'. Just as Atget was the photographic complement to Proust and Brady to Stephen Crane, Kirstein wrote, Evans was the complement to contemporary writers such as William Carlos Williams, John Dos Passos, and Ernest Hemingway — a generation of Americans who had turned their backs on Europe "to attack the subject matter of their own country in their own time."

It was no accident, Kirstein suggested, that since knowing Hart Crane in the midst of his work on *The Bridge,* Evans had gone on to collaborate with James Agee, "whose verse, springing at once from Catholic liturgy, moving pictures, music and spoken language, is our purest diction since Eliot," for "Evans' eye is the poet's eye. It finds corroboration in the poet's voice." In conclusion, Kirstein urged that the photographs "should receive the slight flattery of your closest attention."

Perhaps never before had a writer demanded such high respect for a photographer's work. Evans was as pleased as he could be. "I had heard from Via that you felt thoroughly well over Lincoln's introduction," wrote Agee from Frenchtown, "and needless to say, I wish also I might see it (the book I was thinking; the writing also) while it's being put together."

Kirstein was also involved in the selection of the photographs. Both he and Evans were determined to give the utmost attention to the sequence of images in the book. In this, their mutual interest in the art of film was central. Evans approached the task as a frustrated filmmaker and Kirstein as a connoisseur and friend of the Russian director Sergei Eisenstein and the American Harry Potamkin, both outspoken theorists of the subtle art of image sequencing. They believed in the power of the montage — the message that was not literal but that was given voice by the juxtaposition of images. Kirstein's strategy was to arrange the photographs in a rhythm of ironic contrasts, a strategy he perceived at the core of Evans' vision. "A clumsy 'For Sale' sign clamped to a delicate pillar, a junk pile before a splendid gate," he wrote, "are living citations of the Hegelian theory of opposites."

The essayist was more politically concerned than the photographer. Kirstein wanted the photographs to represent the most important social conflict in America since the Civil War; his political feelings were a personal synthesis of both Communist and right-wing southern agrarian theories, both philosophies representing a protest against American capitalism and its attendant sins of materialism. To Kirstein, Evans' photographs were the perfect vehicle for this sophisticated critique. Evans, though, was less concerned with what his photographs might symbolize than with what they actually were: pure record. Their sequence, he felt, should be guided by their formal aesthetic qualities. His overriding intention was for the book to retain an anonymous style, to avoid an obvious political point of view. "The physiognomy of a nation is laid on your table," Kirstein concluded. And that was enough.

As the pictures fell into place, the full range of Evans' consciously impartial document was indistinguishable from Kirstein's multicritical social agenda. At some point, they agreed to give the book the deceptively plain, sweeping title of *American Photographs*.

Helen Levitt, who was now sharing Walker's kitchen darkroom, volunteered to assist him in printing his exhibition photographs. Eventually, agreeing to split the rent in half, they found an apartment where Helen could live and they both could work on 93rd Street and Third Avenue. As Walker's voluntary assistant and darkroom-mate,

Helen witnessed the comings and goings of his closest collaborators during the busy summer of 1938 at both 92nd and 93rd street. Kirstein dropped in once when Helen was visiting at 92nd Street, expressed his approval of Meade "Lux" Lewis' jazz playing on the Victrola, engaged in a quick exchange with Walker, and was gone. When Frances Collins came over, she and Walker would retire to the next room, leaving Helen to look at a book. Frances was worldly and intellectual; she could punctuate her conversation with French and Italian expressions and discuss the relative merits of Shelley and Blake. In the midst of Walker's varied social life, Helen knew her boundaries. Only when Jim Agee was there was she included as an intimate party to their jokes and banter, even though, as she later confessed, she often had no idea what they were talking about.

Helen admired Walker for his taste, his wit, and his artistic integrity, but she resisted becoming his disciple. In her blunt streetwise way, she held her own ground and complemented his fastidiousness. She let him play Henry Higgins to her Eliza Doolittle by attempting to refine her Brooklyn accent (he fondly corrected her pronunciation of the word *bottle*). Expanding her literary taste, he read aloud passages from *Ulysses,* including the sexually explicit Gertie MacDowell section. He lent her his cameras, took her out to dinner, and at least once when she was short of cash — though short himself, as usual — he handed her a fifty-dollar bill.

Jim Agee never failed to include Helen when he invited Walker to Frenchtown, where he continued to entertain all forms of distraction from his agonizing effort to describe their experience in Alabama. Whenever they met, Jim and Walker exchanged reading material that somehow bore relation to their creative quests of the moment, from Sigmund Freud to the Goncourt brothers to Céline, and ideas for new projects proliferated. One came as a result of a prowl through the attic in Frenchtown, where they came upon a trunk full of old letters. Jim thought they should publish them anonymously, as examples of a pure, uninhibited, native American writing style. Each one, they believed, was as flawless a work of art as a dream.

While printing photographs for his retrospective, Evans was also occupied with the selection and sequence of the photographs for the sharecropper book, *Three Tenant Families,* now due at Harpers on August 1. The deadline passed without a manuscript. Working fitfully, Agee requested an extension of another month. Aswell's subtle reminders that their agreement was a matter of business only made Agee more nervous. "I had more or less forgotten the book was going to be for sale," he told Evans. In July, Evans sent him an adjustable rubber date stamp to help sharpen his awareness of the passing time. By mid-August the deadline had been extended to November 1, or at the very latest December 1, for publication in early 1939. But by mid-September Agee told Evans he was thinking of beginning the book all over again: "I am wanting and hoping I may find a way of doing the whole thing new from start to finish."

If Agee's book was still a long way from completion, Evans' museum exhibition was fast approaching. "I wish you the luck of one good explosion of excitement over the show," Agee wrote to Evans. "I imagine it might solve everything."

As his opening day drew near, Evans became increasingly nervous. He had made his final selections for the accompanying book and it was too late to make any changes there, but he could still make alterations in the exhibition.

On September 26, the evening before the show was scheduled to open, it had still not been hung. At Evans' request, Beaumont Newhall provided a large worktable and a paper cutter in the gallery, where Evans and Kirstein planned to spend the evening; it was clear to Newhall that he was not invited to join them. The next morning, when he returned to make sure everything was in order, he found on the floor a few empty Coca-Cola bottles and a litter of paper, slender silver-gray picture edges trimmed at the eleventh hour. Evans and Kirstein had arranged one hundred photographs around the walls in a continuous horizontal line. The smaller photographs were framed or simply overmatted; the larger prints were mounted on board and pasted flat on the wall with rubber cement. The arrangement of the images in clusters — frame houses, signs and billboards, shopfronts, architectural fragments, industrial landscapes, and fourteen photographs of the Alabama tenant farmers — gave a more literal thematic cohesion to Evans' subject matter than the book's pointed sequence. Finally, at the exhibition's climax, an oversize photograph of a tumbledown Victorian Italianate building that had become the Tuscaloosa Wrecking Company loomed large over the rest, like a benediction.

"American Photographs" opened to the public on a warm Saturday, September 27. The underground galleries at Rockefeller Center were far from ideal. A bank of plate-glass windows gave onto the sunken outdoor skating rink. Opening the fall season at MoMA along with "American Photographs" was an exhibition of prints by Georges Rouault and, from the design department, "Useful Objects under Five Dollars." At the reception, Evans could not to be found. Charles Fuller later learned that he had come to the door of the galleries, thought better of entering, walked around the block a few times, and gone home.

Evans could not explain his feelings about this great event at the apex of his career. At last his hopes of making a photographic portrait of America had been realized. Yet somehow, along with the obvious pride he felt in his achievement came a certain disappointment. He felt tight, suppressed, embarrassed. The show was full of his private feelings, now open to the public.

No one was better prepared to understand his mixed reaction than Agee, whose reluctance to finish *Three Tenant Families* now approached pathological proportions. "Simply by being published, bound, reproduced," he wrote to Evans upon receiving his complimentary copy of *American Photographs,* the photographs "have a strange thin illusion of part-death, which must or may be why you are partly disappointed." Both Agee and Evans were deeply suspicious of museums in general, of the role they played in bringing subversive material into the arms of the establishment, thereby sapping that material of its life and its power. To have the image of Allie Mae Burroughs hanging on the wall of a museum was to admit that their worst fears had come true. "The world has not the slightest idea what to do with these productions," Agee said, "can neither throw them away nor have them around, and so he has invented a sort of high-honorable day nursery or concentration camp for them, so that they will not be at large." Nevertheless, Agee wished to reassure his friend that the book was altogether a triumph. "It is one of the only 'great' and 'honest' or 'uncompromised' books of anywhere in this time, that I know of. It is also dangerous and I am very curious to see how far the dangerousness of so dangerous a thing can carry."

At Agee's request, Evans forwarded his reviews to Frenchtown as they steadily mounted. Critical attention was not lacking; Mabry had done his job well. Writing for the *New York Times,* Edward Alden Jewell noted the difference between Evans' work and that of his fellow documentary photographers simultaneously on view in the city. "There is . . . nothing of the evangelical in Walker Evans' approach," Jewell wrote. "He does not carry along with him the reformer's zeal when with superb artistry he photographs a mass of motor derelicts, a cluttered slum, a row of ramshackle huts, a small town main street eye-sore, the grimace of a jig-saw boarding house in ruins." Carl Van Vechten, with whom Evans had shared afternoons at Muriel Draper's ten years earlier, wrote in the *Herald-Tribune* that "if all America except Evans' photographs were razed they would tell our story." David Wolff of *New Masses* described the work collectively as "facts, . . . given the merciless edge of truth." Comparing Evans to the growing numbers of commercial photographers on assignment for *Life,* who had "corrupted our taste into a desire for hasty titillation," he saluted Evans' integrity and independence: "The very real pressure of . . . success, Walker Evans has resisted with all the force of his art." The poet William Carlos Williams wrote in *The New Republic* that Evans' photographs "pack a wicked punch." Moreover, he believed that Evans' integrity of vision was crucial in confronting the problems of his time. "The artist must save us," Williams wrote. "He's the only one who can."

But to many, *American Photographs* seemed an attempt not so much to save as to vilify, and to criticize a country that was in desperate need of optimism and national pride. In the *New York Times Book Review,* S. T. Williamson complained that Evans "has succeeded with his camera in doing what cultists of the ugly have done with paint and etching needle." The *Washington Post* called the exhibition "a parade of dreary, drab, and depressing scenes." A photography journal in Boston reassured its readers that Evans worked with a jaundiced eye that reflected his "own mental state and does not depict the mental state of the world." The *San Francisco News* stated simply that the work was "unnecessary and cruel." Agee was right in suggesting that the photographs were dangerous. They left viewers face to face with a place that was hauntingly familiar but that until then they might not have realized was their own country. "Through the intensity of his vision," Tom Mabry explained in *Harper's Bazaar*, "our ordinary world appears invisibly changed into its ultimate and classic form."

Other critics argued that even if the photographs were not really sinister, they were overvalued. Pare Lorenz delivered the sharpest blow in his review for *The Saturday Review of Literature*. As Evans' colleague at the Resettlement Administration, Lorenz had constructed his own version of Evans' artistic development, arguing that "until Professor Stryker employed him, along with Russell Lee, and Dorothea Lange, and Arthur Rothstein and Ben Shahn, Mr. Evans had not found the wave-length of his vision." He thought it important to mention that almost half the photographs in the exhibition "were paid for by the U.S. government" and added that "if you will buy the U.S. *Camera Annual* and look at the collection of FSA pictures . . . Mr. Evans' work becomes a little less mysterious than Mr. Kirstein tries to make it." Other critics agreed that Kirstein's essay was overly literary and pompous. The *Times Book Review* called it "a boiled shirt introduction." Roy Stryker saw the show and "liked it a lot," but, he told Evans, "I wish that Kirstein's article had been as good as the photographs."

When *American Photographs* reached the photographer Ansel Adams in California, he was shocked to see what the Museum of Modern Art was putting forward as great American photography. Adams, who was born the same year as Evans, was pursuing an entirely different goal. Integrating his avocation with his love of nature and especially the wilderness areas of California, he had photographed in the high sierras, and it would not be long before he had made spectacular views of Yosemite Valley from each of its most dramatic outlooks. As far as he was concerned, the beauty of America and the strength of its resources were best expressed through the elegant portrayal of its natural scenery. Walker Evans' junked cars, ruined mansions, and torn movie posters were an insult to his national pride. "I think the book is atrocious," he wrote unequivocally to his friend Georgia O'Keeffe. "Just why the Museum would undertake to present that book is a mystery to me." To Edward Weston, his West Coast neighbor and mentor in the photography of nature, Adams declared that "Walker Evans' book gave me a hernia. I am so goddam mad over what people from the left tier think America is."

Weston did not agree with Adams. In the late 1930s, his own work was shifting from a photography of pure nature to the broader landscape of American culture in decline. When he learned of *American Photographs,* he wrote immediately to Beaumont Newhall, "I want the Walker Evans book. He is certainly one of our finest. When I see a photograph reproduced that I like, I usually find it is by Walker Evans." Two years later he would travel the same River Road along the Mississippi as Evans had, photographing the ruined plantations.

"American Photographs" was dismantled on November 18, 1938. Elodie Courter, the head of the museum's circulating exhibitions, made arrangements right away for a nationwide museum tour. The first stop would be the Chouinard Art Institute in Los Angeles. A slightly larger group of 120 photographs were mounted on Masonite and fitted on the back with hanging rings. Following the explicit instructions of the artist, Courter enclosed a checklist of the photographs in the exact order in which they should be hung, in eighteen small groups. To make it difficult for the borrowing curator to deviate from the suggested order, a single label was provided for each group. At the same time, the book (now in a British edition as well) was distributed throughout the country, at the price of $2.50.

In New Orleans, Paul Ninas' friend Christine picked up a copy of *American Photographs* in a bookshop and noticed that on the page preceding the title page there appeared the initials J.S.N. She bought the book and presented it to Paul Ninas, who in turn showed it to Jane, to whom it was indeed obliquely dedicated.

7 *Love Before Breakfast*

As the first photographer to be given a one-man show at the Museum of Modern Art, Walker Evans won an unprecedented distinction. It was like having "a calling card," or better yet, "a passport," he later said, but with passport in hand, he still faced the question of where to travel next. Was his museum exhibition to mark the formative years of a long, venerable career or the summary of a brief but brilliant one? Would the acclaim he now received challenge him to take greater risks or relax him into a creative stasis? No matter what, "American Photographs" would go down in history as his signal achievement, establishing him as an artist and the very notion of documentary photography as an art.

If "American Photographs" gave Evans a disturbing sense of finality, he had enough unsatisfied ambitions at the end of 1938 to keep him from feeling complacent. He planned to continue work on his photographic portrait of the urban American scene. He still held out hope for a Guggenheim fellowship. For the longer term, he might find a position as photography editor or consultant with one of the new picture magazines — *Life, Look, The Saturday Evening Post.* Meanwhile, the Alabama book was still pending. Only one thing was clear: money was short, as usual.

For Jim Agee the future was equally tentative. He and Alma married a few weeks before Christmas 1938 and were living in French-town. While Agee enjoyed a wave of paternal sentiment toward his young bride, he sought from Evans a steady rudder that might keep him on course. In typically circuitous, apologetic prose, he offered to make Evans a Christmas gift of the Alabama book's text, at least as far as he'd gotten on it. "If you'd like it (and if you wouldn't by all means say so) I'd like to give you something which will be delayed, and will necessarily have a few strings attached: it might also seem indecently egoistic . . . that is, when I'm done with it, whatever there is of the manuscript of the book." The strings he referred to were only that he might need to borrow the manuscript back "for a good while at a time."

Agee was still working on his manuscript, and Alma, who had no secretarial experience, was in the process of typing it. Faced with Agee's illegible longhand and his constant efforts to improve on the manuscript, she soon lost heart. Charles Fuller, in a typically expansive gesture, offered his own secretary, Alice Morris, to see the task through to completion. Morris was well suited to the challenge. She was an avid reader of modern fiction and an aspiring writer herself, and she was ready to throw away the conventional life her eastern boarding-school education had prepared her for to work with men she felt were brilliant. Evans set her up in the living room of his apartment with a typewriter and a stack of Agee's manuscript pages. Morris quickly learned that deciphering Agee's eccentric punctuation and miniature scrawl was an act of devotion; his words seemed to go in and out of focus, as if, she recalled, "they were dancing on the head of a pin." Evans hovered nearby to make sure that every word, comma, and period was exactly as Agee had written it, even if it appeared to be a mistake.

In making a gift of his manuscript to Evans, Agee was moved by his desire for an almost impossible level of oneness with his coauthor. At the peak of his work on *Three Tenant Families*, Agee imagined them to be inseparable halves of a whole. He had read enough about psychology and known enough of the romantic friendships between boys at boarding school to acknowledge that his longing had homosexual overtones. At the time, his and Evans' love for each other was perhaps stronger than either of them had for a woman, whether or not they confessed as much to each other or anyone else. Instead of consummating their relationship directly, they made their sexual connection vicariously, through women, a trend that had its beginnings in Evans' love affair with Agee's sister Emma and that had continued in his involvement with Agee's former wife, Via.

For Evans, connecting with Agee through his women was a roundabout way of expressing his love for him; it was also a way of exploring Agee's tremendous appeal to women, which he admired. For Agee, the connection had another meaning. He subtly encouraged these affairs as part of his impossible campaign to break down all barriers, both physical and emotional, between the people he loved, between those people and his own powers to empathize. His incurable desire to observe while participating colored every aspect of his life and work and invaded his relationships with everyone he knew. On several occasions throughout the spring and summer of 1938, he had tried to organize weekends of group sex in the house in Frenchtown, but most of his friends, one remembered, either refused or grew bored with his repeated invitations.

Whether or not Evans got involved in the Frenchtown orgies, Agee later became obsessed with the idea of witnessing his best friend in bed with his new wife, as if to take a trend that had arisen unconsciously to its logical extreme. From the evidence of his letters to Evans, it is clear that his obsession became a troublesome distraction for all three of them. "However much or in whatever ways you happen to like each other," he wrote, "good: I am enough an infant, homosexual, or post-dostoevskian to be glad. However much you don't, that's all right too."

Walker and Alma were not fond of each other. They represented the opposite poles of Jim's psychological makeup. Walker could not understand what Jim was doing with a woman who was so clearly his intellectual inferior; Alma found Walker intimidating and over-refined. But Jim was determined to join them together, and finally one day in Frenchtown, under his irresistible pressure, all three of them took their clothes off and began to fumble awkwardly with one another on the bed. In less than five minutes Jim realized his mistake, collapsed on a chair in the corner, and wept. His chronic problem, Walker later reflected, was to include other people in thoughts that were his alone: "He was blind in the heart and in the genitals."

Evans may have appeared to be more considerate of other people's privacy than his reckless, impulsive friend, but he had his own quiet way of intruding on it. Agee encouraged him in his next photographic project, one he had been mulling over for some time: to make portraits of people with a hidden camera on the New York subway. The idea was born of his desire to strip portrait photography of its artificial conventions, to thumb his nose at the studios of Steichen and Cecil Beaton, and to provide a sober counterpoint the disingenuous smiling faces arrayed in the window of the small-town studio photographer. In many ways the subway project was the photographic equivalent to Agee's idea for a book of anonymous letters; it embodied the same sense of immediacy and the flawlessness of innocence. It all but disclaimed the role of the artist.

And so, on the brink of a certain degree of fame, Evans literally went underground. He was determined to capture his subjects completely unawares, in the privacy of their daydreams, when their vanity was for a moment suspended. But a fear of being caught in the act deterred him from taking off on his own. If the subjects discovered what he was up to, the picture would be ruined and the confrontation awkward, if not dangerous.

To Helen Levitt, photographing in the subway (even though it was in fact against the law) was not daunting. Evans' difficulties looked to her more like a case of his usual inertia. Prodding him along, she volunteered to ride the subway with him as the photographer's foil. During the colder months of 1938, the two would set out for several hours of subway travel on the Lexington Avenue local, as he later described, "down among the torn gum wrappers into the fetid, clattering, squealing cars underground."

In order to work inconspicuously, Evans did not use flash equipment in the subway car's dim available light but slowed his shutter speed down to a risky one fiftieth of a second. He painted the bright chrome parts of his 35mm Contax camera matte black, tucked its body under his coat with the lens slyly protruding between two

Walker Evans Jr., c. 1900

Jessie Crane Evans in her
wedding dress, 1900

Walker Evans, Walker Evans Jr.,
and Walker Evans III, c. 1907

Walker Evans III

The Evans house in Kenilworth

Walker Evans III, yearbook picture,
Phillips Academy, Andover, 1922

Walker Evans at work, Darien, Connecticut, summer 1929, by Paul Grotz

Hart Crane, by Evans

Walker Evans, 1929–1930, by Grotz

Paul Grotz, 1929–1930, by Evans

Lincoln Kirstein, by George Platt Lynes

Ben, Judith, and Tillie Shahn,
23 Bethune Street, New York,
c. 1931, by Evans

Jane Smith Ninas,
Belle Grove, Louisiana,
1935, by Evans

James Agee, Old Field Point, summer 1937, by Evans

James Agee and Mia Fritsch, 1942, by Helen Levitt

Walker Evans, c. 1940, by Levitt

Herbert Solow and John McDonald, Croton-on-Hudson, by Evans

John Jessup and Wilder Hobson, by Evans

Jane's barn with porch addition, Old Lyme, Connecticut, 1940s, by Evans

Isabelle Boeschenstein Evans, 1961, by Walker Evans

Walker Evans, 1971, by Arnold Crane

Walker Evans at work, Hale County, Alabama, October 1973,
by William Christenberry

Walker Evans at his last lecture, April 8, 1975, by Edward Forman

buttons, and rigged the shutter to a cable release on a slender cord that led up to his right shoulder, down his sleeve, and into the palm of his hand. Sitting beside him, Levitt would feel him stiffen his back, his camera aimed at his captive and unsuspecting subjects, and know that he was about to squeeze the trigger. Every so often, they disembarked onto a station platform for a cigarette break.

At each station the photographer's subjects rearranged themselves. Framing two people in one shot, Evans toyed with real or imagined loves or alliances, impossible dialogues or unknown hostilities. Later, in his darkroom, he could crop his images, join two neighboring shots in a single frame, or divide his duets into solos, then shuffle the individual faces and lay them out again like a deck of cards. The entire social spectrum of New York was at his fingertips: messenger boys, schoolteachers, bank clerks, grandmothers, street sweepers, garage mechanics, and half-wits. From a horde of unposed portraits emerged a patchwork of native intelligence and natural beauty, expectation and resignation. In each city-worn face Agee saw a ruined child, "the wrecked demeanors of the mind / That now is tamed and once was wild."

Like Agee, Evans was having an orgy of the imagination without the risk of personal involvement. "The guard is down and the mask is off," he said of his unwitting subjects, "even more than when in lone bedrooms (where there are mirrors). People's faces are in naked repose down in the subway." But while he could gaze at the faces of his subjects with all the visual lust of the voyeur, their thoughts remained hidden from him, like those of "the ladies and gentlemen of the jury," or the strangers who visited his exhibition at the Museum of Modern Art, bringing with them a host of unknown associations and convictions and then passing judgment.

When "American Photographs" embarked on its national tour in January 1939, radical changes were in the works at the Museum of Modern Art. Anticipating the opening of the museum's first permanent home at 11 West 53rd Street, its directors were poised to expand its already ambitious program in every way. The presidency of MoMA passed from A. Conger Goodyear, who had served since it opened in

1929, to the thirty-year-old Nelson Rockefeller, the second son of Abby Rockefeller, already an active committee member. With Rockefeller in charge, the small family atmosphere of the museum's first ten years was suddenly overtaken by a corporate mastermind. The aspiring politician immediately saw the need for his own team of "efficiency experts" as well as the abrupt dismissal of what he considered "dead wood." Many faithful staff members felt their foundations shaken with the imminent possibility of a total bureaucratic overhaul of their departments.

The opening of the new building, designed by Edward Durell Stone, was also the occasion of MoMA's tenth birthday. Rockefeller hired a publicity expert to organize a radio program, which included Edsel Ford, Walt Disney, and FDR expounding on the museum's critical role in American culture. The opening exhibition, "Art in Our Time," encompassed the full spectrum of the contemporary visual arts — painting, sculpture, prints, and drawings, as well as a section of photographs called "Seven Americans," organized by Beaumont Newhall.

Newhall chose seven photographs by Walker Evans for the exhibition. The other photographers represented were Ansel Adams, Brett Weston, Ralph Steiner, Berenice Abbott, Man Ray, and Harold Edgerton. Newhall's idea was to give each photographer his own space in the gallery, delineated by his own wall color. Ansel Adams' Western landscapes, for example, were shown on a green-tinted wall, Evans' selections on dull red. If Evans was less than enthusiastic about being but one of seven Americans in the first place, he was definitely displeased with Newhall's installation plans, especially the color scheme. Through a third party, he insisted on controlling the installation of his photographs. Newhall vividly recalled the dispute. "'Mr. Evans,' I was told, 'will exhibit his photographs only on condition that he be allowed to hang them himself, but not in your presence.'" There was no arguing with him; as Newhall by then knew, Evans "was a man of strong opinions." Newhall obligingly arranged for him to enter the museum after hours to rehang his pictures. Alone in the galleries, he dry-mounted each one on a large sheet of pure white board and placed them edge to edge so that no dull red showed between them.

Seven thousand guests had received engraved invitations to the gala white-tie opening of the museum on May 10. The list included New York City's prominent socialites as well as celebrities from the worlds of art and film such as Salvador Dali and Lillian Gish. Frances Collins, with her enduring Vassar idealism, resented the fact that several of the lower-ranking staff members were not on the guest list. Seizing the opportunity to poke fun at the museum's new president, she called on her friend Joseph Blumenthal of the Spiral Press, who had printed the book *American Photographs* as well as many other museum publications, and asked him to make a substitute invitation to the ball. Blumenthal produced a four-page "French fold," on the front of which the motto "Oil that glitters is not gold" (a reference to the source of Rockefeller's wealth) appeared under a drawing of a crown. Inside, elaborate script requested the honor of the recipient's presence at "the semi-public opening of The Museum of Standard Oil," and added below, "Better dresses 5th floor." Blumenthal "designed it and I wrote this abominably impudent 'invitation,'" remembered Collins. "It was kid stuff, let's face it."

Kid stuff or not, Collins' practical joke helped to spell the end of her career at MoMA. Lincoln Kirstein got hold of one of her invitations and showed it to Rockefeller. Dressed in a severe black evening dress for the opening party, Collins met her fate when Kirstein kissed her and said, "This is the kiss of death." Shortly afterward, Collins was fired. It was up to Tom Mabry to deliver the unfortunate news that Kirstein's friend Monroe Wheeler would be taking over her department.

A few days later, Mabry got the ax as well. These sudden dismissals were particularly disturbing to those who knew that Alfred Barr was in Europe at the time, researching a major Picasso retrospective, and seemed to have nothing to do with the changes in his staff.

The tenth anniversary of the Museum of Modern Art coincided fortuitously with the New York World's Fair, which opened in April 1939. Throughout the spring and summer thousands of tourists flocked to the city to see the fair, a popular alternative to travel in Europe, where Hitler's threats to Poland had forced the other European nations into alliances and everyone was poised for war. Holger Cahill, who had been acting director of MoMA, was in charge of an enormous survey of American art for the fair called "American Art Today." For many months before, local directors of the WPA art program throughout the country had been making selections to present as candidates for the show. Cahill, with the help of Dorothy Miller, his new bride, had deftly whittled masses of WPA art down to a mere one thousand objects. From the New Orleans group, organized by the Arts and Crafts Club, he had chosen a painting of a cemetery by Jane Smith Ninas.

By now an expert in subterfuge, Walker had been secretly corresponding with Jane since early that year. One of her classmates from Sophie Newcomb, Marion "Billie" Rainey, had recently married and moved to Connecticut with her husband, Clark Voorhees, a sculptor. Through Billie, Walker and Jane were kept informed about each other. After dedicating *American Photographs* to Jane, Walker began to send little notes to her via Billie, who would enclose them in her own letters.

Ever since Walker had left New Orleans nearly three years earlier, Jane had blocked him out of her mind, as if the affair had never happened. But when she saw her initials on the dedication page of *American Photographs,* she was shocked out of her self-imposed amnesia. The dedication was indisputable evidence of Walker's lingering devotion. And with the arrival of his amorous notes, tucked between the folds of her friend's letters, Jane knew that the embers of the romance were there to be stirred. Furthermore, there was no denying that her marriage to Paul Ninas was beyond repair. Between his drinking and his extramarital love affairs, Jane had reached her limit. Meanwhile, the Voorheeses were encouraging her to visit them in Connecticut, and with her painting on view at the fair, she had a good excuse to visit New York. So when she found that her old boarding-school classmate Mona Kraut was willing to travel with her, Jane borrowed Paul's rickety old Chevrolet and headed north, with Mona at the wheel, in June.

Apprised of her travel plans, Walker told her to call him as soon as she reached Old Lyme. His excitement at the prospect of seeing her again was mixed with a dread of being unprepared. On the twenty-second of June he wrote a frantic note to Billie Voorhees demanding to know exactly when Jane might be arriving. A few days later, the phone rang at 441 East 92nd Street. It was Jane calling from a pay phone in the country store in Hamburg Cove, Connecticut. "Bless you for calling" was the first thing Walker managed to say at the sound of her voice, and there followed a halting, excited conversation. "Darling you are terrible on the phone and so am I," he wrote to her the next day, proposing that they meet that Friday. He would take the train up to Saybrook in the morning, and they would spend the day together.

At the sight of her errant lover, Jane was struck equally with passion and the sting of Walker's last departure from New Orleans. "I cried all night" following their brief reunion, she recalled — tears both of relief at knowing that their love had survived the distance and of fear of the unknown ahead. Was Walker worth the pain he had already caused? And how much more was to come? But Walker persisted. Over the next few weeks he went up to Connecticut several times to take her out for lunch or a drive. By the middle of July, still in Connecticut, Jane had gained enough confidence to take him up on his constant suggestion that she come to New York. "Like a gambler with all his money, I took the plunge. This is it. I'm going," she told herself.

Mona, who had already called on Walker during a visit to the city to see her brother, encouraged her daring. Together she and Jane decided to surprise Walker. On a hot midsummer afternoon they found the building on East 92nd Street quiet. Mona rang all the doorbells, but no one answered. Having visited the building before, she knew how to reach the internal stairway to the roof, which was right outside Walker's kitchen window. She made her way up the stairs and through the window into the apartment, and let Jane in the front door. Like a pair of schoolgirls rather pleased with their prank, they made themselves at home. It was not long before Walker arrived, but to everyone's embarrassment, he was accompanied by Frances Collins. They all carried on as if nothing were wrong, but Frances graciously took her cue and was the first to leave. Perhaps she knew that this pretty, round-cheeked young woman with the slight southern accent was the one Walker referred to when he said there was someone else. In bed with Jane that night, Walker took a strand of her long brown hair, wound it around his ring finger, and said, "With this hair I thee wed."

Whether or not Frances was ready to end her love affair with Walker, she was not prepared to admit openly that the end was not entirely her own choice. In July she wrote to Marga Barr, then in Italy with Alfred, "Within 24 hours of leaving [the museum], I had the courage and ruthlessness to bring to a sharp and inalterable end two and a half years of intimacy with Walker, so that by Sunday night . . . I'd cut free from the wreckage and encumbrances that had been holding me down and stepped into a brave new world." She related that she had spent the following week in New York feeling gay and lighthearted, "so glad to be free of Mr. Nelson Rockefeller *and* Mr. Walker Evans that I had no room in my cheerfulness to worry about where to turn next." Frances' husband, Pete Collins, was spending the summer at Yaddo, the artists' and writers' colony in Saratoga Springs. By midsummer, Frances found him looking better than ever, as she told Marga, "more healthy, more handsome and serene than in all the years I've known him." But her renewed enthusiasm for her marriage was brief. Soon after writing these words, she divorced Collins, married another writer, Jim Smythe, and moved to Ohio.

Jane never returned to New Orleans, in spite of Paul Ninas' persistent pleas that she do so. Her mind was made up; their marriage was over, and she was determined to stay with Walker. She asked Paul to pack up her clothes, her books, her paints and brushes, and send them to New York. For the first time in his thirty-six years, Walker found himself living with a woman as husband and wife.

Jane was a stranger to his city, an artist with no reliable means of supporting herself. Other than the Voorheeses, she had no friends and no family nearby. In New Orleans she had been immersed in the intimate ambiance of the French Quarter, where her circle of artist friends met frequently and supported one another's efforts and where in her daily rounds she knew all the shopkeepers by name. In New

York, to Helen Levitt's amusement, she wondered if she needed a personal introduction to the neighborhood butcher.

Walker left Jane in charge of the kitchen, but he reigned supreme over the aesthetic aspects of their conjugal life. He loved to find old pieces of furniture and polish them up or fashion them to his special needs. He transformed an old bureau into a housing for the radio by drilling neat little holes for the knobs and painting it matte black. He found dinner plates in a restaurant supply store — pure white. "Everything was pure white," remembered Jane, except for those things that were black or gray. "I had to fight to get some color in there." She planted a little flower garden on the roof. She eventually managed to introduce some striped slipcovers to the bedroom, and she upholstered a green velvet cushion for the top of Walker's fragment of a wooden Ionic column, turning it into a footstool. After a while, she had the temerity to hang some of her own colorful paintings on the living room wall, where Walker had never thought to hang his photographs.

Walker had already covered much of his wall space with densely packed bookshelves, a library that ranged in content from recent paperback novels to rare first editions of classics by Henry James and French literary journals he had carefully preserved from the year he spent in Paris. He also had a sizable antique postcard collection, which he kept neatly filed in shoeboxes, and scrapbooks pasted with pages of advertisements and other printed matter he had cut out of magazines or picked up off the street — ticket stubs, can labels, invoices, letterheads, odds and ends he had accumulated over the past decade and classified as "printed ephemera." Occasionally Jane came across a child's drawing or a handmade costume Walker had fished out of the trash (in much the same way that Jim Agee would search through public trashcans for other people's letters). One day he came home with a large black rubber ball and placed it with thoughtful deliberation in a white compote. He also had a small collection of doorknobs. And for some reason Jane never understood, he kept part of the engine of his mother's car behind the clothes hamper in the kitchen.

By the time Jane arrived there, the building at 441 East 92nd Street had become the home of artists, photographers, and filmmakers. Edwin Locke moved in downstairs. Jay Leyda and his wife, Si-Lan Chen, still lived in the apartment directly in front of Evans', but the two couples did not see much of each other. As much as he admired Leyda as a filmmaker, Evans had never been sympathetic to his Communist ideals. Via Agee recalled that while she and Jim would march off to Communist party meetings just to see what they were like, "Walker was too mature for all that." In the late 1930s the Leydas were holding such meetings in their apartment. As political loyalties divided after the Moscow trials and with the rise of Stalin, the Leydas' pro-Communist stance was all the more pointed, and it was clear to all of the residents that the building was being watched by the FBI.

When it came to politics, Evans' sympathies were more in keeping with the writers and editors of *Partisan Review*. Under the new editorship of Fred Dupee, Philip Rahv, Dwight Macdonald, and William Phillips, in 1938 the journal had turned away from the kind of leftist political writing that had characterized its first two years. These men still considered themselves radicals, but having witnessed the outrages of Stalinist communism, they resolved to remain independent of the Communist party. Returning to the spirit of the nonpartisan "little magazines" of the 1920s, they decided that the literature they published would not be at the service of politics any more than it would succumb to the pressures of commercialism and academia. James Agee contributed to the literary tone of the first issue under the new editorship (August-September 1938) with an autobiographical short story "Knoxville: Summer of 1915"; his fellow contributors included the poets Delmore Schwartz and Wallace Stevens.

Lionel Trilling, a professor of English at Columbia, wrote frequently for *Partisan Review;* his wife, Diana, was the book critic for the equally liberal *Nation.* By 1940, Evans and Agee were both often included in evening gatherings at the Trillings', which typically consisted of a few people sitting around in a circle engaged in lively, opinionated discourse on the war in Europe, its ideological implications, the future of liberal thought, high art, and popular culture. Conversation often turned to who was moving left and who was moving right, whether being anti-Communist meant being pro-Fascist, or whether being anti-Stalinist meant that a person had reneged on his liberal ideals. If anything, the *Partisan Review* crowd was sympathetic to Stalin's arch-adversary, Leon Trotsky, and some had been actively involved in his work. At the Trillings', Evans met John McDonald, a writer with strong political convictions who had been Trotsky's assistant during his exile in Mexico. McDonald's wife, Dorothy Eisner, a painter, was also in Mexico at the time. Among the same crowd Evans met Eleanor Clark, a novelist who had married Trotsky's former private secretary. He also made friends with the passionate, melancholy Herbert Solow, a writer who had organized the American Committee for the Defense of Trotsky.

For Evans, the circle around the Trillings, which also included the poets and writers Edmund Wilson, Mary McCarthy, and Elizabeth Hardwick, represented the height of literary sophistication to which he had always aspired. But at times the *Partisan Review*'s intellectual bias was too strong for him. His own intelligence was intuitive, not deductive. Furthermore, the *Partisan Review* crowd was not immune to insularity. More than occasionally conversation grew introverted and self-centered. Highly competitive among themselves, the members of the group were overly concerned with the question of who was worthy of their journal and who was not. The writer Alfred Kazin commented that they were "interested in the people around them to the point of ecstasy."

Evans was also friendly with a certain group of writers for Time Inc. In the company of Wilder and Peggy Hobson, he spent evenings that inevitably turned musical, mostly to the tune of improvisational jazz. Jack Jessup, a writer for *Fortune,* and his wife, the former Eunice Clark (Eleanor's sister), gave famous dinner and after-dinner parties, where there was plenty of alcohol and the mood was usually light-hearted, rife with sophisticated New York gossip, Ivy League in-jokes, and punning repartee.

As far as Jane was concerned, the best parties of that era were going on right upstairs at Dorothy and Harry Harvey's. It was Dorothy who had discovered the building on East 92nd Street — she had spotted it from a boat on the East River — and taken it upon herself to renovate it and attract an interesting group of fellow tenants. Dorothy came from a wealthy family in Chicago and had traveled abroad. In the early 1930s she and her two sisters had lived in Paris and had come to know some of the artists and writers of the emerging surrealist movement. Many of the friends they had made there — Marcel Duchamp, Marc Chagall, Ossip Zadkine, Matta, Max Ernst, and André Breton among them — fled the war in Europe for the safe harbor of New York and now frequently gathered in the Harveys' living room. One day, as Jane recalled, Breton made a date to see Evans in his darkroom. After looking at Evans' photographs and seeing his penchant for torn posters, fragmented words, and junk, Breton declared that he had a surrealist turn of mind.

By far the most frequent visitor to Walker's and Jane's apartment was Jim Agee. He would arrive at almost any hour of the day or night, on the spur of the moment, longing to talk, to share a piece of music, a poem, or his latest idea for a new magazine, film, or novel. One of his pet ideas at the time was for the movies. Building on the significant advance of "talkies," Agee developed the concept of "feelies," which would give the audience all the physical sensations they witnessed on screen through vibrations in the seats. Jane thought Jim was brilliant, and funny too, but she was not the only friend to recall that in his verbal excess and intensity, "he could also be incredibly boring." His enthusiasm for the movies led him to describe single shots or sequences exhaustively, as if he had written the script himself. His conversation was always lubricated by a drink and a Lucky Strike, often by several of both. When Jane and finally Walker would stagger off to bed, he would as often as not follow them there, settle on the edge of their bed, and continue his uninterruptible stream of thoughts.

Jim's desire for late-night talks with Walker was especially urgent in 1939. Alma was pregnant, and he was anxious about the prospect of a child. At the same time he was in the final stages of preparing *Three Tenant Families*, which he had now given a new title: *Let Us Now Praise Famous Men*, a line in the Bible he had kept in mind since his student days at Exeter. With mounting trepidation about turning in his manuscript to the editors at Harpers, he would read passages aloud, begging for Walker's judgment as to what should stay and what should go. The book had grown far beyond the conventional boundaries of a documentary essay about tenant farmers. It included an apology for the journalist's endeavor, a meditation on the limits of words and the dangers of photography, an account of his travels with Evans through the South and the search for their subject, a confession of helplessness in the face of their subjects once found, and the most exhaustive description of the people, their food, shelter, clothing, and every condition of their daily life that journalism had ever known. Still, as far as he was concerned, it did not seem to approximate the experience of being there. His literary efforts sometimes felt to him like a sham. If it were possible, he would throw out his pages and pages of words and replace them with real evidence, and he said so in the book's preamble. "If I could do it, I'd do no writing at all here. It would be photographs; the rest would be fragments of cloth, bits of cotton, lumps of earth, records of speech, pieces of wood and iron, phials of odors, plates of food and excrement."

While Agee toiled over his manuscript, Evans was overseeing the printing and engraving of the photographic plates for the book. Resigned to the limits of Harpers' budget, he drew from the layout of his sharecropper albums and made a selection of thirty photographs. During the summer of 1939 he was a regular visitor to the engraving plant to ensure that no detail, no nuance, was lost from his carefully crafted images. Flogging his memory for the sensual reality of that summer in Alabama, now three years back, he strove to match the intensity of Agee's prose and to do justice to an experience that was all the more extraordinary in retrospect. Studying every plate, he gave instructions to the engraver. The wrinkles on the Burroughses' bed-sheets did not show up clearly enough; could he make them sharper? Could he show more clearly the tear in the pillowcase? Could he bring out the texture of the wooden wall and the objects around the fireplace? Could he soften the lines on Allie Mae's face, sharpen the creases on Bud Fields' overalls? Under Evans' scrupulous direction, several of the plates had to be made over again entirely, while small imperfections in others were painstakingly corrected. As Aswell said, "I doubt if any engraver's plates were ever made under such careful and loving scrutiny."

In August, Agee relinquished his text to Edward Aswell and waited anxiously for his response. His doubts about the quality of the work and the inadequacy of his talents in the face of his subject had not abated. Like Evans on the eve of *American Photographs,* he felt the terrible weight of his own high standards. At the same time he was plagued with guilt about exposing the sad lives of innocent people to the public eye. He had changed the names of his subjects — the Burroughses had become the Gudgers, the Fieldses had become the Woodses, and the Tingles had become the Ricketts — but this was not enough. He wrote to Aswell that he wished the book to be as inexpensive as possible (he suggested the unrealistically low figure of $1.50); he hoped that the paper would be cheap and that the whole thing would disintegrate in a few short years. Finally he suggested that the book be bound in cardboard and covered in plain black Bible cloth, as *American Photographs* had been.

In spite of his doubts, Agee was certain that no one in a commercial publishing house could improve on one word of his text. It was not long before he learned that the editors were suggesting certain cuts, in an effort to make the book more like conventional documentary studies of the Depression, such as the one produced by Caldwell and Bourke-White. A memorandum had been circulated to that effect at Harpers, as Aswell reluctantly informed the author. Changes that the editors considered to be minor, "in order to meet the practical requirements of publication," as Aswell phrased it, Agee considered blasphemous. In his opinion, the integrity of the entire work was threatened, and he would not stand for it.

Evans, who knew his friend well enough not to tamper with a word of his text even if Agee begged him to, probably did nothing to dissuade Agee from a confrontation with the publishers. They made a date with Aswell, hoping to reason with the editors, to bring them around. Agee said he would go along with the changes as long as Harpers agreed to publish the editors' critical memorandum in the same volume. However sincere this offer was, it was not greeted warmly. Meanwhile, the publisher had also unwittingly insulted Agee's coauthor. The engravers, in their effort to perfect one of the photographic plates, had touched it up and in so doing removed the fleas from the Burroughses' bed.

Negotiations between Agee and the editors of Harpers had reached an impasse. After several days of soul-searching, Agee decided he was still determined to find a publisher that would accept his text as it was, and he withdrew the book from Harpers. On October 3, Aswell wrote a letter to Agee giving him conditional release from the contract, leaving him free to take his work elsewhere. Technically, without such an agreement, Harpers had the right to publish the work as the editors saw fit. If Agee did succeed in placing the book with another publisher, that publisher was obliged to repay Harpers $500 of the author's $700 advance and to reimburse it for the cost of the engravings.

Until that better day should come, the book was briefly previewed in the October issue of a new liberal journal, *Common Sense*. Selden Rodman, the chief editor, selected five photographs and a piece of the text from the section "On the Porch." Meanwhile, Agee pleaded with Evans to play a greater role in editing and shaping his prose, even suggesting at one point that he might incorporate something *Evans* had written about Allie Mae Burroughs. But Evans resisted. The manuscript's greatness and its flaws, its compassion and its fury, were the writer's alone, and Evans knew that however complementary his and Agee's talents and vision were, he should not interfere. "I wouldn't touch it," he later said. "I saw things that needed to be done. But I thought that it was too great and that its faults had better be left in it."

The disappointments of the fall of 1939 prompted Evans to apply again to the Guggenheim Foundation for a fellowship. He proposed to continue the kind of work he had presented in *American Photographs* but now to concentrate more on people and cities. The result would be "a catalogue of people and environments of this time, general and anonymous, national rather than regional." The critical acclaim of *American Photographs* made the difference, and Evans was awarded his first Guggenheim fellowship, with a stipend of $2,000, in the spring of 1940.

Expecting to spend the better part of the year on the road, Evans sublet his apartment. But just as he and Jane were ready to go south he was struck with acute appendicitis (or "appendisodomy," as he called it), and he spent the next few months recovering with his sister and brother-in-law, then living in the affluent Maryland suburb of Chevy Chase, and later, back in New York, in a room in the Hotel Wales. Jane visited Alice Morris and the critic Harvey Breit in their little apartment, where they set up an army cot for her on the only available piece of floor, under the piano. By the time Evans had recovered his strength, his Guggenheim fellowship period was almost over, with little work to show for it, and the money was gone. He was soon to lose his studio on 93rd Street as well. Helen Levitt was off to Mexico, accompanied by Alma Agee, who was taking her one-year-old son, Joel, and leaving Jim for good.

Evans lost little time in finding a basement studio below a grocery store at 1681 York Avenue. He also promptly applied for a renewal of his Guggenheim. During his convalescence, he had been mulling over the photographs he had made in the subway three years earlier. Now he intended to focus his efforts on his next book, which he would call *Faces of Men*. The book, a collection of unposed portraits of contemporary Americans, made on the street with a hidden camera in a "semiautomatic" fashion, would go one step beyond *American Photographs* in its claim to objectivity.

Pondering the idea, Evans selected two dozen subjects from the subway negatives and enlarged them as single faces, severed from their context, to march in his melancholy street parade. The seeds of his huge portrait project were beginning to come to life. In his Guggenheim application, he stated his intention to intersperse text in the sequence of pictures, a verbal grab bag of the kind Agee might have proposed: "I want to collect a series of literary texts, some just captions, some longer, and arrange a sequence of pictures and words. Some of this I want to write myself, some I want to be literally overheard spoken sentences or conversations."

On April 1, 1941, Evans was awarded $1,000, a six-month extension to his Guggenheim. By this time he could also finally look forward with some confidence to the publication of *Let Us Now Praise Famous Men*. Eunice Clark Jessup, acting as a part-time literary agent, had brought the Alabama book to the attention of Paul Brooks, a young editor at Houghton Mifflin, in Boston. Brooks, who had been a year ahead of Agee at Harvard and remembered his distinguished work for the *Advocate*, recognized the unique quality of the Agee-Evans collaboration. Furthermore, he was willing to risk publishing the work unchanged in its entirety, as long as certain words that were "illegal in Massachusetts" were deleted. According to Brooks, "Walker was very helpful in urging Jim to be reasonable," and the deal was made. "Let me tell you how greatly I envy you the privilege of publishing this book," Edward Aswell wrote to Lovell Thompson, senior editor at Houghton Mifflin, upon receiving the news. "It was a great blow to me personally that things turned out as they did. Agee is certainly one of the most remarkable writers I have ever known and the only one now living who, I feel sure, is an authentic genius."

By the time Agee and Evans were wrapping up the final details of their book with Houghton Mifflin in the spring of 1941, they were willing to balance their demands with concessions. Evans wished for the photographs to be placed one to a page, on the right-hand side only, as they had been in *American Photographs*. The expense of production made this proposal unacceptable to the publishers. However, they did agree to replace the fleas that Harpers' engraver had removed from the Burroughses' counterpane. Houghton Mifflin's printer dutifully reproduced them with an engraver's tool. When the authors learned that the book jacket was to be a brown-tinted close-up photograph of tilled earth (by an uncredited photographer), Agee ventured to Robert Linscott, who was handling the book's production, their jointly held opinion on the subject — "We had hoped the jacket might be as plain as possible print and paper" — while conceding that the question was "out of our territory." Houghton Mifflin agreed that it was, and the photograph remained.

The editors were also at pains to adhere to Agee's highly specific order of the text. As the galleys arrived in stacks in the mail, Agee seized his last opportunity to make revisions. Linscott grew alarmed at the rising costs in time and money of a book he had been led to believe was finished. On March 4 he wrote to Agee, "I hope . . . that it won't be necessary to continue to make changes at this rate all the way through as it is going to run into a pretty heavy charge for excess corrections." Production time for the book ran longer than expected; Houghton Mifflin shifted sights to a late-summer publication date.

On July 18, 1941, Paul Brooks wrote to Agee to say that the first copy had just come from the press and would be forwarded immediately to New York. Agee and Evans had their own list of special friends and potential critics to receive advance copies of the book. In their personal notes accompanying the review copies, they emphasized that the photograph section was an integral part of the whole, to be addressed as equal to the text. "We are anxious to make it clear to everyone that this isn't an 'illustrated' book," explained Agee to Linscott, "that the photographs and text are a collaboration, each of full importance in communicating our subject." Finally, there was nothing more for them to do but wait for their readers' response.

As they might have predicted, the response was mixed. Several of the reviews were devastating, mainly to Agee. While Evans' photographs rose above the overkill of Depression reportage, Agee's verbosity and passionate empathy seemed to many critics undisciplined, self-centered, and out of date. For the *New York Times*, Ralph Thompson summarized this view: "There never was a better argument for photography. Mr. Evans says as much about tenant farmers . . . in his several dozen pictures as Mr. Agee says in his entire 150,000 words of text."

Those who were personal friends of Agee and Evans treated the text more sympathetically. Jack Jessup wrote a carefully considered review for *Time*, praising the directness and honesty of Evans' photographs as well as the power of Agee's prose. "Parts of the book come as close to reproducing the actual as words and pictures can," he wrote. At the same time, he did not hide his doubts about the book's problems, mainly concerning the writing: "Agee's chief failure is one Photographer Evans scrupulously avoids: he clumsily intrudes between his subject and his audience, even when the subject is himself." Harvey Breit, who had spent many an evening talking to Jim late into the night, devoted his September column in *The New Republic* to the book, concluding that "whatever the case, whether attracted or repelled, whether for or against, it is a rich, many-eyed book that ought to be looked into." Selden Rodman urged readers of *The Saturday Review* to try it, with the warning that it was a book that would not appeal to the average reader. "Take the opening pages," he wrote.

"If the reader does not like the kind of naked realism which is the truth as Walker Evans' camera-eye sees it, he is through before he even reaches the text." Lionel Trilling was almost alone in his ability to see beyond the book's immediate experience and to proclaim its place in history. Writing for *Kenyon Review,* he called it "the most important moral effort of our American generation."

These generally positive and well-placed reviews did little to boost sales, however, to no one's surprise. The war in Europe was spreading; American troops might soon be sent to join the Allies. There was nothing less on the minds of the American reader, nor more gratefully forgotten, than the Depression. *Let Us Now Praise Famous Men* sold about six hundred copies in its first year of publication. Not much later, it could be found on the remainder shelf for as little as nineteen cents. To Agee, this was all as it should be. The book's commercial failure meant that he had succeeded in protecting his subjects from journalistic exploitation and himself from the sins of success.

Agee was in love again, this time with a tall, sturdy Austrian, Mia Fritsch, who was a member of the research team at *Fortune.* He was still married and sending money to Alma and Joel in Mexico, but there was little chance of their return.

Though both Walker and Jane were reluctant to legalize their happy cohabitation, new insecurities had cropped up, which the prospect of marriage seemed to assuage. Jane was single again, having obtained a divorce from Paul Ninas earlier that year, and Walker, as an unmarried man, was eligible for the military draft. It appeared unlikely that the United States could stay out of the world war, and Walker felt no urge to play his patriotic part in it. In October 1941 they decided on the spur of the moment to get married.

They announced their intentions to Walker's family while they were visiting the Brewers in Chevy Chase. Walker's mother had left Washington to move in with the Brewers following a wild shopping spree in Europe, which had depleted her savings. Walker coolly informed his family of his wedding plans but insisted that they not participate. Instead, he invited Charles Fuller, who was stationed in Washington on an architectural job for the government, to be their only witness at a brisk Methodist ceremony in Rockville, Maryland. On the way back to Chevy Chase, Walker predicted that his sister would produce nothing more than an ordinary bottle of champagne from People's Drugstore to celebrate the occasion. Sure enough, the drugstore champagne was there to toast the newlyweds; they duly popped and drank it, and that was the end of that. Jane and Talbot Brewer were relieved that Walker had finally married. In spite of being a divorcée, Jane was, in their view, a nice girl from a proper background, and a great deal more compatible with the family than the dubious arty type they might have expected Walker to bring home. Even his mother seemed not to mind that her only son finally belonged to another woman.

For her part, Jane was not eager to confront her parents with the man who had helped to cause her divorce. Nevertheless, when the newlyweds traveled to the Midwest to visit Philip Rahv, who was teaching at the University of Chicago, she bravely proposed that they go on to Fond du Lac to visit her family. But Walker refused; he had things to do in Chicago, he said, and he sent Jane off with an unlikely excuse for his absence. For one reason or another, the opportunity for Walker to meet Jane's parents never arose again.

Like their first outings together, up the River Road, Walker and Jane's honeymoon was the result of a photography assignment. Since the spring of 1941, the indefatigable Ernestine Evans had been trying to engage Walker in a new book project. A journalist named Karl Bickel was writing a traveler's history of the west coast of Florida and needed a section of photographs. Ernestine unequivocally recommended Walker Evans for the job. "He's the most difficult artist except [Edward] Weston in the country to deal with; but also he's so damned difficult and uncommercial that his product is endlessly interesting," she wrote. Still enjoying a rest from the trials of publishing *Let Us Now Praise Famous Men*, Walker was reluctant at first to encourage Ernestine's efforts. But, typically, Ernestine would not take no for an answer. "Now [Evans] says he can't and won't," she reported to Bickel, "but I am allowing him another three days to reconsider."

Upon reconsideration, he decided the assignment was hard to turn down. For one thing, he needed the money — the funds from his Guggenheim fellowship extension were running dangerously low — and for another, the project would allow him to spend a few weeks of winter traveling the coast of Florida with Jane.

Though the subject matter of Bickel's book (natural history and early Florida history) held little interest for Evans, the project offered an opportunity for cultural satire. Having been the winter hideaway of millionaires in the boom-time 1920s, Florida's coastline now carried the tainted aura of big-time bankruptcy. In its new incarnation, Florida was rapidly becoming the most densely populated middle-class retirement state in the union. In the cracks between the extravagant past and the overcrowded present, Evans found what he wanted. Along the waterways, Spanish haciendas and byzantine palaces were falling into ruin, while in trailer parks retirees sat contentedly on the porches, overlooking fake flamingos and unlikely flora, and discontented-looking tourists had their pictures taken in front of plastic palm trees and pelicans.

Jane took out her sketchpad in Tampa, where they visited the Ringling Brothers circus, wintering in the South. Walker photographed the elephants in rehearsal, absurdly posed in a daisy-chain formation, and the spindly-necked, cow-eyed giraffes, coupled and caged, matching the slender palm trees. He loved the old circus wagons, with their pseudo-Baroque figures and carved wood friezes chipped and eroding after years of cross-country travel. Jane knew enough never to suggest to Walker what he should photograph, but it was another matter to ask him to make a picture for her to work from. In Tarpon Springs, she had the urge to paint a picture of a hollow sponge-diver's suit hanging, like an augury of death, from a shopkeeper's shingle. The photographs Walker made of it were among the best he brought home.

For Evans, *The Mangrove Coast*, as the book was called, was a winter vacation and a few badly needed dollars in his pocket, but assignments like this were far too few to keep a married man and his wife feeling secure. The honeymooners were on the beach on December 7 when the radio announced the stunning news that the Japanese had bombed Pearl Harbor. The next day the United States joined the war in full force. Insecurity of one kind or another prevailed as FDR enlisted troops in 1942. Rationing was imposed. Even photographic film was harder to come by. Friends included one another when they had saved enough ration tickets for a nice thick steak, which Evans craved. Jane planted a victory garden on the Voorheeses' land in Connecticut and tended it like a nurse.

Many people Evans knew, including Ben Shahn, were in Washington again, looking for war work or drumming up war-related projects. There seemed to be several possible entrées for Evans, and with Shahn's encouragement he went down to discuss them. People related to the Museum of Modern Art who had supported him in the past — Tom Mabry, Henry Russell Hitchcock, Eddie Cahill — were all there to help connect him to a paying job. There was poster work with one government organization; there was an opening for an officer in a navy darkroom. Evans was even desperate enough, he told Jane, to have dinner with Roy Stryker, whose historical section had merged with the Office of War Information. But no jobs came of this brief descent on Washington.

Finally, in the spring of 1943, Evans got a job that was worth waiting for, one that would exercise his unsatisfied urge to write. During the war Wilder Hobson was placed in charge of the arts and entertainment section of *Time* magazine, otherwise known as the back of the book. With a number of staff writers on military leave, Hobson found a place for Evans as a contributing editor. His first assignment was as movie critic.

Time was twenty years old when Evans first appeared on its masthead. It was the first magazine launched by Henry Luce, beginning in 1923, and it was also the first magazine of its kind — a weekly digest of world and national news. Luce's partner, Briton Hadden, had been mainly responsible for what soon became known as Timestyle, a predictable set of literary effects which the writers of its brief essays learned to exploit. Hadden had even come up with his own vocabulary, borrowed from various foreign languages. During the 1920s, for example, he introduced *tycoon*, from the Japanese word meaning "great lord." Timestyle was cogent, witty, and worldly-wise. It had a way of suggesting that its writers knew what they were talking about, intimately. Writers used it to imply an impudent familiarity with famous figures by candidly describing their character and physical appearance and including their nicknames in parentheses, such as "the tennis champion Helen ('Poker Face') Wills." Personalities were almost invariably awarded a list of adjectives strung before or after their names, preferably adjectives beginning with the same letter, such as "mocking, mordant, misanthropic George Bernard Shaw." Another Timestyle idiosyncrasy was the backward-running sentence, with the main subject and verb at the end, such as "Forth from the White House followed by innumerable attendants, Mr. and Mrs. Warren Harding set out." Writing for *Time* was hardly an opportunity for creative writing or in-depth reporting; nor did it lead to fame — no writer was given a byline. But it was an exercise in clarity, wit, and persuasion as well as an opportunity to air one's opinions.

When Evans joined the editorial staff in the spring of 1943, Jim Agee had written the film column for a year and was now dividing his criticism between *Time* and *The Nation*. James Stern, an Englishman who joined *Time*'s editorial staff just a few months before Evans, remembered the day he passed Jim Agee's office and noticed him bent over his desk, with Evans beside him, equally intent, getting his lesson in the basics of Timestyle.

It was a stroke of good timing that Evans was hired the same year that T. S. Matthews became *Time*'s managing editor and promoted a subtle elevation in style. Slender and handsome, Matthews was the son of an heiress to the Procter & Gamble fortune and an Episcopal minister. As a graduate of Princeton and Oxford, he had hoped to become a poet. When Henry Luce hired him as managing editor, he warned his boss frankly that he remained more interested in poetry than politics. Furthermore, he was not afraid to tell Luce that "as a reader and a writer, I consider *Time* badly written, which means, in *Time*'s language, misinformative."

Instead of encouraging rude character sketches and acrobatic prose, Matthews was a strict grammarian and a stickler for clarity. At the same time, he was stuck with the basic format of the typical *Time* article. On any subject, the writers were to give a brief biographical background of their subjects, to run through the information with synoptic efficiency, keeping their prose terse and to the point, and finally to toss in the unexpected word or dash of color.

Evans' interest in film was not limited to high-brow and documentary movies. He came equipped with several years of moviegoing behind him, as well as countless hours of talk with Agee on the subject. Furthermore, his dream of making movies himself still lingered in the back of his mind.

In the early 1940s, war movies were the general fare. Whether fiction or document, romantic drama or musical comedy, few films escaped the ubiquitous theme or context of war. One of Evans' first review columns, in April 1943, featured the documentary *Desert Victory,* a collaboration between 20th Century-Fox and the British Army Film and Photographic Unit. Evans admired the director, David Mac-Donald, a "shy Scotsman," and particularly liked the movie's four-and-a-half-minute real-life sequence of artillery fire, "one thing Hollywood could not supply."

In May of the same year he also thoroughly enjoyed *The Ox-Bow Incident,* featuring Henry Fonda in one of his most famous roles, as a cattle puncher in a small town in Nevada. In "Walter Van Tilburg Clark's excellent sagebrush yarn," Evans found only "the occasional thoughtless detail," like the fake tree constructed for the crucial lynching scene. A vigilant critic of fakery and slickness, he was quick to identify the same problem with *Five Graves to Cairo,* for which "a packaging job of high sheen fails to conceal the fact that there is very little product inside." *Action in the North Atlantic,* starring Humphrey Bogart, was in Evans' opinion "a symphony of heaving, buckling studio sets, dubious ship-model photography and explosions in the sound track." By the same token, wherever he perceived authenticity and understatement, he cheered. In *Bataan,* a Metro-Goldwyn-Mayer war drama, he praised the only moment when the noisy soundtrack falls silent and "for a moment . . . Hollywood's war takes on the tense, classic values of understatement."

Evans was not critical of props and stagecraft when he felt they suited the show. In the color extravaganza *Coney Island,* he cheerfully admired the period-piece scenery and garish color assault. "The Technicolor cameras of this picture will turn many a spectator green with envy," he wrote. "They have been allowed a prolonged fondling of Betty Grable." And when the mood was light, Evans was fluent in puns. Reviewing *Mister Big,* "a fatuous romp celebrating the national affliction known as jitterbugging," he warned, "Mature audiences who commit the indiscretion of attending this picture will be apt to feel that the punishment zoots the crime."

He was not strictly limited to reviewing films. When *Time*'s press column decided to feature an exhibition of the work of the combat photographer Eliot Elisofon at the Museum of Modern Art, Evans was sent to review it. He gave his younger colleague a respectful critique. Combat photography was one thing he knew he could never brave. While other photographers marched into the fray — W. Eugene Smith flew in raids over Tokyo, Robert Capa waded with the troops onto Omaha Beach, and Margaret Bourke-White survived a torpedo attack in the Mediterranean — Evans was safely tucked away with his typewriter on the fiftieth floor of the Time-Life Building at Rockefeller Center. The weekly deadline was his only threat.

As a writer for *Time,* Evans was finally exercising his verbal talent along with his critical eye. For the two years he was employed at the magazine, his social life revolved around his fellow writers and editors, and his conversation, as Jane recalled, was continuously lured back to Time Inc. shoptalk. But for conversation, he could not have hoped for better than that of his colleagues at the magazine — some temporary war replacements, others full-time staff members, all discerning and talented writers: Hamilton Basso, Saul Bellow, Nigel Dennis, John Hersey, Louis Kronenberger, Whittaker Chambers, and Winthrop Sargeant. Almost none were professional journalists or ever wanted to be. Down the corridor of the fiftieth floor, the doors of the writers' offices were almost always open, encouraging a free exchange of information and opinion, ribaldry and gossip. The pay was decent and the hours lenient. To relieve the pressures of work, the writers relaxed over long, bibulous lunches in midtown Italian restaurants. Jimmy Stern recalled one such gathering place in particular:

> The morning hours over, some of us, seldom fewer than four, more often six or eight, breaking open one more pack of Camels, would swiftly fall the fifty floors to the teeming street, and hasten round the

block to the Ristorante del Pezzo. In my memory, no matter how many of us turned up, we invariably sat at one large round table, which Nigel and I called our *Stammtisch,* in this most excellent of Italian restaurants . . . In this civilized atmosphere, its comfort and decor so fin-de-siècle Europe, so remote from that lofty, over-heated clinical cage of our labours, who could help but rest and revel?

In July 1943, when Stern moved over to book reviewing, Evans took his place as art critic, approaching the subject with as much verve as he had the movies. The war hung equally over events in the art world. Evans wrote about the Metropolitan Museum's plans for storing its masterpieces in case of an attack and the National Gallery's exhibition of contemporary war paintings. Wartime gave him ample opportunity to meditate on one of his favorite images, the architectural ruin. During the Christmas season of 1943 he singled out *The Bombed Buildings,* a recently published book containing 270 photographs of war-torn public buildings in London. The book was not so much a protest as an appreciation of the particular aesthetic of the ruined state. Evans called it "a handsome record of destruction" and added his conviction that "many of these charred, strewn, gaping images, signed by such names as Wren, Adam, Nash, Soane, and Stuart, make a moving reaffirmation of their dignity and style. Ruin sometimes adds beauty as well as pathos."

For the most part, Evans seems to have followed his personal interests freely as an art critic. His developing Anglophilia would have suited his Oxford-educated editor, not to mention an American readership now united with Britain in war. Combining this with his fondness for caricature, he devoted one article to the "raffish" Thomas Rowlandson of eighteenth-century England, and another to Rowland Emmet of *Punch,* "a daft satiric cartoonist in the English tradition of Max Beerbohm and Edward Lear," whose theme, the railway, was a favorite of Evans'. He also chose to highlight the humorous drawings of *The New Yorker*'s Whitney Darrow, whose subjects included "the laughable aspects of human underwear, the drastic results of heavy, middle-aged drinking, and the leering onset of sex in very small Boy Scouts," as well as those of the "famous comic master of neurasthenia," James Thurber. Evans took note of the emerging talent of Saul

Steinberg, a Romanian refugee who had just published his first book of wartime drawings. And when George Herriman, the creator of "Krazy Kat," died, Evans praised him as a master of originality as both draftsman and writer: "The Elizabethan talk and supralunar world of Krazy Kat were entirely Herriman's own, a private universe of fantasy, irony, weird characterization, odd beauty." Evans was perhaps not the first critic to compare Herriman's inventive use of language to Joyce's distortions in *Finnegans Wake*. Further endearing Herriman to Evans was his immovable modesty: "He remained effortlessly unpretentious, indestructibly innocent."

As an art critic, Evans did not sway from his deeply held convictions about what gave his own best work its superior edge. Much of this had to do with his lasting suspicion of self-conscious artiness, and it was no doubt for this reason that he favored cartoonists, illustrators, and amateur painters (such as Winston Churchill), all safe from the pretentious "chill" of the art museum. He also wrote about children's art — "Snooksology" — with complete seriousness. And when he did address the great figures in art history, it was almost invariably in the form of a review of a scholarly book, such as Erwin Panofsky's recently published volume on Dürer or the new folio-size book on Leonardo da Vinci published by the Phaidon Press. Always, Evans was attentive not only to the work and the personality of both artist and writer but to the quality of the book's design and production.

He was just as adept as the next *Time* writer at ushering in his subjects on the requisite carpet of adjectives. "Erect, frail, handsome Edvard Munch came from a family of civil servants"; "Stone-deaf, crop-haired, twinkling Dorothy Brett is known to her friends as The Brett"; "In the 1930s affable, active Charles Dana Gibson took to oil painting"; "Aristocratic, cantankerous Edgar Degas was a difficult man" — such chatty introductions as these seem to have been written with the routine lightheartedness of a longtime staff writer.

Time was not the place for Evans to go deeply into the subject of art, even if he had wanted to, but it suited him to keep up-to-date with the galleries and bookstores in midtown and to champion what he felt deserved an appreciative audience. He saved most of his efforts for the things he admired, but occasionally he came upon an opportunity for subtly derisive sarcasm aimed at a long-awaited victim, such as Alfred Stieglitz and his wife, Georgia O'Keeffe.

By this time O'Keeffe was the best-known woman artist in the United States. Her work, Evans had decided, was woefully predictable. "The 16 smooth-surfaced canvases were standard O'Keeffe," he wrote of her exhibition at An American Place in 1945,

> quasi-mystical, highly polished designs inspired by New Mexican land-scapes and still lifes. There was the bald roll and wrinkle of creviced hills, *Black Place III,* suggesting the convolutions of the human brain. There was the shock of a swatch of blue sky seen through the gape of sun-baked bones, *Pelvis III.* There also were canvases which seemed to represent nothing whatsoever in nature: skillfully colored symbolic forms that were sure to stir the imaginations of most gallery-goers.

Evans broadly hinted that O'Keeffe's success, under the steady nurturance of Stieglitz, was a family affair. "Dealer Stieglitz also handles all O'Keeffe sales," he wrote. "These are usually accompanied by a resounding clang of the cash register." But there was more to owning an O'Keeffe than cash, he warned, with the pleasure of popping an exclusive, high-art balloon. "The money must be accompanied by certain spiritual, emotional, and intellectual qualifications satisfactory to Dealer Stieglitz."

As much as Evans enjoyed the opportunity to applaud or to poke fun at the current events of the art world, writing for *Time* was hard work, and conforming to the magazine's style and format over the course of two years was ultimately degrading to his naturally independent spirit. Now he knew better what Agee had suffered over the years at the service of Henry Luce. As he later reflected, "You had to figure out how not to die."

8 *Fortune*

WITH THE END of the war in 1945, Time Inc.'s substitute writers found themselves in the job market again. Evans wrote his last review, on the first postwar art show to be held in Berlin, for the issue of August 20, 1945, and with that his career as a professional critic came to an end. By that time he felt that he had been "drained dry." But for once he did not have to languish in doubt about his next paying job. He was now part of the inner circle of Time Inc.'s editorial staff, and there were many in Luce's media empire who not only believed in his special talents as a photographer but enjoyed having him around. In September 1945 he was transferred to *Fortune* to become the magazine's only staff photographer, a position he would hold for the next twenty years.

While the pay was not as good as *Fortune*'s name suggested, there was not a more luxurious magazine in terms of production quality that a photographer could hope to work for. Its eleven-by-fourteen-inch format was the largest in the industry; its pages were the heaviest. While the classic wide-margin "book" style of *Fortune*'s early years had been somewhat modified by the 1940s, the magazine was still printed by the sheet-fed gravure process, which could seamlessly combine rich matte-finish pages of black-and-white photography and bold display type with glossy full-color graphics and drawings. In particular, *Fortune* had perfected the so-called industry portfolio, in which factories, power stations, dams, and turbines were depicted in the clear light and with the sharp angles of modernist photography, with clouds of smoke and steam enlivening the air around them. Margaret Bourke-White, William Ritasse, Fenno Jacobs, Horace Bristol, and William Vandivert were among those most frequently hired on a freelance basis to peer with their cameras, as *Fortune*'s prospectus put it, into the "dazzling furnaces" of American industry.

The Walker Evans of *American Photographs* might have struck some readers as an unlikely employee of a magazine dedicated to glorifying American finance. At the beginning of an optimistic postwar business boom, his appointment was all the more unlikely. During the war, while Evans was writing for *Time,* a shift had taken place in American photography that was incompatible with his instincts. Photojournalism dominated the profession, keeping pace with the increasing popularity of the picture magazines. *Life, Look, Collier's,* and *The Saturday Evening Post* served a vast and growing audience eager for "real life" stories told in photographs. This trend, which had its beginnings in Depression reportage and government-sponsored documentary projects such as those of the FSA, had a new kind of story to tell. The magazines were blatantly at the service of middle-class values, and as such displayed a supreme confidence in the American economy. They abounded in cheerful reports about the American family, the American teenager, the American housewife, the American commuter, and above all the rising American standard of living. The photography for these stories was brightly lit and often staged, its content dictated by the generally upbeat editorial tone. *Life* especially was known for its sensational photo coverage of poverty, violence, and the oppression of people not fortunate enough to be middle-class Americans. Walker Evans, with his aversion to overstatement, his dedication to the unposed, and his interest in uncovering those aspects of the culture that were cast off, forgotten, or obscured from popular view, was out of date.

But *Fortune* could afford to take the high road. Just as Luce believed that a poet could write about business, the artist with a camera could enhance the interest of and give tone to the same concerns. It had already been proven that *Fortune*'s best employees were often its riskiest ones, James Agee being a prime example. Furthermore, Evans could now add to the already considerable status of *Fortune*'s editorial profile with a Guggenheim fellowship, a one-man exhibition at the Museum of Modern Art, and a book coauthored with Agee to his credit.

At the beginning of his tenure as staff photographer, Evans was usually pressed into service for a particular story for which other visual material had already been gathered. Some assignments were dull: "The Adventures of Henry and Joe in Autoland" required him to make a series of head-on portraits of businessmen at their desks. Others gave him an excuse to visit old friends. One of his first assignments was to expand on a story called "The Boom in Ballet," which included a portrait session with ballet's foremost American impresario, Lincoln Kirstein, as well as informal photographs in the rehearsal halls of Kirstein's New York ballet school.

In general, the writer of a *Fortune* story did not choose his photographer, nor vice versa, but happy coincidences sometimes occurred. In the spring of 1946, Wilder Hobson (having moved back from *Time* to join *Fortune*'s board of editors) was assigned an article on American housing and Evans was asked to research the photographs. Under Evans' editorial direction, "Homes of Americans" became a study in eclecticism. He dug up a photograph of the most minimal of Shaker interiors to compare with Mrs. Cornelius Vanderbilt's architecturally encrusted Victorian drawing room. On a two-page spread he made a patchwork of small photographs, slipping in several of his own, including a photograph of the Burroughses' tenant farmhouse in Alabama. On the next to last page he took the opportunity to showcase a new international-style house in New Jersey designed by his old friend Paul Grotz.

On another occasion Evans was assigned to a story about the Kennecott Copper and Brass Company in Connecticut, a prospect that would have been quite unappealing if the writer had not been his friend John McDonald. As McDonald recalled, it was the morning after a late night of partying that the two of them piled into Evans' jet-black Buick convertible and traveled up to Connecticut to meet the copper and brass people. In order to start the meeting in a friendly way, the journalists planned to meet the executives at the local golf club for a quick round. Evans was not a very good golfer anyway, in McDonald's estimation, and there was no question that his performance was even less impressive when he had a hangover. At his first turn he "whiffed" — his club didn't even touch the ball. A sudden thunderstorm saved him from further embarrassment. Later, in the middle of the informal portrait session with the Kennecott executives at their desks, his camera refused to function. Somehow, *Fortune*'s art department pieced together what remained of the aborted session.

Evans grumbled about the drudgery of some of his *Fortune* work, but from early on he was given at least as much freedom as the magazine's veteran staff writers. Time Inc.'s laboratory assistants took care of his darkroom work, and he was encouraged to direct his job toward some of his own ongoing photographic projects. In the summer of 1946 he drove out to the Midwest "on a felicitous mission," explained Time Inc.'s in-house journal, *FYI*, "to follow, on behalf of *Fortune*, where his sharp eye led him."

Evans was still on the trail of the *Faces of Men* project he had proposed to the Guggenheim Foundation in 1941, and the full-scale portrait of the American scene he had conjured with as early as 1934 remained incomplete. "American city is what I'm after," he had written to Ernestine Evans, "so might use several, keeping things typical. The right things can be found in Pittsburgh, Toledo, Detroit (a lot in Detroit, I want to get in some dirty cracks, Detroit's full of chances). Chicago business stuff . . ." From the photographs he brought back from Detroit and Chicago in 1946 he composed his first two credited portfolios in *Fortune.*

Evans returned to Chicago with the perspective of nearly thirty years in New York. The city was rundown compared to its heyday in the early part of the century, when he first encountered it as a young boy. And from his more mature point of view, he believed it deserved to be. "Chicago is the only great city in the world to which all its citizens have come for the avowed object of making money," he quoted Henry B. Fuller, of his parents' generation, as saying. Demonstrating the ongoing fallacy of that object, he explored various areas of the city that had once been grand and now were neglected. He photographed giant "serio-comic" sculptures on the site of the Century of Progress Exposition of 1933, overgrown with weeds; he discovered a solitary abandoned townhouse on Chicago's South Side, once the city's Gold Coast, its ornate porte-cochère a memento of better days; and from various angles he viewed a crescent of classical columns indiscriminately overshadowed by a towering Pabst Blue Ribbon signboard. All of his images attest to a city impatient for progress for its own sake, without a clear sense of the attendant responsibilities — a city, in the words of Evans, "decaying in a sort of corporeal self-strangulation."

In Chicago and Detroit, Evans also added to his ongoing series of street portraits. Like the photographs he made on the subway, his street portraiture was meant to be "pure record," with the photographer avoiding any personal interaction between himself and his subject. In both cities he abandoned artistic control by assigning himself a fixed position on a downtown street corner and shooting discreetly from waist level, not with a concealed 35mm camera this time but looking down into the viewfinder of a twin-lens reflex Rollie. In Detroit most of his subjects were men in shirtsleeves, a chance, average cross-section of workers passing diagonally across his picture plane in a lottery he called "Labor Anonymous." In Chicago, Evans chose a busy downtown shopping district, where more of his subjects were women, elaborately hatted, furred, and feathered, wearing big dark glasses or squinting into the sun. Marching like armed soldiers for an afternoon of shopping, they headed straight for the camera, unaware of the spy who would take them home to study as the unmitigated evidence of a materialist society. But while Evans aimed at an impartial study, he could not resist rigging the shooting sessions to his own point of view, and the photographs betray his sexual prejudices, held since childhood. While the men in "Labor Anonymous" are hardworking and unpretentious, the women in "Chicago: A Camera Exploration" are frivolous, encumbered, and overbearing.

At the Art Institute of Chicago, the curator of prints, Carl Schniewind, took note of Evans' Chicago photographs when they appeared in the

February 1947 issue of *Fortune*. Schniewind, whose field of expertise
was Old Master prints, believed that photography was integral to his
department's program. He wrote to Evans of the institute's interest
in mounting a small retrospective of Evans' work, adding that he
hoped that the exhibition would be "somewhat like holding a mirror
up to the people of Chicago. I feel they need it." Evans wholeheartedly
agreed. "Let's shake Chicago back down to the swamps from which
it grew," he replied.

Evans' trip to the Midwest was by no means born of a nostalgic
urge. Approaching middle age, he remained determined to leave his
past behind him. By this time what remained of his family was widely
scattered. The Brewers were moving from Washington to Florida
because of Jane's respiratory problems. As her mother's caretaker, she
had reached the end of her patience. After years of Jessie's domineer-
ing manner and constant criticism, Jane suffered a mental breakdown. In the mid-1940s she and her husband persuaded Jessie to
move to southern California, to live near her two younger brothers,
Ralph and Bob Crane, and their families.

When Evans traveled for the first time to southern California in
the summer of 1947, he commanded his sister not to let their mother
know; he was not sure he would have either the time or the inclina-
tion to see her. In the meantime, there was much to distract him
from his family. The trip was sponsored by Florence Homolka, a
Washington newspaper heiress in the midst of a divorce from the
actor Oscar Homolka. John Becker, who had not forgotten Evans'
photography since exhibiting his work in 1931, had recommended
Evans as Florence's private photography tutor.

En route to California by train, Evans was thrilled by the geological
wonders and otherworldly light of New Mexico, which he attempted
to convey to Jane by letter, excitedly describing "the gigantic fantastic
red rock formations under turquoise sky with pure white clouds
floating high. Holy Cats." He was so entranced by the desert scenery
that he tried to capture the experience with his camera, spending
most of one day at the open door between coaches as the train rocked
its way west.

As for Hollywood and Beverly Hills, he was prepared to be cynical.

Well before his train arrived in Los Angeles, "the awful California stuff set in," he told Jane — "oranges, roadside motels, moderne gasa-lube stations, old and croaking people, sunshine, fear, blood, sweat and tears." Evans was less interested in Florence Homolka than in her pocketbook, her connections, and the temporary luxuries of her large house in Beverly Hills, where he was invited to stay — "Gardens, patios, telephones, mirrors, art and books all over the place. Slices of cold roast beef one inch thick, absolutely tasteless." There was plenty of time for him to cast his critical eye around, as well as to escape to the beach. "It is of course spectacular," he wrote to Jane. "High clay bluff, enormous surf, lotsa young beautiful blond tanned boys and girls all tall clear and vacant like the roast beef." The whole experience reminded Evans of his "Riviera period," which made him wince. Sitting poolside at one of the expensive Beverly Hills hotels, eating a club sandwich, attended by a white-coated Filipino waiter, and sere-naded with piped-in music playing an Offenbach waltz, occasionally interrupted by the loudspeaker paging one of his fellow sunbathers to the telephone, he felt as much the outsider as he had in a Paris café twenty years earlier.

But one evening Evans was offered the proverbial insider's view of Hollywood — a private movie screening. The film, "a five-episode contraption," was not especially good, but the evening yet held prom-ise. After the screening Evans was included in a party at the Hal Roach studios, where he recognized such movie-world celebrities as Jean Renoir, Clifford Odets, and Sono Osato. But the brightest star was yet to come. After "a long, mysterious wait," he recounted to Jane, "in trotted a little bouncing white headed man accompanied by a flashing lovely in shy blue evening wraps — Chaplin and Oona." Evans looked on in fascination as Chaplin displayed both his show-manship and his awareness of his magnetic power to hold the room hushed and hanging on his every gesture. A party never began until Chaplin arrived, Evans was later to explain to Jane, and never ended before he left.

A day after having a tooth pulled, Evans braced himself for his last act in California — the dreaded visit to Pasadena to see his mother, "which was a much worse experience than the tooth-pulling, I can

tell you, kiddo," he wrote home to Jane. Having made contact with
the Cranes, he had little choice but to endure three days of their
excruciating company. He suffered dinners, lunches, and road trips,
dull food and suffocating conversation. "I wasn't quite prepared for
the degradation I found — age, relative poverty, mental deterioration — in all of them in the older generation, and deep-dyed narrow
provinciality in the younger ones." The Robert Cranes, he told Jane,
were once "pretty hot stuff," but no longer. "It's really interesting how
fast the top bourgeois crust can melt, and how empty, in this period,
and finished it is anyway."

"Chicago: A Portfolio by Walker Evans" covered eight full pages in
the February 1947 issue of *Fortune*. Evans was generally pleased with
the results, but problems of presentation and layout — most of all
how his pictures seemed to be crowded onto the page — still nagged
at him. But it would not be long before he was granted greater control
over his portfolios. In 1948 he was given new status as *Fortune*'s special
photographic editor. This title coincided with one of Luce's many calls
for a general rethinking of the magazine. Advertising revenue was
down; subscriptions were falling off. Readers complained that the
articles had become fragmented; there were no new ideas. The same
could be said for the look of the magazine. As part of his new plan,
Luce suggested that they offer the readers "light and leading" articles
instructing them on the ways of American business. The managing
editor, Ralph Delahaye Paine, transferred from *Life*, was not inclined
to agree with his boss. "The acres of half-baked, wrong-headed, soft-
headed, trite and repetitious 'light and leading' I have cut out of the
manuscripts of some of my more distinguished associates!" he wrote
to Luce. Paine's aversion to soft-headed, trite, and repetitious writing
was matched by his approval of the impartial realism of Evans'
photographs and the belief that Evans should help to direct *Fortune*'s
new thinking about photography.

Paine informed his staff that Evans' new responsibility was, in loose
terms, "to develop a distinctive photography for the new *Fortune*."
This job, he went on to say, would in some cases put Evans in charge
of the photography and layout of the article, albeit with the final

approval of the art director. At last Evans had been given the kind of editorial power he had sought with Agee at *Life* ten years earlier. His photography would be integrated with his exacting taste in graphic design; the writing from then on would be, in almost every case, his own. And Paine was there to support him. "I bespeak the complete cooperation of both editorial and art department staffs in the important creative task that Walker has undertaken," concluded Paine in his memo to the staff.

For at least a while, Evans took his job as special photographic editor seriously. Here was an opportunity to point out that the quality of photography in the magazine lagged way behind the quality of its writing. Much of the photography being used was just a dated and weakened version of the original style of *Fortune* photography — the stylish black-and-white portrayal of American industry, an approach that Evans disliked but that he acknowledged had had its strength when new. Now he felt that in general the layouts were pinched, the photographs too plentiful, the imagery dull and methodical. In a lengthy memorandum to Paine, Evans spelled out his critique: "You would never use a cluttered, confusing piece of prose. By the same token I would like to see you throw out any photograph that does not properly invite the eye." Acknowledging that the literary mind was in charge of Time Inc., he wished to encourage that mind to alter its thinking about the visual, and to teach his managing editor to "read" a photograph. "*Fortune* photographs should take a long look at a subject, get into it, and without shouting, tell a lot about it."

Evans was describing the kind of photography he not only aspired to personally but hoped to encourage from others. Photography, he had recently declared in a brief written "opinion," "has a voice, in which its tone and style range from declamation to murmur, enunciation to lisp and stutter." Suggesting a literary vocabulary for photographic criticism, he maintained that the masters of the medium "control diction and wield wit and fashion metaphor: they almost can pun, and even do achieve oxymora." He asserted that at its peak, the camera could make poetry. Finally, he wrote, in assessing the quality of a photograph, one should ask that it be "literate, authoritative, and transcendent."

Photographing with precise attention to the commonplace delivered the kind of detached factual record that Evans valued — pictures
that begged the reader to look again. A typical corner of a typical
factory town contained all the wealth of detail a writer needed for
the opening of a classic American story, Evans explained to Paine,
using the example of one of his own photographs: "There is the
profitable and well-run cracker factory in the sweaty part of town,
there is a knot of men talking on the pavement about anything but
crackers, amidst the irrelevant trucks. This is where Mal-o-Mars are
cooked and this is where last week's newspaper meets the gutter too.
And the Strand Hotel becomes Famous for Flavor." This eclectic mix
of information, delivered in even, unspectacular description, exemplified to Evans those photographs that were "quiet and true."

Evans' new status at *Fortune* coincided with a gap in the leadership
of the art department. Will Burtin had left the magazine, and Leo
Lionni, a designer of Dutch birth and Spanish ancestry, was rede-
signing "the book" on a freelance basis. By the time Lionni was made
full-time art director, Evans was well ensconced in his own self-de-
signed program. "For a long time I didn't even know he was part of
my staff," Lionni recalled. "I think he was considered to be sort of
on a retainer, semi-retired — he could come in or not come in. I
didn't see him for weeks at a time." Less of a purist than his Bauhaus-
trained predecessor, Lionni tolerated and even enjoyed Evans' unconventional taste and learned to ignore his working habits. He knew
that Evans had to be given his head. "Whatever he put forward,"
Lionni said, "was fine with me."

In a pointedly offbeat beginning to his career as *Fortune*'s special
photographic editor, Evans' first picture story was a portfolio of
antique postcards drawn from his private collection. On four pages
of gravure-printed color reproductions, the May 1948 issue published
a handful of Evans' most cherished examples, accompanied by his
first credited text for the magazine. In an effort to educate the reader
as to the value of these modest collectibles, he suggested how much
the postcards had to say about the era in which they had first
flourished ("the trolley car period"), the innocent pride of the small-
town dweller in his local courthouse or main street, the truthful,
unglamorous scenes admired by the typical Yankee traveler. Evans

also included an example of the occasional staged melodramas he deemed exceptional. Analyzing this woodland scene of quarreling lovers, he betrayed his delight in its old-fashioned romance, closing his essay with the query "How, with his masculine logic, did that pitiable male come up against the maddening cross-purposes met beneath that intractable sailor straw?"

Evans' new status also gave him an opportunity to introduce the kind of photographer he admired and enjoyed working with to the magazine. When Ralph Steiner returned to New York in 1948 from a stint of moviemaking in Hollywood, his photography portfolio was five years old, "and it might as well have been one hundred," Steiner admitted, so completely had he lost touch with commercial New York. Evans saw his chance to help an old friend who had once helped him, as well as to unload one of his most dreaded and pre-dictable photographic tasks — making the full-page color portraits of corporate heads that were featured in the magazine every month, known around the office as "super face." Steiner easily mastered the demands of this assignment, and he was immensely grateful for the job. Evans kept sending assignments his way and sometimes joined him on his travels. Steiner noted, however, that Evans never showed the slightest curiosity about the results of his efforts, and concluded that he just enjoyed traveling at *Fortune*'s expense.

Evans also gave the photographer Tod Webb several assignments for *Fortune,* one of which was on the New York garment industry. Webb vividly recalled that it happened to be election day 1948 when he set out with Evans for the garment district. The votes had not yet been completely counted, but the eager press, including *Time, Life,* and *Fortune,* had confidently predicted a landslide victory for Dewey over Truman. In a preelection issue, *Life* had even gone so far as to caption a photograph of Dewey as "the next president." Visiting a garment factory, Evans and Webb stood amazed as the news came over the radio that Harry Truman had been elected. Webb remem-bered that the four hundred workers in the vast sewing room mi-raculously brought forth bottles of beer from under their sewing machines, and the two photographers gladly joined in an uproarious celebration.

While his colleagues performed *Fortune*'s assignments, Evans came up with story ideas, but by no means all of them came to fruition. Among the many that never made it onto the page was a photographic portfolio of "street furniture," a term made current by certain English architectural magazines. Fire hydrants, streetlights, mailboxes, park benches, manhole covers, trash baskets, all fell into this category. Whenever Evans came upon an example he thought was especially fine, he took a picture or, lacking his camera, made a note. He covered pages of a pocket spiral notebook with reminders: "DO — Merrit pkwy red signs just before exit 34 (going north) at Long Ridge Road, Greenwich," or "Canal st. kiosk Lex. line NE corner morning sun."

Others of Evans' "patented portfolio ideas" that never appeared in print included the big outdoor sign business, unhappy motoring, business Americana, the awkward age of advertising display, and the business of shopfront lifting. His interest in typography led him into a study of the finer points of "securities art." This could make an interesting portfolio, he explained in a memorandum to editor Hedley Donovan in March 1954: "Three large engraving companies in New York turn out great lots of securities certificates. Very fancy eye-filling stuff. Tearjerking, funny, handsome. Portfolio of samples would be *Fortune*ate. To be luxuriously knockout we might run actual engravings on banknote paper, give the readers a feel of this richness. (We once ran cigar-box art that way, on intaglio, years ago. It was the nuts.)"

By all members of the art department at *Fortune*, Evans was regarded as something of an eccentric. His office, which he shared with the photo editor Seville McCarten, was a small room on the twenty-first floor, right next to the layout room. Predictably, as the deadline for one of his portfolios approached, he would become fanatically attentive to the details of its production. Lionni's assistant, the German-born Walter Allner, attempted to direct him, with little success. "He obviously didn't know how to use a slide rule or calculate enlargements or reductions," Allner explained. Without any training in the techniques of graphic design, Evans could not visualize his portfolio without actually seeing his pictures laid out in several different sizes and arrangements. Tinkering with the possibilities, he would order fifty or sixty photostats. The layout team may have been amused by these methods; *Fortune*'s budget manager, Edward Patrick

Lanahan, was not. When the art department's budget was cut in the early 1950s, Evans was transferred to editorial, but this would not be the end of Lanahan's trials.

At *Fortune*, Evans avoided playing with the team, just as he had in Roy Stryker's historical section. While the general policy around the office was open door and open drawer, McCarten noticed that Evans kept his filing cabinets carefully out of reach of the curious. "A padlocked steel bar was installed from top to bottom of this four-drawer repository of art," she recalled. And while the dress code around the office was casual — even Henry Luce was known to loosen his tie and roll up his sleeves at a meeting — Evans was always buttoned up to the collar. But after all, he did not bother himself with the dull business of in-house meetings or the harried team excitement of going to press. He had his own agenda.

Fortune gave Evans a platform from which to express his values and exercise his eye, and the freedom to travel where his instincts bade him go. He operated as an arbiter of taste, a connoisseur of manmade America. No longer in search of commanding views of small towns like those he had made for the FSA, encompassing detail from where he stood with his camera across the river or down the road and beyond, he now gathered material for his magazine portfolios like a collector of scattered artifacts. He had turned from the prophet of what 1930s America would look like as the past to a retrogressive tastemaker of the 1950s. He singled out objects and features of the American scene as if to rescue them from extinction. "I used to try to figure out precisely what I was seeing all the time," he told an interviewer, "until I discovered I didn't need to. If the thing is there, why, there it is."

With increasing drive, Evans at mid-century sought out the tangible presence of Old World values. On assignment in the summer of 1949, he made a tour of New England hotels. Turning the assignment into an opportunity to reexamine summer scenes from his childhood, he headed north with Jane, all expenses paid. They drove the back roads at a leisurely pace from the North Shore of Massachusetts to the rocky coast of Maine and basked in the vanishing elegance of Victorian hotel life.

In the style of the turn-of-the-century postcard, Evans photographed each rambling wooden building in strong sunlight that
spared no detail. One can almost imagine the hand-drawn arrow
pointing to one of the windows beside the inscription "Our Room."
Then, with his deftest prose, he took the reader inside. Little had
changed since Walker the midwestern schoolboy had first experienced
the charms and embarrassments of the summer hotel; his writing
betrayed his intimacy with the subject as well as the distance he had
learned from the poetry of T. S. Eliot:

> August is their month. These are the weeks they welcome the battle
> for waterfront rooms and the small horrors of dinner table misalli-
> ances. Now the tinkle of the ice-pitchers is louder, the whine of wicker
> heightened. The lending library waiting list is longer for *Point of No
> Return*. Here once more is the fixed, reigning smile worn by the deb-
> utante from Sewickley, Winnetka, Cos Cob. And how to say good
> morning, safely, to the hotel bore? What to do with the forgotten damp
> bathing trunks just at train time?

The more out of step with postwar America a subject was, the more
Evans treasured it. And the more it differed from the hurried, competitive atmosphere of his workplace, the more he was its champion.
From high in the ultramodern Time-Life Building, which Alfred Kazin
described as "a brilliant center magnifying everything like the fluo-
rescent tubes in the elevators, which seethed with excessive brightness," Evans made a case for vintage office furniture — "the roll-top
desk, the scrolled and lettered black-iron safe, the padded and studded swivel chair, the high oaken bookkeeper's perch" — with photographs he had taken in dim, old-fashioned offices he had ferreted out
in Boston, Hartford, and Cincinnati. Riding the local railroad lines
to small towns from Connecticut to Maryland, he made a photographic study of old depots, illuminating their architectural interest:
the conical tower, the mansard roof, the arched ticket window. His
thoughts turned to his childhood in Kenilworth. "He who travels by
rail over the lesser lines of the U.S.A. clangs and shunts straight into
his own childhood," he wrote, noting how the railroad stations now
"seem more and more toylike — as model railroad toys grow more

like the real thing. With only a slight effort of the imagination these encrusted little buildings turn into miniature stage sets, and the people in them become correctly costumed dolls."

To herself, Jane wondered if *Fortune* was spoiling Walker, indulging him in his light schedule and whimsical story ideas. He kept his studio at 1681 York Avenue, but most of his darkroom work was done by assistants. He went to the office every day, but he dawdled all the way, stopping for a long breakfast at Shrafft's. And whenever he went off on assignment, he took as long as possible to get to his destination and back, taking detours and back roads, everywhere alert to his own subject matter; if the season was right, he never failed to pack his golf clubs.

"He was a little on the spoiled side," admitted Leo Lionni. "That's what he wanted. He loved walking around as if he had his own private cloud that stretched out along the corridors when he took his little strolls." Max Gschwind, a designer in the art department, remembered Evans strutting around the offices like "a cross between a stork and a Prussian soldier."

"I once asked Walker how he operated," remembered Ralph Steiner, "since he seemed so little connected with the magazine. He told me that twice a year he would take the managing editor out to lunch and would suggest picture story ideas. They were almost always accepted. And the ideas were usually those which would include a trip that Walker wanted to take." William Hollingsworth Whyte, a young staff writer familiarly known as Holly, also remembered the ease with which Evans got his ideas accepted: "He knew that in Del [Paine] he had a sucker, and he kept him amused." As early in his *Fortune* career as 1947, Evans himself rather boldly confessed to Time Inc.'s *FYI*, "All my life I've wanted nothing so much as leisure."

If Walker Evans was getting spoiled, he was not getting rich. To Jane's despair, however, he was fond of behaving as if he were. Jane never knew how much money he made, only that it was constantly in short supply. While she struggled to keep their household budget in balance, Walker would be off spending the better part of his monthly paycheck on a new shirt or a pair of velvet slippers at J. Press or Brooks Brothers. Holly Whyte, who shared his enthusiasm for well-made shoes, could attest to this special weakness. "It was a big day when we learned that Mr. Piggott of the Peal Company in London would be in New York to see customers," he recalled. Whyte and Evans, both thoroughly enjoying the affectation, would meet Mr. Piggott in a private suite at the Biltmore Hotel to view his wares and settle in for a proper fitting. A few weeks later, their brand-new custom-fitted waxed-calf Peal shoes would arrive in the mail.

As much as Evans delighted in these small luxuries and the appearance of personal wealth, anyone could have seen that he was financially insecure. He had never been inclined to save, and at forty-five he still owned no property. In 1948 the ASPCA bought the building at 441 East 92nd Street in order to demolish it and erect its own building, and the band of tenants the Harveys had assembled ten years earlier was thoroughly dispersed. Under the pressure of a postwar housing shortage, Walker and Jane briefly rented an apartment in a six-story building on Sixth Avenue in the West Village, but Jane complained that the walls were so thin she could hear the neighbors talking and playing music. So they moved uptown again, into Walker's studio, now at 1666 York Avenue, a railroad apartment with no central heating. There was a living room, two narrow bedrooms, and a cramped kitchen, which, in the typical format of New York tenements, also housed a big old-fashioned clawfoot bathtub. In winter they lived in the kitchen, huddling by the warmth of a Factory Florence oil stove, dining on a table Walker had made with the baroque wrought-iron base of an old sewing machine. As decoration, he tacked a row of tools to the mantelpiece of the boarded-up fireplace.

Walker continued to take off on assignments without Jane, but by the late 1940s it had become clear to her that she needed her own escape from New York. For ten years she had painted in a corner of the living room on 92nd Street; at York Avenue she painted in the kitchen. In response to her longing for the country, the Voorheeses asked a neighboring farmer in Connecticut if he would be willing to sell an old garage on his property that he hadn't used in years. The farmer agreed, and Jane bought the garage for fifteen dollars. "Clark and the farmer moved it by tractor down to Clark's land," remembered Jane. "He and I heaved it up onto cement blocks, put a floor in, cut a couple of windows. He dug a well and connected it to a hand pump in a secondhand sink. I had a Franklin stove, a bed, an electric plate, and a bureau. It was my country house."

At first Walker felt no need to intrude on Jane in her Connecticut retreat. He had never been drawn to nature. At night he was even a little afraid of the darkness and the quiet, and in the daylight there didn't seem to be enough to look at. "Too much green stuff!" Billie Voorhees remembered him complaining one weekend, as he prepared to leave for the city a day early.

But after a season or two he began to appreciate the pleasures of country life, and after Paul Grotz designed a screened sleeping porch that more than doubled the space, Jane's studio turned into the couple's weekend cottage. Walker planted a bed of pink and white cosmos, which he told Jane reminded him of his childhood. He also tried his hand at painting, with a box of watercolors Jane had given him for Christmas. He enjoyed handling the paints and brushes, so different from the cold machinery of photography, and he was pleased with the results of his untrained hand.

On summer evenings Walker and Jane would drive up Grassy Hill Road to the top of the hill to watch the sunset. Walker bought a kit to make his own telescope so they could gaze at the stars. Often they joined the Voorheeses for a drink or a barbecue. Walker, as Billie recalled, mixed daiquiris with the panache of a professional bartender while making a terrible mess of her kitchen. On one memorable evening in the midst of an especially hot, dry summer, Walker and Clark were preparing the coals for barbecued lobster when it began to rain. All four of them — Walker, Billie, Clark, and finally Jane — stripped their clothes off and danced in the grass.

For a long time after Jane moved to New York, she and Walker savored the novelty of being together, unencumbered by their former attachments. In the early 1940s Walker's letters to her were alive with sexual innuendo, erotic anticipation, and memories of lovemaking. Their spontaneity, light touch, and lover's confidence attest to the couple's private happiness. "Love, Just got your card. The extra $5 is for your profane thoughts. You ought to see mine. Doing my best to contain them. Hurry. Bang. Wow. W." is the full contents of one urgent note in October 1944. "Miss you like hell; have indescribable thoughts about private intimacies. Come home for demonstration," Walker wrote, care of the Voorheeses, in 1943. And in 1942, "You were lovely in your blue dress at the station."

To Walker, Jane's sensible mind and artistic integrity were a tonic; her lack of social ambition punctured the false veneers and lightened the pressures of city life. While he labored in the towers of midtown and stayed up too late drinking, she escaped to the cleaner air of Connecticut and kept her garden growing. She made an effort to engage in his social life, but she was shy. "I didn't sparkle at parties," she confessed frankly, and when she did accompany Walker out, she often left him early in the evening and took the bus home alone. She enjoyed weekends with John and Dorothy McDonald in Croton-on-Hudson, where she and Dorothy talked about art while Walker and John, who joined *Fortune*'s staff in 1945, talked about Time Inc. Jane also became a close friend with Alice Morris, the dedicated typist of *Let Us Now Praise Famous Men*. But many of Walker's colleagues and friends had no idea that he was married, so often did they see him alone, so rarely did he mention the woman in his life. Verna Harrison, a young researcher at *Fortune* who was soon to become the second Mrs. Wilder Hobson, remembered inviting Walker to New Jersey for the weekend, innocently assuming he was a bachelor. Walker declined, explaining that he was married and adding with a smile that his wife was very beautiful.

Walker enjoyed his measure of independence, but over the years he began to resent Jane's. When he disappeared to his office at random hours or took off in his car on photography assignments or weekends with friends, he wanted to be sure that Jane was at home waiting for him. Alice Morris, who lived around the corner on 93rd Street, was amazed at the way Jane would nervously dash home after a brief visit in case Walker should call from out of town. His fury at not finding her there was not worth the risk of missing his call. In Old Lyme, where she for a while achieved complete autonomy, Jane gradually found herself spending more of her time as Walker's wife, serving him breakfast, lunch, tea, and dinner as well as entertaining his guests.

In spite of Jane's retiring personality, Walker began to regard her in the 1950s as social competition. When he observed her rapport with Jim Agee, Alice Morris, and Wilder Hobson, he accused her of stealing his friends. And although her reputation as an artist was modest compared to his, by the time her paintings were showing at a number of galleries, including Kraushaar in midtown, Walker was not sure that she appreciated the difference in their status. Did she not realize that since they had met, in 1935, he had become a famous photographer? At the peak of his irritation, Walker would declare with mounting irritation, "I don't think you know who I am!"

He became critical of Jane's abrupt manner, her spells of depression, her lack of urban savoir-faire. One evening Jim and Mia Agee invited the Evanses to their apartment for dinner to meet their new friends, Charlie and Oona Chaplin. By then Agee had thoroughly analyzed and praised Chaplin's genius as the brightest star in "Comedy's Greatest Era," his cover story for *Life* in 1949. "The Tramp is as centrally representative of humanity, as many-sided and as mysterious as Hamlet," Agee wrote, "and it seems unlikely that any dancer or actor can ever have excelled him in eloquence, variety or poignancy of motion." To both Agee and Evans, Chaplin was the god of movies; there was no greater honor than his presence among them. But as far as Jane was concerned, the evening was a trial. Mia, who had just had a baby, and Oona, who was expecting one, talked about nothing but children, while Jim and Walker sharpened their wits for the sake of their honored guest, who did not seem to be feeling at his most garrulous or amusing. At her usual bedtime, Jane announced that she was going home. Though he said nothing at the time, "Walker was so furious he wouldn't speak to me for a week," Jane recalled. Forgetting his criticism of Hollywood's awestruck movie moguls a few years back, he haughtily told her, "Nobody leaves before Chaplin!"

Jane's painting began to suffer. It wasn't that Walker told her how to paint — he expressed far too little interest in her work. She was increasingly distressed by the pressure he exerted on her behavior in general, his apparent dissatisfaction with the woman she was. There was a way to answer the phone, a way to behave at parties. She felt herself tighten; her confidence slipped away, her paintbrush felt dead in her hand. "He destroyed me," she later said simply.

But from Walker's point of view, perhaps it was the other way around. He was terrified of nameless emasculating forces, and women were the first in line to blame. He perceived his father as a victim of an overbearing wife; indeed, all of his Crane relations appeared to be caught in this syndrome. "All the women," he wrote to Jane after seeing the Cranes in Pasadena, "have ruled the men right out of their masculinity, independence, courage, will and at last, brains even." Might Jane be doing the same to him? he wondered. Might she be partly responsible for a significant drop in his creative drive in recent years?

While he preened, Jane offered him less of her admiration. He was in the process of making himself into a full-time retiree, dinner guest, and arbiter of taste, but Jane confoundedly remained the girl next door. By the 1950s it was clear to her that he had been "wildly" unfaithful. He would call her at five in the afternoon to say he wouldn't be home for dinner — no explanation. He confessed to one affair; he hinted at others.

To Jane, Walker's growing interest in the rich and powerful was increasing the distance between them. Suddenly it was so important to know the Whitneys, she noticed — an attitude Walker would have scorned as a young man. The rebelliousness of youth was in middle age translated into an exaggerated sense of personal entitlement. Walker seemed to think that the mark he had made in the previous decade was enough to go on. In the eight years between leaving the FSA and joining *Fortune,* he had devoted himself almost entirely to the organization of his work rather than to its production, to dreaming up projects but not to realizing them. In so doing he had lost track of the pulse of his talent; the driving force had deserted him under the pressure of making a living and the surrender of unrealized ideas.

Ever more fastidious about his home, his food, his Brooks Brothers jackets and Peal shoes, Evans behaved, as Lionni noted, as if he had retired by the age of fifty. Charles Fuller, who had done a great deal for Evans over the years, concluded that he was just "a lacemaker." Jim Agee quipped to their mutual friends that Evans had become, by mid-century, "half old master, half old maid."

At the Museum of Modern Art, a new era was under way. Edward Steichen had given up his career as a photographer to become the head of the photography department. Beaumont Newhall, who had placed his wife, Nancy, in charge of the department while he was overseas with the navy, fully expected to reclaim his position when he returned. But by the time his military duties were over, Steichen had already made an impression at the museum with two spectacular wartime exhibitions, "Road to Victory" in 1942 and "Power in the Pacific" in 1945. Aiming to take control of the photography department, Steichen rallied his forces and funds and took advantage of a moment when high attendance and greater revenues were foremost concerns at the museum. When he was appointed in 1947, he hoped that Newhall would serve as his curator; he needed the benefits of his scholarship. But Newhall declined, knowing that he could never work under Steichen's megalomaniacal direction.

Steichen was not a scholar; he was an impresario. His directorship of the department reflected his familiarity with the world of picture magazines and photographic agencies. With Steichen at the helm, the department became known for large-scale topical theme shows, aspiring to "the photographic presentation of all that makes America the country that it is." It also reflected his mission to educate the public by way of lively, easily digested lessons in the photographer's art. He organized small instructive surveys on photographic technique and experiment, such as "In and Out of Focus" and "All Color Photography." Photography was to him "a vital modern means of giving form to ideas." With this criterion, nothing in the eclectic mix of postwar photography escaped his great embrace.

In November 1950, Steichen organized a symposium at the museum that typified the all-encompassing scope of his interest. He called it "What Is Modern Photography?" and invited ten leading American photographers to answer the question in five minutes or less. Along with such diverse talents as his old friend Ben Shahn, the precisionist painter and photographer Charles Sheeler, the abstract expressionist photographer Aaron Siskind, and the fashion photographer Irving Penn, Walker Evans was asked to contribute his opinion. Like many Steichen events, the symposium was well attended. The auditorium was filled, and the entire proceedings were broadcast overseas by the State Department's Voice of America as well as on the local public radio station, WNYC.

While Evans' fellow participants assumed that the question "What is modern photography?" referred to the photography of the present time, he took the question more literally, to mean the recent past, when he was young and "modern" was new. In his brief talk, Evans reminded the audience that the word *modern* meant something altogether different in the 1920s from what it meant in 1950. In the 1920s it meant "atonality and cacophony in music, abstractions and various distortions in painting, incommunicable subjective imagery in poetry and automatic writing in prose." Yet the best artists did not express themselves that way for the sake of being modern. In photography, Evans suggested, as in any other medium, "a good picture shows a relation to its period."

At the beginning of the 1950s, the kind of photography that best showed its relation to the period was that of the emerging beat generation. At the time, political optimism appeared to be pervasive, but its counterpoint was beginning to be expressed by artists and poets who were cynical about the false veneer of a world at peace. As the beats perceived it, the cold war was dominating the culture and dragging it down; a subtly pervasive anticommunism threatened to silence every creative urge. Rebelling against the conservative background of the postwar years, a new school of photographers was forming in New York. They made their living with commercial magazine work and took their own pictures on the street, on the boardwalk, or in the Bowery bars. Using small hand-held cameras in available light, with faster lenses and faster films than Evans had used in the 1920s, they abandoned the trappings of commercial photography, seeking to express the undercurrent of the city and the tension beneath the calm of postwar prosperity. To the new generation, Evans was a model of artistic integrity. His unheroic portrayal of the American scene, his affection for the primitive, and his reticence toward political statement formed a foundation upon which they might build their own photographic visions.

To some members of the audience at the Museum of Modern Art, Evans' presentation was nothing less than superb. Among them was Louis Faurer, a young fashion photographer with a personal sideline in street photography. Faurer had been to see Evans at his office at *Fortune* and had nervously presented his portfolio to the master. "I was afraid of him," Faurer vividly recalled. "I went to bed with his pictures every night." Evans looked over Faurer's photographs with care, relating them favorably to the work of Atget. Faurer was impressed with Evans' manner of speaking, his posture, his dress; even his handsome brass teakettle sitting there on a hot plate "projected his stability and eloquence."

About two years later, Evans met Faurer's friend and colleague Robert Frank, a young photographer from Zurich who had come to New York to pursue a career in magazine photography. By the time he met Evans, Frank had photographed all over Europe and in Peru, but North America was his most urgent subject, and New York City was its heartbeat. "What a town!" was Frank's refrain as he absorbed its rocking contrasts and tragicomic incongruities at every street corner. "It couldn't happen anywhere else."

Frank had first known Evans by reputation. Evans' photographs epitomized a plainspokenness that was thoroughly American, and their satirical edge penetrated what Frank saw as the typical American's inflated nationalistic pride, a pride he wished to puncture. Evans was capable of regarding his own country with ironic detachment. When Frank first encountered his photographs, he thought of André Malraux's phrase "to transform destiny into awareness."

Like Evans as a young man, Frank learned by looking. "I love to watch the most banal things," he explained. "Things that move. A little like a detective. I watch a man whose face and manner of walking interest me. I am him. I wonder what's going to happen." His natural medium was the miniature 35mm Leica, which he used with breathtaking speed and invisibility. He responded to his surroundings as deftly and intuitively as if the camera were an extension of his body. The results were the antithesis of the kind of picture the average photojournalist was paid to do — information-packed, evenly lit images neatly matched to their captions. Frank's photographs were obscure, stealthy, unlikely. In spirit they were close to the bold new paintings of his contemporaries, the abstract expressionists; he worked in big, angry strokes of black, white, and gray. The power of his photographs rested on a minimum of visual information. As Frank once described his mission, he wanted to make pictures that would nullify explanation. To his quick-witted eye, opportunities abounded in New York City. In 1948 he made a photograph of the Macy's Thanksgiving Day parade in which the "strong man" appears as nothing but a distant transparent balloon on a cloudy November day, hovering over puddles reflecting skyscrapers upside down.

Evans was immediately interested in the slouching, thoughtful young Swiss Jew. He saw that Frank's work was original, that its signature was unmistakable. It was as if Frank had taken Evans' own photography a step further, as if his cynicism toward Eisenhower's America was an attitude that only a European could have. His ambition to photograph "how Americans live, have fun, eat, drive cars, work, etc." was on the same scale as Evans' ambitions nearly twenty years earlier. If Frank wanted to pursue his portrait of the American people without financial pressure, Evans suggested, he should apply for a Guggenheim fellowship. Evans offered to contribute his personal recommendation and to help Frank plan his trip.

Evans' feeling for Frank's work undoubtedly related to the many sentiments and interests the two men had in common. They shared a love of books and a determination to make their own, with a passion matched only by their disdain for the *Life* magazine photo story. They preferred the company of artists and writers to that of their fellow photographers. Frank had befriended the beat poets Jack Kerouac and Allen Ginsberg as well as abstract expressionist painters such as Franz Kline, Willem de Kooning, Alfred Leslie, Richard Bellamy, and Miles Forst, who habitually convened at the Cedar Tavern. Like Evans, Frank was married to an artist, the half-English, half-American Mary Lockspeiser. Mary's medium was wood; she carved large mythic figures from logs she found on the beach. Later she would become known for her ceramic sculptures of reclining female figures that seemed to be emerging like phantoms from the sand.

As his social circles broadened to embrace a younger generation, Evans clung ever more firmly to the retreats of the establishment. On the one hand he was intrigued by the new-style bohemia of Robert and Mary Frank's downtown; on the other, he was happy among the comfortably off, middle-aged intellectuals of the Upper East Side. In 1954 Evans was elected to the Century, a private men's club for the art and literary elite that was housed in a generously proportioned McKim, Mead, and White building at 7 West 43rd Street, just off Fifth Avenue. Although he had shunned clubs and organizations for most of his life, he did not mind being counted among that august society of artists, authors, and historians. "I shall *endeavor* to behave well, at least while on the premises," he promised Henry Allen Moe, head of the Guggenheim Foundation and one of his ten sponsors for admission to the Century. Dropping by at lunchtime or in the early evening, he was likely to run into A. Hyatt Mayer, the curator of prints at the Metropolitan Museum; Robert Beverly Hale, the Met's first curator of contemporary art; the *New Yorker* writer Brendan Gill, or the humorist S. J. Perelman. And with them he would enjoy the club's several paneled dining rooms, its art gallery (for exhibiting members' work), its library, and its lofty saloon. For Evans, not the least of the club's privileges was the use of the large marble tub in the downstairs bathroom.

For those who knew Evans well, it was fascinating to watch him migrate from one end of his social life to the other. Without missing a beat, he could move from the gentlemanly murmurs and leather armchairs of the Century Club to a smoky loft on 10th Street where a saxophone whined and the paint was still fresh on the artist's canvas. While his colleagues at *Fortune* thoughtfully dissected American society — Holly Whyte wrote *The Organization Man,* criticizing the shallow values of corporate America; John McDonald wrote *Strategy in Poker, Business, and War,* which demonstrated how frighteningly similar these strategies were; John Kenneth Galbraith outlined his liberal economics in *The Affluent Society;* and Daniel Bell summed up the exhaustion of political ideas in *The End of Ideology* — Evans embraced society's newest rebels, the beat generation.

These new friendships made up for the dissipation of some of his older ones. He rarely saw Ben Shahn, even though Shahn was also frequently employed by *Fortune* for illustration work. With Bernarda Bryson, Shahn had moved to Roosevelt, New Jersey, and they had two children. Even though Evans felt great affection for Shahn, in the red-baiting 1950s he was afraid of associating with an artist of such noticeably socialist ideals. Nor did he see much of Jim Agee. Part of their growing distance could be attributed to geography. Now living with Mia Fritsch, Agee had fathered two little girls and had bought a tumbledown farmhouse and 150 acres in the woods of Hillsdale, New York, to which the family often retreated. Furthermore, his career as a movie critic for both *Time* and *The Nation* had led him to Hollywood, where he spent months at a time working on filmscripts.

Although the spirit of empathy still flickered between Evans and Agee, there was another reason for their distance. As Agee sadly watched Evans become increasingly concerned about hobnobbing with the rich, Evans watched Agee's youthful enthusiasm for drink turning in middle age into a serious disease. Not yet fifty, Agee looked ravaged. His health was ruined by thirty years or more of heavy intake of alcohol and nicotine, and he was by no means beating his addiction. If anything, his behavior had become more outlandish and even violent at times, and his "immoderate supply of moral indignation," as Evans once put it, had become not only self-destructive but harmful to others. At a party one evening, Evans looked on in astonishment as Agee hit a woman over the head with a chair when she confessed that she had faked an orgasm.

In December 1954, Evans received a letter from Agee, writing from the Cottage Hospital in Santa Barbara to say that he was recovering from a heart attack — "a modest edition of coronary thrombosis, which is one of the most majestic things to be afflicted by that I can think of — the least one can do is drop dead, and apparently that is very often done. However, I got off light." He also wanted Evans to know that although the last person in the world he wanted to hurt was Mia, he had a new lover, Pat Scanlon, whom he had met while working for John Huston on the script of *The African Queen.* Pat would be coming to New York, and he wondered if Evans might be free to entertain her.

Despite Agee's reckless love life, he was concerned for the happiness of others. Knowing how difficult Walker could be, he often called Jane just to see if she was all right. He was not the only one to say that he would not blame her for leaving Walker. But she was not willing to give up that easily. She even wondered if they should have a child before it was too late, but Walker would not discuss it.

In an effort to understand if not solve her marital problems, Jane started seeing a psychiatrist, and once succeeded in persuading Walker to join her for a session. "She's competing with me," Walker told the doctor, and he refused to go again. Although he was intrigued by psychological notions, he shared with Agee a deep distrust of the practice of psychiatry, especially on artists like themselves. The likely cost of analysis was the death of the inner muse, and to Evans, being either happier or better behaved was not worth risking that loss. He was intransigent. His quarrels with Jane became more frequent and less easily mended. More than once, Jane escaped to the cramped apartment of Alice Morris and Harvey Breit.

In a gesture reminiscent of some of Jim Agee's maneuvers, Walker began to send Jane off to concerts with *The New Yorker*'s music critic and his onetime colleague at *Time,* the eligible Winthrop Sargeant. In the summer of 1954 he planned a trip to Paris, his first visit since 1927. He would go alone, he and Jane decided; one round-trip passage on the ocean liner *Liberté* was all they could afford. In his absence, Jane and Winthrop saw each other frequently. By the time Walker returned home, they were involved in a love affair.

The following May 16, Agee had a heart attack in a taxicab on his way to a doctor's appointment. The taxi driver rushed him to the nearest hospital, but he was dead on arrival. Three days later, a funeral, a high Episcopal service conducted by Agee's former schoolmaster, the Reverend James Flye, was held at Saint Luke's Chapel in Greenwich Village. Afterward a small coterie of intimates, including Walker Evans and Helen Levitt, drove to the Agees' farmhouse in

Hillsdale to bury him. Later Evans said that Agee had been like an open flame that people warmed themselves on, and that when he died there were some people who wanted to die too, to lie with him in his grave.

Jane could not bring herself to leave Walker so soon after the death of their friend. Perhaps mourning this great loss would reunite them, or at least serve to repair some of the damage of the past few years if they were to part for good. But Walker showed no signs of change. After enduring a few more months of fruitless effort on their marriage, Jane packed her bags and hired a mover to take her things to the Barbizon Hotel. Walker called from the railroad station, expecting to spend the weekend with her in Connecticut. "I'm leaving," she told him simply. "I don't think you like me anymore. Winthrop wants to marry me."

Despite having nearly thrown Jane at Winthrop Sargeant, as Alice Morris would have argued, Walker was furious that she had walked out on him. "Don't fight it," said John McDonald, to whom the separation came as no surprise. Many of Walker's friends hardly knew that Jane had gone, so accustomed were they to seeing him without her. Whenever he spoke of her, which was rarely, his tone was bitter and dismissive. By the end of the decade he would hardly mention her name. For the time being, he led people to believe that the separation was nothing more than a household inconvenience. "Where do you get your sheets washed?" he demanded of his neighbor Elizabeth Shaw.

Alone in his railroad apartment on York Avenue in the winter of 1956, Walker removed the last traces of his life with Jane from his domestic surroundings. She had asked him to throw out whatever she might have accidentally left behind, so when he came across a brand-new pair of ladies' shoes, he put them in the trash. He later discovered that they had belonged to Verna Hobson. "I thought they were Jane's," he explained to Verna by letter. "Into the trash they went, them's was the lady's instructions . . . Now dearest V, get yourself another pair and send me the bill; and please laugh if you can . . . Let us hope someone will enjoy the story, for it has under-and-over-tones that I won't go into."

But underneath the façade of his humor, Walker's damaged pride hurt almost as much as his broken heart. In a letter to Winthrop Sargeant, he could not resist the impulse to strike Jane with the full sting of his fury. In a postscript to Jane, he wrote his final rebuke: "From now on I will consider you dead."

9 *Before They Disappear*

FEW PEOPLE were granted access to Evans' private feelings as he mourned the end of his marriage and the death of his best friend in the same year. But there could be no doubt that this double loss affected him deeply. He had ceased to look after both relationships some years before, and their loss meant the abrupt end of what was probably the happiest and certainly the richest period of his life. One winter day while visiting him at *Fortune,* Robert Frank watched in wonder as Evans suddenly turned toward the window, looked down on the skating rink at Rockefeller Center, and let go a flood of tears.

Subtler evidence of his sadness and regret appeared in the form of his *Fortune* portfolios, disguised as the quiet ravings of an increasingly zealous preservationist. If he couldn't save human life or human love, perhaps he could at least shore up a few relics from the past, things he once might have believed were impervious to change. In 1955 Evans returned to lower Manhattan to photograph the turreted financial buildings and old steel-beamed warehouses, the background of his days in Brooklyn Heights, when he and Hart Crane had wandered around the docks and marveled at the rising skyline. But the place had changed, and its changes were emblematic of the era. City planners across the country had created a monotony of high-rise office buildings, leaving the old downtown sections either derelict or divested of their former vitality. In "'Downtown': A Last Look Backward," published in the August 1956 issue of *Fortune,* Evans warned his readers that the district would never be the same once a score of new construction projects then under way was completed. "The building boom now commencing," he predicted, "will change the face, and a good deal of the atmosphere, of the entire district."

A few months later, in March 1957, Evans produced "Before They Disappear," a photographic homage to the freight-car emblems he had loved since childhood. The portfolio, in color, showed the respectful attention to detail of a boy stamp collector; Evans knew when each emblem had first appeared and how it had been modified over the years. Among his selections was the backward-slanting emblem of his grandfather Crane's company, the Wabash, whose last steam locomotive was about to retire to become a museum piece. Whether or not Evans knew that obscure fact, he was aware that the symbols of his childhood had become historic. "When we can no longer catch sight of the great Chinese red and black double tadpole of the Northern Pacific," he wrote, "or the simple old cross of the Santa Fe, then will a whole world of cherished association have been destroyed. Impiety could go no further."

While he mourned the loss of these treasures of his childhood, he argued vehemently against the idea that his photography might be driven by nostalgia. "I hate that word," he said, and he repeatedly denied any connection with the sentiment. "Pray keep me forever separated from an atmosphere of moist elderly eyes just about to spill at the sight of grandmother's tea set," he wrote. It was a sense of history in the rough he cherished, a sense that he had been better able to master in the days of the Depression, when America's material progress had stalled and the world stood still for his camera, poised for change. In the 1950s, an era that was loath to look backward, the meaning of Evans' enterprise hovered between one misinterpretation and another. He was not an aging social protest artist, nor was he a dewy-eyed sentimentalist. But there seemed to be fewer people around who knew what he was.

In the summer of 1956, *Sports Illustrated* assigned Evans to a story on British sporting events. The story provided an opportunity for him to travel to England for the first time, a prospect he delighted in.

There he would revel in that most civilized of civilizations, taking in at a leisurely pace the famed sporting events of Wimbledon, Henley, and St. Andrews. He would also visit at least two former colleagues from Time Inc. — Tom Matthews, who with his wife had bought a farm in Sussex, and Jimmy and Tania Stern, now living in Dorset. With all of them he would be able to reminisce about their great friend and colleague Jim Agee. And with their collaboration he would help to organize a trust fund for Jim and Mia's three children.

In London, Evans' spirits were lifted by Nora Sayre, a young graduate of Radcliffe College who was the daughter of the writer Joel Sayre. Nora, who had the petite, refined beauty of an English aristocrat, was an aspiring journalist. She and Evans dined together at Wilton's, which Jimmy Stern had recommended. They took a picnic to Glyndebourne to see a Mozart opera ("damned interesting socially and visually too, you bet you betcha," Evans wrote to Stern). Standing on the expansive emerald-green lawn, Evans stole a photograph of his companion when she wasn't looking. Nora entertained his affections but rather nervously maintained her physical distance.

Back in New York, Evans cultivated his social life as a bachelor again. He welcomed invitations to the theater, the Metropolitan Opera, and Carnegie Hall. Among the cultural elite of New York in those days, "everyone knew everyone," as the artist Saul Steinberg recalled. The social scene was an international mix of "rafinati" — refugees like himself, visiting Europeans such as Cartier-Bresson and the poet Stephen Spender, and insatiable travelers such as Paul Bowles and his wife, Jane, were all part of the same social pond in which Walker Evans swam. Eleanor Clark had married the poet Robert Penn Warren and moved to Fairfield, Connecticut, and Evans could count on being invited to their annual New Year's Eve black-tie dinner dance, where he would see the McDonalds, the Jessups, the Dupees, the Herseys, and the Cheevers.

Occasionally he entertained friends on York Avenue. One evening he planned a small dinner party for Sonia Orwell, George Orwell's recently widowed second wife, who was in New York for a visit. Never one to miss an opportunity to enhance her acquaintance with an artist of note, she especially requested that Evans include her friend

Saul, and Evans dutifully invited Saul Steinberg. It would be just the three of them at his apartment. Steinberg turned up at York Avenue in time to watch Evans putting together "a bedraggled little dinner." Sonia was already there. When she thought Steinberg was out of earshot, she leaned toward their host and hissed — "like an amphibian," as Steinberg recalled — "You've got the wrong Saul!" She had meant for Evans to invite Saul Bellow.

Evans also kept up his friendships in the magazine and photography worlds. Ben Schultz, then on the staff of *Sports Illustrated,* was a tireless photography enthusiast who enjoyed nothing more than passing an evening poring over books and prints with Evans. Both men were frequently invited for dinner at the home of the photographers Dan and Sandra Weiner. Jason and Barbara Epstein, the founders of *The New York Review of Books;* George Leighton, an editor at *Harper's,* whose wife was Henry Allen Moe's secretary at the Guggenheim Foundation; and Marvin Israel, the cantankerous, singleminded photo editor at *Harper's Bazaar,* had all become Evans' friends and dedicated admirers.

Evans was always poised to pack his bags and abandon the city at the slightest encouragement. Occasionally, he went by himself to the studio in Old Lyme, which Jane had relinquished, but more often he accepted — and even invented — invitations from friends. "Thank you for your wonderful invitation to Truro," he once wrote to Mary Frank, who with Robert and their two children had rented a summer house on the beach. "I'd love to come." He did, although Mary hadn't actually invited him. Eliza Parkinson, the niece of one of the three founders of the Museum of Modern Art, had a big house on Fishers Island, a summer haven for rich New Yorkers off the coast of Connecticut, and Evans was often urged to go for the weekend. And he was always welcome to stay with Tom and Ethel Mabry and their two little girls in Stockbridge, Massachusetts, on his way to upstate New York or northern New England. The Mabrys' second daughter, Eliza, was Evans' only godchild. He read to her passages from *Alice in Wonderland* and photographed her, at the age of five, struggling to undress herself on the beach, like a sculpture wrestling its form out of stone.

The well-preserved seaside village of Stonington, Connecticut, became one of his regular haunts during his renewed bachelorhood. Anthony West, an English architecture critic (and the only son of Rebecca West), often invited Evans to his house near Stonington. At dinner one evening, he and his wife, Lily Emmet, reunited Evans with the artist Calvert Coggeshall, a friend since the 1930s, and his new wife, Susanna Perkins. Charles Fuller was spending the summers in Stonington with his second wife, Anne Jones, who had transformed an old church into an art gallery and gave summer exhibitions for many of the artists whom the dealer Betty Parsons was showing in New York, including Coggeshall. Between the Wests, the Coggeshalls, and the Fullers, Evans found many occasions to drive over to arty Stonington from stuffy Old Lyme. "Walker always fled to us," remembered Anne Fuller of those days. "He would come for dinner and stay for a week or two." And he always left something behind — a cardigan or a pair of shoes.

Evans' fondness for driving around backcountry roads, poking into junk shops, and photographing what remained of Victorian and Greek Revival architecture was spurred on by his friends in Stonington. With Anthony West at the wheel of his secondhand Jaguar, he explored the villages of coastal Connecticut. Other haunts were the old mill towns — Willimantic, Putnam — with their small-town prosperity frozen intact since the previous generation, their brick walls and clapboard rowhouses chipped and parched with age. Anne Fuller, a veteran junk collector, was also available for shopping in the roadside barns that advertised antiques.

As the perennial houseguest or dinner guest, Evans found that his eccentric tastes were indulged, his nimble social manner and sardonic wit were appreciated, and his artistic talents were a source of pride, even if his recent photography for *Fortune* was not their most stunning proof. His eye was as sharp as ever. "He practically *was* a camera," remembered Susanna Coggeshall. "He took in everything — unless he was a little tipsy, he was conscious of everything in the room." Lily West admired Walker as a connoisseur of the commonplace; at the same time she noticed that "he had a sweet tooth for the aristocratic."

In spite of these social distractions, which temporarily revived his humor and enthusiasm, it escaped no one's notice that Evans was lonely and bored. In the late 1950s he had the slightly puffy look of a man who habitually drank more than enough. His face was thickening, and he bulged a little around the waist. Whenever possible, he reclined. Most of all, he seemed to lack a focus, a purpose toward which he could apply his talent. To Susanna Coggeshall (whose mother was the first female cabinet member, Frances Perkins), it seemed that he lacked a guiding philosophy, that he just "picked up aphorisms from literary sources." He was also "foolishly atheistic, without a foundation." To Anne Fuller, he seemed "always in despair, in a panic about his work or a woman." He was always reading Proust, as if he identified with the epic languidness and agonizing anticipation of *Remembrance of Things Past.* Mary Frank also took note of his Proustian ways. "He built up a tremendous anticipation before an event," she remembered. "He would love to stir up excitement over it. In the same way afterwards he would rethink the event, turning it over and over." In Truro Evans took walks with eight-year-old Pablo Frank while Mary watched from the window. "Walker would stroll along the beach with Pablo and use him as an excuse for meeting women, like having a little dog, or a diplomat." As Mary observed from the window, Evans would keep at a distance from Pablo. Then, if an attractive woman went up to Pablo, he would turn up promptly behind him and strike up a conversation.

In the late 1950s Evans began to collect erotic novels, some recently published, others dating from the turn of the century. *The Amorous Adventures of a Gentleman of Quality, Diary of a Sybarite,* and *Souvenirs d'une gamine vicieuse* were among the books he kept in a small wooden trunk, strapped with brass-studded leather, buckled, and padlocked. This new interest matched his apparent sexual passivity. His flirtations rang a false note. Sandra Weiner resented the way Evans' manner would abruptly change when she entered the room. Others suspected that he was interested only in women he was sure he could never seduce. Anne Fuller watched him skeptically as he propositioned women, including herself, but never followed through. She didn't have the impression that he was homosexual, only that he lacked confidence about his masculinity. His sex drive had inverted into a purely visual lust.

There was no doubt in anyone's mind that Evans was susceptible to feminine beauty; what he did about it was less obvious. One evening at a party he was introduced to Lady Caroline Blackwood, a petite young English aristocrat with a piquant profile and enormous brown eyes. Blackwood was not only beautiful, she also possessed a visual and literary wit, though she was not yet sure of how to use her talents. She was in her early thirties when, having recently divorced the artist Lucian Freud, she came to New York from London in search of interesting company. Evans immediately rose to the challenge and responded with the full battalion of his charm.

"There couldn't be a more wonderful person to show you New York," Blackwood said later. "Walker made you feel as if you were going through life blind — his brilliant eye would notice the tiniest detail." It seemed to her that he lived in a grand style in spite of having no money. She was charmed by his cold-water flat on York Avenue with its bathtub in the kitchen and its old parlor stove. For the greater part of 1957 they dined together as often as three times a week. Walker would grill chicken in his apartment, serve it with a nice wine and a salad, and always light his little suppers with candles. They constantly exchanged reading matter. When Walker had read something he thought Caroline would like — a book or a magazine article — he would hire a taxi to take it to her flat in the east fifties at once. When Caroline was short of money and couldn't pay the rent (in spite of being related to the wealthy Guinness family, she was somewhat short of cash), again Walker made the grand gesture, with money he really could not spare. As she recalled, "He would put the cash in an envelope and send it over in a cab."

Many of Walker's friends had the impression that he and Caroline were having an affair. He took her to the Coggeshalls' house in New-castle, Maine, for a weekend; the Voorheeses met her in Old Lyme. Wherever they went, they impressed people as a fascinating, odd-ball couple. The truth of their relationship was, as Caroline knew quite well, that Walker had a terrific crush on her but it would never amount to anything. As she perceived her ardent escort, he was not so much a womanizer as "a fantasist." He would boast about his various sexual conquests and talk knowingly about what it was like to go to bed with a black woman. His stories struck Caroline as ex-hibitionist. For her part, she felt little physical attraction to him.

Walker looked like Mr. Magoo, in her opinion, and she wished he would stop his boastful storytelling: "It was absurd and awful."

Walker's fantasies also extended to his family history. He told Caroline that he had been born in Boston and was related to the best of the Boston Brahmins. This explained why he was cultivated, and also his natural affinity for the English. Behind this elaborate façade, Caroline saw a man deeply unhappy about his work. "He was ashamed of working for *Fortune;* it was just a way he had to make money. The success of *American Photographs* seemed to be forgotten, and he thought he would not really be noticed until after his death. He accepted this rather bitterly."

Eliza Parkinson was somewhat baffled by the way that Evans constantly felt the need to remind her of his status. "I am an artist," he would assert irritably whenever there appeared to be a shadow of a doubt that he was. Most of all, he seemed to feel the need to distinguish himself from his fellow photographers, since photography was still not generally appreciated as a serious form of artistic expression. It was a commercial art or an amateur's hobby. Either way, photographers lacked the respect for privacy and individual judgment that painters, for instance, were naturally granted. Evans' anger never failed to stir if anyone suggested what he should photograph. One weekend at Fishers Island, Parkinson and her houseguests Courtie and Trini Barnes agreed that it would be fun if he would take their picture. To everyone's astonishment, he responded by retreating into his bedroom, locking the door, and refusing to come out until he was sure his hostess had left the house.

While Evans guarded his artistic independence like a hawk, he had less and less to show for it. His photographs for *Fortune* were hardly the kind of ambitious, all-encompassing views or commanding portraits he had made in the 1930s; they were more like something out of the seasoned artist's sketchbook, an artist whose era had passed. And while Del Paine gave him free rein, his impact on the magazine was limited. Evans ruled over his few pages of photography and text and they were admired and enjoyed, but between the editors' lack of encouragement and specific demands and his own chronic inertia, he had nothing like the influence he had exerted over Roy Stryker's team at the Farm Security Administration. Devoted colleagues like John McDonald felt the magazine did not appreciate what a treasure it had in Walker Evans, or know what to do about it. Evans was contemptuous of *Fortune,* of Henry Luce, of the entire Luce empire, which seemed to him the very model of hypocrisy. In the past it had held out promise as a means of supporting his creative work. But over the years, he realized that it only appeared to support creativity in the process of draining it dry.

Although he painfully felt himself aging as an artist, Evans was beginning to enjoy his role as a mentor to younger photographers. In the early 1950s, Henry Allen Moe suggested that he be made a confidential adviser to the Guggenheim Foundation, in view of the growing number of applications for photography fellowships. In this role, Evans gave Robert Frank his wholehearted support for a fellowship that enabled Frank to make a cross-country road trip in 1955, a trip that would become legendary. Evans also helped the younger photographer to form his plans. "What I have in mind," wrote Frank in his application,

> is observation and record of what one naturalized American finds to see in the United States that signifies the kind of civilisation born here and spreading elsewhere . . . I speak of things that are there, anywhere and everywhere — easily found, not easily selected and interpreted. A small catalogue comes to the mind's eye: a town at night, a parking lot, a supermarket, a highway, the man who owns three cars and the man who owns none, the farmer and his children, a new house and a warped clapboard house, the dictation of taste, the dream of grandeur, advertising, neon lights, the faces of the leaders and the faces of the followers, gas tanks and post offices and backyards . . .

Frank's ideas about photographing America were remarkably like those Evans had sketched out for himself in 1934. But while Frank and Evans had similar intentions, their styles, techniques, and temperaments were quite different. Frank's bleak vision of America made Evans' appear an almost innocent product of a safer, less confusing time. Whereas Evans waited for the sun to brighten the façade of a shopfront before mounting his camera on its tripod, Frank preferred to work in bad weather and dim interiors. With his Leica, he moved stealthily through bars, poolrooms, and back alleys. Whereas Evans stood back and regarded his subject with a penetrating detachment and total control, Frank implicated himself in the risk and sadness of his portrait of America. In every picture the photographer is there, but hiding, crouching, the lone photographer on the road.

When Frank returned from his travels with 750 rolls of film to process and review, Evans encouraged him to publish his photographs as a book and helped to judge their selection and sequence. As Frank's mentor, he felt himself in the role that Kirstein had played for him twenty years earlier with *American Photographs,* as the objective, educated eye, sensitive to the uniqueness of what this young artist was up to, able to steer him subtly in the direction of his art's greatest strengths.

In 1958 the offices of Time Inc. moved from Rockefeller Center half a block west to a forty-seven-story block tower on the Avenue of the Americas. Like most of the senior writers in the editorial department, Evans was offered an office with a full plate-glass window and a spectacular view of midtown New York. He declined the privilege and instead chose a small interior room that was meant for storage. Paul Grotz found his choice typical of Evans' incorrigible will to defy convention. Perhaps it had even more to do with his desire for privacy and his enduring fear of heights.

Grotz was now the art director of *Architectural Forum,* a magazine that Luce had bought in 1932 with the idea that building was going to be the nation's "next great industrial effort." All aspects of design and construction would be addressed to meet what Luce forecast as a revolution in the building business. With his usual desire to preach and prophesy from the pulpit of his magazine empire, he proclaimed that he had bought the respected magazine because "to influence architecture is to influence life." *Architectural Forum* was indeed influential, with a loyal readership in the trade, but as a business enterprise it was nothing but a loss to Time Inc. Luce was resigned to keeping it in the family nevertheless, and there was a frequent exchange of talent and material with his other magazines.

Fortune's editors urged Grotz to make use of the work of his old friend Evans, whose work first appeared in *Architectural Forum* as "The London Look." This was a portfolio of pictures of architectural details that Evans identified as unique to English style, which, as Lady Caroline Blackwood observed, would have gone unnoticed by more casual travelers: a brass doorbell or number plate, a "tophatted" lamppost dating back to gaslight, the famous London cab, never dented and always clean, and chimney pots, "everywhere marching to infinity." All were objects of Evans' admiration, and like almost everything he felt a fondness toward in those days, they were coupled with the imminent threat of extinction.

The preservation theme in Evans' *Fortune* portfolios was by now well established. Another, less obvious stylistic element had entered his writing — a heavy anthropomorphic slant on manufactured objects. To all of his five senses they spoke, often with sexual innuendo. In "The London Look," he described the round shiny brass doorbells with their nipple-size buttons as "glossy, explicit doorbells (PRESS!)." Adding another twist of humor, one doorbell was labeled TOP FLAT. In "Before They Disappear," he claimed that the freight-car emblems seemed to emit the very sounds of railroading, "the attenuated nocturnal moans of steam transportation." Trains and train travel, so familiar to his childhood, were the subject of his most fanciful interpretations. In "The Last of Railroad Steam," he described a railroad yard in Roanoke, Virginia, "where the hippos, the Percherons, and the old elephants are tethered, fed, and bathed — or freed."

As if to empathize with the reflected image of his own aging skin, in the late 1950s Evans increasingly gave loving attention to old surfaces, treating them with the same care with which he bathed and rubbed his feet or eased his shoulders into a Brooks Brothers tweed jacket. He took a new interest in stonemasonry, marveling at its longevity and imperviousness to weather and at the beauty of the effects of age. "Time uses a great obscure formula that has never been fully published, and, let us hope, never will be. It is known, of course, that one Scottish abbey wall, plus nine hundred years, plus a sickle moon, is a foolproof combination," he wrote. For a portfolio on old ocean liners for *Architectural Forum*, he roamed the decks of the RMS *Queen Mary* and the SS *Liberté* to study "how patina is acquired at sea." He concluded that layers upon layers of fresh paint over the years gave the shipboard structures a "cakey, almost edible quality." And during a stroll on East 85th Street, his camera loaded with color film, he made a sampling of wall surfaces, "the restless, cacophonic design created by time, the weather, neglect, and the fine hand of delinquent youth."

With Robert Frank, Evans made a tour of New England mill towns for a picture story that the editor Hedley Donovan had urged him to do — an illustration of William Blake's phrase "these dark satanic mills" translated into the American scene. At the peak of the highly colored New England fall, the two photographers viewed the time-worn mills of Woonsocket, Rhode Island, Putnam, Connecticut, and Exeter, New Hampshire, admiring the warmth of aging brick and clapboard. In his discovery of the beauty of patina, Evans was gravitating subtly toward the power of nature and its imprint on the man-made. As avid as he was about preserving such reminders of times past, he was passionately against their being conserved or improved in any way. Let them show the honest nature of their age. The older the better.

The same rule did not apply to women. The older Evans grew, the younger were the women he pursued. Penny Andrews was nineteen years old when she dropped out of Goucher College to work as an "odd-job girl" at *Fortune* and met Walker Evans for the first time. At fifty-two, he was exactly the same age as her father. Scattered, nervous, passionate Penny took to Walker's old-fashioned charm, and he to her girlish manner and unadorned style. She felt at home in his railroad flat, with its simple furnishings, gathering clutter, and touches of genuine art. Ben Shahn's portrait of Walker now hung on the wall, reminding her that he too had had a youth.

Toward the end of 1958, Evans learned that he would have to have surgery for an ulcer, the affliction that had killed his father. Even Henry Luce was moved to write to him on the occasion of his admission to Roosevelt Hospital for the better part of the Christmas holidays. If Luce could not sensibly wish Evans a Merry Christmas, he could extend all his best wishes for "a bright New Year."

Having been "butchered by daring surgeons" in New York, as he described it to one friend, Walker went to recover with his sister and brother-in-law, who had retired to Anna Maria, an island off the west coast of Florida. He took Penny Andrews with him. They saw Charles Fuller, who was also in Florida that winter, without Anne, drinking heavily. Before the year was out, Fuller would die of a heart attack. Jessie Evans, who had been in a coma for the past five years, would finally die of a stroke in May. In Florida, Walker painted a picture, Penny remembered, of a palm tree with a single dead leaf dangling forlornly from its crown, while she took pictures of sunsets, for which Walker prescribed the right film. He also bought her a box of water-colors and encouraged her beginner's attempts at rendering the tropical scenery.

It was soon after his return to New York in late February 1959 that Evans first met Isabelle Boeschenstein, a twenty-five-year-old Swiss who was spending the year in New York with her husband, Alex von Steiger. Both were graduates of the Kunstgewerbeschule, Zurich's renowned design school directed by Johannes Itten, where Isabelle had studied textile design and Alex photography. In New York, Alex found a job assisting Hans Namuth, whose photographs and films of Jackson Pollock in the act of making his famous drip paintings were already deeply ingrained in the consciousness of the New York art world. Isabelle was working for a clothing designer at Saks Fifth Avenue. One evening when Alex was out of town on a job, Herman Landshoff, a magazine photographer whom Isabelle's father had known in Paris, invited her to dinner to meet Walker Evans. Isabelle's first impression was of a frail little man, tanned from his Florida vacation, reclining gracefully on Landshoff's chaise longue, dressed in a soft gray Shetland suit and a pink chambray shirt.

Isabelle was extremely pretty, "a fairy tale," as Saul Steinberg later described her. Fresh, cheerful, and as neat as a pin, she listened attentively to everything Walker said. She spoke English with charming imperfection and with a gentle lisp, and she laughed and glinted at his playful flattery. Perhaps for Walker it would be a bright new year after all.

Walker wondered if Isabelle had seen *My Fair Lady*, then playing on Broadway. He had enjoyed it so much, he wanted to see it again, but only if she could be persuaded to join him. They would dine first, wherever she wanted. Isabelle suggested an Italian restaurant by the name of Romeo Salta, on West 56th Street, which she thought would appeal to her romantically inclined escort. She was wrong; Walker politely let her know that the place was phony, but he took her there anyway. Later that evening, they laughed as Rex Harrison wondered "Why can't a woman be more like a man?" and Julie Andrews imagined "Wouldn't it be loverly?" and in the darkness of the theater Walker held Isabelle's hand.

Isabelle was the oldest of three daughters, all beautiful, of Hermann Boeschenstein, a successful journalist from Bern. In her sense of order, correctness, and care for the minor detail, she was absolutely Swiss, but she was also restless to break away from the rigid order of Swiss design taught at the Kunstgewerbeschule and curious about the culture of more cosmopolitan cities. As soon as she was old enough, she took the train to Paris. She hung about the sidewalk tables of the Deux Magots as the young Walker Evans had, dressed in Parisian disguise (in the 1950s, black), and watched Jean-Paul Sartre and his lover, Simone de Beauvoir, lingering over their aperitifs and conversation in a cloud of cigarette smoke. Likewise, Isabelle was thrilled with New York. Compared with the tidy, small-scale cosmopolitanism of Bern or Zurich, it was alive with excitement, danger, and irregularities. Now that she had arrived, she doubted that she would ever want to leave.

Alex von Steiger was very interested in meeting Walker Evans, whose work he knew from books. That winter he and his wife became regular visitors to Walker's studio on York Avenue. They sat around the kitchen table listening to old jazz records, looking at books, and talking about photography. Sometimes the von Steigers invited Walker to their little apartment on East 56th Street. He would honor his hostess with a single flower and take his glasses off, hoping to look a little younger than he was. When Alex was out of town, Isabelle visited Walker after work, bringing supper for two. He liked to practice his French on her; there was always something slightly wrong with it, and Isabelle played off his mistakes and made him laugh. He corrected her English and told her what to read — Hemingway, Nabokov; she took him the Olympia Press edition of *Lolita*. In the growing confusion of his living room, he invited her to arrange a still life on his mantelpiece, and for a long time he left it there, just as she had placed it.

As spring came and Walker regained his strength, he felt ready to make photographic expeditions in his new thirdhand Buick Roadmaster convertible. He put the top down and took Isabelle along for the ride. They explored the waterfront and Brooklyn and cruised through the warehouse district below Houston Street. Walker stood on the seat of the car to take pictures. The result of this tour was a portfolio he named after the 1954 movie classic starring Marlon Brando, *On the Waterfront.*

For Isabelle, nothing could have been a more fascinating introduction to the city than touring with the sharply observant, eccentrically focused Walker Evans. To a young woman tired of Swiss perfection, the observations of this American artist were an education. He found beauty in the plain heavyweight architecture of industrial buildings and in their rusted hardware and cracked paint; he recognized style in their iron shutters and wrought-iron hasps. Even in his delicate state of convalescence, he seemed to her youthful, strong, and full of spice. For Walker, Isabelle — fashionably dressed, insatiably curious, and bubbling with enthusiasm about what she saw and whom she met — was a delightful companion. That she was married was of course a situation to which he was well accustomed.

Since Alex von Steiger was on the West Coast on assignment, Walker had Isabelle's exclusive companionship for much of the summer of 1959. They toured the coast of Maine together, visiting the Coggeshalls in Newcastle, the Hobsons on Squirrel Island, and the artist Jack Heliker on Cranberry Island. But there were other women in Walker's life. He remained close to Caroline Blackwood. Even when they didn't see each other, they had long conversations on the phone. With Penny Andrews he maintained an on-and-off romance, according to Penny, but it was on enough for her parents to be concerned. Her mother confessed that she was afraid of her daughter's suitor, even though he seemed to be "a very interesting man." During that summer they took Penny off to Europe, in the hope that her interest in Walker might fade. Walker wrote to her but never signed his letters with love. He asked her to throw them away, and she did.

Toward the end of the year, as Walker's fifty-sixth birthday passed and as the Christmas season approached and the von Steigers were due to return to Switzerland, Walker and Isabelle declared their love for each other. Von Steiger had tolerated their romance, expecting it to pass. But for Isabelle, the prospect of returning to Switzerland with her predictable husband no longer held the slightest interest. She had fallen in love not only with the charming and venerable Walker Evans but with the great city he knew so intimately. "What do you want to do?" he asked her as they approached the inevitable impasse in their relationship. "I want to marry you," declared Isabelle, with a sense of confidence she had hardly known before.

At first Walker was flabbergasted at the idea. It had been four years since Jane had departed and at least twice as many since they had lived happily together. But if his confidence in his suitability as a husband had been shaken, he was nonetheless interested in the benefits of having a wife at home. With Isabelle, perhaps, marriage could be a success. In so many ways she promised to be the opposite of Jane. Whereas Jane had resisted his social life, Isabelle would embrace it. Her pretty figure and musical voice would add charm to any party. She would entertain his friends and flatter them with her enthusiasm for their accomplishments. Youthful and fresh to New York on the one hand, sophisticated and well traveled on the other, she was the perfect foil for Walker's urbane and gregarious way of life. Whereas Jane had confirmed his ties to the Midwest and enhanced his understanding of the South, Isabelle gave him a greater bond to Europe. And while Jane had guarded her time with her painting, Isabelle seemed ready to postpone, if not cancel, her professional goals. Her talents at upholstery, interior design, cooking, and gardening could all be directed toward being the perfect young wife of the famous photographer.

Meanwhile, Evans' reputation was enjoying a revival. In the late 1950s a new generation of readers discovered *Let Us Now Praise Famous Men*. Agee's unfinished autobiographical novel, *A Death in the Family*, was published posthumously in 1957 and won a Pulitzer Prize, and a wave of interest in his writing followed. In response, Houghton

Mifflin decided to reprint *Let Us Now Praise Famous Men* in the fall of 1960, and the book "was reborn like the Phoenix," Evans remembered. Lovell Thompson, the manager of the Trade Department, thought the new edition might be enhanced by a brief memoir of the late James Agee by his friend Walker Evans. During a January holiday in Florida with the Brewers, Evans composed his piece.

By now he was a seasoned essayist, having produced more than sixty art reviews for *Time* and more than a dozen short pieces for *Fortune*. He displayed an imaginative command of vocabulary and a talent for animating the most resistant subject, glibly borrowing aspects of his style from writers he admired — the circumlocutions of Henry James, Joyce's animation of the inanimate, and the sensual detail of Agee himself. As a writer, Evans was perhaps most expert at the brief character sketch, having offered candid portraits of talented friends in the letters of recommendation he had written for the Century Club and the Guggenheim Foundation. Indeed, everything he wrote for *Fortune* was an appreciation of some kind; these essays had become his stock in trade.

In his piece about Agee, Evans maintained the emotional distance his subject had loved him for. He wrote about the impression Agee made as well as what went on behind the surface, about what he said as well as what he meant, and about his gift for empathy, which could at times turn him from one person into quite another. In everything Evans expressed, it was clear that he had thought about his subject long, hard, and often, and that Agee's complexities still provoked him as if the man were still alive. "His Christianity," Evans wrote,

> . . . was a punctured and residual remnant, but it was still a naked, root emotion. It was an ex-Church, or non-Church matter, and it was hardly in evidence. All you saw of it was an ingrained courtesy, an uncourtly courtesy that emanated from him towards everyone, perhaps excepting the smugly rich, the pretentiously genteel, and the police. After a while, in a round-about way, you discovered that, to him, human beings were at least possibly immortal and literally sacred souls.

The republication of *Let Us Now Praise Famous Men* was also an occasion for Evans to make a few changes in the photography section.

To begin with, he doubled the number of pictures, bringing the total to sixty-two. Most of his original choices remained, but he changed his mind about the sequence, cropping, and inclusion of a few. The story of the sharecroppers had lost its immediacy; he was better able to assess his work without feeling for his subjects. In the second edition, the photograph section reads with greater emotional distance and higher aesthetic standards than in the first. Finally, the jacket design was altered to be more in keeping with the idea Agee and Evans had shared about it in 1941. In Florida, Evans played with the graphics, with plain gray backgrounds and brown type. The final result was an elegant and understated black-and-white type on a gray ground. It seems that he also had a hand in writing the jacket copy. No one else would have invited the reader to appreciate the subtle power of the "plain, relentless snapshot."

As he reviewed his old work and his old friend, Evans was on the brink of a new life with a new woman. He pondered the ways in which he might be able to improve on the past, to learn from his mistakes. "I miss you all the time," he wrote to Isabelle from Florida on January 16, "and think delicious improbable thoughts of you, of us together. Plans, for the apartment, for Lyme. How to be happy and poor, as you know how to do. Live well on little. Save well and go to London and Paris." And the next day, "I think more and more of our marriage, of ways to make it a success, of how to make you happy. That will be my purpose and it is something worth working for. You have made me believe in my luck. I will succeed with you. And you with me."

Walker's sister was curious about Isabelle, "but nicely so," he reassured her. "Her reaction is just what I'd hoped for. Delight for my sake." Nursing his own curiosity about his bride-to-be, Walker decided to abstain from sexual relations with her until after the wedding. When Alex left New York, he insisted that Isabelle stay at the Barbizon Hotel, on Lexington Avenue, where all well-bred single young ladies were traditionally safely housed.

Most of Walker's friends were happy to see him relieved of his loneliness, but his marriage to the young Swiss woman was not without its skeptics. Especially among the women who had recently figured in his bachelor life, Isabelle seemed an unlikely choice. To his neighbor Barbara Kerr, she seemed much too social for Walker, whom Barbara regarded as shy, even awkwardly so. Penny Andrews felt that Walker's wonderful ascetic sense of style was compromised by Isabelle's taste for florals and chintz. As for Isabelle's parents, they had heartily approved of von Steiger, who came from a good Swiss family and was a hardworking and attractive young man. Why Isabelle should abandon him and her stable life in Switzerland for an adventure with this middle-aged American artist, they were not at all sure. Her mother was frankly distrustful of him. After meeting him for the first time over tea at her New York hotel, she wept and told her daughter as much. But Isabelle had made up her mind.

For his part, Walker reassured Isabelle that there was nothing to worry about as far as gaining the approval of their many onlookers went. Among the people who most mattered, he was certain, there would be nothing but pleasure in getting to know her. "Just be your nice self," he urged. "Leave things alone, all will be well."

Soon after Walker's return from Florida at the end of January, Isabelle took off for Juarez, Mexico, to obtain a quick divorce. Walker's lawyer, Grenville Emmet, had handled her paperwork. In October 1960, Emmet and his wife's cousin, Mark Schmidt, were the hosts of a very private wedding ceremony at Schmidt's house in Katonah, New York. After a simple lunch and a glass of champagne, the newlyweds drove to New London, Connecticut, to board the Pullman to Boston, first class.

Walker was full of anticipation. As a wedding present, he gave Isabelle a long flowing white nightgown and a matching peignoir. He was hoping to spend his wedding night at the Ritz-Carlton in Boston, but it was full, and the Copley Plaza was a disappointing substitute. The newlyweds dined at the Ritz anyway, and the next day Walker hired a black limousine and a driver to take them on a tour of the city. "Walker wasn't feeling very well," remembered Isabelle, "after all that anticipation. The leaves were on the ground. It was a little melancholy."

Almost immediately upon their return to New York, Isabelle suggested that they move out of Walker's apartment. It was not just that the bathtub was in the kitchen (Walker made a photograph of Isabelle standing in the tub wrapped in a towel, like the star of a 1950s Hollywood comedy); the place was a mess, crammed with a confusion of papers and various collections. And a young woman kept calling; if Isabelle answered the phone, Walker would tell her to say he was not at home.

In October, the couple moved into an apartment on the fourth floor of a townhouse at 163 East 94th Street, a classic New York brownstone, with a fireplace and high ceilings. It was the top floor of the townhouse of Gustav Petersen, a German businessman, and his wife, Vita a painter. The neighborhood included several other artists of note. Robert Motherwell, Giorgio Cavalon, and Richard Lindner lived nearby, and they all knew one another. As part of the same crowd, the Petersens were eager to know the legendary photographer and his new young bride.

During Evans' year of convalescence, Leo Lionni, the art director at *Fortune,* retired and moved to Tuscany, leaving the department to his former assistant, Walter Allner. While Evans occasionally obliged Allner with a run-of-the-mill corporate portrait, he increasingly depended on the flexibility of Del Paine and on the faithful support of Paul Grotz at *Architectural Forum.*

Lacking a healthy crop of new photographs, Evans improvised portfolios from his files. "Come On Down," for the July 1962 issue of *Architectural Forum,* was his third portfolio of picture postcards. In much the same spirit that he and Agee had planned their book of anonymous letters in 1938, he accented the authenticity of his collection of summer-hotel cards by quoting the concise messages of their original senders: "Here till the tenth. Come on down," or "Too bad, but you would not come see what you missed." When possible, he also devised portfolios out of photographs he had already made. "Primitive Churches" was one such piece, comprising photographs of Alabama and South Carolina dating back to 1936 expanded by more recent examples from Massachusetts and Maine. Barbara Kerr, then an editor at *Mademoiselle,* pieced together a story from Evans' photographs of Third Avenue antique stores, "Collector's Items," and married it to a chatty piece on browsing by the English professor Malcolm Bradbury.

Considering how little new photography Evans was producing, some of the editors of *Fortune* began to have their doubts that he was worth keeping. "But he had this other feather in his bow," explained Holly Whyte. "He could write." In 1963 Evans summoned all his journalistic skills as well as his indignity in a preservationist diatribe for *Life*. The piece was inspired by the news of the impending demolition of the Pennsylvania Railroad Station. In its place would be a high-rise office building; the old depot would be reduced to a low-ceilinged, fluorescently lit underground station. Bad enough that this grand old monument to the American railroad, with "its Herculean columns, its vast canopies of concrete and steel," was about to be reduced to rubble; worse that this act of vandalism was like so many others. "America's heritage of great architecture is *doomed*," was Evans' headline in the July 3 issue of *Life*. "*It must be saved.*"

> The disaster that has befallen Penn Station threatens thousands of other prized American buildings. From east to west, the wrecker's ball and bulldozer are lords of the land. In the ruthless, if often well-intentioned, cause of progress, the nation's heritage from colonial days onward is being ravaged indiscriminately — for highways, parking lots, new structures of modernized mediocrity.

In reviewing his files for examples of doomed architecture, Evans came up with good news and bad. The United States Hotel in Saratoga ("the last word in nineteenth-century elegance") had been razed in 1945. However, an antebellum mansion in Tuscaloosa, which had been the office and depot of an auto wrecking company when Evans first encountered it in 1936, had been restored by a Baptist church.

While the eclectic American architecture that Evans loved faced the wrecker's ball in the early 1960s, two events in the works at the Museum of Modern Art would serve to resurrect his classic style of the 1930s. Edward Steichen was organizing a retrospective of the photography of the Farm Security Administration, dramatically titled

"The Bitter Years." It was Steichen's belief that a new generation, "which has problems of its own," would benefit from seeing the vivid evidence of the Depression. Rexford Tugwell was brought in to cast his blessing on the exhibition, and Roy Stryker showed up to advise on the hanging of the show. Stryker had never believed that the photography of his historical section belonged in a museum. So immune was he to the notion of a photograph as a valuable work of art that in recent years he had gone through the early negatives of Evans and Shahn and actually punched holes through the ones he considered to be rejects. At the museum he marched around espousing this and denouncing that in his rough western twang. The department research assistant who trailed after him recalled that "every other word was *goddamn.*"

Evans had been agitating for a new edition of *American Photographs* for some time. Elizabeth Shaw, the head of publicity at the museum, remembered that he talked to everyone about it and made it everyone's responsibility to see that it was done. Ultimately, the project fell on the shoulders of Monroe Wheeler, Frances Collins' successor as the director of publications. The new edition, published in 1962, was virtually the same as the first, but there were a few subtle differences. The dust jacket displayed a photograph (*Wooden houses, Boston, 1930*) rather than just type; the titles of the pictures were moved from the back of each of the two sections to the page opposite each photograph; and the dedication page with the initials J.S.N. was removed. In its place was a brief foreword written by Wheeler, who dedicated the book to the "many young people" who had encountered it in libraries and found it not only "an extraordinary example of photographic art, but . . . an indispensable visual chronicle." Wheeler added an explanation of why the photographs seemed even more important in retrospect than they had when they were made: "Evans contemplates the present as it might be seen at some future date." To mark the publication, Steichen's assistant curator, Grace Mayer, selected fifteen photographs from the book for a small exhibition.

Among the "many young people" who discovered Evans' photography at the time was an artist by the name of William Christenberry, who had been born in Tuscaloosa, Alabama, in 1936, just three months after Agee and Evans found their way to the county court-house in Greenville and first made the acquaintance of the Bur-roughses, the Fieldses, and the Tingles. Twenty-three years later, Christenberry picked up the new edition of *Let Us Now Praise Famous Men* in his favorite bookshop in Birmingham and recognized his grandmother's neighbors in Hale County, Frank and Flora Bee Tingle.

Within the year Christenberry had moved to New York to look for a job. He had learned that Walker Evans was a senior editor at *Fortune* magazine. One day when he found himself in the neighborhood of the Time-Life Building he was seized by the impulse to enter the skyscraper and walk right up to the woman at the reception desk. "'Excuse me ma'am,'" he recalled himself inquiring, "'but does a Mister Walker Evans work here?' And she picked up this *huge* direc-tory. 'Evans, eighteenth floor,' she said, and before I could say another thing she'd called up there. Fortunately for me, he was on vacation."

A few months later Christenberry gathered his courage to call Evans on the phone. He told him that he was from Alabama and that he knew a lot about the families in *Let Us Now Praise Famous Men.* Christenberry recalled that Evans was very interested in what he knew about the Tingles and immediately suggested that they meet. Evans was also moved to help the serious, innocent young man from the South survive in New York. Before long he had found him a job as a file clerk in the photo library of Time Inc.

At about the same time, Marvin Israel introduced Evans to Diane Arbus, who was then working as a freelance photographer for *Har-per's Bazaar* and other fashion magazines. Arbus was the daughter of wealthy Jewish New Yorkers in the fur trade and the founders of Rus-sek's department store. She had grown up in an overstuffed apart-ment in a towering building on Central Park West, but from early on she was irresistibly drawn to the city's underworlds. Israel had shown her Evans' subway portraits, and in the frightening candor of this work she detected a kindred spirit.

But when Israel took Arbus to the door of Evans' apartment for the first time, she was too frightened to go in and sent him on with her pictures. Evans was immediately impressed. Soon afterward, with Evans' encouragement, Arbus became a regular visitor to the apartment to share her latest work. Evans envied the outright daring of this outwardly shy, nervous, inarticulate young photographer. "My favorite thing is to go where I've never been," said Arbus. Photography was her open ticket to get there, as it had been for Evans in his youth. He still used photography as an excuse to get behind the scenes, but compared with the subject matter Arbus was seeking out, his work was tame. When she met Evans in 1961, Arbus was taking her camera to nudist camps, to the dressing rooms of performing transvestites, topless dancers, and sword swallowers, and to the homes of midgets and freaks. Even without searching for such obscure locales, she made portraits of strangers on the streets of New York and in the act revealed them to be the aberrant products of a sick society. She could make a carefully trained curl of hair or the arch of a plucked eyebrow look grotesque, as if behind this façade lay a terrible secret. Her pictures spoke to the malcontents of her own generation, who were eager to expose the ills of American life, and she eventually won an impressive reputation.

In the 1960s, the pleasure of new faces for Evans alternated with the loss of old friends. In the spring of 1963 he learned that Wilder Hobson was on his deathbed. Years of heavy social drinking had taken their toll on a friend Evans had once described as "a seriously happy man." Hobson had produced one important book on American jazz, which was his passion, and two novels, which went unpublished and unnoticed, respectively. Otherwise he had labored for *Fortune, Time,* and later *Newsweek,* editing and writing and for the past several years leading the life of a commuter, returning home to Verna and his two children in Princeton. But like many men and women of the generation who came of age in the days of Prohibition, Hobson never got over the forbidden thrill of drinking and never learned to resist it.

With Isabelle, Walker made his way to Princeton to say goodbye. Percy and Nancy Woods, neighbors of the Hobsons', invited them to stay. Nancy was the daughter of the poet Allen Tate and could gossip with Walker about poets and writers of his generation as if she had known them all intimately. Percy, a psychologist, lent his wry observations. Night after night with the Woodses, Walker would talk and drink until almost dawn. After two or three nights Isabelle left for New York, but Walker was reluctant to go.

Wilder's children, Archie and Eliza, were amazed at the way Walker vigilantly stood by as their father was dying. He was the only visitor outside the family whom the hospital would allow into the intensive care unit, where Wilder lay. The nurses could not resist him, and probably did not know that he carried a flask of whiskey in his belt. "When you get through this, old Hobson and old Evans will get together again," Walker would say, but Archie could hear the doubt in his voice.

When Wilder finally died, Walker stayed for the wake, which lasted ten days, and the funeral, which was packed with old friends. The church's choir sang spirituals in Hobson's honor. When the crowd gathered outside after the service, Walker saw Jane for the first time since their divorce, standing on the steps of the church. He walked up to her, took her hand, and kissed it, then quickly turned to resume his conversation, without a trace of inner conflict.

When Walker went home, Isabelle felt that he was a changed man. She had not noticed how much he drank before; it might have seemed a lighthearted habit, but now it was serious. They had recently moved from the Petersens' house on East 94th Street to an apartment in a remodeled brownstone on East 85th — a depressing little place, Isabelle thought. It seemed to stand for the lull in Walker's work, the sadness of losing his friends, and his growing attachment to alcohol.

10 *Message from the Interior*

OTHER THAN SHOWING AN OCCASIONAL flurry of energy over
a picture-story idea, Evans had all but quit working for *Fortune* by
1964. Most of the people who over the years had made working for
Time Inc. a pleasure for him, if not a privilege, had died or departed.
Herb Solow died on Thanksgiving Day of that year. Jim Agee and
Wilder Hobson were already dead; Jimmy Stern and Tom Matthews
had left for England. For Evans, the fabric of company spirit was
wearing thin.

As he gained the stature of a veteran staff member, his condescension toward some of his younger colleagues became pointed. He
remained as elusive as he had been toward his colleagues at the FSA
thirty years earlier. Among others, Walter McQuade, who wrote for
both *Fortune* and *Architectural Forum,* never succeeded in breaking
through the barrier of his seniority. In 1964 Evans and McQuade were
paired for a story on Boston, part of a series on American cities that
Henry Luce had devised. McQuade spent most of the winter traveling
to and from Boston, gathering information on the history, economics,
and architecture of the city, but Evans only dropped in with Isabelle
for a few days in January, long enough to make some pictures and
accept McQuade's invitation to dine at the Ritz-Carlton. When the
check came, McQuade reached for his wallet; Evans grandly offered

to pay the tip. Extracting a fresh green note from his pocket, he folded it several times over until it was a small wad in the palm of his hand and pressed it into the waiter's hand as he glided to the door.

Fortune's financial department found it increasingly difficult to justify supporting a staff photographer who seemed to do whatever he pleased, if he did anything at all. The budget director, Patrick Lanahan, was known to be intolerant of staff members who appeared to take advantage of the magazine's expense accounts and benefits. He was particularly displeased with Evans when he learned that he had used the loan he had requested for medical leave in 1960 to purchase a secondhand Jaguar. Over lunch one day, Walter Allner warned Evans that he was facing increasing demands for routine photography, such as the dreaded corporate portraits. Otherwise he was in danger of being considered too much of a luxury. "But Walter," Evans protested, "I thought *Fortune* could afford a luxury!"

Allner was well aware that Evans considered the corporate portraits beneath his dignity; they were a task he had routinely succeeded in passing on to Ralph Steiner, Dan Weiner, and other photographers better suited to it. The corporate chief was bound to be a very busy man; the photographer could expect to be treated brusquely and told that his subject had only a few minutes to spare. But Evans could not be pressed into working fast, and to be treated like a journeyman photographer was for him a bitter pill. Though his work was generally skilled and competent, quite often, according to Allner, the results of his portrait sessions were unsatisfactory.

If Evans was beginning to seem like an unnecessary luxury at *Fortune*, his work was elsewhere in demand. Hugh Edwards, now the curator of photographs at the Art Institute of Chicago, organized a small exhibition of his photographs to open in November 1964. The majority of the twenty photographs on view were recent, some made on assignment for the Container Corporation, some on self-assigned projects for *Fortune*, some on visits with friends. Most of all, the Chicago exhibition showed Evans' inexhaustible eye for interiors. These photographs were for him a form of portraiture, an expression of the people who arranged and inhabited the rooms, at least as telling as their faces, especially if they weren't there. "I do like to suggest people sometimes by their absence," he once said. "I like to make you feel that an interior is *almost* inhabited by somebody." By the 1960s, that somebody was no longer an Alabama tenant farmer, a Kentucky coal miner, or a shrimp fisherman in Biloxi, Mississippi. Evans was more inclined to intrude on the artist or the heiress or the friend with a country house. The Chicago exhibition included his photographs of Mrs. Mabry's dining room, Robert Frank's living room, and an unspoiled Victorian parlor that Ben Shahn had led him to in Oldwick, New Jersey.

As a guest, Evans noticed everything. His eye was ever alert to the detail that gave the room its special character and the personal stamp of its inhabitant. He campaigned against museum reproductions and professionally decorated rooms; he flattered his hosts with his sure eye for the quality of their particular taste. He would inquire about the fabric of the curtains, admire the curve of a certain chair, or covet an antique silver box or the first edition of a book he might have read twenty years before. Sometimes his enthusiasm for an object so disarmed his hosts that they found themselves rather unexpectedly giving it to him — as a friend recalled, "One was expected to make the sacrifice" — a gesture that Evans rarely protested. His flattery contained a twist. There were certain things he believed would be better loved, better understood, in his hands than in someone else's.

Before the exhibition at the Art Institute closed in January 1965, Evans accepted Hugh Edwards' invitation to go and see it. His only request was that Edwards line him up with a nice young man to assist him on a road trip of a few days. Edwards came up with David Swan, a young architect and amateur photographer who was a frequent visitor to the institute's photography department.

Evans' main objective was to get to Galena, Illinois, a railroad town in the northwest corner of the state that had remained remarkably intact since its heyday in the nineteenth century. As one guidebook described it, Galena contained "a résumé of the nation's architectural experience." Its share of Greek Revival houses was particularly impressive. But upon arriving in Galena, Evans found its charm too obvious to be interesting material for his camera. Quickly finding his way to the edge of town, he photographed the old baggage carts baking in the sun on the railroad tracks.

From Galena, Evans and Swan traveled on to St. Louis, which had fared less well than Galena over the years. Its downtown was in ruins, and the well-to-do had abandoned the city neighborhoods for the suburbs of Clayton and Ladue. As Swan recalled, Evans had no interest in revisiting the streets where he had once lived and preferred to stay in the old business district. He made photographs in a desultory way. "All he really wanted was a drinking companion, someone to talk to — he was out on a lark," remembered Swan. In a secondhand bookshop in downtown St. Louis, Evans came across a four-volume set of books that he told Swan he had been looking for for years. The only trouble was, he didn't have enough money in his pocket to pay for them. Later Swan returned to the shop and bought the set as a gift. It cost him at least as much as Evans was paying him to drive him south. But it seemed to be the only thing that made their trip to St. Louis worthwhile.

The growing presence of young men and women in Evans' life relieved some of the pain of growing old. To the generation coming of age in the 1960s, the art and life of Walker Evans were a paradigm of a liberal-minded era and an artistic plainspokenness that matched their own search for truth. Given the Cuban missile crisis in 1962, the assassination of President Kennedy in 1963, the race riots in Harlem and Watts in 1965, and the accelerating war in Vietnam, they had reason to doubt the political confidence of the immediate postwar years. Like the generation that had come of age in the 1930s, they felt compelled to speak their minds. At the same time, recent history suggested that they should beware of substituting their own flawed idealism for that of their parents. Walker Evans' gentle-mannered iconoclasm and his skeptical distance from political dogma on the right or on the left struck a note of quiet authority. His photographs of the Depression had outlasted the vicissitudes of New Deal politics, never having been driven by them in the first place. His travels across the country to bring back his own chronicle of its state of mind were an inspiring example to the growing number of young people who, in Paul Simon's words, had "all gone to look for America."

Furthermore, the young Americans of the 1960s held no prejudice against the notion of photography as a legitimate art form. They had grown up with television and movies in "living" color. They had suffered an onslaught of visual excitement that made the classic photographs of Walker Evans seem all the more stately, still, and convincing.

The emerging pop art movement also gave Evans' photography a fresh interest. Long before Andy Warhol made a silk-screen of a Campbell's soup can or Roy Lichtenstein enlarged heartbroken comic-book lovers to more than life size, Evans had perceived the ironic potential of ubiquitous commercial logos and seriocomic art. He was later to quip to the artist Robert Moskowitz, among others, that he had invented pop art. Even though this was far from true, the connection was intriguing. Drawing upon the icons of popular culture, the pop artists were rebelling against the purity of the abstract expressionist painters who directly preceded them. They worked with a self-conscious absence of feeling, whereas Evans had a genuine love for the objects he photographed. But at a moment when a new school of preservationists was battling an increasingly throwaway American culture and pop artists were raising the throwaway to the level of icon, the meaning of junk was up for grabs, and the art of Walker Evans seemed to be at the heart of the dichotomy. His vision of America as a junk culture of advertising, cars, and dereliction had come of age. His preference for the education of the street over that of the art museum or the academy was in fashion. In the early 1960s he began a series of photographs of trash — sometimes literally staring head down into public trashcans. For him, trash was the contemporary equivalent of the ruin.

Evans' longtime passion for picture postcards was part of the same aesthetic. Among a small number of privileged visitors to his apartment on York Avenue, it had become known that his collection was not only vast but highly refined. On several occasions in the late 1950s he had been persuaded to perform his special postcard slide show for friends, flashing the images on the wall in the dark, magnified to life-size proportions, and inviting his viewers to project themselves onto the main streets and boardwalks of turn-of-the-century America. There was no more authentic portrayal of the American scene to be had, he argued. But now postcards carried a poor reputation. To say that a view was like a picture postcard was to be derogatory. In an article in *Fortune*, Evans bemoaned the current "aesthetic slump" of postcard art, which had been reduced to the "quintessence of gimcrack."

> Gone is all feeling for the actual appearance of street, of lived architecture, or of human mien. In the early-century days color photography was of course in its infancy. Cards were usually made from black-and-white photographs subsequently tinted by hand lithography. Withal, the best ones achieved a fidelity and restraint that most color photography printers have yet to match — notably in flesh tints and in the rendering of patina and the soft tones of town buildings and streets.

Within the modest frame of a penny postcard, Evans blended his knowledge of photographic art, graphic design, and American social history. It was this ability that in 1964 led the artist Jack Tworkov, the head of the art department at Yale, to invite his friend Evans to bring his postcard slide lecture to the university. In the small auditorium of Yale's new art and architecture building, a massive piece of 1960s brutalism designed by Paul Rudolph, Evans delivered his lecture on the art of the postcard. The response was enthusiastic among students and faculty alike. Alvin Eisenman, a young professor of graphics, was especially intrigued with Evans' presentation. With Tworkov's wholehearted approval, Eisenman decided to ask Evans to teach at Yale.

Eisenman telephoned Evans at Time Inc. several times. Never finding him in his office, he left one message after another. After twelve attempts, by Eisenman's reckoning, Evans finally returned his call and agreed to go to New Haven to discuss the position.

There was no photography department or degree program at the Yale School of Graphic Design in 1964. Eisenman, however, believed that photography was an essential tool for the graphic designer and made it a requirement in the graphics curriculum. The Swiss designer Herbert Matter had been teaching photography part-time since 1951, and Eisenman believed that Matter's exacting technical approach and minimal verbal comment might be well complemented by Evans' flexible, literary mind for pictures and gift for conversation. Eisenman was also disturbed by the current fashion among university students for large-format nature photography, exemplified by the work of Ansel Adams, Minor White, and Paul Caponigro. Instruction in this kind of work went hand in hand with the "zone system," a method of calculating exposure and development that in its perfectly modulated scale of grays would reveal every blade of grass, every shimmering leaf. Evans would be sure to counteract this trend, for there was nothing that interested him less than nature photography. Most of all, Eisenman wanted Evans to teach his students how to "read" a photograph in terms of both its human and its aesthetic interest. Would he consider the job?

Evans told Eisenman that it was the most interesting assignment he could imagine. As a visiting professor, he joined a faculty that was faithful to Josef Albers' legacy of inventive modernism. Eisenman and Norman Ives taught a rigorous course in graphic design; Herbert Matter and John Hill, an architectural photographer, taught photographic technique. Evans' only teaching responsibility was to give individual weekly portfolio reviews. He commuted to New Haven by train on Fridays and spent most of the day at Yale. One by one the students presented their work to the master in a small windowless room in the Rudolph building.

The idea of being on the faculty at Yale was enough to make Evans blush with pride. He had set his hopes on Yale as a prep-school student almost forty years earlier, and the yearning had never quite left him. His years in the company of Yale, Harvard, and Princeton men at *Time* and *Fortune* had constantly reminded him of the enduring power of Ivy League prestige. Finally, the appointment was the very honor Evans needed to snub his nose at *Fortune,* and it helped him to realize that he was ready to leave Time Inc. for good.

All the same, faithful to the former rebellious student in himself, he was doubtful about his abilities as a teacher and remained distrustful of most forms of the educational system. He also found the quality of his students disappointing at first. They didn't seem to be very well read, nor did they exude the good manners that in his college days had been indigenous in the Ivy League. After an all-day session of examination reviews in January 1965, he wrote to Isabelle, then in Europe, that the experience had been "rather interesting; but

I didn't really like the tone or something about university life and I don't believe I'd wish to go into it full-time. I have only two exceptional students out of thirty, although several others are intelligent. Very few are well-bred, so perhaps that's a thing of the past."

In 1964 Walker and Isabelle planned to spend Christmas with her family in Bern. During the fourteen years of his marriage to Jane, Walker had successfully avoided meeting her parents, but a trip to Europe and a holiday in the company of Isabelle and her two doting and beautiful younger sisters, Christine and Anne-Marie, helped to make Christmas with the Boeschensteins an attractive prospect. In the midst of the Christmas dinner festivities and the joyful babble of the reunited family, his eyes filled with tears.

No doubt Walker was feeling the loss of his own family as keenly as the warmth of Isabelle's. In the fall of that year, his sister, Jane, had died. In recent years her little house in Florida had been his regular retreat, where he recovered from illness or surgery and swam and lounged in the sun when the New York winter seemed interminable. To Isabelle, the Brewers were like a pair of shorebirds, which they watched with avid interest around the Florida saltmarsh — Talbot a heron, Jane a frail stork. Like her brother, Jane had a certain grace, and like him, she knew how to twist a phrase. But they shared few interests, and their visits were not without conflict. After a day or two Jane would begin to pester Walker in little ways, hinting broadly about how he took advantage of their hospitality, reminding him that he hadn't finished college, or boring him with family history. Walker would escape to the beach to read a book.

But even though brother and sister had lacked the warmth of true soulmates, Jane had been all Walker had left of family, and he had depended on her more than he realized. In November, he wrote to Isabelle's father to thank him for his letter of condolence. "As a man of my age, you know how more and more frequent, and painful, death is," he wrote. "It leaves me the only member of the immediate family of father, mother, and two children. *Fin de race*," he concluded, half in jest, as if the Evanses were old European aristocracy.

If Walker really cared about extending the Evans family name, he showed no interest in acting on it with Isabelle. Before they had married, he had made it clear that he did not want children. But when Robert Hale, Walker's fellow Centurian, and his wife had a baby, Isabelle wondered if Walker's feelings toward having one of their own might soften. Robert was about Walker's age, just over sixty, and Nicki, his wife, was not much older than Isabelle. Might this parallel marriage inspire his confidence? "We'd have to send him to Andover and Harvard, and we can't afford it" was one of Walker's arguments against having a child. He assumed, of course, that their baby would be a boy.

As Walker looked forward to retiring from Time Inc. for the greener pastures of academia, he nurtured anxieties. Isabelle was alarmed by the amount he was drinking that Christmas in Bern. In their hotel room she looked on helplessly as day after day he ordered a bottle of Russian vodka with his breakfast tray. By evening it would be drained. The Boeschensteins were paying the bill, but Isabelle cautiously asked the management to keep the liquor tab aside for her to pay. By the end of their stay, it had added up to more than the cost of the room.

After Christmas the Evanses flew to England to visit Jimmy and Tania Stern at Hatch Manor, an old Tudor farmhouse in Wiltshire that Jimmy had recently bought with his inheritance. When they arrived, they were greeted by the news that the White House had just telephoned, trying to reach Evans. As Stern recalled, Evans "had advanced no further than the hall, when, producing a pint-size flask from his overcoat, he let his head fall back, tipped up the flask, took a long pull, let out a gasp, and then declared that this phone call could only mean that an intimate friend of his in Washington had committed suicide." Later, when the White House called again, they learned that there was no need for alarm. President Johnson's cultural team wanted Evans to be one of the "overseers" of photography in the United States. As such, he was invited to attend the White House Festival of the Arts on the following June 14, to be honored along with other noted figures in the fields of art, music, and literature. The transatlantic call was not bad news after all.

But later that night, Stern came across Evans prowling the downstairs hall in search of a vodka nightcap. "It's this darned ulcer," he explained, giving his stomach a stroke. The next day, Stern learned of the myriad pills Evans took. As half a dozen little bottles emerged from his "pillmanteau," Evans explained their various functions to Tania, "like a man proudly exhibiting his stamp collection."

From the Evanses' point of view, the trip to Hatch Manor was a great success. "I haven't seen [Walker] as happy as he was at Hatch for the longest time," Isabelle wrote to the Sterns. "He needs his old friends to stimulate him and fill his soul with love, and in the end there is very little I can do for him." On St. Patrick's Day, Walker himself confessed to Jimmy Stern that the winter had been a hard one: "It is the Ides of March . . . really death time. But not death this time around, we intend not only to survive but to rise, prosper, and lick the world, as you and [Tania] have done." Then, recalling their fond reminiscences of Jim Agee, he wrote, "Il faut pleurer, so much wasted, lost, before used properly. Well what is proper. Maybe what happens is proper."

Speaking of his old friend, Evans might just as easily have been reflecting on the decline of his own creative powers. He quit *Fortune* on May 31, 1965. After twenty years with the magazine, he departed almost unnoticed, and his output during those years had been all but ignored. With the little structure the job had given his life now gone, his drinking reached an alarming level. One evening at York Avenue, John McDonald was so shocked at the amount he was drinking that he strongly suggested that Walker should go to a clinic to be dried out. By the fall of 1965, Walker was willing to admit that he had a problem, and he wanted to conquer it. To that end he booked himself a stay at Regent's Hospital, a discreet clinic for alcoholics on East 61st Street.

He was scheduled to enter Regent's on the evening of November 9, 1965. Less than an hour after sunset, just as his train from New Haven pulled into Grand Central, a huge power failure suddenly and mysteriously blacked out the northeast coast from Pennsylvania to Quebec. Tuning in to the transistor radio that he always carried, Walker was apprised of the details of the disaster, and he decided that his best course was to check into the Vanderbilt Hotel, near the station. Isabelle, who was shopping at Bloomingdale's when the lights went out, easily made her way to Regent's. Finding no Walker, she spent the night in his bed. The next day electricity was restored and Walker settled willingly into his program of rehabilitation. Isabelle went to visit every day, taking books, magazines, and her cheerful babbling of news.

An equally regular visitor was a young man named Leslie Katz, who had just established his own art-book press. A small man with a genial round face, Katz was the son of a successful advertising executive, and he could afford to follow his own rarefied taste in books and bookmaking, publishing works that a commercial house would consider impractical. His first book was a facsimile of the first edition of Whitman's *Leaves of Grass.* Now he was eager to work with a contemporary artist. Margaret Marshall, the literary editor of *The Nation,* suggested that he contact her friend Walker Evans.

Distracting Evans from the pounding fists and mutterings of Regent's other patients, Katz discussed plans for a new book of Evans' photographs, the first to be published by the Eakins Press. The portfolio, Katz hoped, would represent an entirely new standard in photographic books. With an eye to quality and coherence, they selected a small number of photographs, spanning the photographer's career from its beginnings to the present, to be printed on oversize heavyweight stock and bound to a slender spine. Each page would be printed on one side only, interleaved with waxed tissue, and titled in an elegant typeface at a discreet remove from the image. Matching Evans' penchant for the square format of Rolleiflex negatives, the book was an eccentric fourteen by fourteen and a half inches. The generous advance Katz made would cover Evans' charges at Regent's.

Katz and Evans agreed to devote the book exclusively to Evans' photographs of interiors. They selected images as deep in his past as the DeLuzes' kitchen in Truro, the breakfast room at Belle Grove, and the charred ruin of a house near where his mother had lived in Ossining. They also chose more recent photographs made during summer visits with intimate friends, such as one of Eliza Mabry's bedroom in Stockbridge, her pillow guarded by a team of lightly mauled stuffed animals, her toy horses neatly stalled on the lower shelf of her bedside table.

When Walker emerged from Regent's Hospital ten days after his

admission, he was, Isabelle believed, a new man. So convinced was
Walker that he had overcome his drinking problem that he refused
to attend the requisite follow-up session two weeks later. Instead, he
and Isabelle almost immediately went south to Florida to stay with
Talbot Brewer and bask in the winter sun. "We are back," Walker wrote
to Lovell Thompson upon their return in mid-January, ". . . both
having had 'flu in Fla. (Flu in Fla, you may have a song title)."

After a period of hesitation, Evans began to enjoy university life and
his role as resident mentor. Although he distrusted the very idea of
teaching photography and believed that the best photographers were,
like himself, self-taught, he saw the value in setting a personal example. Pressed to define his approach, he stressed "absolute fidelity to
the medium itself." Photography, he told his students, was best at
recording the contemporary scene. It was important to understand
the use of natural, uncontrived lighting and to have a general but
unobtrusive command of technique. He warned them of the dangers
of nostalgia, sentiment, propaganda, and color. "Color photography
is vulgar," he said more than once, and there were few examples that
anyone could find to dispute him with, except perhaps those he himself had made tastefully throughout the twenty years he worked for
Fortune.
    Most of all, Evans stressed that each student must find his or her
own voice. Eisenman remembered his ability to draw a student out
by subtle indirection:

> He would ask a person a question, like "What interests you the most?
> What excites you? Here you are in New Haven, having come from
> somewhere else — what do you see?" A student might say, "It isn't
> anything that has an image, I couldn't photograph that." He'd say, "Oh
> yes, you can. Try to find a way." He kept notebooks of these conver-
> sations that would lead to an idea. He would squeeze the idea out of
> a student and hold the student to it. He would never propose to take
> it literally, nor tell them how to do it. He just said, "If you think about
> it hard enough, you can find a way."

Evans avoided answering any question in a direct or obvious way.
As his student Alston Purvis described it, "He circled around the

subject like a hawk." He would not dwell for long on the subject of photography per se. He led his students away from it, often by suggesting that photography was the most literary of arts and adding that some writers had a photographic eye. He could demonstrate the photographic acuity of writers such as Flaubert, Proust, Henry James, Nabokov, and Joyce.

Nor did Evans present his own photography as an example for his students to follow. While he prescribed his straightforward approach to the medium, he expected them to come up with their own reasons for using it and rejected their efforts to imitate him. Marie-Antoinette Alpert remembered presenting him with a series of pictures she had deliberately made to appeal to his eye, of a dilapidated Victorian house on the seashore. After looking through the pictures briefly, Evans turned the whole pile upside down and said, "Okay, now let's talk about you."

Evans had a knack for drawing out whatever it was that he and the student would both enjoy talking about. Tom Strong remembered his own "absolute delight in finding a teacher who really cared about Binx Bolling," the main character in Walker Percy's *The Moviegoer*. With Alston Purvis, Evans stirred up memories of South Carolina, where Purvis had grown up, and his old friend Julia Peterkin, who was Purvis' cousin. Chris Pullman, another student, came from Wilmette, Illinois, just north of Kenilworth. But Pullman felt that Evans had "transcended his background. He seemed to have arrived from nowhere."

As Walker gained confidence in his role as a professor, he and Isabelle began to consider setting up house nearer New Haven. As it was, he went up for the day and was back in town again by evening, but sometimes he spent the night at the old-fashioned Hotel Duncan, just around the corner from the architecture building. If he had had his fondest wish, their new house would have looked out over Long Island Sound, but he could hardly complain about the acre and a half on secluded Beaverbrook Road that the Voorheeses sold to him for a dollar. In 1965, he and Isabelle demolished Jane's studio and embarked on a plan to build a new house near the site. Isabelle's parents would help them financially; whatever she had saved from her own work would also go into it. She would be in charge of the interior, and

Walker would be responsible for the exterior. "This little piece of land that we own in Lyme is worth quite a lot," Isabelle assured the Sterns. "It is all zoned and overprotected and there will never be an ugly Motel or any Tourist-trap in this whole sacred neighborhood." They hired Robert Busser, a recent graduate of the Yale School of Design, as the architect. It would be a simple frame construction in the modern style, its main feature being a large living room with a high vaulted ceiling and sliding glass doors opening onto a spacious deck. For traditional Old Lyme, it was daringly modern.

Once the house was completed, Isabelle wondered what she would do there. As Walker became more involved in university life, she began to yearn for an interesting job of her own. She was also not sure she wanted to spend most of the academic year in rural Connecticut. So when she was offered a teaching position for the winter term of 1966 at the Kunstgewerbeschule in Zurich, it seemed to her the perfect arrangement. At first Walker resisted the idea; he had a busy year ahead and he wanted Isabelle to be there to look after him. But finally he gave in to her pleas, and she went.

In her absence, several projects kept Evans from feeling deserted. Plans for the book with the Eakins Press were moving forward, and he was also corresponding with Lovell Thompson at Houghton Mifflin about the publication of his subway photographs. Other than a small portfolio in *The Cambridge Review* in 1956 and an even smaller one Marvin Israel had published in *Harper's Bazaar* in 1962, the pictures had languished in his files, unseen for more than twenty years. Houghton Mifflin planned to publish a selection in October.

At the same time, Evans found himself in favor again at the Museum of Modern Art, in a way he had not been since Lincoln Kirstein and Tom Mabry had promoted the exhibition "American Photographs." John Szarkowski, the new director of the department of photographs, was keenly interested in Evans' career. Like Steichen, whom he succeeded in 1962, Szarkowski was a photographer himself. While working in a studio in Wisconsin he had been introduced to Evans' *American Photographs* by his former art history teacher, who strongly recommended that he study it carefully. Szarkowski, who was then learning the deceptive techniques of the commercial studio photographer, was hard-pressed to understand what anyone thought was great about Evans' work. But by the time the book was stolen from him a few years later, he understood better and was ready to go to the considerable lengths necessary to obtain another copy. In 1955 he won a Guggenheim fellowship for a book he was planning on the architecture of Louis Sullivan. In New York that year in a mood of exhilarated confidence, he decided to call on Evans, who he had been apprised might be found in his office at *Fortune.* Szarkowski was in luck. Evans immediately invited him up and appreciatively looked over his portfolio of technically clean, elegantly composed architectural photographs, pausing longest over the best of them and not so long over the not-so-good ones, and said, as Szarkowski remembered, "absolutely the right thing about every picture." But he had seen Szarkowski's work before: unbeknown to Szarkowski, Evans had helped him win his Guggenheim.

Like Evans, Szarkowski loved the work of the nineteenth-century masters of wet-plate photography. By the time he was made director of the department of photographs at the Museum of Modern Art, he had also come to believe in the value of anonymous photographs. He embraced the critical conundrum of "photographer unknown" as warmly as Evans embraced the postcard. On the cover of his first treatise as curator, *The Photographer's Eye,* he placed an anonymous photograph of a bedroom that resembles nothing so much as a classic Walker Evans. But as much as he loved the accidental genius of the medium, Szarkowski appreciated the individual photographer as a wholly conscious artist. He would return the department to the scholarly, contemplative pace of Newhall's day, when it had been enough to consider the work of one photographer at a time. Abandoning the thematic roundups of Steichen's directorship, Szarkowski made his point explicitly in 1963 with his first exhibition, which he called "Five Unrelated Photographers."

In 1966, Szarkowski proposed an exhibition of Evans' subway photographs, to coincide with the October publication of the book. At various times since making these pictures, Evans had attempted to explain his enterprise in words. The fact that the photographs had spent so many years in hiding seemed to call for an explanation. His argument for not having shown them was that he did not wish to expose his subjects before time had transformed them beyond recognition. "The portraits on these pages were caught by a hidden camera," he wrote in 1962, "in the hands of a penitent spy and an apologetic voyeur. But the rude and impudent invasion involved has been carefully softened and partially mitigated by a planned passage of time. These pictures were taken twenty years ago, and deliberately preserved from publication."

Evans' emphasis on respect for his subjects' privacy dated back to his experience with Agee in Alabama. But the twenty-year retirement of the subway portraits had not been as carefully planned as he claimed. When he first started to make the portraits, in 1938, he was concerned that another photographer might steal his idea, one that he was sure was unique, and he showed them to very few people. Soon afterward they became part of a larger project that included street portraits and was to make up *Faces of Men,* the book he proposed in his 1941 Guggenheim application, which never came to be.

In retrospect, the series held its own and even gained power as a piece in its own right. Rather than cropping the pictures close to each individual face, as he had done earlier, Evans showed them framed by the hard evidence of subway travel, like a modern-day Daumier. He pondered several possible titles for the series. "Lexington Ave. Local" was one idea; "The Passengers" was another. Finally, Alice Morris, with her infallible sense of poetry, suggested a phrase from the Book of Matthew: "Many are called, but few are chosen." Toying with the words, Evans finally decided to leave it at *Many Are Called.* He also abandoned all his previous attempts at writing about the photographs and chose a brief essay James Agee had written for *The Cambridge Review* to serve as his introduction. Every one of Evans' subjects, Agee had said, "carries in the postures of his body, in his hands, in his face, in the eyes, the signatures of a time and a place in the world upon a creature for whom the name immortal soul is one mild and vulgar metaphor." Evans dedicated the book to Agee in memoriam. "Isabelle releases me," he wrote to Lovell Thompson, "and I shall give her the portfolio I'm publishing."

It was again Alice Morris who came up with a title for the Eakins

Press book. Visiting Walker and Isabelle in their new house one fall weekend, she suggested, out of the blue, "Message from the Interior." As promised, Walker dedicated the portfolio to Isabelle, and he invited John Szarkowski to write a brief afterword. On the title page he quoted Henri Matisse, *"L'exactitude n'est pas la vérité,"* warning the reader against too casual an understanding of photographic truth. *Many Are Called* was printed in duotone, *Message from the Interior* on a sheet-fed press at Meriden Gravure, a small printing press in Meriden, Connecticut. Rich in blacks and subtle in gray tones, the reproductions matched the technical precision of the original prints. For the binding, Evans and Katz chose a handsome gray linen; the title was in a classic serif face laid in an embossed square.

Nothing could have pleased Evans more than the attentions of his two gentleman publishers. Lovell Thompson, whom Evans referred to as Lovable Thompson, was a veteran editor of the old school, with the kind of thoughtful Bostonian manner and gentle suggestions that instilled calm in his authors. Katz was young and idealistic, eager to learn in the process of working intimately with artists he revered. "Leslie is in love with Walker," Isabelle wrote to Jimmy and Tania Stern, "and the two are lunching at the St. Regis or the Plaza . . . at least once a week." Katz indulged Evans in his appreciation of the art of men's tailoring as much as in the finer points of book production. "If they don't lunch or discuss bindings and papers they pay visits to the English tailors at the Biltmore," Isabelle's report continued. "Walker emerged with a double-breasted blazer. They also bought fur hats."

To help launch the book, Katz introduced Evans to Robert Schoelkopf, a print dealer with a small upstairs gallery on upper Madison Avenue. Schoelkopf was interested in exploring the potential market for photographs. At first Evans balked at the idea, afraid of what he might be expected to do, but after he met Schoelkopf, he told Katz, "He'll be fine." Close behind the publication of *Message from the Interior,* Schoelkopf scheduled an exhibition of Evans' work, the photographer's first New York gallery show since Julien Levy's in 1932.

At the time there was virtually no art market for Evans' photographs, nor was there a market for the work of any other contemporary photographer. The concept of photography as something to be collected belonged mainly to the realm of daguerreotypes, old cameras, and rare nineteenth-century albums of travel and war. Why someone should pay good money for a picture they could just as easily tear out of a magazine, few people could imagine. In 1941 Beaumont Newhall had organized an exhibition of photographs for sale for the modest price of ten dollars at the Museum of Modern Art, hoping to encourage the notion, with little success. Steichen's subsequent directorship had made photographs look more like show business than beautiful objects to take home and contemplate. In the 1950s, Helen Gee's Limelight, the only photography gallery in New York, had kept its doors open only by doubling as a coffeehouse. But the times seemed to be changing. Schoelkopf, with his taste for the work of American painters such as Edward Hopper, George Bellows, and Fairfield Porter, seemed just the man for Walker Evans. To introduce his new artist, Schoelkopf organized a small retrospective of Evans' work in December.

Together, the two publications of 1966 gave Evans' photography a new critical shape and dimension. One book was about the faces of strangers "in naked repose," the other about domestic interiors, richly suggestive of the lives of those who inhabited them or once had. Both, by different methods, were studies in portraiture in the hands of a spy. Both received critical acclaim.

"Gratifying as such attention must be, it is unlikely to turn Evans' head," wrote Brendan Gill for *The New Yorker* in December. "He has known who he is for quite a long time . . . He is as modest as the next man (and at least ten times as shy), but he is under no misapprehension as to the value of the work he has done."

Gill judged his subject well. At the age of sixty-three, Evans felt that the rewards for his work were overdue. Not only was it high time he received the kind of recognition he hadn't known since *American Photographs;* it also seemed reasonable to expect somebody finally to pay him for his work. It was outrageous to him that a few artists, such as Warhol and Lichtenstein, achieved fame and fortune at a young age while most could hardly make a living.

In the late 1960s, Evans alternated between acting on the fantasy that he was a rich man, by charging expensive clothes on credit cards, and being furious at the realization that he wasn't, when the bills arrived. Money was a subject that put him in a foul mood faster than any other. He actively rebelled against the truth of his financial state. Isabelle noticed, as Jane had before her, that the broker Evans was, the more he felt compelled to shop. To pay his bills, he borrowed. His brother-in-law, Talbot Brewer, had long ago proven to be a reliable source of ready cash; Leslie Katz was becoming a steady target; Evans even approached some of his students at Yale for money. Chris Pullman, heir to the Pullman train fortune, resisted Evans' appeal to countersign a loan, perhaps wisely. At this point in his life, Evans did not seem to consider it a duty to honor his debts. As far as he was concerned, he was an artist and the world owed him a living.

In 1966, hoping for brisk sales at his gallery exhibition, he was in an especially expansive mood at Christmastime. He booked a room at the Hyde Park Hotel in London, where he met Isabelle for the holidays. "Isabelle and I are having the time of our lives of course . . . waited on in this luxurious credit-card hotel. Long live the American Express," he wrote to Schoelkopf on Christmas Day.

After Christmas Walker and Isabelle were invited once again to visit Jimmy and Tania Stern at Hatch Manor. Fully aware of Walker's troubles with alcohol the previous year, Jimmy asked him what they should provide for him during his visit. "Since you were thoughtful enough to ask," replied Walker, "the thing I miss most in England is iced tea with meals. Do you have ice. Then a pitcher of cool tea handy with if possible fresh lemon would make me happy. Iced tea, for me, is 1) tranquilizer 2) aphrodisiac 3) mental stimulant. Buckets of *hot* tea breakfast and afternoon!" The Sterns obliged, and it was only after Walker had slipped off to bed that Isabelle, Jimmy, and Tania toasted 1967 with a bottle of Moet & Chandon.

Nineteen sixty-seven proved to be a relatively good year for Evans' bank account. That summer, Nancy Newhall approached Evans on behalf of the Exchange National Bank of Chicago. With a budget of $10,000, she was in charge of forming a photography collection to enliven the barren walls of the bank, and she was eager to include the work of Walker Evans. "I am delighted with your plans to educate the Chase bank," he replied. "They have been educating *me* for so long now."

At about the same time, Evans was completing a commission for the private bank of Brown Brothers, Harriman. John Kouwenhoven, a historian, had requested an Evans portfolio — an epilogue — for the back of his book *Partners in Banking: An Historical Portrait of a Great Private Bank*. For about four years, beginning in 1964, Evans kept camera equipment at the bank at 59 Wall Street, came and went as he pleased, and made photographs of whatever and whoever interested him. In the end, having dragged his feet through most of the job, he had more than a thousand negatives to choose from, and it is clear from the results of his assignment for "the Brownies and the Harries" that he enjoyed aspects of the job. As ever, he sniffed out what he liked — old lettering on an office door, a crowded umbrella stand, a rolltop desk. And in his studies of the banker type (very often photographed from desk level or through a doorway), he was probably thinking about Erich Salomon's photographs of the meetings of German elder statesmen between the wars. What he once referred to as Salomon's "photographic spy work" was very much the kind of thing he was up to, unobtrusively observing the way the banker crossed his legs, held a pipe, or shouldered a telephone receiver.

In 1967 he was also hired by Time-Life Books to make photographs for the "Library of America" series. For the book *The Gateway States,* he was assigned to photograph the oldest remaining houses and families along the Hudson River, from Tarrytown to Albany, from the Vanderbilts to the Van Rensselaers. Because of the extra work the project entailed, Evans hired the artist Robert Moskowitz to make appointments, carry equipment, and load film. From Evans, Moskowitz learned that art took patience. He recalled waiting for a long time for the sun to come out of the clouds and shine for what Evans deemed one magical moment on a row of townhouses in Hudson, New York.

Evans' talents as a photography critic were also enlisted that year, when Louis Kronenberger, his former colleague at Time Inc., asked him to contribute a chapter to *Quality,* a book he was planning on the fine and lively arts. For each of the arts, Kronenberger asked an expert to choose the best work in his field. By September, Evans had selected most of the photographs, ranging from a portrait of his longtime hero Baudelaire by the great nineteenth-century French portrait photographer Nadar to the recent work of Diane Arbus and Robert Frank. But he delayed writing the accompanying essay. "I have picked up two new (for me) words which I shall work into my Quality essay," he wrote facetiously to Kronenberger. "They are: synopia and oxymoron. That will be two hundred dollars extra, but surely you'll agree they're well worth it."

The next year got off to a positive start when, in January, Evans was informed that he was finally to be granted a degree from Williams College — an honorary doctorate of letters, which surprised and delighted him. "Among other things," he told President Sawyer, "that honor means that the time I spent cutting classes in order to read voraciously in the library was not wasted." In June the college acknowledged its dropout as a great artist who had "caught in a single face, a single room, a single street the problems and despair of a decade."

A financial windfall was also in store for Evans in 1968 — the first major sale of his original prints. In Chicago, a photography enthusiast by the name of Arnold Crane was preparing his approach to Evans. By profession Crane was a personal injury lawyer, which suited his combative nature and his flair for performance. He once shaved his head on a lark; then, deciding it made him look formidable in the courtroom, he continued the practice, as often as twice a day. He made his intimidating dome all the more so during his off-hours by draping a generous weight of beaded necklaces to his midriff. In his youth Crane had wanted to be a photojournalist, but, responding to the pressures of his family's expectations, he had gone to law school. In the 1960s he had found a new outlet for his passion: he had begun to collect. He started with books — albums of nineteenth-century travel photographs he found in flea markets and used-book stores. More recently, he had embarked on a programmatic mission to meet and photograph the aging great photographers of the twentieth century — Brassaï and Man Ray in Paris, and Edward Steichen and Walker Evans in their country homes in Connecticut.

Crane's timing was perfect. He met the photographers at the point at which they knew they deserved the serious attentions of a collector but before any other collector had appeared. For the work of twentieth-century masters, he had virtually no competition. The aging photographers found Crane hard to turn away, since he was in awe of his subjects at the same time as he was visibly determined to have his way. Before long he was carting away his heroes' vintage photographs by the trunkload.

Evans was in a receptive frame of mind. Sales from his show at Schoelkopf had not been brisk. At the same time, maintaining his negatives and prints and keeping them in order was becoming a chore. In Crane he recognized the spirit of the mad collector, a man willing to take on unsorted quantities of stuff, just as Evans himself might carry home the contents of a trashcan on the street. Furthermore, Crane's admiration was hard to resist. "To me these people were always quite holy," Crane said of his favorite photographers. Best of all, his checkbook was open, his pen poised.

While Evans was engaged with his various new projects, most of his students had the impression that all was well at home. Isabelle made him happy with her sociable manner and her conscientious and creative housekeeping. She prepared wonderful meals, she planted flowers, she cut the grass, she ironed his shirts (he complained that the laundry ruined them), and she kept the house impeccably clean. She appeared to be the ideal den mother, warmly welcoming his students and colleagues, lovely to look at, always cheerfully composed, doting on her man. Walker seemed to bask in her love. He called her "Little Bird," "Tenderleaf," and sometimes "Is-a-bull." But Billie Voorhees, whose marriage to Clark had broken up, saw things differently. Walker was a handful, as she well knew. He was too much for Izzy.

"Walker couldn't stand to see a woman idle, or simply enjoying herself," said Alice Morris, who had broken up with the philandering Harvey Breit. It was the little things that added up. Morris recalled a typical example: "Once when I was in Old Lyme on a weekend, Izzy was making veal scaloppini and a salad for lunch, and went in to ask Walker whether he would like some mashed potatoes with it. No, the scaloppini and salad would be fine, he said. Then, when we were called to sit down at the table, with the veal piping hot, he said, 'You know, I would like some potatoes.'"

Trini Barnes remembered a time when she and Courtie were invited to a small cocktail party at the Evanses' apartment on York Avenue: "Walker was ordering Isabelle around — 'Get the hors d'oeuvres, get so-and-so a drink, get me such and such a pill,' and after about the fifth command Isabelle came by me dancing like a dog in the circus and gave me a big wink. She had a wonderful sense of humor."

In fact, since before Walker and Isabelle had made Old Lyme their home, their marriage had been in trouble. While Isabelle still enjoyed their New York social life, she was growing tired of playing the child, of being "taken" to parties, of being "allowed" to do this or that. Furthermore, Walker was beginning to distance himself from his New York life and all of its associations, which suited her so well. When he had married her, Walker had encouraged her to dress glamorously, to make the most of her good looks, to be the beautiful young lady on the arm of the older gent. But in Connecticut he urged her to turn to a classic country style — tartan skirts and fitted jackets, and for those country walks, the famously indestructible Abercrombies. During winters in Europe, Isabelle enjoyed finding little boxes for him in flea markets and antique stores, but she was less enthusiastic about the growing collection of chipped and rusty outdoor signs with which he was beginning to decorate their brand-new house. Increasingly, he discouraged her from exercising her own eye on the details of their interior. Every time she hung a picture or placed an object, he would rehang it or put it away.

While Isabelle worked at keeping a perfect house, Walker spent much of his day reclining. He would lie on the sun deck if the weather was fine, on his cot in his workroom if it was not, or escape to the little studio he had built on the site of Jane's old one. He would read or sleep. "Walker read five books a week," remembered Isabelle. He reread Proust, Henry James, Lytton Strachey's acerbic biographies, the latest books by Nabokov, Mailer, and his own friends and colleagues. But not all was highbrow. Sometimes when Isabelle entered his workroom — where she was not invited without knocking — she found him mesmerized by a pornographic magazine.

By 1968 Walker had begun to drink again, an alternative to the heavy doses of brightly colored pills, which he was constantly getting confused. Billie Voorhees remembered a day when Isabelle came over to her house to see if she might borrow a ladder. Walker was up on the roof of his little studio and refused to come down until somebody brought him another drink. Billie, who liked a drink herself, went along with the gag. She and Isabelle had martinis on the ground while Walker had one on the roof, and eventually he was persuaded to climb down. A similar incident occurred one weekend on a visit with Robert and Nicki Hale in Springs, Long Island. In the middle of the night, when Walker's fear of heights had been obliterated by several vodka martinis, he climbed into the Hales' half-built treehouse. He had no recollection of it in the morning.

Walker's drinking was not the only problem Isabelle had to contend with. In the late fall of 1966, while she was away in Switzerland, Walker became infatuated with Marie-Antoinette Alpert, the aristocratic young student from France whose attempts to imitate his photography he had put firmly to rest. They went out for long lunches together. Walker delighted in Marie-Antoinette's accent, her good looks, her candor, and her patient ear for his complaints about his work, his marriage, and his lack of cash. By the time Isabelle returned, the romance between Marie-Antoinette and Walker had been broadly observed by the Yale faculty and students. At the annual spring picnic at the Eisenmans', Isabelle discovered the two in a secluded part of the yard, Marie-Antoinette on a swing, her skirt flying, and Walker leaning against a tree in rapt attention, murmuring *"Belle! Belle!"* From that point onward, Isabelle watched for signs of Walker's infidelity. But it was not easy to determine, given the many young women at Yale and Walker's flirtatious manner, exactly where the threat lay.

Isabelle began to develop stomach problems, as if she had empathetically taken on Walker's ulcer. Her usual buoyancy deserted her; she stopped answering the phone. Worst of all, Walker would not discuss their problems. She could not appeal to his logic; his secrecy and unwillingness to talk seemed to come from family problems deep in his past that had no bearing on the present. Her efforts to communicate were a mental torture. She even contemplated suicide. How else could she escape from a man who was killing her spirit yet to whom she felt bound and responsible? It was impossible to imagine how Walker could manage without her. Facing an emotional impasse, she began to see a psychiatrist in New Haven.

Already Walker complained that Isabelle wasn't taking care of him. The six months she had spent teaching in Zurich had been almost unbearable for him. "Come back, I'm dying," he would say, and he discouraged her from leaving again. From his point of view, Isabelle was not the asset in Old Lyme she had appeared to be in New York. He began to suspect that her primary motivation in marrying him had been to engage in his social life, to gain access to the intellectual and financial powers of New York. Her expensive taste, her eye for material luxuries, he believed might be the main cause of his monetary woes. The world may have owed *him* a living, but it didn't owe his wife one too.

In the midst of a social and cultural revolution that reeled between consumer excess and ardent antimaterialism, Walker, the youth of the extravagant 1920s and the photographer of the Depression, was not sure where he stood. He felt himself to be an aristocrat, and he believed in the persistence of culture and cultural distinction which the rich make possible. However, he felt acutely the sins of social injustice, the plight of the poor. The disparity between these issues still plagued him. He found himself presenting one face to his young friends, another to his old friends; one to the rich, another to the poor. He yearned to relate to his students — their liberated views toward sex, their political open-mindedness, their concern for social issues, all seemed to come with less of a struggle than they had in his youth, when there was nowhere to run from authority. He told them, "We had no strength in union." Now an entire generation coming of age was antiestablishment, and he envied them. But he also disdained the affectation of their dress, their speech, their casually adopted politics. Their style and their philosophy often lacked the substance of his own generation's, he thought, and made him feel old.

But when Evans met a young photographer named Virginia Hubbard in 1968, the distance between their generations seemed irrelevant. Hubbard had recently completed a documentary essay on black tenant farmers in northern Mississippi. She had been deeply impressed by *Let Us Now Praise Famous Men,* but it had not occurred to her that Evans was still alive and that she might meet him. As she went through the grueling process of showing her photographs to various editors in New York, one of them told her that Evans was teaching at Yale and that she should show him her work. She decided to take the advice. When she first saw Evans from a distance, she instantly thought that he was a man in pain. She paused. Then, entering his office in a mood of tense perseverance, she abruptly placed her portfolio on the table in front of him and demanded to know what he thought.

The old man surprised her. To begin with, he liked her pictures. As she sat across from him, his eyes sparkled and the lines in his face seemed to disappear. His comments were witty and sharp, and he moved with the grace of a cat. No doubt his positive response to her pictures had as much to do with Hubbard's lanky figure and square, bony face, and her complete lack of affectation, makeup, and disguise, as it did with the photographs themselves. As she struggled awkwardly with words, her soft voice and southern accent (she was from Montgomery, Alabama) called up distant memories. On the spot, Evans decided to add one of Hubbard's photographs to his essay in Kronenberger's *Quality.* He chose a photograph she had taken of a large unmade bed in one of the farmer's houses, strewn with gentle sunlight.

After Hubbard left, Evans kept in touch with her, and they met again in New York. In Ginni, as he soon called her, he saw the opposite of Isabelle. She loathed the high-rolling social ambiance that Isabelle thrived on. Her strength was in her willful determination to defy convention and her absolute faith in her instincts. Her lack of formal education and her indifference to the who's who of the art and literary worlds endowed her with a surprising power. Like Walker, she understood intuitively the beauty of the castoff and the ruin. She was also, like Walker, foot-loose and unsentimental. She was a runaway, and he wanted to catch her, to save her, the way Agee had wanted to save young Mary Burroughs from her mean older husband. She warned him that she was not by nature monogamous. But he pursued her ardently nonetheless. Moved by feelings quite new to him, he told Ginni he thought they would breed well together. He wanted to father her child.

When Ginni left to live in Alabama a few months later, Walker continued to correspond with her by letter. About two years later, after suffering a nervous breakdown, she answered Walker's pleas to come north again, but only as far as Baltimore, where her parents then lived. By this time she was prepared to suspend her own photographic activities in order to learn as fully as possible from his.

While Isabelle increasingly took off for New York and Europe, Ginni and Walker spent a good deal of time together. Even in a crowded restaurant, it seemed to Ginni that Walker had the ability to close out the rest of the world, so completely was he able to engage her. As always, he had the urge to educate his young lover. He sent her books, Isak Dinesen's *Out of Africa* and Knut Hamsun's *Hunger*. Ginni longed to know more about Agee, but Walker was too conscientious toward the memory of his friend to answer her questions quickly or directly. Over time, and as thoughts suddenly occurred to him, he attempted to describe what Agee was like. To Ginni, in retrospect, it seemed "an ongoing, mumbled conversation."

Walker wanted Ginni to meet Ben Shahn, but the night before they planned to go to Roosevelt, New Jersey, Bernarda Shahn called Walker with sad news. His old friend had died. Walker drove down to Roosevelt to see Bernarda but did not attend the funeral. To console himself, he drove on to Atlantic City and then Cape May. "I got much afraid because Ben Shahn died," he wrote to Isabelle, who was in Europe at the time.

Soon after Ben's death, Bernarda donated all of his photographs to the Fogg Art Museum at Harvard. Davis Pratt, the Fogg's photography curator, organized an exhibition of the work in November 1969. To honor the occasion, he invited Evans to speak to his students about Shahn's photography.

In typical form, Evans asked the students not to stand at attention but to gather themselves around on the floor and ask plenty of questions, for he had not prepared a speech. In a spirit of intimate recollection and spry humor, he honored the memory of his old friend. "This man was a humanist par excellence," he said, appealing to the younger generation's humanitarian outlook. He told them what it had been like to starve in shabby bohemian flats in New York, and how it had really been to work for the government during the Depression, and he reminded them that history was inevitably a subjective report of the facts. The Depression was a spellbinding subject for the photographer — that was one way of looking at it. But if given the opportunity to photograph the British royal family behind the scenes, he himself would not turn it down. No matter what the subject, it was the privileged view from the interior that was the photographer's domain.

Shortly after he made his tribute to Shahn, Evans received the shattering news that Tom Mabry had hung himself. Evans had seen him through a nervous breakdown twenty years earlier, when he had fled from New York City to recover in the Berkshires. Finally Mabry had resolved to return to Kentucky, to claim the farm where he had grown up, to work the land himself. Right after Christmas, Evans went alone to stay with his mourning family. On New Year's Day he photographed a large, square, empty armchair. The bulk and insensitivity of its shape seem to make a prisoner of a skinny avocado plant dancing limply behind it. We are in a stranger's house, but no one seems to be at home.

The deaths of his closest friends provoked Evans' anger as much as his grief. As if to repay the dead for deserting him, he began to trade in the treasures of his past friendships. As Hubbard recalled, Shahn was barely in his grave before Evans took the portrait he had made of him in Truro in 1930 off the wall and began to make arrangements to sell it. At about the same time he cashed in on his friendship with Agee by selling Agee's letters to a manuscript dealer in Chicago. His personal copy of the Black Sun Press edition of Hart Crane's *The Bridge* also found its way into the secondhand book market. And before long Evans was retrieving the first editions of *Let Us Now Praise Famous Men* that he had given to various friends years before.

He would ask them if he could borrow the book, then return to them the new edition. None of this made up for the fact that Agee's precious gift of more than thirty Christmases before, the manuscript of the book, had been lost somewhere in Evans' moves from one studio to another.

Evans wanted to let go of his past; at the same time, he feared losing control over it. He was haunted by the letters he had written to Jane over the years, which he suspected she had kept. When he encountered her at Dorothy Eisner's gallery opening in 1968, he demanded to see them, but Jane knew better than to let him. Instead, she offered her perpetual feeling of regret about the end of their marriage, and he admitted his own. "But you know I've never been faithful to anything," he told her, "but my negatives."

11 *A Penitent Spy*

BY THE LATE 1960s, the influence of Walker Evans on a younger
generation of American photographers had proved to be as profound
as it was subtle. For an artist who never sought disciples, Evans had
acquired an extraordinary range of them, far beyond his university
classroom. Although other photographers of his generation, such as
Ansel Adams, acquired imitators, the transparency of Evans' vision
allowed room for all kinds of personal expression. Emmet Gowin's
portraits of his wife and family in the candid light of the back yard
in summer, Joel Meyerowitz's surreally charged street photography,
Lewis Baltz's deadpan topographics, and William Eggleston's apparently offhanded pictures of suburban Memphis were not imitations
of Evans' photography, but these artists derived from his example the
courage to use the medium directly, to let its idiosyncrasies, its infor-
malities, and its candor lead them to the distillation of their own
private realities. All acknowledged his influence.

John Szarkowski's 1967 exhibition "New Documents" at the Museum of Modern Art, which introduced the work of Diane Arbus,
Garry Winogrand, and Lee Friedlander, helped to demonstrate the
currency of Evans' photographic aesthetic. These three young photographers represented a new documentary approach, which Szarkowski described as "the belief that the commonplace is really worth

looking at, and the courage to look at it with a minimum of theorizing." Like Evans, they loved photography for its ability to reveal the subject in all its fascinating nakedness, to tell all but the moral of the story. "Their aim has been not to reform life," Szarkowski suggested, "but to know it." Among this generation of photographers, too young to have seen the exhibition "American Photographs," a new edition of the book was urgently in demand.

In 1970 Szarkowski began to make plans for a Walker Evans retrospective at the Museum of Modern Art. His original idea was to organize an exhibition in conjunction with two publications, a new edition of *American Photographs* (the third) and a selection spanning Evans' forty-five-year career, with an eye to showcasing his later and lesser-known work. In order to make his selection for the second book, Szarkowski wanted to see everything — hundreds and hundreds of photographs dating from the 1920s to the present, tearsheets from magazines, and negatives that Evans had never bothered to print.

The Evans photographic archive was by now scattered among various closets and vaults from Old Lyme to Washington, D.C. The Library of Congress held the negatives he made for the Resettlement Administration (except the ones he made at the time for himself), and he housed his personal archive of negatives and prints in various states of order in his studio in Old Lyme, in his apartment on York Avenue, in a footlocker at the Century Club, and no one knew where else. As Szarkowski recalled, "He was a little like W. C. Fields was rumored to be about his money, keeping dollars in every bank in the U.S. Walker had these caches of negatives everywhere, and he would forget where they were, or claim to."

To pay for the archival research and darkroom work necessary to review Evans' career, Szarkowski won a grant from the New York State Council on the Arts. Charles Rodemeyer of the museum staff was given the task of proof-printing two of everything. While Rodemeyer worked at the museum, Jim Dow, a recent graduate of the Rhode Island School of Design, helped Evans sort and retrieve old negatives and make exhibition prints. Dow had been in awe of Evans ever since he had seen *American Photographs* as a student at RISD. With his

classmate Emmet Gowin, he had made Evans the subject of a graduate paper and had studied in depth the prints Evans made for the
Resettlement Administration. Having just inherited a small fortune
from his father, he volunteered to work for Evans in exchange for
one set of new exhibition prints rather than wages.

Arnold Crane, eager to participate in the great event, suggested that
the museum show only vintage prints; it was welcome to borrow
them all from his collection. By this time, Crane said, he owned eleven
or twelve hundred prints. But Szarkowski, who had seen selections
from Crane's collection on view at the Sidney Janis Gallery, remained
unconvinced. "There were an awful lot of bad prints in that show, I
thought. They were vintage, all right. They were mustard colored,
peanut-butter colored, faded . . . And here and there a pretty good
print. I saw no reason to get involved." Evans agreed with Szarkowski:
"Walker didn't care if they were old prints or new prints, as long as
he felt they were good." The exhibition would consist of modern
prints made under his supervision and vintage prints from his own
and the museum's collections.

Dow quickly learned how difficult it was to make a successful print
from one of Evans' negatives. Though Evans had never considered
himself a technician, over the years he had developed his own refined
approach to processing his pictures, which was difficult for anyone
else to follow. His negatives were of widely varying contrast and
density; each one seemed to require its own chemical formula. When
Dow took his first efforts to the museum, Szarkowski told him he
was on the wrong track. The prints had too much contrast; it was as
if he were making them for the more abstract photography of Harry
Callahan, his former teacher at RISD. Evans' work called for an entirely different chemistry. Dow learned that at one point Evans had
used a formula called Anadol, a "compensating" developer. He managed to find a paper that had approximately the creamy white quality
of the kind that Evans had used in the 1930s, Illustrator Special Azo.
Over time and with practice, Dow learned to bring out the subtler
contrasts of a soft-grade paper, to "dodge" and "burn" the negative
under the enlarging lamp to achieve the luminosity and softly graded
gray scale of Evans' best prints with a similarly apparent effortlessness.

As Szarkowski brooded over his picture selection, he realized that the bulk of Evans' work since 1938 was much less impressive than he had expected. However, there were forgotten treasures of the early 1930s — the dockworkers in Havana, the Victorian houses in Ossining and upstate New York, the DeLuze house in Truro. And the eighteen-month period Evans had spent working for the FSA in the mid-1930s had been even more productive than Szarkowski had thought — "an astonishing creative hot streak," he called it, that had never been fully treated. Many photographs that had not been published in either *American Photographs* or *Let Us Now Praise Famous Men* deserved to be seen. Ultimately, Szarkowski fulfilled the form of a retrospective survey, selecting photographs as early as those published in the Black Sun edition of *The Bridge,* circa 1930, and as late as those of the Coggeshalls' bedroom in Newcastle, Maine, circa 1967. But nearly half the exhibition space was devoted to the unpublished wealth of Evans' classic period, 1935–36. Meanwhile, the reissue of *American Photographs* would have to be postponed for budgetary reasons.

Evans greeted Szarkowski's suggestions with an open mind. He enjoyed the rediscovery and reinterpretation of pictures he had made more than thirty years earlier. In his choice and order of photographs, Szarkowski presented an artist less studied and self-conscious than the one Kirstein had attempted to create in *American Photographs.* Whereas Kirstein had compared Evans' photography to poetry, Szarkowski was more inclined to agree with Evans' recent claim that it was "strictly prose." He regarded Evans as an interpreter of an era that was now history, and as the creator of "a new set of clues and symbols, bearing on the question of who we are." Furthermore, he was attentive to the sequences of the artist's development. Instead of placing each photograph as an amplification or inverted symbol of the next, as they had been in *American Photographs,* and keeping the specifics of its time and place in the back pages, Szarkowski's sequence moved through town and country in roughly chronological order, with title and date directly below each picture.

The exhibition was scheduled to open on January 27, 1971. Evans was honored with the museum's most prominent venue, the first-floor galleries. To offset the potential monotony of viewing more than two hundred small black-and-white pictures, Szarkowski had mural-size prints of twelve of the photographs made.

Evans anticipated the event with enthusiasm. The artist who had shied away from the opening of "American Photographs" in 1938 now wished to be surrounded with friends, admirers, and lovers past and present at the black-tie dinner on January 26, the eve of the opening. This dinner, attended by eighty-eight guests, including Alfred Barr, Julian Levy, Dorothy Miller, Diane Arbus, and Robert Frank, was a gala event. Szarkowski had urged the poet Robert Penn Warren to prepare a toast to his friend of twenty years. In his deep Kentucky accent, Warren recalled his impression of Evans' photographs when he first saw them, in 1941. "The world that Walker caught so ferociously in his lens thirty years ago was a world I had known all my life," said Warren.

> Facing his pictures then, I found, at first, pleasure in simple recognition, but as I pored over the pictures, it began to dawn on me that I had not known that world at all. I had walked down those roads, dusty or muddy according to season. I had stopped before those log cabins or board shacks and been barked at by the hound dog. I had swapped talk with those men and women, by the rock hearth inside or squatting on my heels under a white oak or a chinaberry tree, according to latitude. But staring at the pictures, I knew that my familiar world was a world I had never known. The veil of familiarity prevented my seeing it. Then, thirty years ago, Walker tore aside that veil; he woke me from the torpor of the accustomed.

Warren compared Evans' vision of the South with that of such writers as William Faulkner and Katherine Anne Porter. He commended the work for its exactitude and at the same time its implied complexity and compared its naturalism to that of Charles Dickens.

Moved by the praise of his distinguished friend, and by the presence of so many admirers in one room, Evans rose to speak. "You've made me feel like a king," he said, addressing the entire party. He thanked the poet for comparing him to great writers, but he was now secure enough in his reputation to forgo the literary references that had trailed his work since its first appearance. He invited his guests to abandon their intellectual trappings and approach his photographs with their emotions: "After all, pictures are a matter of feeling, and it's hard for a literary society to understand pictures, because we don't feel. But I'd like you to open up . . . and just receive these, not with your minds, but with your feelings."

The retrospective did much to prove the power of the feelings behind Evans' apparently factual record of American life. But after months of reviewing Evans' career, Szarkowski still found it impossible to identify exactly where his interpretation took over from pure documentary. Getting to know him as a friend did little to uncover the mysteries of his art. Indeed, Evans himself was incapable of explaining what had drawn him with such a clear force to his subject matter and point of view, a point of view so transparent that his public had by now taken it to be their own. "Almost all good artists are being worked through with forces they're not quite aware of," he would offer by way of explanation. As Szarkowski finally confessed in his introduction to the catalogue, "It is difficult to know now whether Evans recorded the America of his youth or invented it."

Szarkowski was not the only one to come to this tantalizing critical impasse. Most of the commentary on the retrospective circulated in one way or another around this central conundrum. "For how many of us, I wonder," wrote Hilton Kramer for the *New York Times,* "has our imagination of what the United States looked like and felt like in the nineteen-thirties been determined not by a novel or a play or a poem or a painting or even by our own memories, but by the work of a single photographer, Walker Evans?"

Speaking for his generation, the young photography critic A. D. Coleman declared how greatly Evans had shaped his impressions of the recent past. Evans' photography, Coleman claimed, "has colored all our memories so that we can no longer separate our fact from his fiction, or vice versa." Coleman also noted the important difference between Evans and his contemporaries. Compared with other New Deal photographers — Dorothea Lange being the strongest example — Evans did not promise or even suggest that a better future for American society was within reach. "The grief Evans evokes may be quieter," Coleman wrote in his *New York Times* review, "but there is no tempering it ever; for Lange dealt with chance, while Evans deals with fate."

Walter McQuade, Evans' former colleague at Time Inc., joined in the chorus for *Life* magazine: "His photographs become a part of our past, whether or not we were ever there." McQuade also thought it fair to tackle a brief description of Evans' contrary personality. "He has an entrancing, self-indulgent wit," he wrote, "a finely polished peskiness, a zone defense of personality traits that makes him even more impenetrable than his pictures." This much might have passed muster with Evans, but McQuade went too far when he wrote that "he was poor, and never quite let his rich friends forget it." When McQuade innocently asked Evans to inscribe his copy of the exhibition catalogue, he received a slap in the face: "Dear Walter, I'm dead broke, and since the world owes me a living I think you ought to do something for me . . . You guys with all the dough damn well ought to give some of it up. Your *Life* review check perhaps? May I remind you, you couldn't have written it without the subject — I'm not letting you forget it."

If only the MoMA retrospective could have granted Evans the ultimate artist's fellowship, enabling him to pursue new projects freely, without the need to support himself, his happiness would have been complete. As much as he enjoyed the new round of critical attention, he resented the way people constantly dragged up his photographs from the 1930s, asking him about the Depression, about working for the FSA, about Agee, as if he weren't a living artist, still churning with ideas.

For Evans, 1971 was a year of transition. By the time his retrospective opened at the museum, his marriage was over. Isabelle was living on East 71st Street in an apartment that Alice Morris had recently vacated, working at Bonwit Teller, and seeing a Freudian psychiatrist four times a week. Although she continued to go up to Old Lyme on most weekends, she had employed a lawyer and asked for a divorce. Walker was equally ready for the end. Perhaps calculating that his financial position would be less threatened if he let Isabelle desert him (as he had let Jane), he made no move. But as Isabelle proceeded with her case, his bitterness grew. He carried his woes to his neighbors in Connecticut, "the way people do when they are going through a divorce," his friend Mary Knollenberg recalled. "They keep repeating what's happening. 'Then she said, then I said.' The whole thing was a bore."

Within weeks of Isabelle's final departure, Evans retired from Yale, having reached the mandatory retirement age. But he was hardly idle. Yale introduced a graduate program in photography that year, and he was invited back as its principal visiting artist. He was to conduct a week-long workshop each fall; he was also invited to accompany students on photographic field trips, to visit classes at the end of each term, and to teach at the Yale summer school in Norfolk, Connecticut. He was also asked with increasing frequency to lecture at other art schools and universities, and he followed his retrospective exhibition to several of the stops on its tour of the country, including museums in Washington, D.C., San Francisco, Boston, and St. Louis.

The market for photographs was expanding as rapidly as Evans' reputation among new audiences. Several photographers of his generation, including Bill Brandt, Henri Cartier-Bresson, and Ansel Adams, were urged to make new prints from their old negatives for what their dealers and representatives hoped would be lively sales. In 1971, at the encouragement of Robert Schoelkopf, Evans produced his first limited-edition portfolio, published by his colleagues Norman Ives and Sewall Sillman. The portfolio included fourteen images, mostly from the 1930s, and was printed in an edition of one hundred.

As the demand for his pictures increased, a string of young admirers from the ranks of Evans' colleagues and students began to assist him. John Hill, who headed the graduate photography program at Yale, helped Evans pack up his apartment on York Avenue when he terminated his lease. Melinda Blauvelt, a graduate student in photography, volunteered her help in preparing a retrospective exhibition of his work at the Yale Art Gallery in the fall of 1971. Evans also had the assistance of Jerry Thompson, a young photographer who had gone to Yale for the main purpose of studying photography with him. At twenty-six, the soft-spoken Texan was older than his fellow graduate students, and he and Evans quickly developed a relationship beyond the university. By the end of the fall term, Thompson had made himself indispensable and more or less moved into the house in Old Lyme.

Evans invited Thompson to make prints from his negatives and to keep any he wanted for himself. Thompson also helped go through the archives, fishing for things to sell, selecting vintage prints, and searching for negatives that needed reprinting. He would hold up a photograph for Evans' response, which was always fast, decisive, and inscrutable. Neither Thompson nor anyone else, Thompson was sure, was capable of second-guessing him.

Beneath the surface of Evans' disorderly studio, Thompson perceived the evidence of a once fanatically well organized man. The African sculpture project of 1936 filled a wooden cabinet; the negatives from his trip to Cuba in 1933 were stashed in an old valise. There was a box that contained prints and negatives from *Let Us Now Praise Famous Men,* and another with a set of prints from *American Photographs,* filed in precisely the order in which they appeared in the book. And on each negative envelope Evans had noted the timing, aperture, and chemical dilution that rendered the perfect print.

Evans was also working on several new projects. He was thinking about photographing scarecrows (or directing Thompson to do so for him). He was also working on an alphabet comprising photographs of letters he liked on public signs, each one different. Composing pictures meant less to him now than it once had; simply pointing to his subject matter — lifting it from the scene — was enough of a statement.

His passion for photography had transformed into another pursuit, the art of assemblage, which had been with him at least since the days he roamed Brooklyn with Hart Crane and browsed through the picture collection of the New York Public Library with Ben Shahn, piecing together the blasted remnants of his father's profession like an archaeologist. He and his friends had been a fraternity of junk collectors, somewhat secretive, but now Evans felt free to go public. He was gathering a vast horde of castoffs, scavenging for things washed up on the beach, rummaging through trashcans, scooping bits of paper off the sidewalk, picking up the odd bottle cap, cigarette wrapper, or bent soft-drink can. Every day he went hunting for material and brought back a bagful. Just walking between the design building and the Old Heidelberg, his favorite place in New Haven for lunch, Evans would gather a pocketful of trash. In various corners of the house, little piles of rubbish took form, having a logic only their collector could explain. The dining room table was covered with an indescribable carpet of frayed and broken bits and pieces of paper, glass, and tin. Flip-tops had recently appeared on canned beverages, and Evans filled his pockets with the aluminum rings and curled tongues. Bill Christenberry, who watched him at this one day, couldn't imagine what he planned to do with them. At the house in Old Lyme a few weeks later he found out. The flip-top rings were arranged in a fine grid pattern and glued down to a sheet of deep red sandpaper. It looked to Christenberry like ancient armor.

Without warning, Evans enlisted his friends in the pursuit and even the caretaking of his junk collections. On a field trip to Martha's Vineyard, he corralled one of his students into carrying home his latest purchase: $150 worth of lobster buoys. On a visit with Courtie and Trini Barnes in Colorado, he picked up an assortment of nuts and bolts he found on a walk along a defunct railroad track and then charged Courtie with the task of shipping them to New York. One day after visiting Leslie Katz in his country house in Saratoga, he was in an especially insatiable frame of mind, and when he came across a yard sale on his way back to Connecticut, he bought everything. Then, not sure how to cope with it all, he borrowed a truck, drove back to Katz's house, and dumped it on his front lawn.

Evans' collection of signs was also expanding. By the 1970s, he was packing a can of Liquid Wrench and a couple of pairs of pliers in the trunk of his car as a matter of routine. Many a student was roped, willingly or not, into a late-night sign theft. Sometimes it took several clandestine visits to the site to loosen the prize from its mount. Evans proudly displayed some of his recent acquisitions in his retrospective at Yale — signs for Nehi soda and Chesterfield cigarettes, a Coca-Cola sign in the shape of a bottle, and the hand-painted sign "?DO YOU BELIEVE IN JESUS? I DO." On a trip to Maryland with Ginni Hubbard in the fall of 1971, he found a number of identical NO TRESPASSING signs in varying states of disintegration. Heedless of their stern warning, he and Ginni proceeded to lift the notices from the site. As if reconstructing a series of sequential film stills, they lined them up in descending order of disintegration. Bill Christenberry built a long rectangular box for them, to be installed as a single piece on the gallery walls.

Like the subject matter of his photographs, Evans' selection of these objects endowed them with an aura that transcended their original purpose or context. "The point is," as he explained in a wall label, "that this lifting is, in the raw, exactly what the photographer is doing with his machine, the camera, anyway, always."

Free of teaching responsibilities at Yale, Evans accepted an invitation from Dartmouth College to be its artist-in-residence in the fall of 1972. Mathew Wysocki, the director of the program and an avid amateur photographer, had worked long and hard to persuade Evans to come. The plan was for Evans to spend ten weeks living in Hanover, New Hampshire, being available to students but with no obligation to teach a course.

Wysocki's admiration for his guest quickly led him into the role of Evans' personal handmaiden. He drove him all over the countryside, served him tea, arranged his social engagements, and loaned him the odd twenty-dollar bill, never to see it again. Eager to catch on to Evans' creative pulse, he showed him early New England Greek Revival architecture and old graveyards and introduced him to a farm family whose home had an unspoiled country charm he had a hunch Evans would appreciate. Wherever they went, Evans kept his eyes peeled for interesting road signs or advertisements he might wish to take away with him. "Stop the car!" he would command, and, having his pliers always handy, he would prise the sign from its post without a backward glance.

Varujan Boghosian, a collage artist who was a member of the art faculty at Dartmouth, had a studio that Evans loved to explore. A dense thicket of found objects — dead birds, discarded sheets of metal and linoleum, children's toys, broken kitchen equipment — covered every surface. It was to Evans a mesmerizing hoard. Seeing his eyes bulging, Boghosian was inspired to make a present of one of his treasures. But perhaps his most significant gift was his personal assistance in stealing the hand-painted sign from Trott's barber shop on Main Street in Hanover. Evans insisted on embarking on his escapade at four o'clock in the afternoon, in plain view of the police station, to Boghosian's dismay. But somehow he couldn't say no.

Although Evans appeared to be enjoying his stay at Dartmouth, Wysocki and Boghosian noticed that he was frail and easily tired. Over a cup of tea in Wysocki's apartment he would suddenly fall asleep; he was irritable and fussy. Shortly before Christmas, Wysocki was so concerned that he took him to see a doctor. Evans was immediately diagnosed with bleeding ulcers and rushed to the Mary Hitchcock Memorial Hospital in Hanover. After a five-hour operation, the doctor put him in the intensive care unit for one week, where he was not allowed to receive visitors. Ginni Hubbard drove up from Baltimore to see him and eluded the nurses by wearing white so she could visit every day. She would not leave Hanover until Jerry Thompson assured her that he would take care of Evans after his release from the hospital.

Once Evans was out of intensive care, Thompson went to see him every weekend, delivering mail and news from New Haven. Lee Friedlander, at work on a series of photographs of monuments in towns and cities all over America, detoured to Hanover to cheer him along on more than one occasion, and made a photograph of him in his hospital bed, raggedly smiling, with a month's growth of shaggy white beard. Leslie Katz went up from New York. Isabelle, upon hearing the news, felt the familiar pull of Evans' helplessness and considered driving up to New Hampshire, until her psychiatrist firmly ordered her not to. Frances Collins, now Lindley, telephoned regularly from New York with gossip and consolation.

"Dearest F.," Walker wrote to Frances in mid-January with a shaking hand,

> I must apologize — your last, thoughtful telephone call got entangled with three or four hospital-nurse medical medicinal happenings and, I'm afraid, ruined for you by my lack of ability to handle and to juggle everything tactfully, smoothly, graciously and well. That was not like me, a generally tactful, smooth and gracious man — was it? But I've noticed in the past your gift of favorable memory toward me, that man; and your quick grasp of contretempsive situations, and your

knowledge of how to toughen your enormous sensitivity when necessary and keep it all intact through rough and confused going. Well!
No one but you could untangle the above brise and see that reduced,
it all means simply that I love you.

His brush with death seemed to clarify Evans' feelings about his
friends and loved ones. Just before going under the knife, he had
rewritten his will. He was a bachelor again, childless, parentless, and,
with the exception of his sister's son, Talbot Brewer Jr., whom he
hardly knew, without familial heirs. Whom had he loved most in his
life? Who would survive him, and for whom did his love survive?

Wysocki and Boghosian were on hand at the hospital bedside as
witnesses to his last will and testament. Upon hearing what he proposed, they were not entirely sure that his mind was sound. "He
wanted to leave everything to these three women," Boghosian remembered. "Mat [Wysocki] suggested that he leave some of his photographs to the museum [of Modern Art]. 'No!' he roared."

As it was finally written and witnessed by his Dartmouth colleagues, Evans' will named his fellow Yale professor John Hill as
executor and Norman Ives as Hill's understudy. Evans left all of his
camera equipment to Jerry Thompson. The remainder of his estate
was to be divided between his goddaughter, Eliza Mabry, his old love
Frances Lindley, and his last love, Ginni Hubbard. The three heirs
had never met, nor were they likely to in the future, except perhaps
to disseminate the remaining spoils of his life's work.

Evans was finally released from the hospital at the end of January.
He was extremely weak and thin, and it was essential that he not be
left alone at home in Old Lyme. He could eat only small amounts of
food, about five times a day. Jerry Thompson and his girlfriend,
Charlee Mae Brodsky, moved in for three months, Thompson as the
photographer's assistant and Brodsky as cook and housekeeper. Keeping Evans' checkbook for him, Thompson paid himself and Brodsky
a small weekly salary.

Brodsky was amazed at the state of the house. Evans' studio had
spread to every corner. There were rusting advertisements and road
signs everywhere. "You had to try to clear off spaces just to sit down,

or a walkway to get across the floor," she recalled. Various projects were in the works — the material for an assemblage in one corner, a plastic garbage bag full of aluminum flip-tops in another. There were thousands of old postcards. And always there was something they were supposed to be searching for — a vintage Atget print, the negative of his Atlanta "Studio" photograph; had he cropped it with scissors? "Everything was a mess. Bills came, but no one ever opened the mail; they piled up," Brodsky explained. Evans was more interested in recapturing his memories of childhood than in dealing with bills. Like a baby, he dribbled his soup down the front of his cable-knit sweater. Yet in certain respects he insisted that a standard of civilized behavior prevail. Brodsky remembered, "We always had candlelit dinners."

The three of them went on brief outings — to a restaurant in Old Saybrook for lobster, Evans' favorite food; to the private beach club at Black Point; or to the local grocery store. Evans' diet consisted mainly of cream soup, English muffins, and tea. "He always bought three of everything," recalled Brodsky, "as a safeguard. He had no practical household sense, no sense of thrift."

Although his young friends kept him from feeling lonely, Evans was depressed, and he knew that by himself he was incapable of keeping his life under control. He told Alan Trachtenberg, a professor of American studies at Yale, that he thought it would be helpful for him "to talk to somebody." Trachtenberg knew of a therapist who was interested in creative minds and arranged for Evans to meet him. Jerry Thompson remembered that at first the therapist tried to focus on some of the practical details of Evans' daily life that had lately fallen by the wayside — getting his driver's license renewed, filing his tax returns. But soon Evans was thinking up ways of making the sessions more amusing by preparing stories and ideas in advance, some more accurate than others.

Evans' New York years had acquired a certain distance, and he turned increasingly to his neighbors around Lyme for company. Mary Knollenberg, a recently widowed sculptor in nearby Chester, was like a sister to him, and often he would call her at about five in the afternoon and invite himself for supper. With the sharp-witted and

intellectually astute Knollenberg, Evans enjoyed a good deal of rail-
lery. They talked about everything but her work. "We never talked
about my sculpture," Knollenberg remembered. "I don't think he
admired women's work. He asked me once, 'Do you think I'm a male
chauvinist pig?' 'Yes, I do,' I think I said."

If Evans didn't call Knollenberg, he would call Adele Clement, a
reclusive artist with an uncanny eye for the treasures of nature. She
displayed a large iridescent bug on her mantelpiece and kept dead
songbirds in her freezer. Evans also spent many an evening at home
on the phone with Frances Lindley, continuing their snappy dialogue
about books and people and reflecting on his own curious turns of
mind and heart. "This thought sprang into my head," he scribbled
to Frances in the middle of May. "Ginni H. apealed [sic] to the highest
aspect of my nature — the animal."

In spite of his physical frailty and spells of depression, Evans was
still enthusiastic about his ongoing projects. One idea in the works
was a book of selections from his postcard collection, which he hoped
Hilton Kramer would help him edit. Kramer had been urging Evans
to write his memoirs. "He was such a great raconteur," Kramer
thought, he would be sure to write a fascinating account. Evans took
the idea seriously enough to spend the next several months reading
the memoirs of people of his own generation, which were just beginning to be published, and he became discouraged. "They're all
lies," he told Kramer, and frankly admitted, "I would write lies too."
Instead he urged Kramer to join him in the appreciation of the
"honest," small-town, turn-of-the-century American postcard.

Evans was also experimenting with a new and intriguing piece of
photographic equipment. The publicity department at Polaroid Corporation had made him a gift of one of the new SX-70 cameras,
which instantly spewed forth each color-print-and-negative "sandwich" with a satisfying zap; after that, there was the fun of watching
the image take form. Evans was delighted with his new camera, which
at first he thought was a mere toy. He took it to parties and aimed
it at his friends, often not more than a few inches from their faces.
He packed it on the road and documented signs he hoped to steal.
With the camera's one-step simplicity, he found himself photograph-

ing differently, with a new sense of freedom, almost like a child. And in its miniature glossy square prints, with their milky whites and bloody reds, he managed an unsurpassed directness of expression.

As he warmed to color photography and its potential to depict quietness and melancholy, Evans savored the little color photographs Bill Christenberry had recently made with his Brownie camera in Alabama. In their quiet honesty, "each one is a poem," he stated summarily in a brief appreciation of Christenberry's work for the Corcoran Gallery in Washington.

In the spring, when Evans was invited to give a talk to students at the University of Alabama, he asked Christenberry to go with him. Christenberry flew down from Washington and met him at the airport in Atlanta. On the short flight to Birmingham, Evans said that he wanted to visit some of the places that both he and Bill had photographed, but he did not want to see any of the families they knew in Hale County.

Once settled in the hotel in Birmingham, Christenberry took Evans by car to Selma. They went down Main Street, past the Victorian rowhouses he had photographed and the brick walls which minstrel-show posters had once covered. They went on to Sprott, where the post office still stood at the fork in the road, though it had been remodeled; to Moundville, where Evans had photographed the mayor's office and the general store; and finally up a dirt road as rubbled and dusty as it had been in 1936, to Mill's Hill, where the three families had lived. The Burroughses' house was gone — just a pile of weeds stood on its site — but the Tingles' house was still standing, and a black woman lived there. Christenberry asked her if she would mind if he went inside. It was so dark, he wondered how Evans had been able to make his pictures. "I'd crack a door or raise a window shade," Evans told him. Both thanked the woman profusely, but they never explained why they were there.

Evans' trip to Alabama set him off on a flood of reminiscences. He told Christenberry that he missed Jim Agee, and he added that he missed Tom Mabry too. "I could tell that a lot of thoughts were going through his head," remembered Christenberry. "I just didn't interrupt them. I didn't think it was right." Later, when Evans was speaking to the students at the University of Alabama, a young woman with a strong southern accent asked him a question. "Walker said, 'Pardon me, I didn't understand,'" Christenberry recalled. "She asked it again, and again, and finally Walker thought for a moment, turned to me, and said, 'Bill, can you please translate that?' Everybody laughed."

By late spring 1973, Jerry Thompson and Charlee Brodsky had enough confidence in Evans' health to move out. Evans was determined to travel to England by himself. He had invitations from Jimmy and Tania Stern in Wiltshire, Tom and Pamela Matthews in Suffolk, Ben deLoache, of the Yale music faculty, in the Cotswolds, and Lady Caroline Blackwood, now married to the poet Robert Lowell, in London. His former student Alston Purvis, who was living in Holland, had encouraged him to spend a few days in The Hague.

The Sterns were not prepared for Evans' beard, which he had grown to cover his cadaverous cheeks. "Tania took one look at him and thought of Rumpelstiltskin," remembered Jimmy Stern, "and I of a frail little Father Christmas, with his flowing white beard, stooped, and covered in cameras." In London, Evans stayed with the Lowells on Redcliffe Square and went with them to their house near Maidstone. He made portraits of the couple, individually and together, which Caroline remembered as an agonizing exercise. Evans' hands were shaking, and she was sure that his wounds were bleeding too.

Evans' physical frailty was in sharp contrast with his appetite for tough, gruesome imagery. The art critic David Sylvester, who escorted him around London, recalled his fascination with a book of photographs they found at the Photographer's Gallery, *Is Anyone Taking Notice?*, by Donald McCullin — full of grainy, gut-wrenching pictures of bodies maimed, starving, amputated, or decomposing in Vietnam, Lebanon, and India. Sylvester was so moved by Evans' interest in the book that he bought it for him on the spot.

As Evans toured around London, he made photographs in the street and from the window of a cab, attempting to capture the essence of English style and English manners; the dark, rushed effect was not unlike that of the photographs Robert Frank had made in London more than twenty years earlier. From London, Evans traveled on to The Hague to visit Purvis. There he kept busy making pictures, poking into the pornography shops, and collecting things off the street. One day he went to Amsterdam and came back with a paper bag full of trash. He laid it out for Purvis and demanded, "Look at that! Isn't it beautiful?" Purvis had to admit that it was, and soon afterward began to make collages himself.

Knowing how interested Evans would be in seeing a grand private interior, Purvis arranged for them to be invited to dinner with the German ambassador, Herr Obermeyer, whom he happened to know. There Evans discovered that the ambassador's beautiful daughter, Ulricha, was interested in becoming a photographer. "I am of course courting the German ambassador's daughter," he reported to Frances Lindley, "who is of course a photographer and may like white beards and lord knows what else. Needless to say I'm having something of a 'good time' in the embassy and elsewhere, and am somewhat over-stimulated shall we say."

While his friends worried about the state of his health, Evans was having a wonderful, invigorating time abroad, filling his eyes with new sights and his mind with new projects. He had an idea for a book he would call *A Smattering of English,* a title he couldn't resist sharing with Alston Purvis, while swearing him to secrecy. "I want to spend a year working in London," he told Jimmy Stern — a promise of his return.

Back in Old Lyme in the fall of 1973, Evans celebrated his seventieth birthday with a small party of mostly local friends, including Mary Knollenberg, Adele Clement, Jerry Thompson, and Leslie Katz. Later that fall, Ginni Hubbard, still living in Baltimore, went to see him with her infant son, Ezra, whom she had conceived with another man.

Thompson, Ives, and Hill, among others, kept Evans involved in events at Yale. He often poked his head into the office of the Art and Architecture Building or the American Studies Department, where the secretary knew him and pampered him with cups of tea. Among the new arrivals that fall was Michael Lesy, who had been hired as a substitute teacher for Alan Trachtenberg's American studies course. At twenty-five, Lesy was interested in how photography might tell

American history in a new way. His first book, *Wisconsin Death Trip*, published earlier that year, had done exactly that. For several months Lesy had mined the archives of the photographer Charles van Shaick at the Wisconsin Historical Society, and he had compiled a bizarre portrayal of small-town American life in the late Victorian age. To make sense of what he saw, Lesy searched local newspapers for contemporaneous accounts of murder, arson, insanity, suicide, and disease. Between the photographs and the documents, he developed a historical thesis that set the social history of the period on its ear.

Lesy knew Evans' work well but had never met the man. One day in the American studies office, a small bearded figure sat down at the table beside him. Lesy noticed that Rose, the secretary, immediately began to make a fuss over him. "He's got a nice tweed coat on, and it's warm out," Lesy remembered noticing, "and he takes out of his inside pocket a handkerchief, puts it down very carefully on the table, opens the handkerchief sort of like he's opening up this little packet of love letters, and inside is this smashed soft-drink can! And I'm thinking, this is so weird, and then Rose says, 'Michael, have you met Walker Evans?'"

Before long, Lesy and his wife, Liz, became regular visitors to Evans' house in Old Lyme, helping out with chores and errands. Ginni Hubbard had the impression that Evans was especially drawn to Lesy, that in some way he saw his own youth reflected in the young man. It was not only that Lesy was, like Evans, an image scavenger; he was a cultural rebel, disaffected, ruthless, and with no interest in joining the Yale establishment. For Lesy, keeping Evans company was an education, just by observing what he saw, what moved him. "He'd go into a grocery store," Lesy recalled, "and come out with these foam rubber sponges they put on wands to clean bottles — he'd come out with a bouquet of them, absolutely overjoyed."

Lesy also found it fascinating to watch Evans at his exclusive beach club, scavenging for bits of plastic and glass the waves had washed up and wading in the shallow water. "There'd be this old bony guy with a beard and a bag strapped to his abdomen, walking into the sea," recalled Lesy. "He'd stand there with the stuff up to his knees and then come back. Talk about Prufrock!"

At the same time, Lesy noticed Evans' interest in more gruesome visions. He was riveted by *Wisconsin Death Trip,* with its horrifying, mourning pictures of babies, head-on photographs of lunatics, and solemn group portraits of small-town societies. Occasionally and indirectly, he expressed his boredom with the gentlemanly tone of the university classroom. At one of his graduate seminars at Yale, he surprised his students by praising the work of a young woman who photographed herself naked, her legs held wide open and her genitals exposed, then enlarged the photos to life size and cut and gauged them with pins and needles. "This was not erotic work," one student recalled. "This was gruesome work . . . and I remember him singling it out."

In the spring of 1974, the historian Jacques Barzun wrote to Walker Evans to inform him that the National Institute of Arts and Letters had voted to confer on him the Award for Distinguished Service to the Arts. This award, Barzun explained, was presented from time to time to someone who was not a member of the institute and who had "by his production in any genre contributed to the flourishing of the arts." There was not a more distinguished award to be had in America. Evans was more than pleased to join the list of recipients, which included Henry Allen Moe, Alfred Barr, and Lincoln Kirstein.

On May 22, Evans arrived at the institute, at 633 West 155th Street, to accept his award. At lunch he was seated next to his old friend Eliza Parkinson. "You know," he confided to her, "I'm still as poor as a churchmouse, but I'd rather have this." On the stage of the lecture hall for the ceremony, he sat next to Saul Steinberg, who was there to receive the Gold Medal. Steinberg thought his neighbor was Santa Claus in person until the bearded fellow winked and he recognized his old friend. Another old friend, Lionel Trilling, offered a speech in praise of Evans' photography and his ability "to acknowledge the relentless power and mysterious charm of both things and persons, usually commonplace, mostly sad, often cast off, but permitted by the intermediation of his lens to assert the strangeness and dignity of their perdurable being." After that distinguished introduction, the president gave the award to Evans, "whose way of looking at the world," the certificate read in bold capital letters, "has deeply influenced a whole generation of painters and sculptors and photographers, as well as a whole generation of poets and novelists and journalists and architectural historians and moving picture directors."

Four days later, Evans wrote to Trilling from Cambridge, Massachusetts, to thank him for his speech: "I need not say it — how it affected me. Only let me tell you I began to feel it too emotionally there on the dias (or dais?) and had to stop listening."

During Evans' visit to Cambridge, Davis Pratt, the curator of photographs at the Fogg, introduced him to a young photographer named Bobbi Carrey. The three of them dined at Henri IV, an intimate French restaurant. Carrey was beginning to make her reputation as a photographer with a series of blue-tinted cyanotype self-portraits. Her face, her direct gaze framed by a mass of severely tethered dark hair, was superimposed on a field of daisies, emerged darkly from under a circus poster, or dove through the rib cage of an x-ray.

The dinner was a great success. "We hit it off immediately," remembered Carrey. In the course of the evening, it emerged that Evans was overwhelmed by the disorder of his photographic archives, and Carrey offered to spend the summer helping him sort out and safely store his life's work once and for all. Pratt assured Evans that Carrey was experienced and good at it; she had recently done the same for Steichen. Evans could see for himself that Carrey would make bright and interesting company. With his usual business informality, he more or less hired her on the spot and agreed to pay her with cash and with prints.

Carrey spent most of the summer of 1974 living with Evans in Old Lyme. She was going through a divorce, and was glad to be away from home and to avoid an active social life. Evans was in a similar mood. There were few visitors that summer, and he and Carrey kept much to themselves. They talked about men and women and relationships. Their own was strictly platonic. "He couldn't resist making sexual overtures to a woman," Carrey said, "but all he really wanted to do was stroke your hair."

They read a lot; Evans was rereading *Madame Bovary*. They took pictures of each other with the Polaroid. They comforted each other and sparred. They listened to the Watergate hearings on the radio. They went out for lobster dinners or spent the afternoon at the beach club, combing for old glass or plastic or driftwood.

All summer Carrey sorted through the confusion of Evans' prints and papers. Her first task was to make sense of the mess of unpaid taxes and neglected IRS forms, which dated back several years. But she spent most of her time looking over Evans' photographic archives. Whenever possible, she dated the prints, identified them by project or series, and retired them to archival boxes. At the same time she made a detailed inventory.

As she worked, Carrey learned of Evans' perpetual need for money. His pension from Time Inc. was about $8,000 a year. He had no capital, no insurance, no investments that he could divest in case of an emergency. Beyond that, he could count on perhaps $2,000 in print sales. The outlook for increasing sales was not improved by the publication of *Walker Evans: Photographs for the Farm Security Administration* in 1973. The book was published by the Library of Congress, where the negatives resided, without Evans' consent. The copyright for the photographs, which included those he made with Agee in Alabama, was held by the government, which meant that it was in the public domain, and the book not only printed every photograph in a cursory, cataloguing fashion, it also included specific instructions on how to order prints from the Library of Congress for as little as five dollars apiece. Evans was furious; with all the precautions he had taken, the U.S. government had got the better of him in the end, it appeared. The book, which he kept in a brown paper bag, was virtually giving away his greatest work.

Carrey suggested that he meet George Rinhart, a successful young photography dealer she knew through her work with Steichen. To that point, Rinhart had concentrated on nineteenth-century photography. His interest had extended into the twentieth only as far as the last issue of *Camera Work*, he said, and having done very well, he was not sure why it should go any further. But Carrey insisted that he come, and one day in June, Rinhart took the train from New York to Old Saybrook.

As Rinhart recalled, his meeting with Evans got off to an uncomfortable start. "Everyone was quite testy," he remembered. "I explained that I didn't buy the work of contemporary photographers, and Walker said, 'I'll show you why you should' and brought out an original pasteup of *American Photographs*." By the end of the day, Rinhart had picked about forty prints he wished to buy, mainly from the *American Photographs* group, and offered Evans $5,000 for the lot. Evans agreed and, at Rinhart's behest, signed each print before handing it over. "Everybody was terribly happy," remembered Rinhart.

Less than a month later, Rinhart called again. Tom Bergen, an English banker with an interest in photography, had suggested that Rinhart buy Evans' entire collection. He was willing to back Rinhart for three quarters of the cost. There was virtually no precedent for such a sale by a living photographer. "Would you think of selling it all?" Rinhart asked Evans over the phone. "How much?" was Evans' reply.

Later that summer, Rinhart drove out to Old Lyme in his Rolls-Royce Silver Shadow. He offered Evans $100,000 for his entire estate of photographs (about 5,500 prints), to be paid in two installments — $50,000 by or before October 31 of that year, the remaining $50,000 by October 31, 1975. Evans had never possessed a sum of money of that size. He hardly paused before accepting Rinhart's offer. "He was like a child about it," recalled Rinhart. "He literally hopped around with excitement. He talked about going to Europe. He talked about buying a Rolls-Royce."

Evans didn't tell his friends about his deal with Rinhart, but many suspected that a sale was in progress. Mary Knollenberg had an idea that he was arranging some kind of financial deal when he told her one evening over dinner that she would not have to worry about supporting him, that he had taken care of that. But he didn't say how, and she didn't ask. Alston Purvis sensed that something was happening when he stopped in to see Evans at home one day and was politely asked to leave; Evans and Carrey were expecting some other guests at any minute. The silver Rolls passed Purvis on his way out the driveway. Suspecting that Evans might be signing away his life's work without consulting them for advice, John Hill and Jerry Thompson drove out one day to see what was going on. Although they didn't directly accuse Carrey of anything, she could feel their distinct hostility toward her.

By the end of the summer, Carrey had done her job and left for Cambridge. She sensed how dependent on her Evans had become, and she tried to ease her departure by promising to visit him and inviting him to call her anytime. Soon afterward, Jerry Thompson suggested that Evans, who was in the habit of going into New Haven once or twice a week but was no longer a competent driver, come and live with him on a part-time basis. Sharing Thompson's apartment would save him the trouble of driving back and forth. Together they found a two-bedroom apartment in a high-rise building near the University, from which Evans could walk over to the design building and take part in a class for an hour or so before going home for a rest.

One day that fall, Alan Trachtenberg invited Evans to lunch to meet Valerie Lloyd, a curator of photographs at the National Portrait Gallery in London. Immediately charmed by the young Englishwoman, Evans announced that he would take her under his wing while she was there, and that very night he insisted on taking her to Old Lyme. To Lloyd's terror, they hurtled off in his Chevrolet hatchback at top speed, with the hand brake on all the way. As Lloyd gazed at the photographs strewn all over the floor in Old Lyme, it was clear to her that the entire collection was in the process of being carted away. Evans picked up his portrait of Allie Mae Burroughs and gave it to her. Finally Lloyd persuaded him to return to the Trachtenbergs', where they both spent the night, in separate beds. Evans left a note for Alan announcing that he and Valerie were "getting married in the morning."

For the next few days Evans took Lloyd wherever he went, and when he finally put her on the train for New York, he lingered so long and ardently that she was afraid he would lose the end of his nose in the closing door. A few days later he was in New York to escort her around town — to the Museum of Modern Art, to the bar at the St. Regis. He proposed that he go and live with her in England; perhaps with her connections she could find him work over there. When he saw her off at the airport, he urged her to call him from London on his credit card at any time of the day or night.

In September, Rinhart returned to pick up the bulk of his treasure. This included early vintage prints, new portfolios of prints made under Evans' supervision, mockups of books he had never published, copies of books he did publish, including the first editions of *Let Us Now Praise Famous Men* that he had recently collected from his friends. Rinhart also stipulated that he would have the first option to buy Evans' negatives, if Evans should agree to sell them. All together, the contents of Rinhart's purchase filled fifty archival boxes, neatly organized by Carrey. To the question of how good the collection was, Arnold Crane later replied, "They got what I left behind." Certainly the quality was mixed, as would be the case with any bulk sale, but there were a great many treasures, most of them irreplaceable. Evans' print boxes filled the large trunk of Rinhart's Rolls-Royce, and there were still more, which they managed to fit into the back seat. Evans took pictures with his Polaroid of the boxes being loaded. As Rinhart recalled, he was "fidgety."

Those who had taken it upon themselves to look after Evans as he grew old and careless in his ways watched in helpless anguish as he waved goodbye to forty-five years of his creative work. He had cut himself off from any further discovery of his own photography and divested himself of his greatest financial asset — his entire career — in one fast move. His friends were almost unanimously disappointed in his action, and certain that he had been swindled. No one could deny that he needed the money, but the deal could have been handled in a way better suited to a man of modest means and extravagant taste. Evans, however, was thrilled to find that he was worth what seemed to him like a lot of money, and it was only when he saw his archives carried off forever that he began to realize that his small fortune had been won at a personal cost. Indirectly, he confronted the recklessness of his act. He started to drink again. With his Polaroid camera, he photographed signs he found scrawled on the windows of shopfronts. "Going Out of Business," they said. "Must Go." He gave piles of his Polaroids to Ginni Hubbard. "Take them all," he said to her. "At least he can't have these."

By December, Evans' health was declining again, and Thompson found it difficult to keep him from drinking. When he couldn't find company, he would go by himself to the Old Heidelberg restaurant, in the basement of the Hotel Duncan. One evening a student watched silently from a table nearby as Evans began to nod over his unfinished plate of food. A waitress came over and bluntly told him that if he was going to pass out, he should do it somewhere else.

As his seventy-first birthday passed and the Christmas season approached, Evans agreed to go to the New Haven hospital for help with his drinking problem. A day or two after checking in, he fell and broke his collarbone, and he soon came down with pneumonia. The doctors recommended a few weeks' stay at Gaylord, a small hospital in Wallingford, Connecticut, that fostered gentle recuperation. When he was released in February, he was still too weak to hold his camera up. Before leaving the hospital, he told Jerry Thompson that he wanted Ginni and Ezra to come to New Haven and live with him. Within a few days they were there.

In March, Rinhart approached Evans again, this time with an offer to buy the entire archive of his negatives for an additional $50,000. While the cash would not be due until October 31 (along with the remaining $50,000 from the first agreement), Rinhart asked Evans to sign over the negatives in both title and deed immediately, "so that we can begin the process of sorting, indexing, and, hopefully, using these negatives at the earliest possible date." Furthermore, he asked Evans to be on hand to assist in the reproduction of the negatives — as he put it, "upon my request or the request of any persons designated by me, aid and cooperate, to the best of your ability, in the use of and reproduction from these negatives, including supervising such reproductions and signing the prints produced therefrom." All of which Rinhart concluded "with warmest personal regards." Evans signed on the dotted line.

Spring came and Evans' health slowly improved, but he was still extremely weak. Back in his apartment in New Haven, which he now shared with Ginni and Ezra, a day nurse for the baby, and Thompson, who was in and out, he felt his thoughts turning to the country. In his absence over the winter, a young woman named Dale Vosburgh, a friend of Adele Clement's, had lived in the house in Old Lyme rent-free. He asked her if the dogwood was in bloom, how the daffodils were, whether the peepers were in the pond.

Evans had not fully recovered from his illness when he was invited to talk to a group of Harvard and Radcliffe students in Cambridge on April 8. Alvin Eisenman, among others, tried to discourage him from making the effort. But he was determined to go. A network of students and friends was organized to ensure that he got there safely. Thompson put him on the train in New Haven; a student took the day off to ride with him to Boston; Norman Ives' son met him at the station and took him to the Ritz-Carlton.

In Cambridge that evening he felt tired. At the podium, dressed in a glen plaid suit, his sharp eyes peering at his audience over the top of his glasses and his long white beard neatly brushed, he looked as old as the hills. In his usual manner, he declined to give a speech and invited his audience to help him along. "Do a little work with your own mind on mine, such as it is, what there's left of it," he urged. In the middle of his first reply, looking out at his eager audience from the podium, he asked if he might sit down. Then for almost an hour he answered questions about how he began his career as a photographer, what it felt like to live through the Depression, how he became famous, what his photography meant, and how it felt to grow old. He warned his young audience not to be carried away by the promise of fame and fortune, he asserted the value of luck and friendship, he spoke of the difficulty of recapturing the past, and he confessed that he thought a great deal about his childhood. At the same time, he explained regretfully that he could not photograph what it was that he felt: "I've gone back far enough to find out that it can't be done, and it's always a letdown . . . Things don't look right. You go up to something that you knew in your childhood, and you are full of feeling about it, and that feeling doesn't come through."

The next day, Bobbi Carrey picked Evans up at the Ritz to take him to the train. From the smell of his room she could tell he had been smoking marijuana. She thought he did not look well. Jerry Thompson met him in New Haven and took him home to bed. Evans called Valerie Lloyd in London and told her that the Harvard lecture had been a great success. He was in high spirits. But he looked terrible.

Later that evening, Thompson summoned Ginni Hubbard to come and sit by Evans' side and left them alone to talk. Michael Lesy, now teaching at the University of Louisville, was scheduled to arrive the next day to give a lecture, and Evans was looking forward to seeing him. "When is Michael's plane arriving?" he wanted to know. With pen and paper ever handy, he wrote down Hubbard's answer. A few moments later, he suffered a massive stroke. Hubbard immediately called an ambulance and they rushed to the hospital. Evans was brain dead. Five hours later his heart stopped beating.

In his obituary for the *New York Times,* Hilton Kramer called Walker Evans "one of the greatest artists of his generation." He died a famous man, but it was fame at the cost of being widely misunderstood. "To no other figure of our time," Kramer wrote, "does Rilke's dictum about the paradox of celebrity — that fame is but the sum of mis-understandings that accumulate around a well-known name — apply with greater force." In conclusion, he predicted that it would be some time before Evans' work would be fully understood, "even by those who now mourn his passing."

In his will, Evans had requested that there be no funeral, no memorial service of any kind. He asked that his body be cremated and his ashes scattered over Long Island Sound. Fulfilling his first duty as executor, John Hill took Evans' ashes to Black Point and let the wind carry them away. Friends wrote to each other and called each other across the country and overseas. Many people who con-sidered themselves close to Evans were aware of each other for the first time. Having had what seemed to be an intimate relationship with him, Jerry Thompson realized that there were rooms upon rooms of Evans' life he would never know.

Respectful of his wishes, the heirs held no formal service, but spontaneous memorial parties were held among his closest friends. Ginni Hubbard, Mary Knollenberg, and Adele Clement, all feeling like widows, commiserated and reminisced over a long candlelit din-ner with a table set for four, holding a place for Walker, as if he might be resurrected. "I suppose a lot of people loved Walker," said Knollenberg. "He had that mysterious magical thing that some crea-tive people have, and you either love that thing or die — what else is it for?"

The literary remains of this mysterious magical man lay in un-sorted confusion in the house in Old Lyme. John Hill made photographs of details of the interior — shelves of books collected and read over more than forty years, the clothes closet with racks of shoes, and a work in progress, a washbasin full of beer tabs with a sign on the rim: "Please do not disturb the arrangement of tin beer caps in this wash bowl." Jerry Thompson took away the cameras that Walker had willed to him. Walker had wanted Ginni Hubbard to have his Chevrolet. Other friends went into his closet and divided up his clothes. Letters were returned to his old girlfriends. Bill Christenberry, his fellow sign thief, was appointed honorary curator of the sign collection. Lee Friedlander, who shared Walker's love of old-fashioned erotica, was given his leather trunk full of pornography. Ginni Hubbard rescued some of his first halting, self-conscious attempts at fiction writing. Dale Vosburgh, who was still living in the house, bought it from the estate and by so doing inherited the residue of Walker's unfinished work. Piles of flip-top rings and ticket stubs were everywhere, and the crawl space was crammed with moldy driftwood. The spirit of Walker Evans could still be felt in these things, but the inimitable art of their selection died with the man.

Notes

Bibliography

Index

Notes

The following abbreviations are used in the notes:

WE — Walker Evans
JA — James Agee
AAA — Archives of American Art, Smithsonian Institution
Beinecke — Yale Collection of American Literature, Beinecke Rare Book and Manuscript Library, Yale University
Houghton — Houghton Library, Harvard University
MoMA — Museum of Modern Art, New York
Mugar — Department of Special Collections, Mugar Memorial Library, Boston University
Ransom — Harry Ransom Humanities Research Center, University of Texas at Austin
Tamamint — Tamamint Institute Library, New York University

1. A MIDWESTERN CHILDHOOD

page

1 "Privilege": "The Thing Itself Is Such a Secret and So Unapproachable," interview with WE, *Yale Alumni Magazine*, February 1974, p. 15. "He liked to imply": Mary Knollenberg, interview with the author, February 21, 1991, Chester, Conn.

2 "the moral": Hilton Kramer, "An Era Lives in Photos at Evans Show," *New York Times*, January 28, 1971.

page

2 "This attraction": "Walker Evans, Visiting Artist," transcript of discussion with students, University of Michigan, October 29, 1971; in Beaumont Newhall, ed., *Photography: Essays and Images* (New York: Museum of Modern Art, 1980), p. 314.

4 "representatives of the fashionable set": *St. Louis Post-Dispatch*, January 15, 1900, p. 2.

5 "A phantasm": Henry Adams, *The Education of Henry Adams* (New York: Modern Library, 1931), pp. 466–67.

6 "uniform right through": John Gunther, *Taken at the Flood: The Story of Albert D. Lasker* (New York: Harper & Brothers, 1960), p. 75.

7 "I'se in town": Brendan Gill, *A New York Life: Of Friends and Others*, p. 303.
"Sales to Caucasians": Colleen Brown Kilner, *Joseph Sears and His Kenilworth*, p. 143.

8 "He who travels": WE, "The U.S. Depot," *Fortune*, February 1953, p. 138.
"and the ting ting ting": WE, "Along the Right-of-Way," *Fortune*, September 1950, p. 106.
"like old ditties": WE, "Before They Disappear," *Fortune*, March 1957, p. 141.

10 "Time to Re-Tire": Theodore Crane, interview with Eve Harris Noake, December 7, 1986, Springfield, Vt.

11 *Babes in Toyland*: WE, interview with Paul Cummings, October 13, 1971, Old Lyme, Conn.; transcript, AAA. A shorter version of this interview appears in Paul Cummings, *Artists in Their Own Words* (New York: St. Martin's, 1979).
"atmosphere of flannels": WE, "Come on Down," *Architectural Forum*, July 1962, p. 96.
"confessions and descriptions": Cummings interview, AAA.

12 "bright but inattentive": application card, Loomis Chaffee School Archive, Windsor, Conn.

13 "a bunch of babies": Cummings interview, AAA.
"rather a strange fellow": Dudley Britton, interview with the author, February 1, 1991, Pleasantville, N.Y.

14 "out of adjustment": N. H. Batchelder to W. M. Irvine, November 10, 1920, Mercersburg Academy Archive [MAA], Mercersburg, Pa.

page

14 "cordial consent": Batchelder to Irvine, January 7, 1921, MAA.
"in no sense bad": Batchelder to R. J. Mulford, November 10, 1920, MAA.

15 "typical American boy": Mercersburg Academy Catalogue, 1920–21, MAA.
"I am *very anxious*": WE to W. M. Irvine, December 4, 1920, MAA.
"of good habits": Edward Cady to Irvine, January 11, 1920, MAA.
"certainly bright enough": Harvey Robison to Irvine, January 7, 1921, MAA.
"gives the impression": N. H. Batchelder to Irvine, January 7, 1921, MAA.

16 "merely temporal": L. E. Lynde to Irvine, July 27, 1921, MAA.
"manner in the classroom": Frederick S. Allis, *Youth from Every Quarter*, p. 402.

17 "a nice fellow": Jack Watson, interview with the author, October 29, 1990, Baltimore, Md.
"E is for Evans": Yearbook, Phillips Academy, Andover, Mass., 1922.

19 "just walked in": Cummings interview, AAA.

20 "a pathological bibliophile": Ibid.
"were taught": Malcolm Cowley, *Exile's Return*, p. 33.

21 "Just look who": Cummings interview, AAA.

2. PARIS AND NEW YORK

25 "Paris was a great": Cowley, *Exile's Return*, p. 135.

26 "lay stacked": Noel Riley Fitch, *Sylvia Beach and the Lost Generation*, p. 14.
"it burst over us": Janet Flanner, *Paris Was Yesterday*, p. x.

27 "She sensed": Cummings interview, AAA.
"It was like": Dwight Macdonald, *Against the American Grain*, p. 125.
"not for me": Cummings interview, AAA.

28 "Stare": Jerry Thompson and John T. Hill, eds., *Walker Evans at Work*, p. 161.

29 "Who could be": Leslie Katz, "Interview with Walker Evans," *Art in America*, March-April 1971, p. 84.
"a deportment": Charles Baudelaire, *The Painter of Modern Life and*

page

Other Essays, Jonathan Mayne, ed. (New York: Da Capo, 1986), pp. 13, 2, 3.

30 "plastered from top to bottom": Gustave Flaubert, *Madame Bovary,* Alan Russell, trans. (New York: Penguin, 1982), p. 85.
"She loved the sea": Ibid., pp. 49, 50.

31 "and sort of asked": Cummings interview, AAA.

32 "He was a little": Dorothy Grotz, interview with the author, March 1, 1990, New York, N.Y.

33 "a usable past": Van Wyck Brooks, "On Creating a Usable Past," *Dial,* April 11, 1918, pp. 337–41.

34 "We just had fun": Paul Grotz, interview with the author, March 1, 1990, New York, N.Y.

35 "a sketch of manners": Baudelaire, pp. 1, 5.
"Both of us looked": Iago Gladston to John Szarkowski, n.d., private collection.
"somewhat guiltily": Cummings interview, AAA.

37 "Modernistic photography": M. F. Agha, "A Word on European Photography," *Pictorial Photographers of America* (New York, 1929), n.p.
"restful" compositions: Ibid., Editorial Comment.

38 "artiness": Cummings interview, AAA.

39 "Very good": Ibid.
"That's the stuff": Thompson and Hill, *Walker Evans at Work,* p. 24.

41 "in his raving way": Katz, "Interview," p. 83.

43 "how a Bach fugue": Louis Unterecker, *Voyager: A Life of Hart Crane,* pp. 270–71.
"aristocracy of taste": Ibid., p. 227.
"the loud-speaker stuff": Hart Crane, *The Bridge,* p. 22.

44 "sorting securities": Hart Crane to Malcolm Cowley, November 1928, Hart Crane papers, Beinecke.

45 "I fake it": Unterecker, *Voyager,* p. 569.
"always a very cocky": Dorothy Grotz interview.

49 While an earlier generation: Ben Shahn, *The Shape of Content,* p. 37.
"on sheets as large": Crane to Cowley, February 26, 1929, Crane papers, Beinecke.

50 "It is a remarkable": Crane to Joseph Stella, January 24, 1929, Crane papers, Beinecke.
"which would be too steep": Crane to Harry and Caresse Crosby, August 30, 1929, Crane papers, Beinecke.

page

50 "à l'americain": WE, interview with Phillip Horton, n.d., Crane papers, Beinecke.

3. EXPOSURE

53 So great was their sense: Cummings interview, AAA.

54 "in fact quite a success": Byard Williams, *Williams College Alumni Magazine*, 1931, p. 30.

"All he had": WE, tape recording of discussion of the exhibition "Ben Shahn as Photographer," November 13, 1969; courtesy of Harvard University Art Museums.

55 "the good shoemaker": Bernarda Bryson Shahn, *Ben Shahn* (New York: Harry N. Abrams, 1972), p. 127.

"a certain malaise": Thompson and Hill, *Walker Evans at Work*, p. 70.

56 "She couldn't say no": William DeLuze, telephone interview with the author, March 25, 1992.

"a kind of saint": Judith Shahn, interview with the author, June 21, 1991, Truro, Mass.

57 "I am going to publish": Thompson and Hill, *Walker Evans at Work*, p. 70.

"the blended babel": *Creative Art*, December 1930, pp. 453–56.

58 "a Harvard Miscellany": Mitzi Berger Hamovitch, *The Hound and Horn Letters*, p. xi.

59 "He invaded you": Katz, "Interview," p. 83.

"This undergraduate": Ibid.

61 "Swift chance": WE, "The Reappearance of Photography," *Hound and Horn*, September 1931, p. 136.

"Contemporary photographers": Charles Flato, *Hound and Horn*, October–December 1933.

"a perfectly transparent": Paul Zweig, *Walt Whitman: The Making of a Poet* (New York: Basic Books, 1984), p. 10.

64 The Lincoln Memorial: J. B. Wheelwright, "Cinque Cento Charles," *Hound and Horn*, Fall 1930, p. 138.

"My first article": J. B. Wheelwright to Lincoln Kirstein, November 16, 1931, Hound and Horn papers, Beinecke.

65 "like postcards": Lincoln Kirstein, *Flesh Is Heir*, p. 318.

page

67 "one of those glorified": M. F. Agha, John Becker Gallery brochure, April 1931. Artist's file, Dept. of Photographs, MoMA.

"I will let": Thompson and Hill, *Walker Evans at Work*, p. 50.

69 When *The Brown Decades:* Hamovitch, *Hound and Horn Letters*, p. 146.

"Suddenly": WE, "The Reappearance of Photography," p. 126.

70 "general note is money": Ibid., p. 127.

"will always appear": Ibid.

71 "phony to the fingertips": Cummings interview, AAA.

72 "When I was twenty-one": Benjamin Cheever, ed., *The Letters of John Cheever*, p. 304.

73 "When it comes": WE, Horton interview, Beinecke.

75 "Romantic journalism": Thompson and Hill, *Walker Evans at Work*, p. 74.

"I am beginning": Ibid., pp. 74, 34.

76 "the barnacles": Katz, "Interview," p. 84.

78 "Mural controversy": Lou Block, interview with Harlan Phillips, May 1965; transcript, AAA.

79 "I feel perfectly sure": Walter Goodwin to Carleton Beals, April 26, 1933, Carleton Beals papers, Mugar.

"Beneath the tropical": Carleton Beals, *The Crime of Cuba*, p. 399.

80 "half savage, forgetful": Gilles Mora and John T. Hill, *The Hungry Eye*, p. 78.

81 "It's a grand place": WE to Carleton Beals, Mugar.

"I often felt": Ibid.

82 "a real Cuban": Ibid.

83 "baseball and cigarette cards": Nicholas Jenkins, ed., *By, With, To, and From*, p. 47.

84 "pure Walker Evans": excerpt from Lincoln Kirstein diaries, March 1930, private collection.

"probably incurable": James Thrall Soby, "The Muse Was Not for Hire," *Saturday Review*, September 22, 1962, p. 57.

"out of Walker Evans": Morris Werner to Lincoln Kirstein, June 27, 1933, Hound and Horn papers, Beinecke.

85 "These wooden houses": Lincoln Kirstein, "Walker Evans Photographs of Victorian Architecture," *The Bulletin of the Museum of Modern Art*, December 1933, p. 4.

4. SOUTH

86 Evans read about: WE to Jay Leyda, November 22, 1933, Jay Leyda collection, Tamamint.

87 "one of those government": WE, tape recording on Ben Shahn, Harvard University Art Museums.

"Look, Ben": Hank O'Neal, *A Vision Shared,* p. 44.

"that split second": Colin Westerbeck, "Ben Shahn, Artist as Photographer," *Connoisseur,* October 1982, p. 100.

88 "The problem": WE, tape recording of interview with Sedat Pakay, June 1968, MoMA collections.

Jacoby was regarded: Leo Seltzer, telephone interview with the author, February 25, 1991.

89 "a fathead": WE to Leyda, February 21, 1934, Tamamint.

"Florida is ghastly": Thompson and Hill, *Walker Evans at Work,* p. 98.

"an oddly invisible": Frederick Lewis Allen, *The Big Change,* p. 131.

90 "American city": Thompson and Hill, *Walker Evans at Work,* p. 98.

91 "during a prowl": Dwight Macdonald, "The Communist Party," *Fortune,* September 1934, p. 69.

"made a fascist": Michael Wreszin, *A Rebel in Defense of Tradition,* p. 30.

92 "How it scraggled": JA, "The American Roadside," *Fortune,* September 1934, p. 53.

"next to unassisted": JA and WE, *Let Us Now Praise Famous Men,* p. 11.

93 "People do get": Cummings interview, AAA.

94 "He seemed to model": WE, "James Agee in 1936," *Famous Men,* p. xlii.

"in due time": Ibid., p. xli.

"How many blocks": Walter MacQuade, interview with the author, November 13, 1990, Great Neck, N.Y.

95 "The weariest river": David Madden, ed., *Remembering James Agee,* p. 134.

"old Americans": Bill Ferris, "A Visit with Walker Evans," in Karl G. Heider, ed., *Images of the South.*

101 The affair, which lacked: WE diary, June 28–29, 1935; courtesy of Jane Sargeant.

"They looked like": Paul Grotz interview.

page

103 "We were full": Elizabeth Sekear Rothschild, interview with the author, June 19, 1991, Hastings-on-Hudson, N.Y.

108 "which seems to me": WE to John Franklin Carter, August 17, 1935, Roy Emerson Stryker papers, AAA.

109 "I wanted the kids": Roy Stryker and Nancy Wood, *In This Proud Land,* p. 11.

"to direct the activities": Ibid.

110 "at his knee": WE, tape recording on Ben Shahn, Harvard University Art Museums.

"Mr. Walker Evans' photographic": Charles F. Fuller to Fred L. Parker, October 3, 1935, National Personnel Records Center, St. Louis, Mo.

"he showed the greatest": Wilfred S. Lewis to Parker, October 4, 1935, National Personnel Records Center.

111 "*No politics* whatever": Thompson and Hill, *Walker Evans at Work,* p. 112.

"A bitter edge": James Guimond, *American Photography and the American Dream,* p. 121.

112 "We were quite": Stryker to WE, December 10, 1935, Stryker papers, AAA.

114 "kept his white gloves on": Elizabeth Sekear Rothschild interview.

"Do you think Jane's": Jane Sargeant, interview with the author. The author's interviews with Jane Sargeant were conducted between July 1990 and December 1994 in Salisbury, Conn., and by telephone. Hereafter they are cited as "Sargeant interviews."

115 "to show deterioration": Stryker to WE, February 1936, Stryker papers, AAA.

"a big Boy Scout": Elizabeth Sekear Rothschild interview.

116 "like magic": Katz, "Interview," p. 87.

117 "Your monthly expenditures": Stryker to WE, March 24, 1936, Stryker papers, AAA.

117 "Carolina and Georgia": Thompson and Hill, *Walker Evans at Work,* p. 98.

5. THREE FAMILIES

118 "Very sorry": JA to WE, March 1936, James Agee papers, Ransom.

120 "full of vitality": Madden, *Remembering James Agee,* p. 54.

page

120 "one day": Ibid., p. 37.

121 At the end of June: Roy Stryker to Eleanor Traecey, June 29, 1936, Stryker papers, AAA.

122 "Feel terrific personal responsibility": Father James Harold Flye, ed., *Letters of James Agee to Father Flye*, p. 92.

123 "the pressure upon us": JA and WE, *Famous Men*, p. 373.
"the light so held": Ibid., p. 38.
"hotter than hell": JA to Via Agee, n.d., general collection, Manuscripts Division, Department of Rare Books and Special Collections, Princeton University Libraries.

124 "up a loose": JA and WE, *Famous Men*, pp. 25, 28, 27, 31.

125 "small sweet peaches": Ibid., pp. 362, 363.
"Walker setting up": Ibid., p. 364.

126 "in a one-piece dress": Ibid., pp. 364, 365.
"of family snapshots": Ibid., p. 369.

127 "have to act any different": Ibid., p. 64.
"According to our employers'": Ibid., p. 372.
"some Communists": Ibid., pp. 373, 375.

128 "You understand": Ibid., p. 371.

129 "all the narrow": Ibid., pp. 377, 7.

130 "to see or to convey": Ibid., p. 232.
"wild fugues and floods": Ibid., p. 145.

131 "a thin constellation": Ibid., pp. 170, 171, 163, 164, 165.

132 "earnest wish": Ibid., p. 156.

133 "master of the brood": William Stott, *Documentary Expression and Thirties America*, pp. 286, 344n.
"rather that of": JA and WE, *Famous Men*, pp. 59, 62.
"the long vertical": Ibid., p. 276.

134 "[her] eyes go to": Ibid., p. 372.

135 "It must out-soup": Margaret Bourke-White, *Portrait of Myself,* p. 81.
"like a motion picture": Vicki Goldberg, *Margaret Bourke-White,* p. 168.

136 "Visitors were always": Bourke-White, *Portrait of Myself,* pp. 133, 134.
"I never touch": WE, interview with William Stott, April 19, 1971, Old Lyme, Conn.; transcript, courtesy of William Stott.

137 "I want you": JA and WE, *Famous Men*, p. 64.

138 "I Sure was": Flora Bee Tingle to WE, n.d.; courtesy of Harry Lunn.

6. AMERICAN PHOTOGRAPHS

139 "Tugwell Has Staff": *New York Times,* November 17, 1936, p. 1.
"the human element": *New York Times,* June 18, 1936 (clipping).
"Roosevelt's clay pigeon": Pare Lorenz, telephone interview with
the author, April 22, 1991.
"cookie-cutters": O'Neal, *A Vision Shared,* p. 10.

140 "The revelation": F. Jack Hurley, *Portrait of a Decade,* p. 90.

141 "Bill posters": Stryker and Wood, *In This Proud Land,* pp. 13, 14.

143 "It's not perfect": WE to Jay Leyda, n.d., Leyda papers, Tamamint.
"a properly negative": WE to Leyda, n.d., Leyda papers, Tamamint.

144 "substitute for my": Gilbert Burck, ed., *Writing for Fortune,* p. 156.
"impossible in any form": Flye, *Letters,* p. 94.
"This little number": JA to WE, n.d., Agee papers, Ransom.
"pessimistic, unconstructive": Stott, *Documentary Expression,* p. 262.

145 "J. Leyda has seen": JA to WE, n.d., Agee papers, Ransom.
"a tenant movie": Ibid., n.d.

146 "Locke-Evans HDQS.": Edwin Locke to Roy Stryker, February 4,
1937, Stryker papers, AAA.
"was damned interesting": WE to Jay Leyda, February 17, 1937,
Leyda papers, Tamamint.
"I am in a hell": Locke to Stryker, February 11, 1937, Stryker papers,
AAA.

147 "working along the flooded": WE to Leyda, February 17, 1937, Leyda
papers, Tamamint.
"Reasons for action": personnel recommendation, March 23, 1937,
National Personnel Records Center, St. Louis, Mo.

148 "exceedingly pretty": Laurence Bergreen, *James Agee: A Life,* p. 185.

149 "younger sons": JA to WE, May 1938, Agee papers, Ransom.
"representatives of the lower": JA, "Six Days at Sea," *Fortune,* September 1937, p. 117.

150 "in a noisy flotilla": Ibid.
"their talent for": Ibid.

151 "With Walker you knew": Via Saunders Agee Wood, interview with
the author, April 24, 1991, Jamesburg, N.J.

152 "present the most exhaustive": WE, application for fellowship, 1937;
courtesy of the Guggenheim Foundation.
"the anthropologist": Ibid.

page
152 "notes for color photography": Bergreen, *James Agee,* pp. 205–7.
153 "two men strike": JA to Archibald MacLeish, November 18, 1937, Agee papers, Ransom.
154 "She happened to see": Roy Stryker to WE, November 18, 1937, Stryker papers, AAA.

"Viking have": C. A. Pierce to JA, December 1, 1937, Stryker papers, AAA.

"those eighteenth-century": WE to Stryker, February 15, 1938, Stryker papers, AAA.
155 "Extra work": WE to Stryker, February 24, 1938, Stryker papers, AAA.
157 "whispering campaign": Tom Mabry, memorandum of conversation with Gilbert Seldes, June 22, 1938, Office of the Registrar, MoMA.
158 "retiring temperament": Tom Mabry, draft of press release for "American Photographs," n.d., Office of the Registrar, MoMA.

"Don't forget": Tom Mabry to Lincoln Kirstein, April 29, 1938, Office of the Registrar, MoMA.
159 "photographic art": Lincoln Kirstein, "Photographs of America: Walker Evans," in WE, *American Photographs,* pp. 192–98.

"whose verse": Ibid.

"I had heard": JA to WE, June 20, 1938, Agee papers, Ransom.
160 "A clumsy 'For Sale'": Kirstein, "Photographs of America," p. 195.

"The physiognomy": jacket copy, WE, *American Photographs.*
162 "I had more or less": JA to WE, July 1, 1938, Agee papers, Ransom.

"I am wanting": JA to WE, September 13 or 14, 1938, Agee papers, Ransom.

"I wish you the luck": Ibid.
163 Charles Fuller later learned: Anne Fuller, interview with the author, April 15, 1991, Princeton, N.J.

"Simply by being published": JA to WE, September 15, 1938, Agee papers, Ransom.
164 "There is . . . nothing": Edward Alden Jewell, *New York Times,* October 2, 1938, section 9, p. 9.

"if all America": Carl Van Vechten, *New York Herald Tribune,* October 16, 1938.

"facts, . . . given": David Wolff, *New Masses,* October 4, 1938, p.

"pack a wicked punch": William Carlos Williams, *New Republic,* October 12, 1938, p. 282.

page

164 "has succeeded": S. T. Williamson, *New York Times Book Review,*
November 27, 1938, p. 6.

"a parade of": *Washington Post,* October 7, 1938.

165 "own mental state": *American Photograph,* December 1, 1938.

"unnecessary and cruel": *San Francisco News,* December 17, 1938.

"Through the intensity": Tom Mabry, "Walker Evans' Photographs
of America," *Harper's Bazaar,* November 1, 1938, p. 84.

"until Professor Stryker": Pare Lorenz, *Saturday Review of Literature,* December 17, 1938, p. 6.

"a boiled shirt": Williamson, *New York Times Book Review,* p. 6.

"liked it a lot": Roy Stryker to WE, November 9, 1938, Stryker
papers, AAA.

166 "I think the book": Russell Lynes, *Good Old Modern,* p. 158.

"I want the Walker": Edward Weston to Beaumont Newhall, September 23, 1938, courtesy of Beaumont Newhall.

7. LOVE BEFORE BREAKFAST

167 "a calling card": Cummings interview, AAA.

168 "If you'd like": JA to WE, December 27, 1938, Agee papers, Ransom.

"they were dancing": Alice Morris, interview with the author, February 5, 1991, New York, N.Y.

169 On several occasions: Verna Hobson, interview with the author,
March 11, 1991, New Gloucester, Me.

"However much": JA to WE, n.d., Agee papers, Ransom.

170 "He was blind": WE, interview with William Stott.

"down among the torn": Sarah Greenough, *Walker Evans: Subways
and Streets,* p. 127.

171 "the wrecked demeanors": JA, *Forum and Century,* vol. 97, February
1937, p. 115.

"The guard is down": Thompson and Hill, *Walker Evans at Work,*
p. 152.

172 "efficiency experts": Lynes, *Good Old Modern,* p. 213.

"'Mr. Evans'": Beaumont Newhall, *Focus: Memoirs of a Life in
Photography,* p. 56.

"was a man": Beaumont Newhall, interview with the author, April
1, 1991, Santa Fe, N.M.

173 Blumenthal produced: Lynes, *Good Old Modern,* p. 207.

"designed it": Ibid.

"This is the kiss": Ibid.

175 "Darling you are terrible": WE to Jane Ninas, June 1939, courtesy of Jane Sargeant.

"I cried all night": Sargeant interviews.

176 "With this hair": Ibid.

"Within 24 hours": Frances Collins to Marga Barr, July 28, 1939, MoMA Archives, Margaret Scolari Barr papers.

177 "Everything was pure white": Sargeant interviews.

178 "Walker was too mature": Wood interview.

179 "interested in the people": Alfred Kazin, *Starting Out in the Thirties,* p. 157.

180 "he could also be incredibly": Sargeant interviews.

181 "If I could do it": JA and WE, *Famous Men,* p. 13.

"I doubt": Edward Aswell to Lovell Thompson, July 18, 1940, Houghton Mifflin collection (uncatalogued), Houghton.

182 "in order to meet": Ibid.

183 "I wouldn't touch": Stott, *Documentary Expression,* p. 264.

"a catalogue": WE, application for fellowship, 1940; courtesy of the Guggenheim Foundation.

"appendisodomy": WE to Ernestine Evans, n.d., Ernestine Evans papers, Rare Book and Manuscript Library, Columbia University.

184 "I want to collect": WE to Henry Allen Moe, February 1, 1941, Guggenheim Foundation.

185 "illegal in Massachusetts": JA and WE, *Famous Men,* p. xlvi.

"Walker was very helpful": Paul Brooks, telephone interview with the author, June 20, 1991.

"Let me tell you": Aswell to Thompson, July 18, 1940, Houghton Mifflin collection (uncatalogued), Houghton.

"We had hoped": JA to Robert Linscott, May 14, 1941, Houghton Mifflin collection (uncatalogued), Houghton.

"I hope": Linscott to JA, March 4, 1941, Houghton Mifflin collection (uncatalogued), Houghton.

186 "We are anxious": JA to Linscott, n.d., Houghton Mifflin collection (uncatalogued), Houghton.

"There never was": Ralph Thompson, *New York Times Book Review,* August 19, 1941.

page

186 "Parts of the book": John Jessup, *Time*, October 13, 1941, p. 104.

"whatever the case": Harvey Breit, *New Republic*, September 15, 1941, p. 349.

"Take the opening pages": Selden Rodman, *Saturday Review*, August 1941, p. 6.

187 "the most important": Lionel Trilling, *Kenyon Review*, Winter 1942, p. 99.

188 "He's the most": Ernestine Evans to Karl Bickel, n.d., Ernestine Evans papers, Rare Book and Manuscript Library, Columbia University.

191 "the tennis champion": Robert Elson, *Time Inc.*, p. 85.

"as a reader": Ibid., p. 66.

192 "shy Scotsman": WE, "The New Pictures," *Time*, April 12, 1943, p. 95.

"Walter Van Tilburg Clark's": WE, *Time*, May 3, 1943, p. 94.

"a packaging job": WE, *Time*, May 24, 1943, p. 98.

"a symphony": WE, *Time*, June 7, 1943, p. 92.

"for a moment": Ibid.

"The Technicolor cameras": WE, *Time*, June 21, 1943, p. 54.

193 "a fatuous romp": Ibid., p. 55.

"The morning hours": James Stern, "Walker Evans, a Memoir," *London Magazine*, August-September 1977, p. 9.

194 "a handsome record": WE, "Among the Ruins," *Time*, December 27, 1943, p. 73.

"raffish": WE, "Ribald Rowly," *Time*, September 20, 1943, p. 70.

"a daft satiric": WE, "Emmet of *Punch*," *Time*, August 2, 1943, p. 50.

"the laughable aspects": WE, "Laughing Tiger," *Time*, October 11, 1943, p. 74.

194 "famous comic master": WE, "Men, Women, and Thurber," *Time*, November 15, 1943, p. 38.

195 "The Elizabethan talk": WE, "Among the Unlimitless Etha," *Time*, May 8, 1944, p. 94.

"Snooksology": WE, "Snooksology," *Time*, February 28, 1944, p. 75.

"Erect, frail": WE, "Expressionism's Father," *Time*, February 7, 1944, p. 78.

"Stone-deaf, crop-haired": WE, "Brett's Stokowskis," *Time*, May 8, 1944, p. 93.

"In the 1930s": WE, "Frankly Romantic," *Time*, January 1, 1945, p. 65.

page

195 "Aristocratic, cantankerous": WE, "Secret Sculptor," *Time*, January 15, 1945, p. 65.

196 "The 16 smooth-surfaced": WE, "Money Is Not Enough," *Time*, February 5, 1945, p. 86.

"You had to figure": WE, interview with William Stott.

8. FORTUNE

197 "drained dry": WE, interview with William Stott.

198 "dazzling furnaces": Guimond, *American Photography and the American Dream*, p. 90.

200 "on a felicitous mission": *FYI*, January 13, 1947, Time Inc. Archives, New York.

"American city": Thompson and Hill, *Walker Evans at Work*, p. 98.

"Chicago is the only": WE, "Chicago: A Camera Exploration," *Fortune*, February 1947, p. 121.

202 "somewhat like holding": Carl Schniewind to WE, February 11, 1947, Art Institute of Chicago.

"Let's shake Chicago": WE to Schniewind, September 2, 1947, Art Institute of Chicago.

"the gigantic fantastic": WE to Jane Evans, August 18, 1947, courtesy of Jane Sargeant.

203 "the awful California": WE to Jane Evans, August 21, 1947, courtesy of Jane Sargeant.

"Riviera period": WE to Jane Evans, August 22, 1947, courtesy of Jane Sargeant.

"a five-episode contraption": Ibid.

"which was a much worse": WE to Jane Evans, September 9, 1947, courtesy of Jane Sargeant.

204 "The acres of half-baked": "Milestones," *FYI*, February 11, 1991, Time Inc. Archives.

"to develop": Thompson and Hill, *Walker Evans at Work*, pp. 182, 181.

205 "You would never": Ibid., p. 181.

"has a voice": WE statement, n.d., Dept. of Photographs, Art Institute of Chicago.

206 "There is the profitable": Thompson and Hill, *Walker Evans at Work*, p. 181.

page

206 "For a long time": Leo Lionni, interview with the author, January 22, 1992, New York, N.Y.

"the trolley car period": WE, "Main Street Looking North from Courthouse Square," *Fortune,* May 1948, p. 102.

207 "and it might as well": Ralph Steiner, *A Point of View,* p. 27.

208 "DO — Merrit pkwy": WE, spiral notebook, Dept. of Photographs, J. Paul Getty Museum.

"patented portfolio ideas": Thompson and Hill, *Walker Evans at Work,* pp. 184, 185.

"He obviously didn't": Walter Allner, interview with the author, March 9, 1992, New York, N.Y.

209 "A padlocked steel bar": Seville McCarten to the author, June 24, 1992.

"I used to try": WE, "Puritan Explorer," *Time,* December 15, 1947, p. 73.

210 "August is their month": WE, "Summer North of Boston," *Fortune,* August 1949, p. 75.

"a brilliant center": Alfred Kazin, *New York Jew,* p. 56.

"the roll-top desk": WE, "Vintage Office Furniture," *Fortune,* August 1953, p. 123.

"He who travels": WE, "The U.S. Depot," p. 138.

211 "He was a little": Lionni interview.

"a cross between": Lesley K. Baier, *Walker Evans at Fortune,* p. 12.

"I once asked": Steiner, *A Point of View,* p. 28.

"He knew that in Del": William Hollingsworth Whyte, interview with the author, June 14, 1991, New York, N.Y.

"All my life": WE, "Perfectionist," *FYI,* January 13, 1947.

212 "It was a big day": Whyte interview.

"Clark and the farmer": Sargeant interviews.

213 "Too much": Marion Voorhees, telephone interview with the author, February 23, 1991.

214 "Love, Just got": WE to Jane Evans, October 19, 1944, courtesy of Jane Sargeant.

"Miss you like hell": WE to Jane Evans, April 18, 1943, courtesy of Jane Sargeant.

"You were lovely": WE to Jane Evans, June 18, 1942, courtesy of Jane Sargeant.

"I didn't sparkle": Sargeant interviews.

page
215 "I don't think": Ibid.
"The Tramp is": JA, *Agee on Film,* vol. I (New York: Putnam, 1958), p. 9.
"Walker was so furious": Sargeant interviews.
216 "He destroyed me": Ibid.
"All the women": WE to Jane Evans, September 9, 1947, courtesy of Jane Sargeant.
"wildly" unfaithful: Sargeant interviews.
217 "a lacemaker": Anne Fuller, telephone interview with the author, March 6, 1991.
"half old master": John McDonald, interview with the author, August 23, 1990, Cranberry Island, Me.
"a vital modern means": Edward Steichen, introduction, "What Is Modern Photography?," November 20, 1950, tape recording, MoMA, Department of Photographs.
218 "atonality and cacophony": WE, "What Is Modern Photography?," November 20, 1950, tape recording, MoMA, Department of Photographs.
219 "I was afraid": Louis Faurer, interview with the author, September 16, 1991, New York, N.Y.
"projected his stability": Edith A. Tonelli and John Gossage, *Louis Faurer: Photographs from Philadelphia and New York,* p. 9.
"What a town!": Anne Wilkes Tucker and Philip Brookman, *Robert Frank: New York to Nova Scotia,* p. 20.
"to transform destiny": Ibid., p. 31.
"I love to watch": Vicente Todoli, *Robert Frank: Fotografias/Films,* p. 38.
220 "how Americans live": Tucker and Brookman, *Robert Frank: New York to Nova Scotia,* p. 20.
221 "I shall *endeavor*": WE to Henry Allen Moe, February 25, 1954, Guggenheim Foundation.
222 "immoderate supply": WE, interview with William Stott, transcript.
"a modest edition": JA to WE, n.d., Agee papers, Ransom.
223 "She's competing": Sargeant interviews.
224 Later Evans said: Michael Lesy, interview with the author, February 22, 1992, Amherst, Mass.
"I'm leaving": Sargeant interviews.

page

224 "Don't fight it": McDonald interview.

"Where do you get": Elizabeth and Sam Shaw, interview with the author, April 11, 1991, New York, N.Y.

"I thought they were": WE to Verna Hobson, March 15, 1956, courtesy of Archie Hobson.

225 "From now on": Sargeant interviews.

9. BEFORE THEY DISAPPEAR

226 One winter day: Eugenia Parry Janis and Wendy MacNeil, *Photography Within the Humanities,* p. 65.

227 "The building boom": WE, "'Downtown': A Last Look Backward," *Fortune,* October 1956, p. 157.

"When we can": WE, "Before They Disappear," p. 141.

"I hate that word": Katz, "Interview," p. 87.

"Pray keep me": WE and Malcolm Bradbury, "Collector's Items," *Mademoiselle,* May 1963, p. 182.

228 "damned interesting": WE to James Stern, July 1, 1956, courtesy of James Stern.

"everyone knew everyone": Saul Steinberg, interview with the author, May 29, 1991, New York, N.Y.

229 "a bedraggled little dinner": Ibid.

"Thank you": Mary Frank, telephone interview with the author, June 10, 1991.

230 "Walker always fled": Anne Fuller, telephone interview with the author, June 10, 1991.

"He practically *was*": Susanna Coggeshall, telephone interview with the author, September 23, 1992.

"he had a sweet tooth": Lily West, interview with the author, April 16, 1991, New York, N.Y.

231 "picked up aphorisms": Coggeshall interview.

"always in despair": Fuller interview.

"He built up": Frank interview.

232 "There couldn't be a more": Caroline Blackwood Lowell, interview with the author, September 30, 1991, Sag Harbor, N.Y.

"a fantasist": Ibid.

233 "He was ashamed": Ibid.

page

233 "I am an artist": Eliza Parkinson Cobb, interview with the author, April 13, 1991, New York, N.Y.

234 "What I have in mind": Tucker and Brookman, *Robert Frank: New York to Nova Scotia,* p. 20.

235 "next great industrial effort": Elson, *Time Inc.,* p. 187.

236 "tophatted": WE, "The London Look," *Architectural Forum,* April 1958, p. 114.

"glossy, explicit": Ibid.

"the attenuated nocturnal": WE, "Before They Disappear," p. 141.

"where the hippos": WE, "The Last of Railroad Steam," *Fortune,* September 1958, p. 138.

"Time uses a great": WE, "These Dark Satanic Mills," *Fortune,* April 1956, p. 139.

237 "how patina": WE, "Ship Shapes and Shadows," *Architectural Forum,* October 1958, p. 122.

"the restless, cacophonic design": WE, "Color Accidents," *Architectural Forum,* January 1958, p. 111.

238 "a bright New Year": Henry Luce to WE, December 19, 1958, Time Inc. Archives.

"butchered by daring surgeons": WE to John Mason Brown, February 13, 1959, Houghton.

"a fairy tale": Steinberg interview.

241 "a very interesting man": Penny Andrews, interview with the author, October 22, 1990, New York, N.Y.

"What do you want": Isabelle Storey, telephone interview with the author, August 20, 1990. The author's interviews with Isabelle Storey were conducted between February 1990 and December 1994 in Boston, New York, and by telephone. Hereafter they are cited as "Storey interviews."

242 "was reborn": Ferris, "A Visit with Walker Evans," in Heider, *Images of the South.*

"His Christianity": WE, "James Agee in 1936," *Famous Men,* p. xliv.

243 "I miss you": WE to Isabelle Boeschenstein, January 16 and 17, 1960, courtesy of Isabelle Storey.

"but nicely so": WE to Isabelle Boeschenstein, January 17, 1960, courtesy of Isabelle Storey.

244 "Just be your nice": Ibid.

"Walker wasn't feeling": Storey interviews.

page

245 "Here till the tenth": WE, "Come On Down," *Architectural Forum,*
July 1962, p. 96.

246 "But he had": Whyte interview.
"its Herculean columns": WE, "Doomed," *Life,* July 3, 1963, p. 52.
"the last word": Ibid.

247 "which has problems of its own": Edward Steichen, *The Bitter
Years,* p. iii.
"every other word": Davis Pratt, interview with the author, September 5, 1991, Cambridge, Mass.
"many young people": Monroe Wheeler, "Foreword," in WE,
American Photographs, 2nd ed. (New York: Museum of Modern
Art, 1962).

248 "'Excuse me ma'am'": William Christenberry, interview with the
author, October 31, 1990, Washington, D.C.

249 "My favorite thing": Diane Arbus, *Diane Arbus* (Millerton, N.Y.:
Aperture, 1972), p. 1.
"a seriously happy man": WE to Committee on Admissions, The
Century Association, February 5, 1957, courtesy of Archie Hobson.

250 "When you get through": Archie Hobson, interview with the author,
February 12, 1991, Brooklyn, N.Y.

10. MESSAGE FROM THE INTERIOR

252 "But Walter": Walter Allner, interview with the author, March 9,
1992, New York, N.Y.
"I do like to suggest": Cummings interview, AAA.

253 "One was expected": Jane Mayall, interview with the author, May
5, 1994, New York, N.Y.
"a résumé of": *Illinois, A Descriptive and Historical Guide,* American Guide Series (Chicago: A. C. McClury, 1939), p. 333.

254 "All he really wanted": David Swan, interview with the author, May
7, 1991, Chicago, Ill.

256 "aesthetic slump": WE, "When 'Downtown' Was a Beautiful Mess,"
Fortune, January 1962, p. 100.

257 "rather interesting": WE to Isabelle Evans, January 31, 1965, courtesy of Isabelle Storey.

page

258 "As a man of my age": WE to Hermann Boeschenstein, November 5, 1964, courtesy of Isabelle Storey.

259 "We'd have to send him": Storey interviews.

"had advanced no further": Stern, "WE, a Memoir," p. 18.

260 "It's this darned": Ibid.

"I haven't seen": Isabelle Evans to James and Tania Stern, January 12, 1965, courtesy of James Stern.

"It is the Ides": WE to James and Tania Stern, March 17, 1965, courtesy of James Stern.

262 "We are back": WE to Lovell Thompson, January 16, 1966, Houghton Mifflin collection (uncatalogued), Houghton.

"absolute fidelity": Louis Kronenberger, *Quality: Its Image in the Arts*, pp. 169, 208.

"He would ask": Alvin Eisenman, interview with the author, March 27, 1992, New Haven, Conn.

"He circled around": Alston Purvis, interview with the author, March 14, 1991, Brookline, Mass.

263 "Okay, now let's talk": Marie-Antoinette Robert, telephone interview with the author, summer 1993.

"absolute delight": Tom Strong, interview with the author, March 27, 1991, New Haven, Conn.

"transcended his background": Chris and Esther Pullman, interview with the author, January 25, 1992, Cambridge, Mass.

264 "This little piece": Isabelle Evans to James and Tania Stern, May 26, 1965, courtesy of James Stern.

265 "absolutely the right thing": John Szarkowski, interview with the author, October 5, 1991, East Chatham, N.Y.

266 "The portraits on these pages": WE, title, *The Cambridge Review*, no. 5, March 1956, p. 16.

"carries in the postures": JA, "Introduction," in WE, *Many Are Called*.

"Isabelle releases me": WE to Lovell Thompson, February 25, 1966, Houghton Mifflin collection (uncatalogued), Houghton.

267 "Leslie is in love": Isabelle Evans to James Stern, March 12, 1966, courtesy of James Stern.

"He'll be fine": Leslie Katz, interview with the author, New York.

268 "Gratifying as such": Brendan Gill, "The Art of Seeing," *The New Yorker*, December 24, 1966, p. 26.

page

269 "Isabelle and I are having": WE to Robert Schoelkopf, December 25, 1966, courtesy of Jane Schoelkopf.

"Since you were thoughtful": WE to James Stern, December 27, 1966, courtesy of James Stern.

"I am delighted": WE to Nancy Newhall, August 13, 1967, Dept. of Photographs, MoMA.

270 "the Brownies": Storey interviews.

271 "I have picked up": WE to Louis Kronenberger, September 17, 1968, courtesy of Emily Kronenberger.

"Among other things": WE to President Sawyer, June 19, 1968, Williams College Archive.

"caught in a single face": transcript of awards ceremony, June 9, 1968, Williams College Archive.

272 "To me these people": Arnold Crane, interview with the author, May 7, 1991, Chicago, Ill.

"Walker couldn't stand": Alice Morris to James Stern, n.d., courtesy of James Stern.

273 "Walker was ordering": Courtlandt and Trini Barnes, interview with the author, May 2, 1991, Santa Fe, N.M.

"Walker read five books": Storey interviews.

274 *"Belle! Belle!"*: from "The Swing," an unpublished short story by Isabelle Storey, courtesy of Isabelle Storey.

275 "Come back": Storey interviews.

"We had no strength": "The Thing Itself," *Yale Alumni Magazine*, p. 15.

277 "an ongoing, mumbled": Virginia Hubbard, interview with the author, May 3, 1991, Taos, N.M.

"I got much afraid": WE to Isabelle Evans, March 19, 1969, courtesy of Isabelle Storey.

278 "This man was a humanist": WE, tape recording on Ben Shahn, Harvard University Art Museums.

279 "But you know": Sargeant interviews.

11. A PENITENT SPY

280 "the belief that the commonplace": John Szarkowski, wall label, "New Documents," February 28–May 7, 1967, Dept. of Photographs, MoMA.

page

281 "He was a little": Szarkowski interview.

282 "There were an awful lot": Ibid.

283 "an astonishing creative": John Szarkowski, *Walker Evans*, p. 14.
"strictly prose": Stewart Dill McBride, *Times Union* (Albany, N.Y.), June 5, 1975.
"a new set of clues": Szarkowski, *Walker Evans*, p. 20.

284 "The world that Walker": Robert Penn Warren, tape recording, Evans dinner, January 26, 1971, MoMA Archives, sound recording #71.4.
"You've made me feel": WE, ibid.

285 "Almost all good artists": "The Thing Itself," *Yale Alumni Magazine*, p. 12.
"It is difficult": Szarkowski, *Walker Evans*, p. 20.
"For how many": Hilton Kramer, "An Era Lives in Photos at Evans Show," *New York Times*, January 28, 1971.
"has colored all": A. D. Coleman, "Did He Find the Real USA?," *New York Times*, February 14, 1971. p. no.

286 "His photographs": Walter McQuade, "Visual Clues to Who We Were, and Are," *Life*, March 5, 1971, p. 12.
"Dear Walter": WE to Walter McQuade, March 3, 1971, courtesy of Walter McQuade.
"the way people do": Knollenberg interview.

290 "The point is": Thompson and Hill, *Walker Evans at Work*, p. 229.
"Stop the car!": Mathew Wysocki, interview with the author, February 21, 1991, Hamden, Conn.

291 "Dearest F.": WE to Frances Lindley, January 15, 1973, courtesy of Charles Lindley.

292 "He wanted to leave": Varujan Boghosian, telephone interview with the author, January 25, 1991.
"You had to try": Charlee Mae Brodsky, telephone interview with the author, April 25, 1991.

293 "He always bought": Ibid.
"to talk to somebody": Alan Trachtenberg, interview with the author, March 18, 1993, New York, N.Y.

294 "We never talked": Knollenberg interview.
"This thought sprang": WE to Frances Lindley, May 15, 1973, courtesy of Charles Lindley.

page
294 "He was such a great": Hilton Kramer, telephone interview with the author, March 2, 1993.

295 "each one is a poem": WE, introduction to William Christenberry, Corcoran Gallery of Art, Washington, D.C., 1973.
"I'd crack a door": Christenberry interview.
"I could tell": Ibid.

296 "Tania took one look": Stern, "WE, a Memoir," p. 26.

297 "Look at that!": Purvis interview.
"I am of course": WE to Frances Lindley, September 10, 1973, courtesy of Charles Lindley.
"I want to spend": WE to James Stern, August 29, 1973, courtesy of James Stern.

298 "He's got a nice": Lesy interview.
"He'd go into a grocery": Ibid.
"There'd be this old": Ibid.

299 "This was not erotic": Leo Rubinfein, interview with the author, February 26, 1991, New York, N.Y.
"by his production": Joseph Mitchell to the Members of the Institute, October 22, 1973, National Institute of Arts and Letters Archives.
"You know": Cobb interview.
"to acknowledge the relentless": Lionel Trilling, transcript of presentation to WE of the Award for Distinguished Service to the Arts, National Institute of Arts and Letters Archives.

300 "I need not": WE to Lionel Trilling, May 28, 1974, Lionel Trilling papers, Special Collections, Columbia University Library.
"We hit it off": Bobbi Carrey, interview with the author, March 15, 1991, Boston, Mass.
"He couldn't resist": Ibid.

301 "Everyone was quite testy": George Rinhart, telephone interview with the author, March 2, 1993.

302 "Would you think": Ibid.
"He was like a child": Ibid.

303 "getting married": Valerie Lloyd, interview with the author, December 2, 1990, Bath, England.

304 "They got what I left": Crane interview.
"fidgety": Rinhart interview.
"Take them all": Hubbard interview.

page

305 "so that we can": George Rinhart to WE, March 11, 1975, town clerk, East Lyme, Conn.

306 "Do a little work": Lincoln Kaplan, "Walker Evans on Himself," *Exposure,* February 1977, p. 15.

307 "When is Michael's plane": Hubbard interview.

"one of the greatest": Hilton Kramer, "Walker Evans: A Devious Giant," *New York Times,* April 20, 1975.

"I suppose a lot": Knollenberg interview.

308 "Please do not disturb": Thompson and Hill, *Walker Evans at Work,* p. 221.

Bibliography

BOOKS BY OR WITH WALKER EVANS

Agee, James, and Walker Evans. *Let Us Now Praise Famous Men: Three Tenant Families.* Boston: Houghton Mifflin, 1941.

Beals, Carleton. *The Crime of Cuba.* Philadelphia: J. B. Lippincott, 1933.

Bickel, Karl. *The Mangrove Coast.* New York: Coward-McCann, 1942.

Crane, Hart. *The Bridge.* Paris: Black Sun Press, 1930; New York: Liveright, 1930.

Evans, Walker. *African Negro Art.* Four bound portfolios. New York: Museum of Modern Art, 1935. Also in Radin, Paul, and James Johnson Sweeney. *African Folktales and Sculpture.* New York: Pantheon, 1952.

———. *American Photographs.* With an essay by Lincoln Kirstein. New York: Museum of Modern Art, 1938.

———. *Many Are Called.* With an essay by James Agee. Boston: Houghton Mifflin, 1966.

———. *Message from the Interior.* With an essay by John Szarkowski. New York: Eakins Press, 1966.

———. *Wheaton College Photographs.* With a foreword by J. Edgar Park. Norton, Mass.: Wheaton College, 1941.

Kouwenhoven, John A. *Partners in Banking.* Garden City, N.Y.: Doubleday, 1968.

Kronenberger, Louis, ed. *Quality: Its Image in the Arts.* New York: Athenaeum, 1969.

Sloan, Alfred P., with photographs selected by Walker Evans. *My Years with General Motors*. Garden City, N.Y.: Doubleday, 1964.

EXHIBITION CATALOGUES AND MONOGRAPHS

Baier, Lesley K. *Walker Evans at Fortune*. Wellesley, Mass.: Wellesley College Museum, 1978.

Brix, Michael, and Birgit Mayer. *Walker Evans: America, Pictures from the Great Depression*. Munich: Schirmer Mosel, 1990.

Chevrier, Jean-François, Allan Sekula, and Benjamin H. D. Buchloh. *Walker Evans and Dan Graham*. Rotterdam: Witte de With, 1992.

Greenough, Sarah. *Walker Evans: Subways and Streets*. Washington, D.C.: National Gallery of Art, 1991.

Hill, John T., ed. *Walker Evans: First and Last*. New York: Harper and Row, 1978.

Maddox, Jerald C. *Walker Evans: Photographs for the Farm Security Administration, 1935–1938*. New York: Da Capo, 1973.

Mora, Gilles, and John T. Hill. *The Hungry Eye*. New York: Harry N. Abrams, 1993.

———. Walker Evans: *Walker Evans: Havana, 1933*. New York: Pantheon, 1989.

Papageorge, Tod. *Walker Evans and Robert Frank: An Essay on Influence*. New Haven: Yale University Art Gallery, 1981.

Rosenheim, Jeff L. *Walker Evans and Jane Ninas in New Orleans, 1935–1936*. New Orleans: Historic New Orleans Collection, 1991.

Southhall, Thomas W. *Of Time and Place: Walker Evans and William Christenberry*. Fort Worth: Amon Carter Museum, 1990.

Szarkowski, John. *Walker Evans*. New York: Museum of Modern Art, 1971.

Thompson, Jerry, and John T. Hill, eds. *Walker Evans at Work*. New York: Harper and Row, 1982.

GENERAL REFERENCES

Allen, Frederick Lewis. *The Big Change*. New York: Bantam, 1965.

Allis, Frederick S. *Youth from Every Quarter: A Bicentennial History of Phillips Academy, Andover*. Hanover, N.H.: University Press of New England, 1979.

Ashdown, Paul, ed. *James Agee: Selected Journalism.* Knoxville: University of Tennessee Press, 1985.

Bergreen, Lawrence. *James Agee: A Life.* New York: Dutton, 1984.

Bourke-White, Margaret. *Portrait of Myself.* New York: Simon and Schuster, 1963.

————, and Erskine Caldwell. *You Have Seen Their Faces.* New York: Viking, 1937.

Britton, John. *Carleton Beals: A Radical Journalist in Latin America.* Albuquerque: University of New Mexico Press, 1987.

Burck, Gilbert, ed. *Writing for Fortune.* New York: Time Inc., 1980.

Cheever, Benjamin, ed. *The Letters of John Cheever.* New York: Simon and Schuster, 1988.

Cowley, Malcolm. *Exile's Return: A Literary Odyssey of the 1920s.* New York: Viking, 1951.

Elson, Robert T. *Time Inc.: The Intimate History of a Publishing Enterprise, 1923–1941.* New York: Time Inc., 1968.

Fitch, Noel Riley. *Sylvia Beach and the Lost Generation: A History of Literary Paris in the Twenties and Thirties.* New York: Norton, 1983.

Flanner, Janet. *Paris Was Yesterday.* San Diego: Harcourt Brace Jovanovich, 1988.

Flye, Father James Harold, ed. *Letters of James Agee to Father Flye.* Boston: Houghton Mifflin, 1971.

Gill, Brendan. *A New York Life: Of Friends and Others.* New York: Poseidon, 1990.

Goldberg, Vicki. *Margaret Bourke-White: A Biography.* New York: Harper and Row, 1986.

Guimond, James. *American Photography and the American Dream.* Chapel Hill: University of North Carolina Press, 1991.

Hamovitch, Mitzi Berger. *The Hound and Horn Letters.* Athens: University of Georgia Press, 1982.

Heider, Karl G., ed. *Images of the South: Constructing a Regional Culture on Film and Video.* Athens: University of Georgia Press, 1993.

Hodgins, Eric. *Trolley to the Moon: An Autobiography.* New York: Simon and Schuster, 1973.

Hurley, F. Jack. *Portrait of a Decade: Roy Stryker and the Development of Documentary Photography in the Thirties.* Baton Rouge: Louisiana State University Press, 1972.

Janis, Eugenia Parry, and Wendy MacNeil. *Photography Within the Humanities.* Danbury, N.H.: Addison House, 1977.

Jenkins, Nicholas, ed. *By With To and From: A Lincoln Kirstein Reader.* New York: Farrar, Straus, and Giroux, 1991.

Kazin, Alfred. *New York Jew.* New York: Knopf, 1978.

———. *Starting Out in the Thirties.* Boston: Little, Brown, 1965.

Kilner, Colleen Browne. *Joseph Sears and His Kenilworth.* 2nd ed. Kenilworth, Ill.: Kenilworth Historical Society, 1990.

Kirstein, Lincoln. *Flesh Is Heir: An Historical Romance.* Carbondale and Edwardsville: Southern Illinois University Press, 1975.

Levitt, Helen. *A Way of Seeing.* New York: Horizon, 1965.

Lynes, Russell. *Good Old Modern: An Intimate Portrait of the Museum of Modern Art.* New York: Athenaeum, 1973.

Macdonald, Dwight. *Against the American Grain.* New York: Random House, 1962.

Madden, David, ed. *Remembering James Agee.* Baton Rouge: Louisiana State University Press, 1974.

Maharidge, Dale, and Michael Williamson. *And Their Children After Them.* New York: Pantheon, 1989.

Neuman, Alma. *Always Straight Ahead: A Memoir.* Baton Rouge: Louisiana State University Press, 1993.

Newhall, Beaumont. *Focus: Memoirs of a Life in Photography.* Boston: Little, Brown, 1993.

O'Neal, Hank. *A Vision Shared.* New York: St. Martin's, 1976.

Primm, James Neal. *Lion of the Valley: St. Louis, Missouri.* Boulder, Colo.: Pruett, 1990.

Rodman, Selden. *Ben Shahn: Portrait of the Artist as an American.* New York: Harper and Brothers, 1951.

Shahn, Ben. *The Shape of Content.* Cambridge, Mass.: Harvard University Press, 1957.

Steichen, Edward. *The Bitter Years.* New York: Museum of Modern Art, 1962.

Steiner, Ralph. *A Point of View.* Middletown, Conn.: Wesleyan University Press, 1978.

Stott, William. *Documentary Expression and Thirties America.* New York: Oxford University Press, 1973.

Stryker, Roy, and Nancy Wood. *In This Proud Land.* Greenwich, Conn.: New York Graphic Society, 1978.

Todoli, Vicente. *Robert Frank: Fotografias/Films, 1948–1984,* Barcelona: Sala Parpallo, 1985.

Tonelli, Edith A., and John Gossage. *Louis Faurer: Photographs from*

Philadelphia and New York, 1937–1973. College Park: University of Maryland Press, 1981.

Tucker, Anne Wilkes, and Philip Brookman. *Robert Frank: New York to Nova Scotia.* Houston: Museum of Fine Arts, 1986.

Unterecker, John. *Voyager: A Life of Hart Crane.* New York: Farrar, Straus, and Giroux, 1969.

Watson, Steven. *Strange Bedfellows: The First American Avant-Garde.* New York: Abbeville, 1991.

Wreszin, Michael. *A Rebel in Defense of Tradition: The Life and Politics of Dwight Macdonald.* New York: Basic Books, 1994.

Index

Abbott, Berenice, 28, 83, 172; influence on WE, 47–48

abstract expressionists, 220

Action in the North Atlantic (film), 192

Adams, Ansel, 172, 257, 280, 287; on WE, 165–66

Adams, Henry, 5

advertising: WE's father's career in, 5–7, 10; WE's attitude toward, 21, 30, 43–44

Advocate, The, 93, 185

Affluent Society, The (Galbraith), 221

African Queen, The (film), 223

Agee, Alma Mailman, 148, 155, 180; marriage to Agee, 167–68; dislike for WE, 169–70; leaves Agee, 184, 187

Agee, Emma, 101, 169

Agee, James, 92–95, 161, 228, 260, 277; "The Great American Roadside," 92; prose style of, 92; interest in photography, 92–93; meets WE, 93; friendship with WE, 93–95, 161, 180, 217, 222–23; appearance and manner of, 94–95; assignment on southern tenant farmers, 119–38; problems with text of *Three Tenant Families*, 144–45, 151–52, 161, 162, 163, 168; relations with Alma Mailman, 148, 155; assignment on Caribbean cruise, 149–50; WE photographs, 151; plans for book from sharecropper story, 151–52; sense of partnership with WE, 152, 168–69; contract with Harpers for *Three Tenant Families*, 155, 183; moves to Frenchtown, N.J., 155, 161, 168; Kirstein on WE-Agee collaboration, 159; on WE's *American Photographs*, 163–64; marriage to Alma, 167–68; romantic feelings for WE, 168–70; suggests subway photography project to WE, 170; as collector of castoffs, 177; "Knoxville: Summer of 1915" story, 178; and *Partisan Review*, 178; enthusiasm for movies, 180, 192; retitles *Three Tenant Families*, 180 (*see also Let Us Now Praise Famous Men*); seeks WE's aid as editor, 183; withdraws from Harpers contract, 183; Alma leaves, 184; *Let Us Now Praise Famous Men* published, 184–87; and Mia Fritsch, 187, 215, 222, 223; writing for *Time* and *The Nation*, 191, 196; work for *Fortune*, 199; alcoholism and declining health

Agee, James *(con't)*
of, 222–23; death of, 223–24, 251; re-
vival of reputation, 242; wins Pulit-
zer for *A Death in the Family*, 242;
and WE's *Many Are Called*, 266; WE
sells letters of, 278
Agee, Joel, 184, 187
Agee, Olivia Saunders ("Via"), 93, 95,
118, 145, 148, 149, 150, 151, 155, 169, 178
Agha, Mehemed Fehmy, 37, 67
Alabama: Agee-Evans documentation
of tenant farmers of, 123–38, 141
Alabama, University of: WE lectures at,
295
Albers, Josef, 257
Allner, Walter, 208, 245, 252
Alpert, Marie-Antoinette, 263, 274
"American Art Today" (New York
World's Fair of 1939), 174
American Committee for the Defense
of Trotsky, 179
American Economic Life (Tugwell), 108
"American Photographs" (Evans):
MoMA mounts exhibit, 157–60, 162–
66, 167; catalogue for, 158–60, 173,
174 (*see also American Photographs*);
opening of, 162–63; Agee on, 163–64;
reviews of, 164–65; national tour of,
166, 171
American Photographs (Evans), 158–60,
173, 174, 182, 183, 185, 198, 233, 235,
264, 268, 281, 283, 288, 302; aesthetics
of, 158–60, 165–66; dedicated to Jane
Smith, 174; new edition of (1962),
247; third edition of (1970), 281, 282,
283–86
American Place, An (gallery), NYC, 38,
196
Anderson, Margaret, 20
Andrews, Penny, 237, 238, 240, 241, 244
Appalachian tenant farmers, 122–38
Arbus, Diane, 248–49, 271, 280, 284
Architectural Forum, 235–36, 245
architectural photography: WE's New
England project with Kirstein, 64–
68, 70–71; WE's Victorian, 64–69, 85,
87; camera requirements for, 67–68;
WE's assignment by Fuller in New
Orleans, 95–99; WE's for preserva-
tion, 209–10, 236, 246–47, 253
Architectural Record, The: publishes
WE, 57
architecture: international style, 62;
WE's enthusiasm for Greek Revival,
64–69, 76–77, 85, 95–99, 230, 253,
290; Kirstein's concern for preservation, 85; southern antebellum, 96–
99; WE's preservation concerns, 209–
10, 236, 246–47, 253; WE's values in,
209–10
Arthurdale, W. Va., 105–8
Art Institute of Chicago, 201–2; WE exhibit at (1964), 252–53
Aswell, Edward, 154, 162, 181–82, 185
Atget, Eugène, 47–48, 69, 159, 219;
influence on WE, 70–71
Ayer, N. W., 76

Baker, Josephine, 25
Balanchine, George, 158
Ballet Caravan, 158
Baltz, Lewis, 280
Barnes, Courtlandt "Courtie," 233, 289
Barnes, Trini, 233, 273, 289
Barr, Alfred, 62–63, 100, 157, 173, 299
Barr, Marga, 63, 151, 157, 176
Barzun, Jacques, 299
Basso, Hamilton, 193
Bataan (film), 192
Batchelder, Prof., 12, 13, 14, 15
Batista, Fulgencio, 82
Baudelaire, Charles, 29–30, 35, 84, 271
Bauhaus, 33, 36
Beach, Sylvia, 25, 26–27
Beals, Carleton, 78–80
beat generation: WE and, 218–21, 222
Beaton, Cecil, 170
Beauvoir, Simone de, 239
Becker, John, 67, 202
Becker Gallery, 63; exhibits WE, 67
Beerbohm, Max, 194
Bell, Daniel, 221–22

Bellamy, Richard, 220
Belle Grove Plantation, La., 97–98
Belle Hélène Plantation, La., 97
Bellow, Saul, 193, 229
Bellows, George, 268
Bergson, Henri, 38
Bickel, Karl, 188–89
Bigelow, Mrs. Albert, 51
blacks: segregation of, 7–8, 10; cultural
    history of, 100
Black Sun Press, 28, 51–52, 278, 283
Blackwood, Lady Caroline, 232, 233,
    240, 296
Blake, William, 237
Blauvelt, Melinda, 287
Bliss, Lillie P., 62
Block, Lou, 77, 78, 102
Blumenthal, Joseph, 173
Boeschenstein, Hermann, 239
Boeschenstein, Isabelle, 238–41, 258–59,
    260, 263–64, 267, 269; WE compares
    with Jane Smith, 241; takes Euro-
    pean teaching post, 264; marital
    problems with WE, 272–75, 277; di-
    vorce from WE, 286–87
Boeschenstein family: WE visits in
    Europe, 258
Bogart, Humphrey, 192
Boghosian, Varujan, 290–91, 292
Bombed Buildings, The, 194
Boston: WE's photography of architec-
    ture in, 65–66
Boston Public Library: murals of, 59, 78
Bourke-White, Margaret, 67, 79, 84,
    120, 193; *Eye on Russia*, 135; com-
    pared with WE, 135–36; coverage of
    the Depression with Caldwell, 135–
    36, 154, 182; at *Fortune*, 198
Bowles, Jane, 228
Bowles, Paul, 228
Brady, Mathew, 61, 112, 159
Brains Trust, 103
Brandt, Bill, 287
Braque, Georges, 37, 71
Brassaï, 271
Breit, Harvey, 184, 186, 223

Breton, André, 180
Brett, Dorothy, 195
Brewer, Jane Beach Evans, 4, 12, 24,
    187, 188, 202; marriage of, 19–20;
    death of, 258
Brewer, Talbot Magruder, 19–20, 24,
    40, 187, 188, 202, 258, 262, 269
Brewer, Talbot, Jr., 292
Bridge, The (Crane), 40–41, 43–44, 49–
    52, 57, 73, 159, 278, 283; WE's photo-
    graph for, 49, 50, 51, 57, 73
Bristol, Horace, 198
Britton, Dudley, 13
Brodsky, Charlee Mae, 292
Brooklyn Bridge, 41
Brooklyn Heights: WE in, 32, 40–45
Brooklyn Museum: WE exhibited at, 76
Brooks, Paul, 184–85
Brooks, Van Wyck, 33
Brown, Slater, 44, 51
Brown Brothers, Harriman, 270
Brown Decades, The (Mumford), 68
Bryson, Bernarda. *See* Shahn, Bernarda
    Bryson
Burroughs family, 125–34, 137, 142, 145,
    163, 181, 182, 183, 199, 248, 277, 295,
    303
Burtin, Will, 206
Busser, Robert, 264

Cady, Edward, 15
Café Sélect, Paris, 27
Cahill, Holger "Eddie," 174, 190
Caldwell, Erskine: assignment with
    Bourke-White on southern poverty,
    135–36, 154, 182
Callahan, Harry, 282
Cambridge Review, 264, 266
cameras: Leica, 34, 35, 87, 105, 219, 235;
    view, 67–68, 105, 111–12, 115, 129, 147;
    Deardorff view, 105, 111; Contax, 170–
    71; Rolleiflex, 261; Polaroid SX-70,
    294–95, 300, 304
Camera Work, 39, 301
Camp Nitgedaiget, N.Y., 91–92
Capa, Robert, 192

Caponigro, Paul, 257
Carlsen, Carl, 74, 83
Carrey, Bobbi, 300–301, 302–3, 306
Carter, John Franklin, 104, 108
Cartier-Bresson, Henri, 153, 155, 287
Cavalon, Giorgio, 245
Cedar Tavern, N.Y.C., 220
Céline, Ferdinand, 161
Century Club, 221, 242, 281
Cézanne, Paul, 62
Chagall, Marc, 180
Chambers, Whittaker, 193
Chaplin, Charlie, 25, 203, 215
Chaplin, Oona, 203, 215
Cheever, John, 102, 228; sexual encounter with WE, 71–72
Chen, Si-Lan, 148, 178
Chicago: WE portfolio on, 200–202, 204–5
Chouinard Art Institute, Los Angeles, 166
Christenberry, William, 248, 289, 295, 308
Chrysler Building, N.Y.C., 34
Churchill, Winston, 195
cinema. *See* movies
Civil War photography, 61, 112, 159
Clarence White School, N.Y., 46
Clark, Eleanor, 179, 228
Clement, Adele, 294, 297, 305, 307
Coburn, Alvin Langdon, 37
Cochran, Gifford, 95–96
Coggeshall, Calvert, 230, 232, 240
Coggeshall, Susanna Perkins, 230, 231, 232
cold war, 218
Coleman, A. D., 285
Collier's, 198
Collins, Frances. *See* Lindley, Frances
Collins, Pete, 176
combat photography, 193
Common Sense, 183
Communists, American, 87–88, 160, 178–79; Camp Nitgedaiget, N.Y., 91–92; and 1950s reaction, 218
Condé Nast, 37, 67

Coney Island (film), 192
Contax camera, 170–71
Cornell, Joseph, 83
Courter, Elodie, 166
Cowley, Malcolm, 25, 44, 51
Crane, Arnold: purchases WE prints, 271–72, 282, 304
Crane, Charles S., 2–4, 20
Crane, Clarence, 41
Crane, Grace, 41, 42
Crane, Harriet Thorp, 3
Crane, Hart, 40–45, 61, 63, 72, 73–74, 75, 83, 159, 226, 278, 288; friendship with WE, 41, 42–45; travels to Europe, 44–45; and publication of *The Bridge*, 49–52; returns to New York, 49–52; death of, 75
Crane, Jessie Beach, 3
Crane, Ralph, 202
Crane, Robert, 202, 204
Crane, Salmon, 2–3
Crane, Stephen, 159
Creative Art: publishes WE, 57
Crime of Cuba, The (Beals and Evans), 78–83, 156
Criterion, 20, 58
Crosby, Caresse, 28, 49, 50, 51
Crosby, Harry, 28, 49, 50, 51
Cuba: WE in, 78–83, 120, 288; WE revisits with Agee, 150
Cummings, E, E., 44, 51
Cunningham, Imogen, 76
Curry, John Stuart, 92

daguerreotypes, 268
Dali, Salvador, 173
Darrow, Whitney, 194
Dartmouth College: WE teaching at, 290–91
Daumier, Honoré, 87
Davenport, Russell, 144
da Vinci, Leonardo, 195
Deardorff view camera, 105, 111
Death in the Afternoon (Hemingway), 81
Death in the Family, A (Agee), 242
Degas, Edgar, 195

de Kooning, Willem, 220
deLoache, Ben, 296
DeLuze family, 56–57
Dennis, Saul, 193
Depression, 53–54, 75, 86; WE on, 2; WE's candid photography with Shahn of poor in NYC, 87; photographic projects to document effects of, 89–90, 103–17; WPA programs, 102–3; *Fortune* series on, 119; films about, 142–45, 147; and the rise of photojournalism, 198; MoMA mounts photographic retrospective on, 247; WE lectures at Harvard on, 277–78
Desert Victory (film), 192
Detroit: WE portfolio on, 200–202
Deux Magots café, Paris, 29, 239
Dewey, Thomas, 207
Dial, The, 20, 58
Dickens, Charles, 284
Dietz, Lorna, 44
Dinesen, Isak, 277
Disney, Walt, 172
Doherty and Company, Henry R., 40, 44
Donovan, Hedley, 208, 237
Dornbush, Adrian, 104
Dos Passos, John, 159
Dow, Jim, 281
Draper, Muriel, 60–61, 71
Draper, Paul, 60
Duchamp, Marcel, 180
Dupee, Fred, 178, 228
Dürer, Albrecht, 195
Dust Bowl: RA film project on, 142–44

Eakins Press, 261, 264, 266–67
Eastman, Max, 81
Edwards, Hugh, 252, 253
Eggleston, William, 280
Eisenman, Alvin, 256, 257, 262, 274
Eisenstein, Sergei, 88, 160
Eisner, Dorothy, 279
Elisofon, Eliot, 193
Eliot, T. S., 20, 21, 41, 58, 73, 210

Emmet, Grenville, 244
Emmet, Lily, 230
Emmet, Rowland, 194
End of Ideology, The (Bell), 222
Epstein, Barbara, 229
Epstein, Jason, 229
Ernst, Max, 180
Eisner, Dorothy, 179
Evans, Augustus Heaslip, 2
Evans, Emanda Brooks, 2
Evans, Ernestine, 78, 81, 89, 90, 102, 104, 110, 115, 116, 117, 139, 200; seeks government work for WE, 102
Evans, Isabelle. *See* Boeschenstein, Isabelle
Evans, Jane Beach. *See* Brewer, Jane Beach Evans
Evans, Jane Smith. *See* Smith, Jane
Evans, Jessie Crane, 202, 204; marriage of, 2, 3, 4; social ambitions of, 9; husband leaves, 11, 12; moves to NYC, 12, 14; demands on WE, 24, 30–31, 41; death of, 238
Evans, Mabel, 2
Evans, Mary Anne Lawrence, 2
Evans, Walker (*see also* AESTHETICS AND SUBJECTS; EXHIBITIONS AND PUBLICATIONS; PHOTOGRAPHIC ASSIGNMENTS; WRITING AND EDITING ASSIGNMENTS): adult appearance and demeanor of, 1–2; birth of, 2, 4; family background of, 3–4; childhood of, 4–22; in St. Louis, 4–7; in Kenilworth, Ill., 7–10; reading tastes of, 9, 20–21, 29, 89, 231, 263, 273, 277, 300; childhood appearance of, 9–10; in Toledo, Ohio, 10–12; father leaves family, 11; loss of virginity, 11; first camera of, 11–12; education of, 12–19; at Loomis Institute, 12–15; at Mercersburg Academy, 15–16; at Phillips Academy, 16–19; adolescent appearance of, 17; joins secret society, 17–18; lack of contact with girls, 18; at Williams College, 19–22, 23; discovery of avant-garde in the arts, 21;

Evans, Walker *(con't)*
works in New York Public Library,
23–24; writing ambitions of, 24; in
Paris, 24–31; French influence on, 28–
30; early photographic interests, 31,
33–36, 55; travels to Mediterranean,
31; moves to New York City, 31–51;
friendship with artists, 33; and controversy of pictorialist vs. modernist
photography, 35–39; concern for career, 40, 54; friendship with Hart
Crane, 41, 42–45; experiment with
horticulture, 46; photographic
friendships and influences, 46–48;
friendship with Ben Shahn, 48–49,
54–57 (*see also* Shahn); and illustration for *The Bridge*, 49–52, 57, 73; at
Shahn's Cape Cod home, 54–55;
Shahn portrait of, 55, 237, 278; at
Draper's salon, 60–61; on New England architecture tour, 64–69; sexual
encounter with John Cheever, 71–72;
sailing tour on *Cressida*, 73–75; concern over fame vs. privacy, 84; pen-
ury during Depression, 86–87; candid photography with Shahn of
poor in NYC, 87; and Communists,
87–88, 178; interest in cinema, 88–89,
90, 142–44, 147, 192–93; meets Agee,
93; friendship with Agee, 93–95 (*see
also* Agee); relations with Jane Smith
Ninas, 96–99, 100–101, 104–7, 113, 114–
15, 174–79; brief affairs, 101; work for
RA, 103–17 (*see also* Resettlement Administration); travels to rural Alabama with Agee on assignment, 119–
38; RA work owned by U.S.
government, 121, 147–48, 153–54, 301;
editing photographs from Alabama,
141–42; and prospect of film project,
142–44, 147; covers Mississippi
floods, 145–47; dismissed from RA,
147; home at 92nd St., 148, 177–78; affair with Frances Collins, 151, 175–76;
affair with Via Agee, 151; applies for
Guggenheim fellowship, 152, 156, 167,
183, 200; interest in younger women,
155–56, 237, 274, 303; relations with
Helen Levitt, 155–56; reviewing work
at age thirty-four, 156; status from
first MoMA one-man photography
exhibit, 167; Agee offers *Three Tenant Families* to, 168–69; Agee's romantic feelings for, 168–70; relations
with Alma Agee, 169–70; begins subway portraits project, 170–71, 184; dis-
pleasure with "Seven Americans" exhibit, 172–73; conjugal existence with
Jane Ninas, 176–80; as collector of
castoffs, 177–78, 288–90; and *Partisan
Review*, 178–79; and the Trillings,
178–79; association with N.Y. literary
and artistic crowds, 178–80; awarded
Guggenheim (1940), 183–84; and
WWII, 187, 190, 193; marries Jane
Smith (Ninas), 187–88; honeymoon
assignment in Florida, 188–90; with
Time, 190–96, 197, 198; socializes
with *Time* writers, 193–94; with *Fortune*, 197–200, 204–9 (*see also Fortune*); and the rise of photojournalism, 198; sexual prejudices of, 201;
travels to California as photography
tutor, 202–4; promotion to photographic editor at *Fortune*, 204–9; co-
worker response to at *Fortune*, 208–
9; nostalgia for prewar America,
209–11; financial concerns, 211–12,
268–69; indulgence in luxuries, 211–
12, 216–17, 268–69; and Jane's Connecticut retreat, 212; moves to tene-
ment on York Ave., 212; changing
relations with Jane, 213–16; failure to
produce new work, 216; resentment
of women, 216; social climbing by,
216, 221, 222, 253; and MoMA's
"What Is Modern Photography?"
symposium, 218–19; and beat generation, 218–21, 222; relations with
younger photographers, 218–21, 274,
276–77, 287, 297, 300–302; joins Century Club, 221; looses touch with

der friends, 222; breakup with Jane, 223, 224–25; and death of Agee, 223–24; and death of friends, 226–27, 249–50, 251, 278–79; bachelor social life, 228–30; drinking by, 230–31, 250, 254, 259, 269, 274, 304, 305; erotica collection of, 231, 297, 308; relations with women, 231–32; fantasies of, 232–33; as mentor of photographers, 233; concern for his status, 233; dislike for work at *Fortune*, 233, 234; mentorship of Robert Frank, 234–35; ulcer surgery and convalescence, 237–38, 240, 245; relations with Isabelle Boeschenstein, 238–41; compares Isabelle with Jane, 241; revival of reputation, 241–43; marriage to Isabelle, 243–45; move to 94th St., 245; influence on new generation, 248–49; perceptive eye as houseguest, 253; solicits gifts from friends, 253; influence on 1960s generation, 254–55, 275–76, 280; teaching at Yale, 256–57, 262–63, 269, 276, 287; death of sister, 258; visits Isabelle's family in Europe, 258–59; disinterest in offspring, 259; White House honors, 259–60; quits *Fortune*, 260; undergoes alcoholism treatment, 260–62; moves to Old Lyme, Conn., 263–64; publishes subway portraits, 264–66; acclaim from new publications, 268–69; money borrowing by, 269, 286; income from picture sales, 269–70, 271–72, 287; Williams awards doctorate to, 271; marital problems with Isabelle, 272–75, 277; interior decorating tastes, 273; lectures at Harvard, 277–78; sells mementos from friends, 278–79; retrieving negatives from RA, 281; divorce from Isabelle, 286–87; fetish for organization, 288; stealing of road signs, 289–91; artist-in-residence at Dartmouth, 290–91; repeat ulcer surgery and recovery, 291–93; writes will, 292; uses Polar-

oid SX-70 cameras, 294–95, 300, 304; revisits Alabama for lecture, 295–96; grows beard, 296; visits friends in Europe, 296–97; teaches graduate seminars at Yale, 297, 299; receives Award for Distinguished Service to Arts, 299–300; organizing his archives, 300–303; financial concerns of, 301; sells his estate's photographs, 302, 303–4, 305; declining health of, 304–5; sells his negatives, 305; final lecture at Harvard, 306; death of, 307; cremation and disposal of remains, 307–8; bequeath of his cameras, 308

AESTHETICS AND SUBJECTS (*see also specific assignments and publications*): aims, 1–2, 56, 61, 67–68; society's castoffs, 43, 83; impersonality, 56, 111, 206; appeal of decay, 66; interiors, 71, 252–53, 261; posters and movie bills, 72–73, 117; Tahitians, 75; decorative lettering, 81, 288; antique postcards, 83, 177, 206, 245, 255–56, 292, 294; anonymous art, 83–84; distaste for the modern, 84, 209–10; and documenting spirit of the Depression, 89–90; southern antebellum architecture, 97–99; West Virginia rural poverty, 106–7, 109; documentary approach, 111; telescopic photography, 111–12; billboards, 113, 115–16; Alabama rural poverty, 130–35; portraits of tenant farmers, 133–34; compared with Bourke-White, 135–36; editing of Alabama sharecropper pictures, 141–42; in *American Photographs*, 158–60, 165–66; Kirstein on, 159–60; *Let Us Now Praise Famous Men*, 161–62, 181; subway portraits, 170–71, 184, 264, 265–66; at home, 177; concern for authenticity of images, 182; quest for objectivity, 184, 206; cover for *Let Us Now. . .*, 185; taste as film critic, 192–93; wartime architectural ruin, 194;

Evans, Walker *(con't)*
  taste as art critic, 194–95; and the rise
  of photojournalism, 198; street portraiture in Chicago, 201; as photographic
  editor of Fortune, 205–6, 208; portfolio ideas for *Fortune*, 208; typography, 208; architectural preservation, 209–10, 236, 246–47, 253;
  railroad stations and yards, 210–11,
  236; influence on younger photographers, 218–21, 280, 287, 300; *Fortune*
  portfolios reflect his sadness, 226–27;
  against sentimentality and nostalgia,
  227; erotica, 231, 297, 308; aging surfaces, 236–37; as prose stylist, 242,
  246; second edition of *Let Us
  Now . . .*, 243; influence on 1960s
  generation, 254–55, 280; and American throwaway culture, 255; color
  photography, 262, 295; difficulties
  with printing from negatives of, 282–
  83; quality of earlier work, 283; on
  emotive response to pictures, 285;
  art of assemblage, 288–90; interest
  in the gruesome, 296, 298–99

  EXHIBITIONS AND PUBLICATIONS
  (see also major titles): first, 57; in
  Creative Art, 57; in *The Architectural
  Record*, 57; in *Hound and Horn*, 58;
  first gallery, at John Becker Gallery,
  67; at Julien Levy Gallery, 75–76; at
  Albright Gallery, Buffalo, 76; at
  Brooklyn Museum, 76; *The Crime of
  Cuba*, 78–83, 156; first at MoMA
  (1933), 85, 87; *Let Us Now Praise Famous Men*, 155, 181; MoMA acquires
  works for collection, 156–57;
  MoMA's "American Photographs,"
  157–60, 162–66, 167; *American Photographs* catalogue, 158–60; "Seven
  Americans" at MoMA, 172; *Faces of
  Men*, 184, 200, 266; *The Mangrove
  Coast*, 189–90; "Chicago," 200–202,
  204–5; *Fortune* portfolios, 200–202,
  204–5, 226–27; "Before They Disappear," 226–27, 236; "Downtown,"
226–27; "The Last of Railroad
  Steam," 236; "The London Look,"
  236; *On the Waterfront*, 240; reprint
  of *Let Us Now . . .*, 242–43; "Come
  On Down," 245; "Primitive
  Churches," 245–46; using old material for portfolios, 245–46; in *Mademoiselle*, 246; *American Photographs*
  reprinted, 247; at Art Institute of
  Chicago, 252–53; *Message from the Interior*, 261, 267–68; *Many Are Called*,
  264, 265–66, 267; in *Cambridge Review*, 264; in *Harper's Bazaar*, 264;
  in *Partners in Banking*, 270; in *The
  Gateway States*, 270; MoMA 1970 retrospective, 281, 282, 283–86; third edition of *American Photographs*, 281–
  86; retrospective at Yale Art Gallery,
  287; *Walker Evans . . .* (FSA), 301

  PHOTOGRAPHIC ASSIGNMENTS:
  for MoMA and the Metropolitan,
  63–64; Kirstein obtains, 63–68; New
  England Victorian architecture project, 64–68; on South Seas cruise, 73–
  75; Fuller obtains for, 76–77; Rockefeller Center frescoes, 77–78; in
  Cuba, 78–83, 120; for *Fortune* on
  Communists, 91–92; for Fuller in
  New Orleans, 95–99; MoMA African
  sculpture collection, 99–100, 102, 113;
  from Resettlement Administration,
  103–17, 121; in West Virginia coal
  country, 105–8, 109; permanent position with RA, 110–17; with Agee on
  southern tenant farmers, 119–38, 141–
  42; on Mississippi floods, 145–47; for
  Fortune on Caribbean cruise, 149–50;
  subway photographs, 170–71, 184,
  264, 265–66; on honeymoon in Florida, 188–90; at *Fortune*, 197–200, 204–
  9, 245; as photographic editor at *Fortune*, 204–9; antique postcard
  portfolio for *Fortune*, 206–7; New
  England hotels, 209–10; for *Sports Illustrated*, 227–28; for *Architectural Forum*, 236–37, 245; tours New Eng-

land mill towns, 237; for Container Corporation, 252; for "Library of America," 270

WRITING AND EDITING ASSIGNMENTS: reviews for *Hound and Horn*, 69–70; reviews for *Time*, 190–96, 242; reviews photography exhibits for *Time*, 193; as art critic, 194–95; edits "Homes of Americans" for *Fortune*, 199; as editor at *Fortune*, 204–9, 242; promoting photographers at *Fortune*, 207; memoir of Agee for *Let Us Now . . .* reprint, 242; preservationist article for *Life*, 246; for *Quality*, 270–71

Evans, Walker, Jr. (father), 2; marriage of, 2, 3, 4; training of, 3; career of, 5–7; leaves family, 11, 14; finances WE's trip to Paris, 24; horticultural enterprise of, 46; death of, 84–85

Evans, Walker (grandfather), 2

Fairchild, Christine, 98–99, 101, 113, 166
Falke, Grace, 104
farmers: problems during Depression, 103–4; WE and Agee project on tenant, 119–38; film projects on, 142–45

Farm Security Administration (FSA), 153 (*see also* Resettlement Administration); publishes *Land of the Free*, 156; MoMA mounts photographic retrospective from archives of, 246; and Library of Congress's *Walker Evans*, 301

Faulkner, William, 284
Faurer, Louis, 219
Fauves, 62
Fernandes Castro, José, 80
Fields family, 125–28, 134, 142, 145, 181, 182, 248
Film and Photo League, N.Y., 87–88
films. *See* movies
Fitzgerald, Robert, 120, 144
Five Graves to Cairo (film), 192
Flaubert, Gustave, 29, 30

Florida: WE's honeymoon assignment in, 188–90
Flye, Father James, 122, 144, 223
Fogg Art Museum, Cambridge, 277–78
Fonda, Henry, 192
Forbes, Charles Henry, 16
Forbes, Ruth, 65
Ford, Edsel, 172
Forst, Miles, 220
Fortune, 68, 73; WE illustrates article on American Communists, 91–92; Agee's work for, 92, 118; Agee-Evans assignment on tenant farmers, 119, 121, 141, 153, 154; staffing changes at, 144; WE and Agee assignment on Caribbean cruise, 149–50; quality of, 197–98; WE joins as staff photographer, 197–200; freelance photographers for, 198; assignments for, 199; WE promoted to photographic editor, 204–9; WE's antique postcard portfolio for, 206–7; WE promotes photographers at, 207; WE's unprinted portfolio ideas for, 208; WE indulged by, 211; writers for, 221–22; WE's portfolios reflect his sadness, 226–27; WE's dislike for work at, 233, 234; WE's architectural preservation portfolios, 236–37; WE's diminishing service to, 246, 251–52, 257; WE quits, 260; WE's color photography at, 262
Frank, Mary, 220–21, 229, 231
Frank, Pablo, 231
Frank, Robert, 219–21, 226, 234–35, 237, 253, 271, 284, 296
Freud, Lucian, 232
Freud, Sigmund, 161
Friedlander, Lee, 280, 291, 308
Fritsch, Mia, 187, 215, 222, 223
Fuller, Anne, 230, 231
Fuller, Charles, 76–77, 110, 168, 187–88, 217, 230, 238; gives WE assignment in the South, 95–96
Fuller, Henry B., 200

Galbraith, John Kenneth, 221
Galdson, Iago, 35, 54
Gauguin, Paul, 62
Gee, Helen, 268
Gibson, Charles Dana, 195
Gide, André, 27
Gill, Brendan, 221, 268
Ginsberg, Allen, 220
Gish, Lillian, 173
Goncourt brothers, 161
Goodwin, Walter, 79
Goodyear, A. Conger, 171–72
Gowin, Emmet, 280, 282
Grable, Betty, 193
Greek Revival architecture: WE's enthu-
  siasm for, 64–69, 76–77, 85, 95–99,
  230, 253, 290
Greenwich Village, NYC, 33
Grotz, Paul, 33–34, 35, 40, 42, 45–46,
  48, 74, 101, 235, 245
Grunberg, Solomon, 44
Gschwind, Max, 211
Guggenheim fellowships, 220, 242, 265,
  266; awarded to Hart Crane, 73; Agee
  applies for, 152; WE applies for, 152,
  156, 167, 183, 200; WE awarded (1940),
  183–84; photography fellowships, 234
Gurdjieff, George, 60
Guys, Constantin, 35

Hadden, Briton, 190
Hale, Nicki, 259, 274
Hale, Robert Beverly, 221, 259, 274
Hamsun, Knut, 277
Harcourt, Brace and Company, 154
Hardwick, Elizabeth, 179
Harmon, Mr., 124
Harper & Brothers, 154–55, 162, 183
Harper's Bazaar, 157, 165
Harriman, George, 195
Harrison, Rex, 239
Harvard Society for Contemporary
  Art, 59, 63, 76
Harvard University: WE lectures at,
  277–78, 306
Harvey, Dorothy, 179–80

Harvey, Harry, 179–80
Heckscher Building, NYC, 62
Heliker, Jack, 240
Hellmann, Geoffrey, 91, 92
Hemingway, Ernest, 25, 159, 240; WE
  meets, 80–81
Hersey, John, 193, 228
Hibbon, Tom, 116, 127
Hill, John, 257, 287, 292, 297, 302, 307, 308
Hine, Lewis, 109
Hirsch, Stefan, 38
Hitchcock, Henry Russell, 65, 190
Hitler, Adolf, 173–74
Hobson, Peggy, 150–51, 179
Hobson, Verna Harrison, 214, 224, 240
Hobson, Wilder, 144, 150–51, 179, 190,
  199, 215, 240, 249–50, 251
Hodgins, Eric, 119, 144
Hollywood: WE's response to, 202–4
Homolka, Florence, 202, 203
Homolka, Oscar, 202
homosexuality: WE and, 71–72, 168–69,
  231; Agee and, 168–69
Hopkins, Harry, 102–3
Hopper, Edward, 57, 85, 268
Houghton Mifflin: publishes *Let Us
  Now Praise Famous Men*, 184–86; re-
  prints *Let Us Now . . .*, 242; publish-
  es *Many Are Called*, 264
Hound and Horn, 58, 59, 61, 63, 64, 68;
  WE reviews for, 69–70
Hower, Henry, 11
Hower, Louise, 11, 14
Hubbard, Virginia, 276–77, 289, 291,
  292, 297, 298, 305, 306, 307, 308
Hubbell, Lindley, 24
Hurwitz, Leo, 142
Huston, John, 223

Ingersoll, Ralph, 92, 144
Israel, Marvin, 229, 248, 264
Itten, Johannes, 238
Ives, Norman, 257, 287, 292, 297

Jacobs, Fenno, 198
Jacoby, Beatrice, 101

Jacoby, Irving, 88, 101
James, Henry, 60, 177, 242, 273
Javitz, Romana, 83
Jefferson, Thomas, 25
Jennings, Oliver, 74, 75
Jessup, Eunice Clark, 179, 184, 228
Jessup, Jack, 179, 186, 228
Jewell, Edward Alden, 164
Jews: and American Communist movement, 91–92
Johnson, James Weldon, 100
Johnson, Lyndon B., 259
Johnson, Philip, 63, 85
Jones, J. Jefferson, 79, 81
Joyce, James, 21, 26–27, 28, 47, 195, 242

Kahlo, Frida, 78
Kandinsky, Wassily, 38
Kasebier, Gertrude, 37
Katz, Leslie, 261, 267, 269, 289, 291, 297
Kazin, Alfred, 179, 210
Kelly, Martin V., 10
Kenyon Review, 187
Kerouac, Jack, 220
Kerr, Barbara, 244, 245–46
Kertész, André, 76
Kirstein, Lincoln, 58–69, 72, 74, 76, 83, 97, 161, 173, 199, 235, 264, 283, 299; publishes WE, 58; encouragement of WE, 58–59, 61, 68, 72–73; meeting with WE, 58–59; artistic interests of, 59; background of, 59; and the MoMA, 63; obtains WE assignments, 63–68; New England architectural photography project for WE, 64–69, 70–71, 85; *Flesh Is Heir*, 65; WE photographs, 72; and Rockefeller Center frescoes controversy, 78; on WE's interests, 83, 84; concern for architectural preservation, 85; essay on WE in MoMA *Bulletin*, 85; exhibits WE at MoMA, 85; and WE's *American Photographs* catalogue, 158–60, 162, 165; and WE-Agee collaboration, 159
Kline, Franz, 220

Knollenberg, Mary, 287, 293–94, 297, 302, 307
Kouwenhoven, John, 270
Kramer, Hilton, 285, 294, 307
Kraut, Mona, 174
Kronenberger, Louis, 193, 270–71, 276

Lanahan, Edward Patrick, 208–9, 252
Land of the Free (FSA), 156
Landshoff, Herman, 238
Lang, Fritz, 145
Lange, Dorothea, 111, 139–40, 165, 285; photography of migrant workers, 111, 140
Lang Syne Plantation, S.C., 90
Lasker, Albert, 6
Lawrence, D. H., 21
Lear, Edward, 194
Lee, Russell, 110, 165
leftist politics, 178–79. *See also* Communists, American
Lehmbruck, Wilhelm, 63
Leica, 34, 35, 87, 105, 219, 235
Leighton, George, 229
Lenin, V. I., 77
Leslie, Alfred, 220
Lesy, Liz, 298
Lesy, Michael, 297–99, 306–7
Let Us Now Praise Famous Men (Agee and Evans), 155, 180–87, 214, 276, 283, 288; drafts of, 144–45, 151–52, 161, 162, 163, 168, 180; contract with Harpers for, 155, 180, 183; WE's selections for, 161–62; Agee offers WE manuscript of, 168–69; title for, 180; expanded themes of, 180–81; contract with Houghton for, 184–86; cover for, 185, 243; reviews of, 186–87; remaindered, 187; new generation discovers, 241–42; reprint with memoir and new pictures, 242–43, 248; WE retrieves first editions for sale, 278–79, 304
Levitt, Helen, 155–56, 160–61, 177, 184, 224; assists WE, 160–61; and WE's subway portraits, 170–71

Levy, Julien, 47, 63, 284; gallery of, 63, 155

Lewis, Wilfred S., 110

Leyda, Jay, 87, 88, 89, 143, 145, 147, 148, 178

Liberté (ship), 237

Library of Congress: holding WE negatives, 281; *Walker Evans: Photographs for the Farm Security Administration*, 301

Lichtenstein, Roy, 255, 268

Life, 152–53, 167, 198, 205, 215; first issue of, 140; and WE's MoMA 1938 exhibit, 157; sensationalism of, 198; WE's preservationist article for, 246; reviews WE MoMA retrospective, 286

Limelight gallery, 268

Lindley, Frances Strunsky, 151, 158, 161, 173, 175–76, 247, 291, 294, 297

Lindner, Richard, 245

Linscott, Robert, 185, 186

Lionni, Leo, 206, 211, 216, 245

Lippincott, J. B.: and WE's Cuban project, 79, 82

Lissitzky, Ed, 36

Little Review, The, 20, 58

Lloyd, Valerie, 303, 306

Lloyd-Smith, Parker, 68

Locke, Edwin, 145–47, 178

Lockspeiser, Mary. *See* Frank, Mary

Look, 167, 198

Lorenz, Pare, 142, 147, 165

Louisiana: WE's assignment by Fuller in, 95–99

Louisiana Purchase Exposition, St. Louis (1904), 4–5

Loveman, Sam, 44

Lowell, Robert, 296

Luce, Henry, 91, 93, 94, 144, 190, 191, 196, 197, 198, 204, 209, 234, 235, 236, 238

Lynd, Robert and Helen, 110

Lynes, George Platt, 76

Mabry, Eliza, 229, 261, 292

Mabry, Ethel, 229

Mabry, Thomas Dabny, 28, 67, 99, 156, 157, 158, 165, 173, 190, 229, 253, 264, 278, 295

MacDonald, David, 192

Macdonald, Dwight, 27, 93, 178; article on Communists for *Fortune*, 91–92; resigns from *Fortune*, 144

Machado, Gerardo, 78–79, 82

MacLeish, Archibald, 68, 81, 153, 156

Madame Bovary (Flaubert), 30, 300

Mademoiselle, 246

Maillol, Aristide, 63

Mailman, Alma. *See* Agee, Alma

Malraux, André, 219

Mangrove Coast, The (Bickel and Evans), 188–89

Many Are Called (Evans), 264, 265–66, 267

Marshall, Margaret, 261

Matisse, Henri, 48, 267

Matta, 180

Matter, Herbert, 256

Matthews, Pamela, 296

Matthews, Tom S., 191, 228, 251, 296

Mayer, A. Hyatt, 221

Mayer, Grace, 247

McCarten, Seville, 208

McCarthy, Mary, 179

McCullin, Donald, 296

McDonald, Dorothy, 214, 228

McDonald, John, 179, 199–200, 214, 221, 224, 228, 234, 260

McQuade, Walter, 251, 286

Metropolitan Museum, NYC: WE photographs for, 63; and WWII, 194

Mexico: revolutionary art of, 77, 78

Meyerowitz, Joel, 280

Middletown (Lynd), 110

Millay, Edna St. Vincent, 47

Miller, Dorothy, 100, 151, 174, 284

Miller, Lee, 76

Mill's Hill, Ala.: Agee and WE document families of, 125–38

miners: problems during Depression, 105

Mississippi: WE documents floods, 145–47

Mister Big (film), 193
modernism, 36, 37–38; at MoMA, 62
modernist photography, 34–35, 37, 57–58, 198; WE on, 70
Moe, Henry Allen, 221, 229, 234, 299
Moholy-Nagy, Laszlo, 36
MoMA. *See* Museum of Modern Art
Morris, Alice, 168, 184, 214, 215, 223, 224, 266, 272, 286
Moskowitz, Robert, 255, 270
Motherwell, Robert, 245
Mount Pleasant, Penn.: WE photographs, 107–8
movies: posters as WE subject, 72–73, 117; WE's interest in, 88–89, 90, 142–44, 147, 192–93; Tugwell project on Dust Bowl, 142–43; on tenant farmers, 142–45; on the Depression, 142–45, 147; Shahn and WE project for RA, 143; Agee's enthusiasm for, 180, 192; about WWII, 192
Mumford, Lewis, 68
Munch, Edvard, 195
Munson, Gorham, 45
Murnau, F. W., 75
Museum of Modern Art, NYC: opening of, 61–63; "American Sources of Modern Art" exhibit, 77; WE's photographs exhibits at, 77; "Murals by American Painters and Photographers" exhibit, 78; WE's first exhibit at (1933), 85, 87; WE photographs African sculpture collection, 99–100, 102, 113; acquires WE photographs for collection, 156–57; "Photography: 1839–1937" exhibit, 157; establishes photography department, 157; new building at 53rd St., 157, 171, 172; WE's "American Photographs" exhibit (1938), 157–60, 162–66, 167; Nelson Rockefeller assumes presidency, 172; "Art in Our Time" tenth anniversary exhibit, 172–73; "Seven Americans" exhibit, 172–73; WE's friendship with staff of, 190; wartime exhibits, 217; Steichen heads photography department, 217–18; "What Is Modern Photography?" symposium, 217–19; "The Bitter Years" exhibit, 247; exhibits WE's subway photographs, 264, 265–66; "Five Unrelated Photographers" exhibit, 265; "New Documents" exhibit, 280–81; WE retrospective (1970), 281, 282, 283–86
Mydans, Carl, 111, 140

Nabokov, Vladimir, 240, 273
Nadar, 271
Namuth, Hans, 238
Nation, The, 178, 191
National Gallery: and WWII, 194
National Institute of Arts and Letters: honors WE, 299–300
Naushon Island, Mass., 65
New Deal, 86–87, 110, 122. *See also* Resettlement Administration
New England: WE's architectural photography project with Kirstein, 64–69, 70–71, 85, 87; WE photographs old hotels, 209–10; WE tours rural Connecticut, 229–30; WE tours mill towns, 237
Newhall, Beaumont, 162, 166, 217, 268; and MoMA "Seven Americans" exhibit, 172
Newhall, Nancy, 217; purchases pictures from WE, 269–70
New Masses: reviews WE, 164
New Mexico: WE photographs, 202
New Orleans: WE's assignment by Fuller in, 95–99; WE revisits, 113–14
New Republic, The, 81; reviews WE, 164; reviews *Let Us Now . . .*, 186
New York: WE's architectural photography project with Kirstein, 64–68; WE's architectural photography project for Fuller, 77; 1950s school of photography, 218–20; WE photographs Hudson River towns for "Library of America," 270
New York City: WE moves to, 31–51; as

New York City *(con't)*
cultural center, 32–33; architecture
in, 33, 34; WE's subway portraits,
170–71, 184, 264–66; 1950s art scene
in, 220–21; WE's *Fortune* portfolios
on, 226–27; WE photographs water-
front, 240
New Yorker, The: reviews WE, 268
New York *Herald Tribune*, 157; reviews
WE, 164
New York Public Library, 23–24, 288;
WE visits picture collection, 83
New York Review of Books, The, 229
New York Times, 157; reviews *Let Us
Now . . .*, 186; reviews WE MoMA
retrospective, 285–86; obituary for
WE, 307
New York World's Fair (1939), 173–74;
"American Art Today" exhibit, 174
Ninas, Jane Smith. *See* Smith, Jane
Ninas, Paul, 96, 98–99, 101, 113, 114, 166,
174

Oak Bluffs, Mass.: WE photographs, 70
Obermeyer, Herr, 297
Odets, Clifford, 203
Office of War Information, 190
O'Keeffe, Georgia, 37, 38–39, 166; WE
reviews, 196
Opferr, Emil, 73–74
Opferr, Ivan, 73–74
Orage, A. R., 60
Organization Man, The (Whyte), 221
Oriente (ship), 149–50
Orwell, George, 228
Orwell, Sonia, 228
Osato, Sono, 203
Outerbridge, Paul, 76
Ox-Bow Incident, The (film), 192

Paine, Lyman, 63, 65
Paine, Ralph Delahaye, 153, 204, 206,
211, 233, 245
Panofsky, Erwin, 195
Paris: WE in, 24–31; expatriates in, 25,
28; photographers in, 28; "staring"

as pastime in, 28–29; Atget's images
of, 47–48; School of, 62
Parker, Dorothy, 25
Parkinson, Eliza, 229, 233, 299
Parsons, Betty, 230
Partisan Review, 178–79
Penn, Irving, 218
Pennsylvania Railroad Station, NYC,
246
Percy, Walker, 263
Perelman, S. J., 221
Perkins, Frances, 231
Peterkin, Julia, 90, 263
Peterson, Gustav, 245
Peterson, Vita, 245
Pfeiffer, Pauline, 81
Phelps, Fanny, 9
Phillips, William, 178
Photo-eye, 70
Photographer's Eye, The (Szarkowski),
265
photography: architectural (*see* archi-
tectural photography); modernist,
34–35, 37, 57–58, 70, 198; reputation
of, 35–36; commercial application of,
36; pictorialist, 36, 37, 70; advances
and experiments in, 36–37; WE's career choice, 40, 54; early influences
and friendships of WE, 46–48; WE's
aim at social commentary, 56; Civil
War, 61, 112, 159; MoMA's elevation
of, 62–63; as medium to document
the Depression, 89–90; Resettlement
Administration projects, 103–17, 121;
WE's telescopic, 111–12; comparison
of approaches to Depression subjects, 135–37; MoMA establishes department of, 157; WE's status from
first MoMA one-man exhibit, 167;
combat, 193; rise of photojournalism, 198; MoMA's "What Is Modern
Photography?" symposium, 217–19;
beat generation and, 218–19; WE's
influence on, 218–21, 248–49, 254–55,
274, 276–77, 280, 287, 297, 300–302;
"zone system," 257; color, 262, 295;

growing market for, 267, 287; printing WE's negatives, 282–83
photojournalism: rise of, 198
photo-secessionists, 39
Picasso, Pablo, 37, 48, 173
pictorialist photography, 36, 37; WE on, 70
Pierce, C. A., 154
Plow That Broke the Plains, The (film), 142–43
Polaroid SX-70 cameras, 294–95, 300, 304
Pollock, Jackson, 238
pop art, 255
Popular Photography, 157
Porter, Fairfield, 268
Porter, Katherine Anne, 284
postcards: WE's enthusiasm for antique, 83, 177, 206, 245, 255–56, 292, 294; WE's *Fortune* portfolio, 206–7
Potamkin, Harry, 160
Pound, Ezra, 25, 58
Pratt, Davis, 277, 300
Proust, Marcel, 32, 159, 231, 273
Pulitzer Prize: awarded to Agee, 242
Pullman, Chris, 263, 269
Purvis, Alston, 262–63, 296, 297, 302
Puvis de Chavannes, Pierre, 59, 78

Quality, 270–71, 276
Queen Mary (ship), 237

RA. *See* Resettlement Administration
Rahv, Philip, 178, 187
railroad stations and yards: WE photographs, 210–11, 236
Ray, Man, 28, 47, 172, 271
Reed, Joseph Verner, 17, 18, 89
Renoir, Jean, 203
Resettlement Administration (RA) (*see also* Farm Security Administration): WE's work for, 103–17, 121, 122, 140, 141–42, 145–47; property rights to Evans work, 121, 147–48, 153–54, 301; WE's furlough to work with Agee, 121, 124; bureaucracy of, 139; histori-

cal section of, 139–40; scandal over fraudulent documentation, 140; cutbacks at, 147; WE dismissed by, 147; acquiring WE archives for publication from, 281; quality of WE's work for, 283
Richardson, H. H., 62
Riis, Jacob, 109
Rinhart, George: purchases WE's estate, 301–2, 303–4, 305
Ritasse, William, 198
River, The (film), 147
Rivera, Diego, 77, 78, 83, 102
Roach, Hal, 203
Robison, Harvey, 15
Rockefeller, Abby (Mrs. John D., Jr.), 62, 172
Rockefeller, Nelson, 62–63, 176; and frescoes project at Center, 77; and MoMA's tenth anniversary, 172, 173; assumes presidency of MoMA, 172
Rockefeller Center, N.Y., 83; WE photographs frescoes at, 77–78; MoMA exhibit of "American Photographs" at, 162–63
Rodchenko, Alexander, 36
Rodemeyer, Charles, 281
Rodin, Auguste, 37
Rodman, Nancy, 91
Rodman, Selden, 183
Rogers, Dorothy, 32, 45, 46
Roh, Franz, 70
Rolleiflex camera, 261
Romains, Jules, 89
Roosevelt, Eleanor, 104, 105, 106
Roosevelt, Franklin Delano, 86, 172; New Deal programs, 102–3
Roosevelt, Theodore, 4
Ross, Cary, 71
Rothstein, Arthur, 111, 165; manipulation of photographic subjects, 136–37, 140, 143
Roualt, Georges, 163
Rowlandson, Thomas, 194
Rudolph, Paul, 256
Russell, Joe, 81

Sachs, Paul, 62
St. Louis: 1904 Exposition at, 4–5; during WE's childhood, 4–5
Salomon, Erich, 270
San Francisco News, 165
Saratoga Springs, N.Y.: WE photographs, 69, 70
Sargeant, Winthrop, 193, 223, 224, 225
Sartre, Jean-Paul, 238
Saturday Evening Post, The, 167, 198
Saturday Review of Literature, The, 165; reviews *Let Us Now . . .*, 186–87
Sayre, Joel, 228
Sayre, Nora, 228
Scanlon, Pat, 223
Schaick, Charles van, 298
Schmidt, Mark, 244
Schneider, Isidor, 45
Schniewind, Carl, 201–2
Schoelkopf, Robert, 267, 268, 272, 287
School of Paris, 62
Schultz, Ben, 229
Schwartz, Delmore, 178
Scott, Sir Walter, 7
Scribner's, 154
Sears, Joseph, 7
segregation: in WE's childhood, 7–8, 10
Sekear, Elizabeth, 103
Sekear, Peter, 102, 113–14, 115
Seldes, Gilbert, 157
Seven Oaks Plantation, La., 97
Shahn, Ben, 74, 78, 83, 165, 190, 218, 253; friendship with WE, 48–49, 54–57; WE's studio with, 54; Cape Cod home of, 54–55; portrait of WE, 55, 237, 278; and Rockefeller Center frescoes, 77; *The Passion of Sacco and Vanzetti*, 78; learns photography, 87, 102; WE shares space with, 102; government work for, 104, 110, 111; film project for RA, 143; leaves wife for Bryson, 143; looses touch with WE, 222; death of, 277
Shahn, Bernarda Bryson, 102, 103, 143, 222
Shahn, Ezra, 83, 143

Shahn, Judith, 48, 56, 83, 143
Shahn, Tillie Goldstein, 48–49, 143
Shakespeare and Company (bookstore), Paris, 25–27, 28
Shaw, Elizabeth, 224, 247
Sheeler, Charles, 218
Sidney, Silvia, 145
Sidney Janis Gallery, 282
Sillman, Sewall, 287
Simon, Paul, 254
Siskind, Aaron, 218
Skolle, Hanns, 33, 54, 57, 67, 74, 75
Smith, Jane: relations with WE, 96–99, 100–101, 104–7, 113, 114–15, 151, 166, 174–79, 279; *American Photographs* dedicated to, 174, 247; correspondence with WE, 174; separates from Paul Ninas, 176; moves in with WE, 176–77, 179–80; on Agee, 180; marries WE, 187–88; honeymoon in Florida, 188–90; sees WE spoiled by *Fortune*, 211; studio retreat in Connecticut, 212–13, 214, 229; changing relations with WE, 213–16; exhibits her work, 215; breakup with WE, 223, 224–25, 279
Smith, W. Eugene, 193
Smythe, Jim, 176
Soby, James Thrall, 84
solarization, 36
Solow, Herbert, 179
South: WE interest in documenting rural, 89–90; WE's assignment by Fuller in, 95–99; RA assignment for WE in, 115–17, 118; Agee-Evans assignment on tenant farmers, 119–38
Special Skills program, 104, 110
Spender, Stephen, 228
Spiral Press, 173
Sports Illustrated: British assignment for WE, 227–28
Stalin, Josef, 178, 179
Stearns, Albert, 16, 18
Steichen, Edward, 170, 264, 268, 271, 300, 301; WE reviews, 69–70; heads

MoMA's photography department, 217–18, 247

Stein, Gertrude, 25

Steinberg, Saul, 195, 228, 229, 238, 299

Steiner, Ralph, 46–47, 60, 61, 67, 142, 172, 207, 211, 252; WE hires for *Fortune*, 207

Stella, Joseph, 50

Stern, James, 191, 193–94, 228, 251, 259, 260, 264, 269, 296, 297

Stern, Tania, 228, 259, 260, 264, 269

Stevens, Wallace, 178

Stieglitz, Alfred, 37–39, 41, 196; WE meets, 39; WE on, 196

Stone, Edward Durrell, 172

Story of Mankind, The (Van Loon), 88

Strachey, Lytton, 273

Strand, Paul, 38, 39, 142; influence on WE, 39–40, 48

Strong, Tom, 263

Stryker, Roy Emerson, 165, 190, 209, 234, 247; relations with WE, 108–10, 111, 112–13, 115, 116, 117, 119, 121, 124, 140, 141, 145, 147; growth of department at RA, 139–40; fires WE, 147; and rights to WE's photographs, 147–48, 153–54; efforts to see WE's work published, 154–55

Subsistence Housing, 104, 105

Sullivan, Louis, 265

Sullivan, Mrs. Cornelius J., 62

Sun Also Rises, The (Hemingway), 27

surrealists, 180

Swan, David, 253

Sylvester, David, 296

Szarkowski, John, 264–66, 267, 280–81; and 1970 edition of *American Photographs*, 281, 282, 283–86

Tabu (film), 75

Tahiti: WE's photographs in, 75

Tate, Allen, 249

tenant farmers: Agee-WE documentation of lives of, 119–38 (*see also Let Us Now Praise Famous Men*); living conditions of, 121–22; film projects on, 142–45

Tennessee Valley Authority, 119

Thayer, Scofield, 20

Thompson, Jerry, 287–88, 291, 292–93, 297, 302, 303, 304, 305, 306, 307, 308

Thompson, Lovell, 185, 242, 262, 264, 266, 267

Thompson, Tommy, 74

Thomson, Virgil, 25, 142–43

Three Tenant Families (Agee): problems with text of, 144–45, 151–52, 161, 162, 163, 168; contract with Harpers for, 155, 183; offers manuscript to WE, 168–69; retitled, 180 (*see also Let Us Now Praise Famous Men*)

Thurber, James, 195

Time: reviews *Let Us Now . . .*, 186; history of, 190; style of, 190–91; WE as critic for, 190–96, 197, 198; Agee writing for, 191

Time Inc., 179, 197, 200, 235, 236, 251, 257, 259

Tingle family, 125–28, 138, 142, 145, 182, 248, 295

Tobey, Mark, 60

Trachtenberg, Alan, 293, 297, 303

Traecey, Eleanor, 121

transition, 58

Trilling, Diana, 178, 179

Trilling, Lionel, 178, 179, 299–300; reviews *Let Us Now . . .*, 187

Trotsky, Leon, 179

Truman, Harry, 207

Tugwell, Rexford, 103, 104, 105, 108, 111, 139, 140, 247; and film project on Dust Bowl, 142–43

Tworkov, Jack, 256

typography: WE's interest in, 208

Ulysses (Joyce), 21, 26, 161

Uncle Sam Plantation, La., 97

Vachon, John, 141

Vanderbilt, Mrs. Cornelius, 199

Vandivert, William, 198

Van Dyke, Willard, 147
Van Gogh, Vincent, 62
Van Loon, Hendrik Willem, 88
Van Vechten, Carl, 60, 164
Vicksburg, Miss.: WE photographs, 115–16
Victorian architecture: WE's photogra-
    phy of, 64–69, 85, 87
view camera, 67–68, 105, 111–12, 115,
    129, 147
Von Helms, Freedie, 101
Von Steiger, Alex, 238, 239, 240, 241,
    243, 244
Von Weigand, Charmion, 50
Voorhees, Clark, 174, 176, 190, 212, 213,
    232
Voorhees, Marion "Billie" Rainey, 174,
    175, 176, 212, 213, 232, 272, 274
Vosburgh, Dale, 305, 308

*Walker Evans: Photographs for the Farm
    Security Administration* (Library of
    Congress), 301
Wall Street: stockmarket crash, 45, 53
Warhol, Andy, 255, 268
Warren, Robert Penn, 228, 284; on WE,
    284
Washington Post, The: reviews WE, 164
Wasserman, Max, 147
Waste Land, The (Eliot), 41
WE. *See* Evans, Walker
Webb, Tod: WE hires for *Fortune,* 207
Weiner, Dan, 229, 252
Weiner, Sandra, 229, 231
Werner, Morris, 84
West, Anthony, 230
West, Rebecca, 230
Weston, Edward, 166, 172, 188; on WE,
    166
Weyhe's Gallery, 63
Wheeler, Monroe, 173, 247
Wheelwright, John Brooks, 64–65, 68, 85
White, Clarence, 37

White, Minor, 257
White House Festival of the Arts, 259
Whitman, Walt, 25, 61, 261
Whyte, William Hollingsworth, 211, 212,
    221, 246
Wickes, Kitty, 154
Wilde, Oscar, 60
Wilder, Archie, 250
Wilder, Eliza, 250
Williams, Byard, 54
Williams, William Carlos, 159, 164
Williams College: WE attends, 19–22,
    23; awards WE doctorate, 271
Williamson, S. T., 164
Wilson, Edmund, 179
Winogrand, Garry, 280
Wisconsin Death Trip (Lesy), 297–98,
    299
Wolff, David, 164
Woods, Nancy, 249–50
Woods, Percy, 249–50
Woolf, Virginia, 21
Works Progress Administration
    (WPA), 102–3; and "American Art
    Today" exhibit at World's Fair, 174
World War II, 173–74, 187, 190, 197; WE
    avoids service, 187, 193; U.S. enters,
    190; films about, 192; combat photog-
    raphy, 193; and the art world, 194
Wysocki, Mathew, 290, 292

Yale Art Gallery: WE retrospective at,
    287
Yale School of Graphic Design: WE
    teaches at, 256–57, 262–63, 269, 276;
    WE retires from, 287
You Have Seen Their Faces (Caldwell
    and Bourke-White), 154

Zadkine, Ossip, 180